Praise for
THE GREAT TAX WARS

"Steven Weisman has done what I previously thought impossible—he has made the history of taxation interesting, even fascinating. From a temporary tax that raised only a fraction of all federal revenues during the Civil War to the main source of government funding during World War I and after, the income tax has been paradoxically the fairest but most controversial of American taxes. This fine book explains how and why that came to be."

—James M. McPherson, author of *Battle Cry of Freedom*

"Steven R. Weisman brings a dry subject to vibrant life by putting the tax debate in the political and social atmosphere of its times and by focusing on the often colorful individuals who made this history happen."

—Steve Forbes, *The Wall Street Journal*

"Tells us how the debate over the levy was at the core of national politics for that crucial period from 1860 to 1920, and how, in many ways, the tax changed government itself. . . . Provides an important context for anyone seeking to understand today's tax debates." —*BusinessWeek*

"A fascinating tale, brilliantly told, that features a colorful cast of heroes, including Abraham Lincoln, William Jennings Bryan, Theodore Roosevelt, and Woodrow Wilson."

—Walter Isaacson, author of *Benjamin Franklin*

"*The Great Tax Wars* is a wonderful, sweeping narrative of how America became a modern nation. Weisman presents an exciting, original, and important history. It's a great story that also happens to provide a fresh and compelling perspective on the battles that roil—and shape—our politics today." —Daniel Yergin, author of *The Prize*

"With *The Great Tax Wars*, Mr. Weisman uses our tax history to show the rise of progressivism. His work reminds us of several truths relevant to the current global and domestic political scene." —*Financial Times*

"Compelling . . . *The Great Tax Wars* proves that the income tax indeed changed America." —*The Christian Science Monitor*

"Weisman's history of America's love-hate relationship with the progressive income tax is lucid, balanced, and anything but deadly. Who knew that the political battles that preoccupied Abraham Lincoln and Woodrow Wilson could shed so much light on today's tax-cut debate?"
—Sylvia Nasar, author of *A Beautiful Mind*

"A lively account. . . . Mr. Weisman rescues the reputations of William Jennings Bryan and his populist supporters, whom the respectable classes denounced as extremists."
—*The Economist*

"[Weisman] has the ability to explain complicated subjects in ways that non-mavens can grasp. . . . [He] leavens his history with little anecdotal gems. . . . *The Great Tax Wars* is useful reading for anyone interested in understanding what tax debates are all about."
—*The New York Times*

"Steven Weisman combines superb use of American history with his great command of current events to show us the political, social, and economic forces that brought us the income tax and how it changed the country. With a cast of characters from Lincoln through Woodrow Wilson and beyond, this absorbing book, with originality and intelligence, captures some of the most important controversies of the nineteenth century and connects them to the political debate of our own time."
—Michael Beschloss, author of *Reaching for Glory*

"Surprisingly satisfying . . . Weisman's book about the ideology of taxation, not its economics, manages to pepper a history of congressional debates, 1040 forms, and bureaucrats from the Internal Revenue Service with lively characters and indignant wit. . . . Bright writing and admirable research."
—*Newsday*

"Masterful is too tame a word for this exciting book."
—Anthony Lewis, author of *Make No Law*

"If you have ever paid an income tax, this epic work will show you why. I wish I had read this book when I became chairman of the Senate Finance Committee."
—Daniel Patrick Moynihan

"This is history written on a grand scale, a fresh and arresting account of the half century of turmoil and insurgency that shaped our modern tax system and modern America itself."
—Donald L. Miller, author of *City of the Century*

LINCOLN—TEDDY ROOSEVELT—WILSON

HOW THE INCOME TAX TRANSFORMED AMERICA

THE GREAT TAX WARS

STEVEN R. WEISMAN

SIMON & SCHUSTER PAPERBACKS

NEW YORK   LONDON   TORONTO   SYDNEY

SIMON & SCHUSTER PAPERBACKS
Rockefeller Center
1230 Avenue of the Americas
New York, NY 10020

First Simon & Schuster Paperbacks edition 2004

SIMON & SCHUSTER PAPERBACKS and colophon are registered trademarks
of Simon & Schuster, Inc.

For information regarding special discounts for bulk purchases, please contact
Simon & Schuster Special Sales at 1-800-456-6798 or business@simonandschuster.com

Designed by Jan Pisciotta

Manufactured in the United States of America

10 9 8 7 6 5 4 3 2 1

The Library of Congress has cataloged the hardcover edition as follows:
Weisman, Steven R.
    The great tax wars / Steven R. Weisman.
        p.   cm.
    Includes bibliographical references and index.
    1. Income tax—United States—History. 2. Taxation—United States—History. I. Title.
HJ4652 . W556   2002
336.24'2'097309034—dc21   2002070486

ISBN 0-684-85068-0
       0-7432-4381-1 (Pbk)

FOR MY MOTHER

AND IN MEMORY OF MY FATHER

CONTENTS

Introduction

———✎———

THIS IS A BOOK ABOUT SIX DECADES OF BATTLES over wealth, power and fairness that led to one of the most important progressive achievements in the making of modern America— the establishment of the income tax.

At its core, the story of the origins of the income tax revolves around the rise of the great American fortunes. Picture, if you will, one of the few places that this history can be experienced: the great citadels of wealth of the Gilded Age—the gothic and beaux arts mansions on the banks of the Hudson River north of New York City, built by the families named Rockefeller, Vanderbilt and Gould. When you walk through the wooded estates, gardens, mirrored ballrooms, libraries and vaulting corridors of these homes, you can almost experience what was intended by their builders as a tranquil refuge from the clanging ambitions of the industrial era, a time when the United States was becoming a world power, with tens of millions of new immigrants coming to its shores to find opportunity and better lives. You can also imagine these places as fortresses against the great social upheaval that accompanied the accumulation of the vast wealth behind them—the protests, strikes and demands for justice by farmers, workers and the poor, all of which led to an outburst of reforms after the turn of the last century.

The tension between these two forces is at the core of this book's narrative.

Why focus on taxes? They are admittedly a distasteful necessity in the governing of any society. Few taxpayers look on the obligation to pay them as a "glorious privilege," in the words of that supreme moralist President Woodrow Wilson. But the fact is that Americans argue almost incessantly about taxes. While our debates are framed by dry sets of numbers, percentages and tables, they involve the most deeply felt and passionate moral and personal sentiments. It could hardly be otherwise. No other aspect of government is as intrusive to the average citizen. Few subjects reflect as many conflicting attitudes toward the role that government plays in our lives.

My purpose in this book is to write not so much a history of taxes as a history of how we think about taxes and the way that Americans, from the beginning, sought to strive toward different standards of equity and justice for society and its individual citizens.

With the subject of taxes goes, inevitably, some well-known truisms. "Nothing in this world is certain but death and taxes," Benjamin Franklin wrote in 1789, the definitive comment on their inescapability. Another familiar aphorism was enunciated in 1819 by Chief Justice John Marshall in *McCullough* v. *Maryland:* "That the power to tax involves the power to destroy . . . is not to be denied." Marshall's formulation expresses as well as anything an enduring American sentiment that has helped ignite the Revolutionary War, the first tax protests of a new nation and the tax revolts of today. Another formulation, from Associate Supreme Court Justice Oliver Wendell Holmes, Jr., summarizes a concept that would be endorsed by most Americans in the age of terrorist threats and the social safety net. "Taxes are what we pay for civilized society," Holmes declared in 1904. The justice, or at least the just purpose, of our taxation system is what sustains its popular support and the willingness of Americans to pay their taxes faithfully and honestly.

These themes are from history, but they echo in our politics today. When Ronald Reagan rode the crest of a tax revolt and won the presidency in 1980 with a pledge to cut income taxes across the board, he ushered in a new era of arguments over taxes and budgets that continues to energize our politics. Since then, the income tax has been at the center of every presidential election, including the 2000 campaign that elected George W. Bush to the White House and led to his own sweeping tax cut enacted in his first year in office. Senator John F. Kerry, the Democratic presidential candidate, promised in 2004 to repeal some of the tax cut, and the issue is certain to echo through November and into the next presidency.

My training for this book has been as a political reporter, not a historian. The idea for it came to me in 1996, when that year's presidential election was unfolding with a residue of anger over President Bill Clinton's record of raising income tax rates on the wealthiest citizens in 1993. Some candidates favored repealing that tax increase and even replacing the entire progressive tax system with a single "flat tax"—in effect, the same tax rate on all Americans, no matter what their incomes were. I began wondering about the antecedents of what I still think is a consensus in American society that wealth should be taxed directly, and in direct proportion to its size. Where did the idea of taxing citizens according to their ability to pay get started? The most popular histories of the populist and progressive movements of the late nineteenth and early twentieth centuries do little more than mention the income tax in passing. Instead, the main political histories of that era tend to focus on other reforms, such as regulation of banks, railroads and trusts, as well as on the rise of the labor movement, environmental conservation, the beginning of consumer issues like food safety and the spread of political reforms, such as the direct election of senators and limits on the power of big-city political machines.

What I want to accomplish here is to tell the story of how the income tax became established, using the words of the chief actors to underscore the origins of our tax debates of today. What I want is for readers to listen, hear and experience these arguments as they would if the disputes were in the pages of the newspapers, magazines and news broadcasts and perhaps even the television talk shows of today.

I could have begun the story of the income tax at any of a number of places. Taxing the incomes of citizens, after all, dates from biblical and Roman times. Certain kinds of taxes on incomes were also a feature of government in the Colonial era. But the modern American income tax has resulted from what I call the Great Tax Wars, beginning with the Civil War and the emergence of the modern American industrial state and concluding with the end of World War I. It was in this interval that the rise of huge aggregates of wealth and corporate power, combined with the drive for social equality, tore at the national fabric and led to the reforms of the progressive era. These dramatic struggles unfolded amid the two bloodiest outbreaks of hostilities at home and overseas and the worst economic collapse the nation had experienced before the Great Depression.

In these sixty years, the income tax was actually enacted three different times before it became established in the form we know today. Its first incarnation came as Abraham Lincoln and his Treasury Secretary, Salmon Chase, sought to raise the money to save the Union while addressing popular resentment against those wealthy Americans who profited from the conflict. When the first income tax was enacted, during the Civil War, it was widely seen as both a necessity and a loss of innocence. Representative Justin Morrill of Vermont, chairman of the taxation subcommittee of the House Ways and Means Committee, took to the floor and quoted from John Milton's *Paradise Lost*, comparing the American taxpayer to Adam and Eve, driven by the exigencies of war "from our untaxed garden, to rely upon the sweat of our brow for support."

The income tax was rescinded by Congress after the war, though there were those who warned that it would be needed again in times of emergency. Then came the worst economic collapse in American history until that time, the Panic of 1893. The tax was re-enacted in 1894, in part because of the driving advocacy of the populist hero Representative William Jennings Bryan of Nebraska. A year later, the United States Supreme Court declared the tax unconstitutional, plunging the high court into one of the worst controversies it has endured and handing Bryan a major issue in his unsuccessful campaign for President in 1896.

For nearly a decade, the problem of the tax's constitutionality served as a barrier to its revival. The turn of the century brought an outpouring of progressive reforms under President Theodore Roosevelt, who established his reputation as a trustbuster and took on the great combinations of wealth as he seemed to grow more radical in his politics with each year that he was in the White House. Toward the end of his term, Roosevelt proposed a reintroduction of the tax to counter the excessive power of great wealth, although he did little to get it enacted. Then in 1909, as part of a deal over tariffs with President William Howard Taft, a resolution to amend the constitution and permit the tax was adopted by Congress. Few expected the amendment to be approved by three-quarters of the state legislatures. But a Republican Party split under Taft, between progressives and conservatives, led to a sweep of statehouses by reformers in 1910 and a quick ratification of the Sixteenth Amendment just as Woodrow Wilson took office in 1913. The tax was quickly enacted in Wilson's first year. Then, once again, it became a vehicle to pay for war. As America sent its young men to fight in Europe, the tax's top rate was raised to an extraordinary 77 percent.

Another theme of this book has to do with the antecedents of today's debate over trade, investment and America's role as a global power. As the United States rose to become a mighty industrial power, the principal means for financing the government while fostering economic growth at home was the protective tariff. Duties on imports raised prices of clothing, machinery and other necessities by as much as 50 percent. Tariffs were a silent consumer tax clearly more punishing to those families of modest means. Without this protection, American industry might have grown at a much slower rate. But as Americans became prosperous, they began to see that their compelling economic interest lay not in protecting industry but in lowering the cost of the goods they purchased. Farmers, workers and eventually small businessmen and professionals came together to demand lower tariffs. As they succeeded, revenues had to be found elsewhere. The income tax was the means they turned to.

I have mentioned a few axioms about taxes underlying this book. But if there is one overarching theme to my approach, it probably comes from the incomparably wise and acerbic Progressive Era writer Ambrose Bierce and *The Devil's Dictionary* he published in 1911. Here is Bierce's great definition of politics: "A strife of interests masquerading as a contest of principles. The conduct of public affairs for private advantage." When it comes to taxes, one must write about both the collision of "private advantage" for both sides and also what I would say are the two basic conflicting principles in our arguments over taxes. These I would call, on the one hand, justice, and on the other, virtue.

Justice first. Proponents of the income tax historically favor taxing the rich according to their ability to pay—the higher the income, the higher the tax rate. The income tax is thus a kind of leveler. It was not seen in its early years as a vehicle for redistribution of wealth. But it softened the edges of the distribution of wealth in the interest of justice and fairness—and among progressives, in the interest of maintaining a certain level of social stability. The income tax, in this view, is desperately needed to underscore the idea of social justice in the distribution of rewards and sacrifice in our society.

Virtue second. Opponents of the income tax, by contrast, see wealth as a product of hard work, thrift, ingenuity and risk-taking.

These ideas form the foundation of our economic system. They are what make the system legitimate in the eyes of Americans, in a way no less powerful than the legitimacy commanded by our political system. The connection between wealth and what I would call virtuous behavior has been put forward by American leaders from Abraham Lincoln to Theodore Roosevelt to the presidential poet laureate of modern capitalism, Ronald Reagan, for whom taxing wealth at excessive rates also distorted the incentives that make an economy thrive. Taxing wealth in proportion to the greatness of that wealth, in this view, has been seen over the years as a kind of punishment of virtue.

Depending on their political leanings, readers will no doubt find themselves leaning to one side or the other of this divide. But most readers, I suspect, will also probably admit to themselves that they agree with elements of both points of view. My intention here is to present the gripping story of the clash of these two ideas and the personalities embodying them. By shedding light on the past, the story of the origins of the income tax can illuminate the challenges as Americans face the future and how to pay for it.

CHAPTER ONE

"Circumstances Most Unpropitious and Forbidding"

The Civil War Begins

"MONEY!" ABRAHAM LINCOLN EXCLAIMED. "I DON'T know anything about 'money.'"

The President was typically modest, evasive and adept at feigning ignorance when he did not want to be pinned down. At a meeting with a delegation of New York bankers and financiers well into the Civil War, Lincoln fully understood that the United States needed money to save the Union. So did Lincoln's anxious Treasury Secretary, Salmon P. Chase. From the conflict's outset, the Union had had to fight while nearly broke. Chase's initial estimate after the taking of Fort Sumter was that the war would cost $320 million. After all, most experts figured at the time, the war could not last long—"two or three months at the furthest," the *Chicago Tribune* predicted—so the Treasury Department's first proposal was for three-quarters of the money to be borrowed from banks. Once the war was over, the money would be repaid quickly, Chase and others thought. But after the first months passed, the optimistic predictions unraveled, leaving the Treasury only $2 million on hand in the summer of 1861. While Union soldiers reeled from defeat after defeat, the banks balked at the administration's demands for loans, especially at the federal requirement that loans be paid in gold and silver.

Lincoln and Chase had a basis for thinking that the Union's credit was good and its eventual prospects even better. The North's strengths in fighting the war derived from a two-to-one advantage over the South in population, income and wealth. The Union side also had a 300 percent advantage in railroad miles, a powerful industrial foundation and vast holdings of unoccupied public land, including the gold-producing regions of the West. But these were assets not easily transformed into the cash to equip and send armies into battle. For months the banks warned Lincoln and Chase that reliance on borrowing when the future was uncertain was risky and potentially inflationary. One such warning was delivered to the Treasury Secretary when he traveled to New York for a private meeting in 1861 with the barons of capitalism at the New York Customs House near Wall Street, where financiers gathered from across the Northeast region. The Secretary was there to discuss the sale of new twenty-year bonds, but the low interest rate of 7 percent and the request that the bonds be purchased in gold unsettled the bankers in the room. They felt that the Treasury Department was looking on them as some sort of bottomless reserve, when the banks' solvency was actually very precarious.

Chase comprehended their situation at one level, but he also viewed the banks' reluctance to buy the bonds as arrogant and unpatriotic. The Treasury Secretary knew about the dangers of inflation, but he did have a war to fight, and he would do what was needed. He warned that, if necessary, he was prepared to print money to pay for the war, even if the price of a breakfast rose to $1,000. The banks were sympathetic, but they wanted to know about the prospects of repayment. At one point, James Gallatin of National Bank of New York, the son of Thomas Jefferson's Treasury Secretary, spoke up.

What if more military reverses occurred? What if Britain or France intervened on the side of the Confederacy? What if the war went on not for months but for years? Another banker threatened to stop doing business with the federal government altogether unless Washington did something to shore up federal finances. His comment came across to the Treasury Secretary as a threat.

"No!" Chase fired back. "It is not the business of the secretary of the Treasury to receive an ultimatum, but to declare one if necessary."

By the end of 1861, Chase and Lincoln pried $150 million from the banks at 7.3 percent interest, but at great cost to the solvency of both the banks and the nation. As the men at the Customs House had feared, their reserves were so far gone that they had to suspend payments in gold and silver to their own customers. Soon afterward, the federal government followed suit, unable to honor its own payments with gold. These were brutal blows to Union credit. Without revenues, the federal government would not be able to turn to the banks again for more loans. More revenues meant only one thing: more taxes. That requirement would mean a new kind of tax, with far-reaching impact on the nation's finances.

Within the next six months, on July 1, 1862, Lincoln signed the first federal income tax in United States history. It was a momentous piece of legislation, rivaling, in its way, the abolition of slavery, the Homestead Act, the establishment of a national currency and federal bank regulation. Enactment of an income tax ushered in a new era of thinking about who should pay, who should sacrifice and who should gain from the federal government at a time of war. It established what until then was considered a revolutionary principle: the idea of taxing rich people at a higher rate compared to the rate for people less well off. Yet once established, that principle became a permanent feature of the American political and economic landscape.

———

The story of how the financial crisis of the Civil War led to a progressive income tax is a story not simply of war but also of the tumultuous economic and political change brought on by a new industrial age. The tax was essential to saving the Union and freeing the slaves. And although the tax was repealed shortly after the war ended, it left a monumental legacy by redefining the relationship between wealth and fairness. The Civil War income tax was a benchmark for how much America had been transformed in the first half of the nineteenth century. It established a foundation for the changes to come in the century's second half and for the years after that.

The tax that was enacted during the heat of a national crisis resulted from many decades of growth and change. Before the Civil War, the United States was populated primarily east of Kansas and on the Pacific coast. It was dominated by small business and farmers dependent on staples and manufactured goods from abroad. Americans kept their investments in their communities, and they used local currencies issued by their own banks. Thousands of different paper currencies, some issued by banks and some simply bogus, circulated as money among Americans. The national government was tiny, with little power to oversee this chaos. The government delivered the mail, collected tariffs and oversaw foreign affairs, but did little else. The Army when Lincoln took office had about 16,000 men, barely enough to protect Americans from Indians. Such was Washington's complacency that in June of 1860, the House Ways and Means Committee eliminated $1 million from a naval appropriations bill to repair and equip vessels. "I am tired of appropriating money for the army and navy when, absolutely, they are of no use whatsoever," said one member of Congress.

Complacency was perhaps understandable. No serious external threat cast a shadow on the prosperity achieved by America in the first half of the nineteenth century. After 1815, nothing seemed to stand in the way as Americans conquered, settled, annexed and purchased new territory, quadrupling the nation's size and population. Exports grew nearly two-and-a-half times in 50 years, to $243 million. In the South, King Cotton dominated world markets, supplying the mills of New England and Europe and enriching shippers, lenders and other middlemen based in New York. From 1817 to 1837, the output of the textile industry in New England rose from 4 million yards of cotton cloth to 308 million. The system of interchangeable parts revolutionized the production of machinery and arms, enabling the United States to surpass Britain in industrial might. Factories required workers. Waves of immigrants joined with Americans from the farm regions to pour into the great American metropolises seeking the means to improve their lot. Crammed into sweat shops, mills, mines and factories, workers grew restive, demanding better wages and conditions and sometimes going on strike.

At the other end of the spectrum, the wealthy of America were no longer simply the owners of large plantations and estates. They were a new breed of businessmen called "merchant capitalists" and "industrialists," people whose wealth was in stocks and bonds rather than property. There were plenty of domestic tensions revolving around economic issues. Farmers and workers regarded the wealthy new class of bankers, lawyers, merchants and speculators as "capitalists" and "bloodsuckers." On the whole, however, Americans were a prosperous people, even though they endured many cycles of boom and bust. Their average income doubled in a half century, and they could afford to buy goods that once had been transported by small ships and flatboats and now arrived on large ships and by roads and rail. New canals and railways enabled farmers to produce and sell their food in what had become for the first time a national market for goods. A revolution in communications allowed news to travel by telegraph. Newspapers and magazines were read by a growing middle class.

Few Americans doubted that these good times were the product of the hard work, industriousness and thrift of the most blessed new citizens of the world. But because there was now a national marketplace, the federal government stepped in to play a critical role by chartering the banks, licensing the corporations, digging the canals and sponsoring the railroads that laid a foundation upon which the nation could grow. To carry out these functions at the federal level required revenue. But on the eve of the Civil War, Americans were not used to paying anything to support their national government except indirectly, through the tariff. The federal excise tax on alcohol had been repealed in 1817. In the 1850s, the federal government obtained 92 percent of its revenues from customs duties imposed on goods imported from abroad. While protecting domestic industry from competing with cheap imports, the tariffs raised the price of nearly all goods consumed by Americans, from clothing to farm equipment. It was the tariff that paid America's way, which is why it was for so long so contentious an issue in American politics.

Tariffs were like a silent sales tax. Though regressive in nature, falling more onerously on the poor than on the rich, tariffs were accepted by Americans because they shared a broad assumption that everyone, producer and consumer alike, gained materially from the government's role in nurturing domestic industry and jobs. Indeed, without tariffs, the United States would have made a much slower transition from its status as a nation with an agrarian-based economy, rich in resources but lacking in capital investment, into the mighty industrial power it became after the Civil War. Debates about the tariff rose and fell throughout the nineteenth century, but without significant damage to the broad consensus in their favor. Democrats supported what Andrew Jackson termed a "judicious tariff," while Whigs, and later Republicans, pushed for higher tariffs to protect industries to fulfill their vision of development and enrich their political base. In the 1840s and 1850s, the anti-tariff forces managed to keep trade barriers reasonably low. Then came the Panic of 1857, a calamitous recession, after which Republicans succeeded in enacting the higher tariffs that they argued were needed to protect jobs and industry from foreign competition.

These were some of the economic conditions on the eve of the Civil War. By the end of the conflict, the Union demand for money to prosecute the war sent tariffs to record levels. American citizens paid higher prices for virtually everything they purchased. To persuade Americans that the wealthy citizens who were prospering from the war would bear more of its cost, Congress and the President turned in 1862 to the income tax, as well as taxes on corporations. Taxes, for the first time, were imposed on people's incomes, at graduated rates. A new bureaucracy was established to collect these charges, the Internal Revenue Bureau.

Taxpaying in wartime, when sacrifice is demanded from everyone, is shouldered more willingly than in times of peace. During the Civil War, it was borne to save the Union and free the slaves. And for the first time, taxation was also conceived and understood as an instrument that reduced inequality in a time of economic upheaval, when new fortunes were being made, in part out of war profits. As one lawmaker put it during a heated tax debate in the House, referring to two families that had grown rich during the war: "Go to the Astors and Stewarts and other rich men of the country and ask them if in the midst of a war [the income tax] is unreasonable. I could not advocate anything else in justice to the middle classes of the country."

———

To many visitors who traveled to Springfield after the 1860 election, Abraham Lincoln seemed overwhelmed.

The President-elect had an unsettling habit of pledging firmly to protect the Constitution and then throwing in a stream of jokes and homespun anecdotes. As the news arrived of one state after another seceding, he was noncommittal about what he planned to do. He had just won a precarious victory with less than 40 percent of the popular vote, and many people around him wondered whether he was up to the challenge of preserving the Union. At the beginning of this strange period of testing, Lincoln, perhaps reflecting some kind of private uncertainty about himself, surprised his friends by suddenly growing a beard.

For all his historic majesty, Lincoln in retrospect is a figure of puzzling contradictions. He was a man of action with doubts about the efficacy of action, a fatalist and an idealist, a farsighted thinker who could be slippery and reactive. We think of Lincoln as a great visionary, but he came across to many of his colleagues as pragmatic. "My policy is to have no policy," he said. The biographer David Herbert Donald attributes to Lincoln in action that quality defined by Keats as "negative capability," the ability to live with uncertainty, doubt, mystery and the avoidance of "any irritable reaching after fact and reason." Yet he could come to a sharp decision when history required.

Lincoln's economic views are more easily definable, but they, too, derived from a mixture of high principle, philosophy and practical politics, as well as from lessons that he had learned from his own life's varied experiences. Long before the war, starting at least when he was in his early twenties, these views embraced rugged individualism and aggressive government—a belief that capitalism rested on both the dignity of labor and state intervention. As the biographer and historian Gabor S. Boritt notes, his image was tailor-made to represent the virtues of hard work in a free society. His nickname, "the Rail Splitter," harkened back to "Old Hickory" for Andrew Jackson and "Tippecanoe" for the war hero William Henry Harrison of the "Log Cabin" campaign of 1840. But it mainly helped Lincoln project himself as a classic self-made man, whose industry would be as good for the country as it had been good for his own soul. He had been a riverboat pilot, country store clerk, soldier, merchant, postmaster, blacksmith, surveyor, small town lawyer and then big business lawyer representing railroads and other powerful interests in the new corporate America.

Lincoln was a philosophical exponent of Henry Clay's so-called "American System," which was rooted in the theories of the first Treasury Secretary, Alexander Hamilton, and which consisted of tariffs to protect industry, a national bank and government spending to promote "internal improvements," from canals to roads to railroads. By investing in these projects, the government would help link the manufacturing of the Northeast to the grain production of the West and the cotton and tobacco production of the South, bringing wealth to all. Clay called the American businessmen thriving in such a system "self-made men," but the term had obvious limits. Government spending on public works and government actions to erect tariff walls around industry clearly gave the meaning of "self-made men" a kind of spin. Call it public improvements or call it pork barrel: Lincoln was good at it.

As a state lawmaker, he fought to bring state money home to his district to improve the Sangamon River near his community of New Salem, Illinois, which was near Springfield, the city that was to become the capital of Illinois, also with his lobbying. To demonstrate that the Sangamon was navigable, Lincoln one day waded into the river, cut back the brush and then took the helm of a visiting steamer to prove his point. In the legislature, he also came up with financial schemes to support dredging, clearing muck and brush from riverbanks and gouging out canals in his part of the state, including a channel to link Lake Michigan to the Mississippi via the Illinois and Chicago Rivers, a project hailed as rivaling the Erie Canal in economic importance. He advocated state debt or the sale of state land to raise money for such projects—even the purchase of federal land followed by its resale to settlers, using the profit for the improvement needed to get his home district's goods to world markets. The historian Gabor Boritt, surveying Lincoln's economic philosophy from its early days, notes the "striking contrast" in his voting for expensive river projects but squabbling over small amounts of money in the regular state budget. "Penny-wise and pound-foolish," says Boritt, "he acted almost as though possessed by a dream."

Public improvements were so vital to Lincoln's philosophy, and to the future of the region he represented, that he even supported—"reluctantly," according to David Herbert Donald—increasing taxes on property, which were the main source of revenue for state and local governments at the time. Not just taxation but taxation with a higher rate for those with higher property values, rather than a flat tax with the same rate for rich and poor alike. He told the Illinois legislature that the graduated tax scheme was "equitable within itself" because it would fall on the "wealthy few" who, "it is still to be remembered . . . are not sufficiently numerous to carry the elections." The tax, however, was not adopted.

By the time Lincoln arrived in Congress in 1847, many of the old economic issues of his early public career had grown passé. President James K. Polk, a Democrat, reduced tariffs to new lows, vetoed several internal improvements measures and presided over the war with Mexico, which was about to add California and New Mexico to the Union. Like other members of the Whig Party, forerunner of the Republican Party, Lincoln opposed the war. He then turned around in 1848 to support the presidential nomination of the soldier who had helped win it, General Zachary Taylor. Lincoln lined up with those Whigs who were opposed to a strong presidency, a stance that would come back to haunt him.

Lincoln honored an informal agreement among rival Whig Congressional aspirants in his home county by retiring after only one term in Congress, returning to his law practice and thinking that his public career was probably at an end. It was as a lawyer that he became known as "Honest Abe," the brilliant courtroom practitioner with a deceptive cracker barrel style and a comfortable income of $2,000 a year, which put him in the top 1 or 2 percent of Americans. He owned $5,000 in real estate and a personal estate of $12,000. Increasingly his practice was taken up with legal problems of the railroads, which he supported as an agent for economic growth.

Slavery was something Lincoln had always opposed as wrong but preferred not to act on, though he sponsored antislavery resolutions as a young legislator and advocated the shipment of slaves back to colonize Africa. But along with the new antislavery group, the Republican Party, Lincoln began to challenge the expansion of slavery to the new territories of the West and to develop his tone of moral outrage. In debates, he stood straight at 6 feet 4 inches, sometimes bending down in a crouch for dramatic effect. His style and eloquence drew the attention of party leaders, who briefly considered him for the 1856 vice presidential nomination. It was Lincoln who contributed the idea of making a party motto out of Daniel Webster's old rebuke to the doctrine holding that states could nullify high tariffs, the forerunner to secessionism: "Liberty and Union, now and forever, one and inseparable."

By the time of his 1858 race for the Senate against Stephen A. Douglas, Lincoln had left his early economic issues behind. The Lincoln–Douglas debates did not address bank regulation, tariffs, immigration, homesteads for farmers or the improvement of factory wages and conditions, the staples of Republican politics since the party's founding a few years earlier. Instead, they argued over slavery, which Lincoln proclaimed to be "a moral, social and political wrong."

Lincoln lost the Senate election but became known across the country as the eloquent advocate of opposition to the expansion of slavery into the American territories and as the leading Republican statesman from Illinois. His only significant rival from the Midwest as a potential national party leader and future presidential nominee was Governor Salmon P. Chase of Ohio, whose delegates defected to Lincoln and helped him capture the 1860 nomination. By the election, slavery was the central issue. But Lincoln's opposition to slavery was a subtle thing, based not simply on moral principle but also on politics, experience and longtime economic philosophy.

Since its founding in 1854, the Republican Party opposed slavery as more than a violation of God's commands. It was seen as a threat to the system of "free labor" and capital responsible for American economic growth, wealth and world influence. Lincoln agreed at all levels. He was a great moralist, to be sure, but he was also a fierce exponent of the so-called labor theory of value—the idea that an individual's ability to work is the foundation of the economy and that the accumulation of capital rests on labor. He believed that "free labor" was sacred not only because it produced wealth but also because it allowed workers to become owners and capitalists—to become wealthy, as he had. Lincoln saw himself as the embodiment of the spirit of individual enterprise. He paid little attention to the increasingly obvious fact that factory workers in growing numbers were mired at the bottom end of the ladder, unable to rise above their station. Lincoln's philosophy was summed up by his statement that wealth automatically accrues when "the prudent, penniless beginner in the world labors for wages awhile, saves a surplus with which to buy tools or land for himself; then labors on his own accounts another while, and at length hires another new beginner to help him."

Campaigning in 1860 in New Haven, Lincoln said, "I am not ashamed to confess that twenty-five years ago I was a hired laborer, mauling rails, at work on a flat-boat—just what might happen to any poor man's son!" The miracle of the system, he declared, was that "there is no such thing as a freeman being fatally fixed for life, in the condition of a hired laborer." From this came the staunch Republican philosophy, delineated by the economists Francis Wayland and Henry Charles Carey, that it was God's law to enable men to work, gain wealth and accumulate private property—and that it was the government's obligation to create and protect the conditions under which men could do so. Capitalism, in this view, was not a selfish philosophy. Rather, it created the conditions for a benevolent society in which the virtues of thrift, hard work, ambition and selflessness would triumph over savagery and yield higher living standards for everyone.

This economic philosophy, the bulwark of the argument against slavery, leads to a skeptical if not hostile perspective toward taxes. Taxing wealth as wealth would later be seen by the exponents of "free labor" as an assault on the very incentives on which the hopes of Western civilization were pinned. That sort of thinking would become clear in due course. For some years now, insofar as they addressed economic issues, Democrats had countered the Republican philosophy of harmony between workers and capitalists with their own view that conflict between the two was inevitable. Indeed, Democrats saw government intervention in the economy through tariffs, public improvements and the like as nothing more than corrupt aid intended to support rapacious monopolies of power and wealth. They clung to this philosophy for some years, though the economic debate was engulfed in 1860 by the issue of slavery and the prospect of civil war.

From the perspective of today, we can see that faith in prosperity has been the abiding theme of Republicans for 150 years. In the years before and after the Civil War, however, Republicans believed that the federal government had a crucial role to play in nurturing wealth. Accordingly, the platform on which Lincoln ran called for a better homestead act to please western farmers and federal aid to improve rivers and harbors to appeal to Detroit, Chicago and the burgeoning cities of the Great Lakes region. Perhaps most important, to placate the fledgling manufacturers of the Northeast, who were struggling to compete with cheaper goods manufactured abroad, the platform urged a higher and more protective tariff. The tariff would effectively raise prices on clothing, farm equipment and many other everyday necessities. Farmers in the South and West, squeezed by these high prices and struggling to sell their own farm products abroad, protested the high tariff. With their electoral clout, they had managed to keep duties relatively low for the two decades leading up to the Civil War.

Tariffs were not called taxes per se, but that is what they were, and what Americans understood the tariff system to be. Tariffs were the main source of federal revenues, and with the victory of Republicans in 1860, Congress and the President were likely to use tariffs to return to the "American system" in which business prosperity was seen as good for everyone.

These were some of the factors that thrust Lincoln to the threshold of the most violent and transforming presidency in American history. None of them prepared him for the crisis he faced as most of the slave states announced that they were seceding from the Union and began seizing federal arsenals within their borders.

———

South Carolina went first.

The state's grievances had been long-standing and not simply focused on slavery. Its major complaint went to the heart of the nation's finances—tariffs. A generation earlier, South Carolina had provoked a states' rights crisis over its doctrine that states could "nullify," or override, the national tariff system. The nullification fight in 1832 was actually a tax revolt. It pitted the state's spokesman, Vice President John C. Calhoun, against President Andrew Jackson. Because tariffs rewarded manufacturers but punished farmers with higher prices on everything they needed—clothing, farm equipment and even essential food products like salt and meats—Calhoun argued that the tariff system was discriminatory and unconstitutional. Calhoun's antitariff battle was a rebellion against a system seen throughout the South as protecting the producers of the North. The crisis was defused with the help of Henry Clay of Kentucky, former House Speaker, and later senator, three-time presidential candidate and passionate advocate of preserving the Union, who persuaded South Carolina to yield on nullification in return for gradually reduced tariffs.

But now the issue was slavery, and there seemed to be no backing down.

Within a day of Lincoln's election, South Carolina, fearing that Lincoln would outlaw slavery in the territories and eventually the South, summoned a state convention to decide what to do about the voters' verdict. In December, the convention voted to secede, and within a month and a half, five more states followed. Soon only a handful of federal installations in the South remained in Union hands. The sitting President, James Buchanan, was not opposed to slavery, but he repeatedly asserted that the federal government could not tolerate the seizure of its property, including the customs houses that collected the tariff revenue on which the government's finances were based. To better defend himself in South Carolina, Major Robert Anderson moved his small garrison on the shoreline at Charleston to Fort Sumter, on a rocky shoal in the harbor. Though Buchanan denied South Carolina's right to secede, he also would not use force to stop it. Instead he sent an unarmed ship, *The Star of the West*, with arms and additional troops to reinforce the fort. After being fired on, it steamed away.

From his base in the governor's office in Springfield, Illinois, President-elect Lincoln found himself consumed with doling out patronage and balancing political interests in forming his cabinet. Lincoln was not simply a stranger to most Americans. He was the first Republican to be elected President and an unknown quantity to the political satraps and brokers in Washington and the big northern states, all of them eager for the federal jobs and contracts enjoyed by the Democrats for the previous eight years.

Lincoln left Springfield on a cold and rainy February 11 for the twelve-day, 1,904-mile journey east to the nation's capital. On the last leg of the trip, from Harrisburg and Philadelphia to Washington, word arrived that someone would try to murder him. Lincoln reluctantly agreed to sneak into the nation's capital from Baltimore disguised in a fake hat and cape, thus opening his presidency on a note of ridicule and perceived cowardice. Yet Lincoln's inaugural was firm and majestic. It sounded a note of economic necessity as well as moral principle by promising "to hold, occupy and possess the property, and places belonging to the federal government." More memorably, Lincoln spoke of his optimism that "the mystic chords of memory" would save the Union when "touched, as surely they will be, by the better angels of our nature."

At the first state dinner shortly after the inauguration, the President kept up the flow of anecdotes and witticisms. Treasury Secretary Salmon Chase recalled later that he felt impatient with

Lincoln's casual behavior until after dinner, when the cabinet withdrew to a private meeting and heard the bad news from a suddenly
not-so-cheerful President. Earlier optimistic reports from Fort
Sumter were wrong, they learned. Far from having enough supplies
to last weeks or months, the garrison was about to run out of food,
and from the scene Major Anderson was warning that it would take
20,000 men to secure the besieged fort. The astonished cabinet was
divided about what to do. The Secretary of State, former senator
and governor William Seward of New York, favored evacuation, and
Chase vacillated.

Lincoln decided that Sumter had to be relieved—peacefully,
with unarmed tugs and whaleboats. On April 12, rebel forces under
General Pierre G. T. Beauregard opened fire on the fort. Anderson
returned fire, and on the following Sunday, April 14, he surrendered, hauling down his flag as Beauregard's forces took over and
permitted the Union troops to embark for New York. As Lincoln
had hoped, if there had to be a first shot, it was the secessionists
who fired it. The Civil War had begun.

As South Carolina's forces took control of the fort, Chase was
discovering that there was no money in the Treasury to fight the
war. Though America had grown to become a mighty economic
power, and though the North's wealth was several times that of the
South, its economy was in dire shape. The Panic of 1857 had ended
a dozen years of growth. It struck after a period of prosperity accompanied by higher prices, speculation and increasing powers accruing
to the nation's banks. Rising prices had resulted also from a surge of
grain exports to Europe as American farmers suddenly filled a gap
when Russian grain was cut off in the Crimean War. Like many other
"panics" of the early days of capitalism, the Panic of 1857 began
with the disclosure of an embezzlement scheme—this one in the
New York branch of an Ohio investment company. The ensuing
wave of alarm set off a run on the banks, selling on Wall Street, a
suspension of gold and silver payments by banks, falling prices, declining trade and a government saddled with deficits and debts. In

boardrooms and government offices, worker protests stirred fear of European-style class warfare. A mob stormed the United States Customs House on Wall Street, threatening to break in.

Economic experts gave many reasons for the sudden collapse in the nation's economic fortunes. But Republicans singled out two major factors. The first was the virtual nonexistence of a federal banking system after President Andrew Jackson killed the federal charter of the privately operated Bank of the United States in 1832. The second factor, said the Republicans, was the low tariffs adopted under pressure from the Democrats in 1846 and again in early 1857. Hard times often breed demands for higher tariffs, and well before the Civil War, Republicans insisted on raising duties to protect ailing industries—especially those, like the devastated iron and steel works of Pennsylvania, represented by powerful members of Congress. Supporters promoted tariffs as a way to expand employment so that Americans wouldn't have to compete with the "pauper labor" of Europe. But the Democrats saw tariffs as a cudgel to subsidize wages and profits in the North at the expense of consumers, especially in the South. The South wasn't as hard hit in the Panic because its farmers could continue exporting cotton while enjoying the ability to import farm equipment from England under the tariffs that had been lowered in the previous twenty years.

The Panic of 1857 devastated the North in several ways. The national income plummeted to $4.3 billion, or $140 per capita, drying up savings that might otherwise have been able to finance government borrowing. Tariff revenues declined because Americans were unable to pay for imports. Borrowing of any kind by the government required Congressional authorization. But there was no central bank—indeed, no strong banking or unified currency system—to make borrowing practical. The banking system consisted of some 1,600 state banks, each operating independently. Some 7,000 different kinds of bank notes circulated, more than half of them bogus. The value of these currencies depended on the solvency of each bank, so that a $10 bill from a bank in Maine might be worth only $8 in Boston or $5 in New York. The government used only hard currency backed by gold, so there was in effect a dual-currency system. ("Gold for the office holders," went the public refrain. "Rags for the people.")

The onset of hostilities in 1861 made all these conditions worse, sending customs receipts plummeting and forcing investors to renege on their commitment to buy government bonds. The banking system at large was in chaos as debtors in the South threatened not to honor their debt repayments to northern banks. Indeed, they were withdrawing their deposits. Lower tariffs and the economic slowdown reduced federal revenues, resulting in federal deficits and deficit projections as far as the eye could see. "The treasury was empty," John Sherman, then an Ohio senator and younger brother of the future Union general William Tecumseh Sherman, later wrote in his memoirs. "There was not enough money even to pay Members of Congress."

The man chosen to deal with these problems was unapproachable, dour and suspicious of others, with a big bald head that some said seemed to radiate intelligence. Salmon P. Chase was a deeply religious man who quoted the Scripture in conversation, liked to recite psalms while bathing and dressing and tended to express his views as dogma. He was also a firm opponent of slavery who believed that abolition was a moral imperative fulfilling the implicit wishes of the nation's founders.

After two terms as governor of Ohio and after losing the Republican nomination to Lincoln, Chase prepared to take his place in the United States Senate, where he felt he could best help the new President face the daunting challenges ahead. That was before the President-elect, a man he had never met, asked him to pay a call in Springfield, Illinois. Ever solicitous, Lincoln came to see him at the hotel when he heard that Chase had just come into town after traveling two days in cramped cars in four railroads from Columbus. Chase later recalled that he had been extremely reluctant "to take charge of the finances of the country under circumstances most unpropitious and forbidding." But Lincoln was impressed with his political skills, declaring that he seemed to be "about one hundred and fifty to any other man's hundred"—a remark that was not seen as especially extravagant in its praise. He nonetheless needed someone of strong intellect and experience to face the biggest financial challenge since Alexander Hamilton rescued an infant nation from insolvency after the Revolutionary War.

Facing his initial problems, Chase had to educate himself and study how to come up with legislation to deal with the crisis. He had some familiarity as a lawyer and former director of various banks. He was a "convinced hard-money man," but that did not mean much in the face of a gigantic financial crisis that included $75 million in debts. More than a third of the debt was in so-called unfunded Treasury notes, which meant there would be no money to repay them when they fell due in less than a year. The notes were considered nearly worthless in the marketplace. Chase reported that they were being traded at "ruinous" discounts.

Under the law as enacted by Congress, Chase had the authority to issue up to $40 million in long-term government bonds at a rate of 6 percent. Also, Congress had raised tariffs before Lincoln's inauguration to try to stem the tide of red ink. In an atmosphere of patriotic fervor after Fort Sumter, many in Washington hoped that Americans would come to the aid of their country by buying bonds. But given the insecurity of the nation's finances, the proposed interest rates on federal debt proved too low to attract customers. Financial markets in this period were engaged in the buying and selling of debt rather than equities. To find purchasers for United States bonds, Chase had to relax the interest rate requirement, selling them at a discount. He also had to resort to still more short-term notes, a risky expedient because the government had to refinance the notes as they fell due a few months later. His hope was to use cash on hand and postpone bill payments to tide the government over until July, when a special session of Congress was scheduled.

In response to Lincoln's emergency summons, Congress convened on July 4, two-and-a-half months into the war. By then Chase had made his first estimate of the war's cost, but it was conservative if not timid. Looking ahead, he forecast that the war would cost $320 million. He proposed $240 million to come from loans and $60 million from revenues from land sales and tariff increases on commodities like sugar, tea and coffee. The remaining $20 million was to come from unspecified taxes. Many economic historians judge the package shortsighted and inadequate. In his 1942 study of American taxation, Sidney Ratner, a pre-eminent scholar of the subject, describes Chase's approach as overly "moderate and cautious." Taxing wealth in any direct fashion was not on Chase's agenda, however. Indeed, he still hoped that any new taxes would last only a year. Congress eagerly adopted Lincoln's proposal to field an army of 400,000 men. The lawmakers actually improved on his request, setting plans to send 500,000 men into battle. Their interest in raising taxes and borrowing was less enthusiastic. Congress ended up authorizing $250 million in notes or bonds, while the revenue-raising measures remained mired in debate.

Any hope that Congress's action on tariffs would be adequate proved to be short-lived, however. It died in a forested and hilly section of northern Virginia, not far from Washington, D.C., near the town of Manassas and the river a few miles to the north called Bull Run.

CHAPTER TWO

"Chase Has No Money . . ."

The Union's Income Tax Is Enacted

FOR MONTHS, LINCOLN'S WORST NIGHTMARE HAD been a Confederate attack on Washington. To its residents, the ill-prepared capital felt like a city under siege, especially after the railroad bridges linking Baltimore with the North were destroyed. Pacing the White House floor, Lincoln was desperate for reinforcements. "Why don't they come!" he exclaimed to his aides. "Why don't they come!" The President had sought to battle the Confederates in Virginia, but the Union troops were ill trained and slow. By the time they got to Manassas, the Confederacy had been tipped off by spies of the North's plans for an engagement and sent in its own reinforcements. Lincoln, assured that the battle would be successful, went to church on July 21.

Rumors of the battle spread through Washington, stirring anxiety everywhere. The new senator from Ohio, John Sherman, decided to ride out toward the battle site with a colleague to see what he could learn. He was part of a large contingent of journalists, politicians and civilians bearing picnic baskets and blankets who thought they could view the battle from a nearby hillside. Sherman, who would become the author of major antitrust and currency legislation in the late nineteenth century, later described how he and a colleague crossed the pontoon bridge into Virginia from Georgetown and heard the sound of distant cannon fire when they got down to Arlington. Speeding back, he went over to the War Department in the evening for news of the battle. "Our Army is defeated, and my brother is killed," Secretary of War Simon Cameron told him.

Lincoln got the word from Secretary of State Seward, who came to the White House with the report that General Irvin McDowell's army was in retreat. "The day is lost," said a dispatch read by Lincoln at the War Department. The disastrous news spread during a hot, humid and rainy day and night in Washington, as residents heard the sound of heavy wagons along Sixth Street. Chase's daughter Nettie woke up during the night to see the first signs of what everyone had been talking about that day. From her window, she took in what she later described as a horrible scene of "gloomy-looking vehicles" rumbling down the muddy street. Like everyone else, the Treasury Secretary's daughter had been hoping for news of a great victory and now could see that the vehicles were ambulances bringing wounded soldiers routed at Bull Run to a nearby hospital. A disorganized horde poured into the city, mud-spattered soldiers, some barefooted and most of them looking panicked. Chase, shocked by the spectacle, had his staff prepare hot coffee for the stragglers and wounded. He felt some responsibility for the debacle, having supported the idea of engaging the Confederates in Virginia to defuse the threat to Washington and recommending the appointment of General McDowell to command the Union Army.

Bull Run dealt a financial as well as a psychological blow, in the form of a collapse of the bond market. In the new crisis atmosphere, the House of Representatives—which under the Constitution has responsibility for originating all revenue measures—rushed quickly to consider legislation to raise taxes as requested earlier by Chase. The House Ways and Means Committee, which is responsible for revenue legislation, had been considering a range of measures, including an increase in the tariffs on tea, coffee and sugar and the taxes on whiskey, beer, carriages, bank bills and other items. After a storm of criticism that these new steps would fall most heavily on the poor, the committee shifted gears and put forward a bill that contained the goal of raising $30 million in "direct taxes"—which meant taxes on real estate, the main means by which states raised money. Each state was to be assessed a sum of money in accordance with its population. (Actually, it was only $20 million, once states that had seceded were dropped out of the total.)

The concept of taxing real estate was immediately offensive to those in Congress who noted that wealth in the form of stocks and bonds would go untaxed. There was an additional problem with a federal property tax—one that would recur throughout the decades whenever an income tax was considered. It related to the United States Constitution, which in Article I, Section 2 states that "direct taxes shall be apportioned among the several States which may be included within this Union, according to their respective Numbers," or population. Property taxes had always been defined in tax law as "direct" taxes on individuals (as opposed to excise taxes on goods). But if each person in each state had to pay the exact same amount of "direct tax" imposed in Washington, there would necessarily be different tax rates imposed in each state, depending on its wealth. This constitutional restriction meant that the wealthiest states could raise the same amount of tax with a low rate as the poorest states raised with a higher rate. The poor states of the West and South would be paying taxes at stiffer levels than their wealthy counterparts.

After the War of 1812, when the first direct taxes were imposed from Washington and apportioned to the states, the direct property tax was anathema in rural areas with sparse taxable property. But America had changed since the War of 1812. Wealth was concentrated more and more in a handful of northern states like New York, Pennsylvania and Massachusetts, where a new class of wealthy had arisen, with its riches tied up in equities and bonds rather than real estate. These changes guaranteed that in the first months of the Civil War, Congress would revive and deepen a classic American debate over whether rich, middle class or even the poor should have an equal tax burden at a time of crisis. Within the Republican Party, the debate pitted the Northeast establishment against its rural base in the West.

The more Congress debated the property tax, the more objections echoed through the Capitol from the farming regions. "The most odious tax of all we can levy is going to be the tax upon the land of the country," declared Representative Schuyler Colfax of Indiana, a future Republican vice president. "I cannot go home and tell my constituents that I voted for a bill that would allow a man, a millionaire, who has put his entire property into stock, to be exempt from taxation, while a farmer who lives by his side must pay a tax." Colfax proposed instead that there at least be a tax on stocks, bonds, mortgages, money and interest—and income earned from them. An income tax.

The proposal for an income tax was based on considerable precedent. England had imposed one in 1799, and some American states that had relied primarily on real estate taxes had begun taxing income in various forms in the 1840s. By 1850, Pennsylvania, Virginia, Alabama, the Carolinas, Maryland and Florida had such taxes, with high exemption levels, generally low rates, and some rates graduated according to the wealth of the taxpayer. They didn't generate significant revenue, but they were seen as a popular way of taxing wealth that escaped real estate taxes. Colfax got enough votes to send the "odious" bill back to the Ways and Means Committee, with instructions to delete the property tax and substitute "internal duties or direct taxation upon personal income or wealth."

Back in committee, lawmakers struggled to get around the continuing constitutional problem barring direct taxes except in proportion to population. If income taxes, like property taxes, were "direct" taxes, lawmakers would have to come up with a way to avoid different tax rates for different states. But how? Representative Thomas M. Edwards, who had been a banker in his native state of New Hampshire, suggested a solution: call the new tax something other than a direct tax. "Why should we stickle about terms?" he asked. "Why should we not impose the burdens which are to fall upon the people of this country equally, in proportion to their ability to bear them?"

Edwards's views were persuasive. An amendment was adopted imposing a 3 percent tax on incomes over $600 a year. Some excise taxes on luxury goods and alcohol were added before the entire tax bill was sent back to the House floor, where it was championed by the courtly chairman of the panel's taxation subcommittee, Representative Justin Morrill of Vermont.

Tall and lanky, with a prominent Roman profile and side whiskers, Morrill had a love of social occasions and a patrician's delight in caring for the terraces, fountains and gardens adorning the Capitol building. He was descended from Pilgrims who had settled in his native state and risen to prosperity as blacksmiths, farmers and operators of a country store. He was widely respected as a legislative tactician and protectionist. His bill had raised tariffs just before Lincoln took office, and he believed that across-the-board tariffs helped farmers as well as industrialists thrive by blocking cheap imports. He reasoned that farmers benefited from protecting industry because factory workers would be able to earn more money and buy food from farms.

But Morrill also had populist leanings. The tariffs he proposed were lowest for necessities like food and highest for luxuries like jewelry. Thus he proved sympathetic to shifting the Civil War's tax burden off the poorer states and onto the shoulders of those in the emerging industrial and commercial sector. "It is a new idea with us to have an income tax," he acknowledged. He seemed to realize that something momentous was happening with this legislation. In his speech to the House, Morrill reflected on the thought that the war was robbing the nation of its long-standing innocence. Quoting John Milton in *Paradise Lost,* he compared the American taxpayer to Adam and Eve, driven by necessity "from our untaxed garden, to rely upon the sweat of our brow for support." The tax bill passed the House on July 29.

Following the procedure outlined in the Constitution, the House bill, with its modest income tax, went to the Senate, where it ran into similar arguments over equity, fairness and the responsibilities of wealth in a time of war. The bill's principal champion was the chairman of the Senate Finance Committee, William Pitt Fessenden, a cantankerous legislator from Maine widely respected for his intellect. Calling for a tax that would be "more equalized on all classes of the community, more especially on those who are able to bear them," Fessenden won adoption of an even stiffer tax rate than the one passed in the House, including a 5 percent tax on incomes over $1,000. The House–Senate conference compromised at a level of 3 percent on income more than $800 earned in 1861, to be paid by June 30 the following year. The final bill adopted the recommendation of the House lawmakers in simply declaring the income to be an indirect tax. At last, said the *New York Herald,* "millionaires like Mr. W. B. Astor, Commodore Vanderbilt . . . and others" would "contribute a fair proportion of their wealth to the support of the national government."

But it did not happen that fast. At the Treasury Department, Salmon Chase greeted the passage of the income tax bill with skepticism, if not hostility. He doubted that merely labeling the income tax an indirect tax made it constitutional. Aside from that, Congress had neglected to create any kind of bureaucracy or enforcement mechanism to implement such a radical measure. The income tax was therefore not collectible. The provision calling for one was thus understood to be more on the order of a recommendation than an edict. Chase chose to ignore it for the time being. He was preoccupied, in any case, with the need to borrow money for the war.

Frustrated by the reluctance of the banks to lend money, Chase turned to other sources, particularly Jay Cooke, a young Philadelphia banker who had a vision that government debt could be marketed to the masses and that he, as the intermediary, could take a share of the sales as commission. Chase had known Jay's brother, Henry, who had been editor of the *Ohio State Journal* in Columbus, as well as Jay's father, a former congressman. Jay Cooke did not behave like the comfortable scion of an established family, however. With his bright blue eyes, full beard and side whiskers, he came across as an almost religious salesman—in this case, of patriotism. His go-getter approach was a refreshing antidote to the attitude of the banks, from whom Chase had to beg for funds.

In the latter half of 1861, the Treasury Secretary managed to squeeze $150 million out of a consortium of thirty-nine New York banks, to be lent in three installments of $50 million in August, October and November and to be paid to the government in gold. The banks, in turn, hoped to sell the debt to the public. With unremitting bad news from the battlefront, however, these hopes went unfulfilled. The first installment was barely subscribed and the second failed completely.

The strain on the banks came to a head on December 30, when, drained of reserves, they stopped honoring payments to their own customers in gold—a step seen as a virtual declaration of insolvency. It was also a slap at Chase for daring to suggest that the banks were evading their responsibilities and for doing little to raise revenues to pay for the war. Two days later, on New Year's Day 1862, the Treasury chief joined his daughters and a house guest to pay respects to the Lincoln family at the White House. He then hurried home to his own open house, deeply upset over the news of the banks' action. He realized that he, too, had no choice but to suspend payments in gold by the government, a terrible blow to the nation's credit.

Word of the financial setback came as reports mounted about the faltering war effort. After Bull Run came Union defeats at Wilson's Creek, Lexington (Missouri) and Ball's Bluff. General George B. Mc-

Clellan, the thirty-four-year-old general in chief of the Union Armies, was ill and virtually incommunicado, with no known plan for any offensive against the Confederates. Congress was increasingly picking up stories of corruption and financial mismanagement, including reports of profiteers making money out of shoddy deals for blankets and other military equipment with the government.

Lincoln was growing impatient with his corrupt War Secretary, Simon Cameron, whom he described to one of his secretaries as "utterly ignorant," "selfish and openly discourteous," and "incapable of either organizing details or conceiving and advising general plans." A New York banker even told the President that if he replaced Cameron the Treasury could raise the $100 million it needed easily. Irked by these reports, Congress investigated and found rampant cases of malfeasance, forcing Lincoln to apologize for the early practice of letting contracts without bids and spending money without authorization. "The people are impatient," the President complained to Quartermaster General Montgomery C. Meigs that winter. "Chase has no money and he tells me he can raise no more; the General of the Army has typhoid fever. The bottom is out of the tub. . . . What shall I do?"

Reluctant to lead Congress, and reluctant to veto measures with which he disagreed, the President maintained a posture of aloof detachment on banking, tax and currency issues. Chase, meanwhile, saw Lincoln as well intentioned, honest—and hopelessly irresolute. He regarded the President's famous pragmatism as "idiotic." On the other hand, the Treasury chief was pleased to be deferred to on financial matters. Indeed, Lincoln told his secretary John Hay that he "generally delegated to Mr. C exclusive control of those matters falling within the purview of his dept." The President also found it useful to be kept in the dark and claim ignorance about finance, especially when meeting with complaining banks.

Though Lincoln did little second-guessing of Chase, the Secretary had no similar hesitation when it came to judgments about the military aspects of the war. Like Lincoln, he was growing skeptical about the abilities of McClellan, Cameron and the "loose and unsystematic" practices that led to waste and corruption in the War Department. The economic situation worsened in late 1861 after the Union seized two southern commissioners on the high seas aboard the British ship *Trent*. The incident was popular at home, but it led to a British embargo on shipping, which threatened supplies of saltpeter from India, the principal ingredient of gunpowder. Fear of Britain siding with the Confederacy led once more to a drop in the bond markets, further weakening the banking system. The melancholy fact was clear: for all the North's wealth, the Union's improvised loan policies and paltry tax schemes were inadequate. Without revenues, the Union was in peril.

At the start of 1862, Chase realized that he had grossly underestimated the costs of the war. His new estimate of the first year's costs was $530 million. Worse, the revenues that were supposed to be coming in from taxes, tariffs and other schemes were falling short. Treasury funds were facing depletion in a matter of weeks, and new taxes could not possibly fill the gap in time. Loans seemed out of the question as well. European lenders balked because shortages of American cotton were shutting down textile mills in Britain and elsewhere. American banks once again demanded that the Union raise taxes rather than demand more loans at low rates.

With no alternatives available, Chase and Lincoln overcame their misgivings and endorsed the idea of simply printing money—$50 million in green paper money that the government would declare to be valid as legal tender, though not redeemable in gold and silver. After an anguished debate, Congress passed the Legal Tender Act in February 1862, providing for $150 million in currency notes that later became known as greenbacks—the first paper money ever issued by the United States government. They were declared to be legal tender for all private and public debts, though not for payment of customs duties or interest payments on federal bonds and notes.

Opponents said the greenbacks were unconstitutional, since

the Constitution mentioned only Congress's power to "coin money," and the word *coin* could not apply to paper. Lincoln and Chase privately agreed. But as one member of Congress put it, "These are extraordinary times, and extraordinary measures must be resorted to in order to save our Government and preserve our nationality." The act also authorized another $500 million in bonds at market price. Despite widespread fears, the greenbacks did not lead to the roaring inflation that would beset the Confederacy, where prices rose 9,000 percent during the war. If anything, their creation put all the more pressure on Chase and Congress to do what the banks wanted all along—raise revenues.

February 1862 was a low point for Lincoln personally. His son Willie fell ill from what was probably typhoid fever, and then his younger son, Tad, also became sick. Lincoln sat up with both boys night after night, soldiering stoically through his duties during the day. When Willie died at the age of eleven on February 20, Lincoln seemed to many around him to be a man lost in grief. A fierce rainstorm blasted Washington at the time of the funeral, and Lincoln shut himself in a room, weeping alone. The President and his wife had earlier lost another boy, Eddie, in Springfield, but the new tragedy sent Mary Todd Lincoln to her bed and ultimately on a long, sad journey into mental instability. Unable to attend the funeral or even look after her surviving son, Tad, she suspended social activities and withdrew from life at the White House while her husband turned increasingly to reading and rereading the tragedies of Shakespeare and the Bible, and to prayer.

The beginning of 1862 also brought the nation's financial problems to a head on Capitol Hill, where the banks—dismayed that the income tax had been uncollectible—were demanding tax increases with increasing insistence. The greenback legislation had been accompanied by an endorsement of $150 million in new revenues. Representative Morrill of Vermont guided a $164 million revenue measure through the Ways and Means Committee—more than three times the sum sought by Chase. Once again, it included a small income tax provision, calculated to raise $5 million. Morrill, who earlier had compared adoption of the tax to the expulsion of Adam and Eve, was still not one to embrace it with enthusiasm. "Unfortunately, internal duties and taxes must reappear," he told his colleagues glumly, acknowledging that the income tax was "inquisitorial" but necessary as a guarantee that capitalists and merchants who did not own real property would share in the obligation to pay for the war. The income tax, he said, would impose "not upon each man an equal amount, but a tax proportionate to his ability to pay." Thousands of salaried employees "would not contribute a penny unless called upon through this tax," he declared. "Ought not men, too, with large incomes, to pay more in proportion to what they have than those with limited means, who live by the work of their own hands, or that of their families?" The *Chicago Tribune* put it more bluntly: "The rich should be taxed more than the poor."

But the newly emerging populist theme of soak-the-rich-to-pay-for-the-war found its most nuanced expression in Representative Thaddeus Stevens, the abolitionist chairman of the Ways and Means panel. Stevens was in many ways the archetypal Republican "radical," a foe of slavery and the plantation aristocracy that depended on it. His family had gained its wealth from a successful iron works in central Pennsylvania, which thrived as a result of the higher tariffs he advocated. Yet the congressman, in his seventieth year, also saw himself as a foe of privilege, whether in the South or among the banks of the North. As one of the smartest and toughest of the old bulls of the House, testy and a little frightening because of his club foot, Stevens ruled over the Ways and Means Committee with an autocratic toughness. Once when one of his members protested that he couldn't vote a certain way out of conscience, Stevens banged his fist on the table and shouted: "Conscience, hell! Throw conscience to the devil and stand by the party."

Stevens had long been convinced of the need for revenue, arguing in 1861 that the only alternative was "annihilation" of the government. "The capitalists must be assured that we have laid taxes which we can enforce, and which we must pledge to them in payment of the interest on their loans, or we shall get no money," he said in the first tax debate. Chase felt that he was being tough on the banks, but Stevens complained relentlessly that the Treasury Secretary was not tough enough. His populism also extended to opposition to the $300 fee that northerners could pay in order to get out of the draft.

Now the chairman of Ways and Means was advocating an income tax with graduated rates according to the "ability to pay," declaring that "it would be manifestly unjust to allow the large money operators and wealthy merchants, whose incomes might reach hundreds of thousands of dollars, to escape from their due proportion of the burden." Stevens could not help mixing his defense of the tax with criticism of Lincoln's handling of the war, which he regarded as passive and confused. The Union should more aggressively attack the rebels and seize their property to pay for the war, he said. "But if the Administration should deem it wise to prolong the war, and suffer the loyal citizens to be oppressed, to show mercy to traitors, the people must expect further and heavier burdens." Americans of "small means" should not have to pay the same as "the large money operators and wealthy merchants, whose incomes might reach hundreds of thousands of dollars." The case for a more equitable system to finance the Union was made a little easier after Grant's victories in Tennessee and the battle between the *Merrimac* and the *Monitor* in early 1862. The bill passed by the House that spring imposed a 3 percent tax on incomes over $600, a direct property tax and a small inheritance tax, also graduated according to the size of the taxed estate.

The makeup of the Senate made the property tax an especially hard pill to swallow. The more sparsely populated farm states, each one with two senators, could be effective in blocking a tax that hit them with higher rates. But the pivotal figure in the tax debate in the upper chamber was Fessenden of Maine. Although a devoted champion of any legislation that protected the manufacturing, fish-ing and shipping industries in the New England region, he also supported imposing the tax burden in an "equalized" fashion. Fessenden was not against the direct property tax, but he and others realized that there were not enough votes in the Senate to keep it in the bill. He was thus forced to guide a bill through the Finance Committee that was more progressive than the one passed by the House. It kept the 3 percent tax on incomes above $600 and up to $10,000 and increased the tax to 5 percent on incomes above $10,000 and to 7.5 percent on greater than $50,000. The inheritance tax was expanded to cover estates of $1,000 or more in value, with rates depending on whether the person inheriting was a parent, descendant, sibling, nephew or other beneficiary. The income tax provoked opposition in wealthy states like New York, where Senator Ira Harris, a Republican, asserted that "the very best men in New York by hundreds, nay by thousands, have been crushed and overthrown" by its imposition. Fessenden carried the day by acknowledging that the United States was groping to "find our way comparatively in the dark" by creating a new tax system that was both fair and effective. "It will be odious, of course, and overwhelmed by all with curses, both loud and deep," he said of the tax bill. "I have made up my mind, however, to put it through in the best shape I can."

The final bill that came out of a House–Senate conference trimmed the income tax increases passed by the Senate, keeping only two rates: 3 percent on incomes above $600 and 5 percent on more than $10,000. (In an important exception designed to help the Treasury Department market federal debt, the income from government bonds was taxed at only 1.5 percent.) Under the new law, the tax was to apply to "annual gains, profits or incomes of any person residing in the United States, whether derived from any kind of property, rents, interest, dividends, salaries or from any profession, trade, employment or vocation carried on in the United States or elsewhere, or from any source whatever."

On July 1, Lincoln signed a sweeping revenue bill. It taxed inheritances, public utilities, distilled spirits, tobacco and banks. It also taxed insurance companies, advertisements, slaughtered cattle, railroads, ferry boats—everything from perfumes and cosmetics to medicines and playing cards. Stamp taxes were imposed on many commercial papers. Also included were gross receipts or dividends of some corporations, from railroads to banks, trust companies, savings institutions and insurance companies. The law's most revolutionary aspect was the provision that would become the first income tax measure ever implemented in the United States. It embodied a new principle at the federal level: that the rich should pay taxes at higher rates than the poor. The law established the Internal Revenue Bureau to collect the tax, set forth the principle of employers withholding the tax, and moved gingerly into the area of defining deductions so that taxpayers paid only what would be defined as their net income. National, state and local taxes could be deducted, for example. Later Congress would allow deductions on such expenses as business costs, interest and losses.

Lincoln's signing the law was front-page news, along with an authorization for a rail and telegraph line between the Missouri River and the Pacific Ocean and a bill to prevent and punish polygamy. But it is doubtful that it was a high-water mark for soaking the rich. One could certainly argue that the tax was more important as a symbol than as a revolutionary change in the nation's tax structure. Lawmakers from the Midwest could tell their constituents that at last the wealthy were paying more of the share of the war, but Congress accompanied the income tax measure with a separate measure to raise tariff barriers, the traditional method of financing government. As a result, consumers continued to suffer higher and higher prices. Morrill had argued that high tariffs were a kind of "reparation" to those hit by business and income taxes. "If we bleed manufacturers, we must see to it that the proper tonic is administered at the same time," he said. "Otherwise, we shall destroy the goose that lays the golden egg."

When George S. Boutwell arrived in Washington on July 16 from Massachusetts to take up his duties as the first commissioner of Internal Revenue, he had not yet read the new tax law, which had been enacted a little more than two weeks earlier. Boutwell, a patent lawyer who had served in the Massachusetts legislature and as governor of the state, faced the challenge of setting up a nationwide bureaucracy rapidly to collect money that had never been collected before. Many people doubted that it could be done fairly or effectively.

Boutwell set up shop in a small room on the Treasury building's first floor, just off Pennsylvania Avenue. When he read the statute, he pronounced the tax provisions "sensible and wise but incomplete and imperfectly thought out." Working day and night, he issued rulings, regulations and forms. For the position of cashier, he tapped an old friend and onetime school principal from Massachusetts, paying him $1,200 (later raised to $1,600) for a job that was responsible for collecting millions of dollars in a matter of months. Staffing for offices outside the city followed the regular dictates of patronage, one of the primary means by which the parties financed their political campaigns. Thurlow Weed, the New York Republican boss, approved the appointees for New York, while Secretary Chase oversaw the jobs handed out to citizens of Ohio. Lincoln personally approved the appointees in Illinois and California.

In his first year, Boutwell worked hard to collect $39.1 million. "My only exercise was a ride on horseback after office hours and before dinner," he recalled in his memoirs, though occasionally he would stop by the War Office for news, sometimes in the evening, frequently running into Lincoln poring over reports as he sat in the cold with a gray shawl over his shoulders.

"Any news, Mr. President?" Boutwell would call over.

"Come in and I will tell you," Lincoln replied.

Back at Treasury, Boutwell's little office was filled with the kind of spirited adventure of a new enterprise. One young aide, John Quincy Adams Griffin, enlivened the proceedings with a sharp sense of humor. The standing joke was an homage, drawn from New Testament, to Caesar Augustus, "in whose reign there went forth the decree that all the world should be taxed."

When letters came in asking about rulings on what constituted taxable revenue, Boutwell and his small staff simply threw them in a basket for discussion later that evening. Would limited business partnerships be covered by the tax? Yes. Would income from pensions also be covered? Yes again. Life insurance premiums would not be deductible, they decided. Gifts such as compensation to a pastor would be taxable, but money spent on restoring fire-damaged property, paid for out of insurance, was not. Slaves emancipated by a master's will were not subject to the inheritance tax.

By the end of the Civil War, the bureau would expand to 3,882 employees, most of them in the field as "collectors" who received the revenue and "assessors" who gave out instructions and listened to appeals on how much each taxpayer owed. These officers received bonuses based on the taxes they collected and were given wide latitude in making their decisions. Assessors, for instance, could increase the amount owed unless the taxpayer took an oath swearing that his own estimate was accurate.

Looking back years later, Boutwell declared himself impressed that a tax as "fair in theory as any that can be laid" achieved surprising compliance. He personally favored an increase in the tax rate on wealthy Americans, but he was proud of his accomplishments. "The people of this country," he said, "have accepted it with cheerfulness, to meet a temporary exigency, and it has excited no serious complaint in its administration."

But as the Internal Revenue staff geared up, the Union's fortunes were unsettled at best. In July, Lincoln had called for 300,000 additional troops. The war was costing a million dollars a day, and Congress faced the need to issue still more greenbacks to make payments. With the federal government still in need of revenues even after passage of the income tax, Congress raised tariffs again on July 14, in part to carry out Morrill's argument that they were "reparation" for the other taxes.

Around the same time, mid-1862, Lincoln had begun moving toward a decision to issue a decree emancipating the slaves in the South. Among the firmest advocates were Boutwell at the Internal Revenue office and his boss, Secretary Chase. At first, Lincoln resisted the recommendations of some of his generals to free slaves in areas they controlled. The President felt such action was politically premature and that it ran counter to his early pledge that he was not waging a war to end slavery where it existed but only to prevent it from spreading to other states. He also feared such a step might drive border states out of the Union and into the Confederacy. But now, at the height of the battle to save the Union, he began to see emancipation as a shrewd political tactic as well as a blow for justice. There was also an economic rationale, in that emancipation would deprive the Confederacy of the labor vital to its financial and tax base. (Lincoln had given some consideration to a scheme of compensating slaveholders for the freeing of their slaves, a step that critics noted would place difficult new strains on the Union treasury.) In July 1862, the President informed his cabinet that, "as a fit and necessary military measure," he intended to declare slaves free when circumstances permitted.

Though Chase was a hawk on war issues and a longtime abolitionist, he told the cabinet that for the sake of the nation's shaky finances, it would be far better to free the slaves gradually, perhaps allowing Union generals to arm them for self-protection. Secretary of State William Seward was even more skeptical, warning that freeing the slaves might anger Americans throughout the North, look like an act of desperation and provoke European intervention in the war.

Lincoln wrestled with his decision at a time of relative hope for the Union's military forces. General McClellan seemed ready at last to deliver on his promise to revive his faltering Peninsula campaign and move on the Confederacy's capital in Richmond, Virginia, where General Robert E. Lee seemed on the defensive. Then miraculously, Lee recovered, counterattacking and forcing the Union to flee. The disastrous failure of the Peninsula campaign was a bitter disappointment at the White House, but it also galvanized Lincoln into transforming the war from a passive approach emphasizing attrition into a scorched-earth strategy that would end only in victory. The irony, as some historians have observed, was that if McClellan had succeeded in the initial stage of the war, the South might have been spared its total destruction, and slavery might even have been preserved for a time.

The Union Army retreated in late August, pushed back by General Stonewall Jackson and other Confederates to the old battlefield of Bull Run, site of the North's first debacle after the start of the war a year earlier. Again Union soldiers manned the fortifications around the nation's capital, where the streets were once more filled with troops and the wounded crowding into hospitals, churches and schools. "The streets were stuffed with ambulances, baggage wagons, artillery and material of war," Boutwell wrote in his memoirs, echoing the observations of his boss, Salmon Chase, of the first Battle of Bull Run the previous year. "The hills were dotted with tents, and the officers and men were discontented and almost in a state of mutiny." With news of one setback after another reaching Washington, Boutwell paid a rare call on Lincoln at the White House to discuss the appointment of revenue assessors and collectors. Lincoln looked coolly over the papers, signed them and asked Boutwell about what seemed to be the collapsing military situation. Like others, the Internal Revenue chief urged replacement of the Union general John Pope, who had recently been transferred from the West.

To Boutwell, Chase and others in the cabinet, Lincoln was especially frustrated because he and many others wanted a battlefield victory before issuing the Emancipation Proclamation. Their reasoning was that freeing the slaves would have maximum political impact if it were seen as announced from a position of strength. General McClellan's victory at Antietam in September gave Lincoln his opportunity. Chase's diaries record an introspective President informing the cabinet of his decision. "I think the time has come now," Lincoln said. "I wish it were a better time. I wish that we were in a better condition." Though the military situation was not ideal, he said, at least the Confederates had been driven out of Maryland, and Pennsylvania was no longer in danger of invasion. Looking around the room, Lincoln said: "I know very well that many others might, in this matter, as in others, do better than I can." If he were satisfied that someone else had more of the public's confidence and that a way existed for that person to take his place, he would agree to it. But there was no such way. "I am here," he concluded soberly. "I must do the best I can, and bear the responsibility of taking the course which I feel I ought to take."

With that, on September 22, the President issued a preliminary proclamation to free the slaves in rebel states. In effect, it was an announcement that the final proclamation would be issued on January 1, 1863. Instead of a gesture of strength, it was widely seen as an act of questionable legality, little effect and an attempt to incite slaves in the South to revolt. But it did redefine the cause for which the North was fighting—not simply to preserve the Union but to extend freedom to all citizens everywhere.

Despite the North's improving situation in the war, the Republican Party suffered major losses in the election in the fall of 1862. The lagging war effort was only one factor. The Emancipation Proclamation was widely disliked in the North as well as the South. Another factor was the chaotic state of the nation's finances, underscored by what was perceived to be a desperate act in issuing greenbacks. Lincoln realized that he had lost the public's confidence as Democrats made an issue of his suspension of the right of trial for those arrested, as well as his freeing of the slaves. An increasingly defiant McClellan, whom Lincoln regarded as both insubordinate and weak, was a focus of frustration at the White House. Furious at the general over his slowness in moving against Lee after Antietam, Lincoln was angered when McClellan cited the fatigue of his horses as the reason. "Will you pardon me for asking what the horses of your army have done since the battle of Antietam that fatigue anything?" he snapped.

Toward the end of 1862, Lincoln was preparing his annual message to Congress, to be transmitted in December. In passages prepared by Chase, he called for Congress to pay "most diligent consideration" to the nation's finances, with the goal of making payments in gold and shoring up the nation's banking system. Mobilizing some of his most eloquent language in support of the cause, the President urged Congress to unite. "As our case is new, so we must think anew, and act anew," he said. "We must disenthrall our selves, and then we shall save our country." Then later that month, at Fredericksburg, the Union Army suffered its worst defeat yet. Joseph Medill, of the *Chicago Tribune,* spoke of the failure of the Army, combined with painfully high taxes, inflation, cotton shortages and government debt, all of it portending "a disastrous and disgraceful termination" of the war.

On top of all these problems, Lincoln's cabinet members fell increasingly to fighting among themselves. The major disputants were Chase and Seward. They disagreed fundamentally over war policies—Seward more sympathetic to making a deal with the Confederacy—and over the role of the New York banking interests in the Union's finances. Their disagreements extended even to such petty matters as patronage. A former governor and senator from New York, Seward had helped to deliver the votes of the nation's wealthiest state to Lincoln in the 1860 election. Wily, affable and shrewd—more likable than Chase—Seward felt from the start of the administration that he had earned the right to be considered its effective prime minister—setting policies, handing out jobs and contracts to friends of his political machine and tutoring the awkward and inexperienced new President on the ways of the world. His high-handed approach irritated Chase tremendously. So did Seward's insistent grip on patronage at the Treasury Department, particularly at the New York Customs House, where hundreds of employees were expected to kick back large percentages of their salaries to the Republican Party. Though Treasury was supposedly Chase's fiefdom, Seward and his New York political boss, Thurlow

Weed, intended to control the cash cow of the Customs House to keep patronage in the state.

Chase's misgivings about Seward reinforced his suspicions of Wall Street and the city's economic barons. The New York economic backbone was linked to the South. Indeed, New York City, with its leading banks tied up in southern credits, its textile manufacturers dependent on southern cotton, and its retail stores dependent on southern markets, was a citadel of Confederate sympathy in the North. The Treasury Secretary even wondered whether Seward, Weed and their Wall Street allies were conspiring to prevent the sale of Treasury notes.

Chase's main difficulties were with Lincoln, however. As the war went on, he began complaining openly to Republicans in Congress of Lincoln's failure to consult the cabinet and of Seward's high-handedness. The Treasury chief's ultimate ambition was to oust Seward as the senior cabinet member over a President he saw as weak. Encouraged by Chase's grumbling, a group of nine Republican senators drew up resolutions calling for reconstruction of the cabinet and asking for a meeting with the President. "What do these men want?" asked Lincoln when he heard about their plots. "They wish to get rid of me, and sometimes I am more than half disposed to gratify them."

On December 19, the President summoned his Congressional critics to a meeting with the cabinet and turned the tables on them. He called on the cabinet members to state whether they had any complaints about disunity or lack of consultation. An embarrassed Chase feared that he would seem disloyal if he repeated the complaints but look dishonest to the senators if he didn't. He replied drily that if he had known he was to be "arraigned" at the cabinet meeting, he would not have attended. Finally he said there had been "no want of unity in the cabinet," though there was a need for more consultation. Chase's allies in the room were flabbergasted. One of the senators was later asked how the Secretary could have made such a statement. "He lied," he said.

Chase now realized that his position in the cabinet was untenable and was ready to say so at his next meeting with the President. Lincoln, however, prided himself on at least keeping his fractious cabinet together and was in no mood to split it apart now. At their private session, the Treasury Secretary told the President that he had found the meeting with the cabinet and the senators to be exceedingly painful. He had come with a letter of resignation. "Where is it?" Lincoln asked. The Secretary pulled it out. "Let me have it," said Lincoln. He snatched the envelope, opened it and read it. "This cuts the Gordian knot," the President said. "I can dispose of this subject now without difficulty." But when Chase got back to his office, a letter from Lincoln was waiting saying that the Secretary's resignation—along with that of Secretary of State Seward—was not accepted.

The clumsy confrontation damaged Chase's reputation irretrievably. From then on, his standing declined in Congress and in Washington generally. Senator Fessenden, an ally of the Secretary on many financial issues, complained about "the weak squeamishness of our friend Chase" and said he would "never be forgiven" for his mishandling of the situation.

On January 1, 1863, Lincoln shook hands with his guests at the White House New Year's Day reception and then escaped upstairs to his office, where he signed the Emancipation Proclamation with an arm stiff from all the handshaking. It was, he later said, his proudest achievement. But it was a dark winter that followed. There was little certainty that the North could stop an invasion by Lee, and the war was costing $2 million a day. The Union armies were in disarray; Britain and France were increasingly upset about the loss of cotton for their textile industries and encouraging a negotiated end to the war. In adversity Lincoln drew strength from his inner reserves of courage and determination. "Lincoln still had much to learn about how to be President," the historian David Herbert Donald writes of this period. But his journey to save the Union seemed to have no end in sight.

CHAPTER THREE

—⌒—

"Every Man's Duty to Contribute"
The Agony of the South

THE SLEEPY CITY OF MONTGOMERY, ALABAMA, WAS not ready for the first meeting of the Provisional Confederate Congress in February 1861. In the three months following Lincoln's election, seven states had seceded from the Union and hastily called conventions to select representatives to send to the new Confederate capital. The delegates arrived to find the hotels dirty, the streets dusty and the statehouse filled with noisy lobbyists and job seekers. The representatives made themselves comfortable in the legislative chamber, where spittoons were set up for their convenience. It was noticeable that most men of ability in the South had gone into the Army, the cabinet or the diplomatic service, leaving behind lawmakers of modest talent to wrestle with how to wage and finance a war of secession in the face of overwhelming odds.

The first order of business was to write a constitution, install a president and authorize a military force of up to 400,000 men to serve for three years—or for the duration of the war, which most people thought—as they did in the North—would be over quickly. The new president, Jefferson Davis, had been a hero of the Mexican War, a former Secretary of War to President Franklin Pierce, and a respected champion of the South as senator from Mississippi. He was a vigorous exponent of the view that the war was, at its core, not a fight to preserve slavery but a struggle to overthrow an exploitive economic system headquartered in the North.

There was a great deal of evidence to support Davis's view of the South as the nation's stepchild. Although the rebel states had seized a military advantage at the beginning of the war, they suffered from a tremendous and lasting financial disadvantage compared to the North. Indeed, economically the North and the South were two different countries, one a growing industrial power and the other an agricultural backwater. In the North, the workforce on farms and plantations had dropped from 70 to 40 percent since 1800, whereas in the South, it remained constant at 80 percent. With 42 percent of the country's population, the South had only 18 percent of the nation's industrial capacity. A quarter of northerners lived in cities, but only a tenth of southerners. New opportunities beckoned immigrants to the North, not the South. The slave states fell behind in manufacturing, railroads, canals and roads. The South's banking structure was even weaker than that of the North. Of course, cotton prices were high, yielding rich incomes for plantation owners. But cotton made even more money for the credit, insurance, warehousing, manufacturing and shipping companies that were based in the North or overseas. Seventy percent of the cotton was exported, and the remainder went to mills in the North and then came back to the South in the form of clothing and other textiles. Indeed, the South had to import two-thirds of its clothing and manufactured goods from outside the region, and southerners paid artificially high prices because of the high tariffs erected at the behest of American industry. The South even had to import food.

The North made nearly all the country's firearms, cloth, pig iron, boots and shoes, an ominous fact, considering the necessity of these things in a war. "Financially, we are more enslaved than Negroes," one prominent citizen said.

From the perspective of the South, the North's economy rested on a kind of state capitalism of trade barriers, government-sponsored railroads, coddling of trusts, suppression of labor and public investment in canals, roads and other infrastructures. Southern slave owners sought to protect and extend slavery, to be sure, but also to secure free trade, overseas markets and cheaper imports. Southern resentment of the tariff system propelled the Democratic Party to define itself as the main challenger to the primacy of the industrial and capitalist overlords of the system.

In the decades before the Civil War, southern politicians, especially southern Whigs, often spoke of the need to build railroads, establish a banking system and make their region more self-sufficient and diverse. But their words never led to results. It was as if slavery served as a kind of narcotic that clouded the South's ability to see its weaknesses clearly and created a comfortable miasma in which all the region's difficulties were seen as perpetrated by a host of evil exploiters and scapegoats, from native southern merchants to Jews. As long as cotton prices rose, the South could be complacent. "Who can doubt, that has looked at recent events, that cotton is supreme?" declared Senator James Hammond in his famous "Cotton Is King" speech of March 4, 1858.

It was tempting for southerners to think that cotton would also rescue them in the war. Jefferson Davis was not so sure. Almost alone among Confederate leaders, he was privately predicting a long and costly fight. Combustible, gloomy, tense, temperamental, autocratic and distrustful of others' ambitions, Davis nevertheless had a sterling reputation for patriotism, intelligence and honesty. But his realism about the war at the outset made him come across to others as weak willed, overly cautious and pessimistic. The men around Davis, unfortunately, thought that the Union would sue for peace after a few punches in the nose. One was Christopher G. Memminger, the man Davis selected to be Secretary of the Treasury. Working in a hot, empty, unswept, uncarpeted and unfurnished room in Montgomery, however, Memminger almost immediately collided with the hard reality of an empty Treasury. Indeed, he got to his office only to find no desk, chair or even paper at his disposal. He paid for the office furniture from his own bank account.

Christopher Gustavus Memminger was a courtly, bewhiskered, German-born lawyer whose officer father had been killed while serving in the army of the Duke of Württemberg. His mother immigrated with her parents to Charleston, South Carolina. After her death, he was reared by a politically well-connected family and then became a successful lawyer and state representative in the South Carolina legislature, where he served as chairman of the lower house's finance committee. An expert on commercial and banking law, Memminger had a solid reputation as an advocate of public education and strict bank regulations.

The new Treasury chief moved quickly to recruit a small group of loyal Democrats from the Buchanan administration to help set up the books and print forms. The first need for the Confederate Treasury was to get hold of cash in the form of gold and silver. Memminger was able to scrounge some cash and bullion from the mint and customs house in New Orleans, the South's financial center, and cobble together loans and gifts from various states, local governments and individuals. It was also difficult to find printers or engravers in the South to produce Confederate notes and currency. A German-born specialist in printing posters and business cards was eventually recruited.

In these first heady days of the Confederacy, Memminger thought there would at least be enough gold to coin money. He enlisted an architectural firm to come up with a design for a gold coin with the goddess of liberty seated, bearing a shield and a staff and flanked by bales of cotton, sugar cane and tobacco. On the reverse side was a chain with fifteen links, which reflected the hope that the seceding states would swell to that number. The letters *C.S.A.* crowned the seal, standing for the Confederate States of America. But before a denomination could be set for the coins, Memminger realized there was not enough gold to produce them. He shut down the mints by June.

To obtain gold for the war, Memminger had to go, like Chase in the North, to where the gold was—the banks. And as in the North, Memminger's demand for bank loans set up a bitter conflict. At the beginning of the Confederacy, it was discovered that all the banks in the South possessed only $26 million in gold, silver and other coins, ranging from Spanish dollars to French napoleons to American half-dollars. About half was in the banks of New Orleans. One of Memminger's first tasks was to figure out ways to secure it. At its initial meeting in Montgomery, the Confederate Congress authorized a $15 million loan from the banks, to be paid off by revenues from a new export duty of one-eighth cent per pound on cotton. The logic was sound. Memminger knew that the South's strength lay in its abundant agriculture production, and he estimated that the Confederacy could export more than $200 million worth of cotton, rice, tobacco and other goods in a year. Revenues generated by an export fee on these goods might be enough to secure hundreds of millions of dollars in loans. The problem was the Union blockade, imposed by Lincoln in April immediately after Fort Sumter.

Historians disagree about whether Memminger was remiss in not acting quickly to export cotton and accrue funds before the blockade set in. E. Merton Coulter argues that if the Confederacy had moved faster to export cotton during the first year of the war, when the blockade was easier to breach, "it might well have made King Cotton an early source of credit at home as well as abroad" and strengthened the value of Confederate currency. Years after the Civil War, a myth arose that millions of bales of cotton sat unshipped on southern docks, costing the Confederacy an opportunity to shore up its finances at an early stage of the conflict. Answering those charges in a newspaper article, Memminger said the story was nonsense. Had such stockpiles existed, he said, "it would have required a fleet of four thousand ships, allowing one thousand bales to the ship!"

In the end, cotton could not bail out the South. The $15 million in bonds, supposedly backed by the cotton export duty, was a hard sell to the banks. It took months to line them up. When they finally agreed, the loans drained their gold reserves and sent them to the brink of insolvency. As for the export tax backing the loan, the Union's naval blockade proved to be so effective that no exports could get out. Memminger tried several times to get congressional approval of further loans backed by the export tariff as the war dragged on. But bowing to the anger of protesting farmers, who argued sensibly that it was not logical to tax exports at a time of blockade, Congress repeatedly rebuffed him. During the entire Civil War, export taxes yielded not tens of millions of dollars, as Memminger had hoped, but only $39,000.

The failure to harness the sources to finance the war was related to another of the South's economic blunders. The Confederates believed that King Cotton was so powerful it could bludgeon Britain and France into helping in their cause. At meetings in Charleston, Savannah, Mobile and New Orleans, planters set on the idea of withholding cotton in order to persuade Britain, which obtained three-quarters of its cotton from the South, to intervene in the war on the Confederacy's behalf. Vice President Alexander Stephens predicted "revolution" in Europe if it could not get cotton. One newspaper, the *Charleston Mercury,* boasted at the outset of the war that the South could bankrupt all the textile mills of Britain and France if those countries refused to recognize the Confederacy. "The cards are in our hands," thundered the paper, "and we intend to play them out." The Confederates even believed that they could coerce New England by withholding cotton.

The idea was misconceived. Britain was indeed feeling an economic pinch. Its cotton supplies by mid-1862 were one-third of normal, and workers were losing their jobs in Lancaster and other mill towns. The Chancellor of the Exchequer, William Gladstone, feared riots and favored intervention on behalf of the South. But in fact the workers did not sympathize with the southern rebellion. They felt more solidarity with workers in the free states than with slave owners in the South, whose cause was looked on more favorably by Britain's aristocracy. The American Civil War thus produced class conflicts abroad as well as at home. Not least of those sympathetic to the North was a German revolutionary named Karl Marx, then living in England, who declared that "the working men of Europe" were on the side of Lincoln, whom he described as "the single-minded son of the working class." In the end, Britain was also afraid of offending the North by violating its blockade, and it was able to get alternative supplies of cotton from India and Egypt.

From the Confederate statehouse, President Davis opposed the boycott of cotton sales, asserting that what the South needed was not threats but hard cash, and he persuaded Congress not to authorize one. But historians such as James McPherson say the embargo "virtually enforced itself." In the spring of 1862, southerners planted about half their usual cotton acreage. Exports to Britain fell to a tiny percentage of their former levels. Whether caused by talk of an embargo or the northern blockade, the loss of exports deprived the South of the ability to earn money from its most precious asset.

The blockade debate illustrates the South's delusions in the financial area. Militarily, the Confederacy had superior generals and skill and the advantage that often accrues to the defending side. It was not so fortunate in its financial leadership. The South's objective was to sow division and irresolution in the North, tap its own agricultural resources and, with any luck, win the assistance of Britain and France. In the end, a multitude of failings kept the South from overcoming the North's tremendous economic and military advantages.

———

When the war began, the South's wealth was estimated at $4.6 billion, a not inconsiderable sum. But most of that wealth was tied up in slaves and land. The South's total banking capital was a paltry $61 million and its total currency only $51 million. The South compounded its problems by printing money and borrowing rather than raising taxes. The Confederacy took its cue not from the United States Constitution but from the Articles of Confederation adopted by the states after the Revolutionary War. One of the tenets the Confederacy embraced was that, since future generations would enjoy the advantages of a war for independence, it was only right for the current generation to borrow money and charge its sons and daughters with at least part of the financial burden of the war. Another argument against taxes was that there was no Confederate money in circulation with which to pay them. The expectation was that the war would be over quickly, and that taxes would take a long time to come in. Any tax system was going to have to be overhauled as soon as they won. Why start one now? Officials feared that southerners, not accustomed to paying taxes to Washington, would hardly be inclined to send their money to Montgomery—or later Richmond, the new capital that the Confederates relocated to in May, a month after Fort Sumter.

The move to Richmond occurred after Virginia joined the secession and extracted a promise from Vice President Stephens that its capital city would become the capital of the Confederacy. Davis opposed the move as expensive and unnecessary, but lawmakers and officials eager to flee the boondocks of Montgomery overrode him. Richmond had the advantage of serving as an important rail and iron-manufacturing center, near the grain-, meat- and food-producing regions of northern Virginia and the Shenandoah Valley. Virginia was the southern state with the largest population and the biggest industrial capacity (including the Tredegar Iron Works), and it had a historic capital building on the James River. Virginia also had the aura of a gentry, as personified by Washington and Jefferson, seen in the South as the models for its own declaration of independence. In Richmond, there was also an advantage, and no small amount of daring, to being near the Confederate Army's crucial positions near the Potomac River, only 110 miles from Washington, D.C.

On a Sunday evening in late May, Davis left for the new capital with an entourage of top officials. As his horses and carriages passed through Atlanta, Augusta, Wilmington, Goldsboro and other towns, crowds turned out to cheer, shouting, "We want Jeff Davis!" and "The old hero!" Though ill and fatigued, Davis managed to make a few appearances along the way. Finally in Richmond, his carriage and four white horses pulled up to the Spottwood Hotel, where Davis and his party prepared to move into offices on the second floor of the United States Customs House, down the hall from the office of the shrewd and genial Secretary of State, Judah P. Benjamin. Arriving separately, Memminger and his aides at the Treasury Department moved into the first floor. Aside from his close aides, the largest part of Memminger's workforce was a contingent of "society belles" recruited to clip and sign Treasury notes in the belief that personal signatures would be a guarantee against counterfeit currency. (Memminger himself did not think that the signing scheme would work.) The women were among the few of their gender to serve in a visible capacity in the Confederacy.

Upon moving to Richmond, Memminger made the first of his many ill-fated proposals for a tax to finance the war: a tax on the owners of property, securities and businesses to raise $15 million for the government. It was "every man's duty to contribute of his substance" to the nation's defense, he declared, adding that taxes were "the only certain reliance" for getting real revenues and the only way of tapping the resources of "the willing and of the unwilling, if there be any such" among the Confederacy's citizens. The tax would be on property, slaves, capital and businesses in each state. The proposal was to allow each state to raise the money by taxing the value of property, slaves, capital and business as it saw fit, using its own tax-collecting machinery and getting a discount if it paid the tax ahead of schedule. A well-known New Orleans banker had recommended to the Treasury that such a tax was a reasonable way to secure up to $30 or $40 million a year.

But in its first display of resistance to taxation, the Confederate Congress balked. Instead, it merely pledged the faith of the Confederate States to provide sufficient revenues to pay the interest and principal on the latest $50 million loan approved on May 16, without saying what revenues would pay them off. It directed Memminger to go out and collect information on property values, revenues and state tax systems to determine what would be a fair form of taxation.

For the time being, the only alternative source of revenue was tariffs. But the South resented high tariffs as a tool of northern interests. High barriers to imports had led South Carolina to try to nullify the tariffs in the 1830s in an early crisis that included talk of secession. As Senator Robert Toombs of Georgia told his state legislature, "There is not an artisan in brass, or iron, or wood, or weaver, or spinner in wool or cotton, or a calico-maker, or ironmaster, or a coal owner, in all the Northern or Middle States, who has not received what he calls the protection of his government on his industry to the extent of from fifteen to two hundred per cent from the year 1791 to this day. They will not strike a blow, or stretch a muscle, without bounties from the government. No wonder they cry aloud for the glorious Union."

Despite this antipathy for trade barriers, the Confederate Congress reauthorized existing United States tariffs in 1861 as they applied to the South, reserving the right to make changes later. Then after Fort Sumter, Memminger proposed duties averaging 12.5 percent on iron, coal, cheese, paper, lumber and other goods, even though the Confederate Army desperately needed the iron and wood for railroads. Memminger assigned five clerks to keep track of imports in New Orleans, the biggest commercial port, but his hoped-for $25 million in revenues fell short because of the blockade. Despite some blockade running, total receipts trickled in at a fraction of projections.

The other expedient tried by Congress was loans from farmers, known as produce loans, which required farmers to sell cotton and other goods to the government in exchange for government bonds. The advantage for the government, faced with the difficulty of collecting revenues from a resistant population, was that produce loans at least got hold of food and cotton for the Army. Farmers complained about low prices and being paid in bonds that diminished in value by the month. But most cotton growers, shut off from regular markets in the North and Europe, were glad to have payment of any kind. At rallies throughout the South, farmers would pledge 2,000 bales of cotton or 3,000 bushels of corn, or rice, sugar and molasses to pay for government loans. As a result, the central and state governments accumulated hundreds of thousands of bales of cotton in storehouses and at farms where it was harvested. They tried to sell it abroad or use it as collateral for foreign loans. Some of the cotton got through the blockade to Europe, and some even got through military lines to the North, where it was exchanged secretly for supplies. But the blockade, combined with croplands destroyed in the war, strangled most of these early financing efforts.

Then came the Confederate's rout of Union forces at Bull Run, thirty miles from Washington, on July 21, 1861.

The South's struggles to get money, like those of the North, rose and fell with the news of battles won and lost. With the decisive victory at Bull Run, the South's cause suddenly burst to life. Within days, Memminger demanded that Congress respond with a real program of revenues. Once again he asked Congress to raise money—not $15 million, as he had requested before, but $25 million in taxes on slaves, real estate and personal property. The taxes were aimed at tapping the total assessed value of $4.6 billion in the South, nearly half of it represented by slaves and most of the rest in real estate. But inevitably the brunt would be borne by the farmers who formed the backbone of the region's economy, and they were not happy. "This Government belongs to the people, and not to a little self-assuming Congress, who had no more right to levy such a tax than you and I have," said a planter quoted in an Atlanta newspaper in 1861.

Aggravating their anger was the same problem of inequity seen in the North. Since some states were richer in property than others, their per capita tax rates were lower than in poorer states. There was no constitutional problem, at least initially. The South omitted the clause requiring "direct taxes" to be apportioned to each state according to population. The resulting "war tax" was pegged at 50 cents per $100 of the value of a person's property, though property worth less than $500 was exempted from taxation. With high hopes for the Treasury, Memminger set up chief collectors for each state and a War Tax Bureau in the Treasury. But the tax turned out to be a sham. Some states did not even try to implement it, arguing that they were under invasion. Others simply borrowed the money themselves and turned the proceeds over to Richmond, claiming that there was not yet enough currency in circulation to collect taxes from the people. The whole idea of avoiding inflation by raising revenues instead of borrowing was defeated by these backdoor borrowing practices.

The way out of the mess was to print paper and still more paper, some of it in the form of long-term bonds and some in the form of short-term notes with low interest rates. The notes were like scrip—in effect, "forced loans" to the soldiers, suppliers, retailers and others that were paid in them by the Confederate government. Confederate currency flooded forth in bigger and bigger amounts, and redemptions deferred further and further into the future. The government tried to encourage people to exchange their short-term notes for higher-denomination bonds, but there were few takers. The first summer of the war, only $1 million in notes were in circulation. By the end of 1861, it was $30 million. The amount reached

$450 million by the end of 1862 and twice that sum a year later. Gold coins and coins of other metals were the only money of any value, and people hoarded them as their value rose. It soon became difficult to make change for amounts less than a dollar. Banks advised depositors to make checks in multiples of $5, and southerners resorted to postage stamps for money, sometimes cutting them in half. Merchants, railroads and other businesses began issuing their own paper currency, known as "shinplasters," though they were nearly worthless. "Great God what a people," said a Mississippi editor, "two hundred and fifty different sorts of shinplasters, and not one dime in silver to be seen!"

With the South's setbacks at Vicksburg and Gettysburg in July of 1863, the value of Confederate money sank further. It sank so low that a northern "greenback" was worth four Confederate dollars, but the government in Richmond appealed to southerners to accept it as an act of patriotism, with some officials threatening that anyone who refused might be arrested. Rumors of the Confederacy repudiating its debts hardly helped shore up public confidence. States, cities and counties made the currency situation even worse by issuing their own debt certificates, even paying the salaries of state lawmakers with state notes and bonds. So did private corporations and individuals, including railways, manufacturers and large retail dealers. All this currency made the Confederate dollar even more worthless. A gold dollar was exchanged for three in paper at the end of 1862. A year later the ratio was 20 paper dollars for every gold dollar, and by the final months of the war, it was in the range of 1,000. For consumers, inflation meant ruinous prices for necessities and luxuries alike. Coffee was worth 4 times its original price by the end of 1861, 25 times a year later, 80 times in December 1863, and by the end of 1864, 125 times. The blockade cut off salt supplies, so Confederate citizens resorted to obtaining salt from seawater. They roasted berries to make their own coffee, used persimmon seeds for buttons, brewed ordinary leaves for tea and made shoes from strong cloth rather than leather.

Confederate money, churning out of the printing presses, was widely derided as "rags" and "fodder." "An oak leaf will be worth just as much as the promise of the Confederate treasury to pay one dollar," declared the *Macon (Ga.) Daily Telegraph*.

Rampant inflation and worthless currency had one important positive effect. It led to a widespread push for the government to raise taxes. Many newspapers and other observers reasoned that even a stiff tax would be less punishing to the consumer and the citizen than the cost of a new round of borrowing. Georgia's senator, Herschel V. Johnson, warned that "universal ruin" would occur if taxes were not raised, and a Georgia editor said, "The Congressman who is afraid of taxing the people, is, and ought to be regarded as a public enemy." The editor of the *Richmond Enquirer* demanded: "For God's sake tax us."

Another impetus behind the demand for taxation was growing resentment over the unequal suffering and burdens brought on by the war. One focus of people's rage was the conduct of the Army. As soldiers moved in to seize horses, food and property, many farmers tried to hide their crops, or they turned to raising cotton and tobacco, which at least wouldn't be eaten by hungry soldiers. Another detested element of unfairness was the rule that allowed at least one white man on every plantation with at least twenty slaves to stay at home and avoid military service. The so-called "Twenty-Negro Law," designed to prevent slaves from running away or rebelling, was eventually modified to require anyone taking advantage of it to pay $500 for the privilege of getting out of the Army. Yet it remained a symbol of the privileges of wealth and property in the South. "Never did a law meet with more universal odium," Mississippi's senator, James Phelan, wrote to Jefferson Davis. Class hatred led to action in some parts of the South. Georgia, North Carolina and other states, along with some local governments, came up with programs of assistance for families facing starvation or malnutrition. The aid was paid for by taxes on the wealthiest plantations, a sign of the readiness in some quarters to consider progressive taxation to alleviate class discontent.

By January 1863, Memminger was toying once again with the idea of a nationwide property tax, but now there was a new problem. It was related to the Confederacy's permanent Constitution, which incorporated some crucial changes from the earlier draft. State legislatures, for instance, were given the right to overrule federal officials on certain issues, and taxes and tariffs designed "to promote or foster any branch of industry" were barred, as were public expenditures to benefit a particular section of the populace. These clauses were a residue of the South's desire to avoid the Union practice of showering largesse on certain industries. In the tax area, the new Confederate Constitution also included the original provision requiring that any "direct tax"—understood as a property tax—had to be "apportioned among the several States" according to their population. Thus, when the Confederate Congress renewed its tax debate in early 1863, lawmakers provoked the same constitutional criticism as they had in the North, with critics warning that wealthy states would be paying a lower tax rate than poor states. Differing property tax rates, in turn, posed the problem of appearing to be in direct violation of the separate constitutional requirement for a "uniform" tax system.

All these factors—class resentment, constitutional problems and the growing demand to do something about inflation—led Memminger to propose that in addition to a property tax, there be a tax on income, as well as the output on farms. He declared that "an ample and permanent tax" was necessary to restore solvency and secure public confidence in the Confederacy's finances, an aim that drew widespread support. The *Richmond Enquirer* ridiculed Congress for failing to act, labeling the lawmakers guilty of "representation without taxation."

An income tax had an additional virtue: it would tax wealth more efficiently. It could also tax wealth earned from war profits, industry and sales. The Treasury Secretary argued that it was entirely "proper" for incomes to be taxed. "Otherwise," he said, "the whole profits of speculation and trade, together with those resulting from skill and labor, would escape contribution." Moreover, farm output could be taxed "in kind"—that is, farmers could hand over a portion of their produce rather than money. Memminger reasoned that the in-kind tax would at least supply the Army with food and matériel, get the government out of the purchasing business and make the whole tax system harder to evade.

The final measure, approved by Congress in April, imposed an 8 percent tax on output on a range of farm products, from cotton and wool to flour, sugar and salt. It also imposed a 10 percent tax on business profits, escalating to 16 ⅔ percent as profits increased. A license tax was also imposed on various professions, including bankers, brokers, distillers, innkeepers, butchers, bakers, physicians and peddlers. The boldest feature was an income tax, with rates differing for salaries and other forms of earning. For salaries, the rate was 1 percent on income more than $1,000 and 2 percent on more than $1,500. Other income was taxed at rates from 5 percent on $500 to 15 percent on income more than $10,000. In addition, an in-kind tax was imposed on farms—at a rate of 10 percent for farm products. In effect, it was a tithe that was to be delivered at depots and then distributed to Treasury agents for eventual use by the Army.

Not surprisingly, it was the in-kind tithe that reinforced farmers' belief that they were being unjustly treated. They saw taxation as falling more heavily on them than on the Confederacy's class of merchants, capitalists and businesspeople. Farmers were especially resentful that they had to pay at such a high rate when salaried workers paid only a 1 or 2 percent income tax. Farmers' antipathy toward the merchant class was hardly new in the South, or indeed anywhere. Taxes "in kind" on produce had inflamed French peasants and helped produce the French Revolution. But in the Confederacy, the farmers' anger created an odd new situation. They were clamoring to pay the income tax instead of the produce tithe. In meetings throughout the South, they demanded its repeal. "We are in favor of a just and equitable system of taxation, so that all classes may bear their burden equally," one farmers' convention declared, denouncing the so-called "tithe system" as punishing "the labor and industry of the agricultural classes."

Another resolution, quoted in the *North Carolina Standard*, pronounced the produce tax "unjust and tyrannical." Another paper called it "a relic of barbarism, which alone is practiced in the worst despotisms." Finally it was argued that the tax was unconstitutional because it violated the clause requiring direct taxes to be apportioned equally among the states. Davis acknowledged the criticism but argued that until a census was taken, the requirement for direct taxes to be apportioned equally need not be followed. Conveniently, the census was perpetually postponed by the Confederacy, and so the constitutional issue never formed the basis of an effective legal challenge.

The in-kind tax not only provoked most of the fury; it also encountered tremendous logistical problems in getting collected— not least because by 1864 nearly a fourth of the Confederacy's 473 collection districts were in enemy hands. Farmers had to deliver sacks of potatoes, grain, sugar, molasses, cotton, wool, tobacco and vegetables to government-owned bins and containers, where assessors were stationed to resolve disputes on what should be turned in. Some of the products went from there to Army supply stations. Cotton, wool and tobacco were held for sale or export. But collection stations were often scenes of chaos and fraud. Because the depots did not have enough sacks, piles of grain were left to rot, and hay was spread out because there was no baling material. The Confederacy unleashed hordes of despised agents to traipse through farmers' fields, demanding their produce. Estimates vary on how much money was actually collected by the in-kind tax. Confederate authorities pegged the amount at $145 million, while other estimates are lower. For all its problems, however, the in-kind tax ended up yielding enough food and produce to keep many destitute and starving soldiers clothed and fed.

As the South's military fortunes sank, starvation and despair spread among its people. More than a dozen cities and hamlets experienced bread riots, with mobs of people raiding shops and depots, shouting, "Bread! Bread! Our children are starving while the rich roll in wealth!" While many Confederate troops fought valiantly until the end, many starving soldiers went to the edge of revolt. The government rushed food to the needy in large cities and elsewhere, averting famine in some instances by selling cotton and other goods through clandestine channels to the Yankees.

At the Treasury Department, Memminger saw quickly that the 1863 tax measure would not be sufficient. The head of the administrative bureau of the War Department wrote in his diary of "the irretrievable bankruptcy of the national finances" and a growing "sense of hopelessness." Reports of robberies and vagabond gangs stealing poultry, meat, cattle and other goods on farms were spreading, as were reports of more and more people dressed in rags. More and more candidates for office began criticizing the authorities and demanding a negotiated end to the war. To do something about the worthless currency, the Confederate Congress passed the notorious Funding Act of February 1864, compelling holders of short-term government notes to exchange them for twenty-year bonds at 4 percent—and to be taxed heavily if they did not comply. But Memminger knew that to prepare for the next round of borrowing, he had to raise at least $100 million in new taxes. The Treasury chief's first instinct was to raise the income tax. In a report from the previous year of 1863, the Confederate Tax Commissioner had argued that the wealthy few had "no moral right to amass fortunes" at the expense of the many fighting in the war. Memminger did not share that populist view, but he did need the revenue.

In February of 1864, southern lawmakers once again resorted to a direct tax, this time imposing a new 5 percent tax on property "of every kind and description," including the value of all land and slaves in the Confederacy. Memminger calculated that this tax would yield $120 million annually, which could be used to support a new $1 billion refinancing scheme. On top of paying a 5 percent tax on property, the owners of jewelry, gold, silverplate, watches and similar personal items had to pay a tax of 10 percent on their value. To capture the money made by speculators and traders, even steeper rates were imposed on profits from trading in farm and manufactured goods and on large profits made by banks, insurance companies, railroads, telegraph companies and joint stock companies. Because of the dire emergency, Congress brushed aside any constitutional problems. There was some debate over whether slaves should be taxed, but Memminger argued that since land and slaves constituted two-thirds of the value of all property in the South, exempting slaves would rule out taxation of "the very property for which they were contending" in the war. Congress also raised the income tax rates to a maximum of 25 percent and increased the tax on business profits that exceeded 25 percent.

In approving the new tax, however, Congress weakened its impact by watering down some of the tax laws passed the year before. For example, they let farmers deduct the new 5 percent tax from the produce they had to turn over to the government in kind. They could also deduct the 5 percent property tax from their income tax payments. The 8 percent tax on farm products was also suspended. Because of these steps, almost nothing was really added to the government's revenues.

The new tax rates were onerous, but Congress did not rest there. In June, the lawmakers raised all tax rates and imposed an additional 30 percent sales tax. This took a toll on Memminger, who had tried without success to get Congress to repeal some of the offsetting tax reductions enacted earlier. Seeing that the new tax increases were undercut by the offsets, adding only a small amount of money to the Treasury, Memminger concluded that he had outlived his usefulness. In his struggle since the beginning of secession, he had been derided for his inability to keep the Confederacy solvent. The *Richmond (Va.) Daily Examiner* had compared the currency to a vile plant called "Memminger's Mammoth Skunk Cabbage."

In Richmond when the cash was low,
And "promises" were all the go,
Then rapid, constant, was the flow
Of the paper currency.

———

Many times the Confederate Congress had entertained the possibility of removing Memminger. But before such a motion could gain steam, he resigned voluntarily, overwhelmed by odds that would have daunted anyone in the job. His biographer, Henry D. Capers, who was his chief clerk, said he would not even try to defend his mentor against charges of "want of sagacity and proper administrative ability." He merely said Memminger was "but an executive officer" who lacked authority, "never more than an officer executing the will of Congress." What Congress did, he said, was contrary to Memminger's "often-repeated and strongly urged recommendations."

In his letter of resignation on June 15, 1864, Memminger cited the "discontent" over his handling of Confederate finances and said he hoped a successor would be "better able" than he had been "to do valuable service to our country." He then retired to his country home in Flat Rock, North Carolina. His successor, George A. Trenholm, was a partner in the investment firm of Fraser, Trenholm, and Company of Charleston, South Carolina, which had served as a financial agent representing the Confederacy in making purchases in Europe. Trenholm was one of the richest men in the Confederacy, controlling as many as fifty blockade runners carrying cotton out of the South to market overseas. Once in office, the new Secretary immediately renewed Memminger's request for increases in the cotton export duty, import duties and property and earnings taxes.

By November 1864, the Union was all but victorious in the war, Lincoln had been re-elected in the North and the Confederacy was all but bankrupt. "Our finances are now a wreck," declared Vice President Stephens. "Past all hope, in my judgment." As the military situation deteriorated into chaos, Congress finally authorized new rounds of heavy taxation. Trenholm even came up with the idea of getting Confederate citizens to donate their own money, jewels, gold and silverplate, securities, heirlooms and food. He made the gesture of donating $200,000 of his own currency and securities. In a last-ditch effort in January of 1865, he pleaded for new revenue measures, including higher taxes on banks and corporations. "We have reached the limit of our issues," he declared. The only alternatives were to print money or "submit to the temporary inconvenience" of more taxes. "To this last policy the support of all wise and patriotic men should be given, and all should unite and bear this temporary inconvenience with cheerfulness."

The military situation was desperate. "Where is this to end?" asked General Josiah Gorgas, who had kept rebel armies supplied with arms and ammunition, as 1865 dawned in January. "No money in the Treasury—no food to feed Gen. Lee's army—no troops to oppose Gen. Sherman. . . . Is the cause really hopeless? Is it to be lost and abandoned in this way?"

Finally, in March 1865, Congress made one more attempt to raise taxes. The lawmakers heeded the earlier call by Memminger and rescinded the provision allowing taxpayers to deduct in-kind payments and income tax from what they owed in property tax. Gold, silver and foreign credits were to be taxed at 20 percent. Profits from buying and selling were to be taxed at 10 percent, in addition to the income tax. Profits exceeding 25 percent were to be taxed at 25 percent. All property, "real, personal, or mixed," was to be taxed at 8 percent. And all remaining taxes were to be raised by an eighth to pay for soldiers' wages. On March 17, Congress passed its last tax bill, imposing a 25 percent charge on all coin, bullion and foreign exchange. But before these taxes could be implemented, the Confederacy collapsed.

From the perspective of history, the Confederacy was vastly outmatched by the North and may never have had much of a chance to win. Its early optimism was misplaced. But surely one of the blunders related to that optimism was the early conclusion that the war could be prosecuted without taxation. In his vast history of the South, the historian E. Merton Coulter concludes that throughout its existence, the Confederacy imposed taxes that raised only 1 percent of its income for use to defend against the North. The expression "too late" is a leitmotif of many instances in southern history, he commented, but "none more appropriately than in taxation."

The sorry story of financing the Confederate cause raised the question of whether a government that believed in decentralization and states' rights could mobilize the resources to prosecute a war. The South was caught in the paradox of its own politics. With their populist leanings, Confederate leaders did not want to raise tariffs. They were sensitive to the slogan in the South that it was "a rich man's war but a poor man's fight." Furthermore, there were built-in limitations on the government's ability to tap the Confederacy's wealth, which was tied up largely in land and slaves. Wealthy southerners did not see themselves as aristocrats and grandees but as victims of exploitation by capitalists in the North. As the Confederate government commandeered the agricultural sector to feed and clothe its soldiers, farmers did not simply protest the burden being thrust on them. They also resented being punished while banks and merchants were not taxed. Congress, in response, then imposed income taxes and bank taxes, but banks complained so loudly that the government had to back off. There were a great many other financial mistakes. The Confederacy never should have let states borrow their way out of the first tax increase. It should not have delayed the first tax imposed for two years. It was a huge blunder to pressure Europe by embargoing cotton sales abroad.

The fact is, however, that although a wiser tax policy might have helped the Confederacy stave off defeat, there was simply not enough wealth in the South to change the course of the war. Higher taxes and more revenue coming into the South might have shrunk the amount of currency in circulation, lowered prices and strengthened the government's credit, making it easier to borrow. But without more Army successes and without the Navy's ability to break the blockade—or the success of diplomats in obtaining intervention from France and Britain to break it—the Confederacy did not have much of a chance.

In the end, the Confederacy collected $198 million in taxes, including $62 million in in-kind payments, $3.4 million in import duties, $5.7 million in duties and taxes on the Mississippi River and $30,000 in export duties: all for a total of $207 million in revenues during the Confederacy. This contrasted with $1.55 billion in debt. As for the flood of currency, there is no certain way to calculate the amount of money issued by states, cities and smaller local governments, but reliable estimates put it at between $1 billion and $1.5 billion.

Looming defeat had many bizarre effects on Confederate leaders. Surely one of the government's most peculiar actions took place in the final months, when Congress approved a measure to draft as many as 300,000 slaves into the armed forces—with the promise of freedom if they served. A war that had been started to preserve the rights of slave owners and to extend the institution of slavery to other states ended with the willingness of the South to give up the institution for which it went to war. The logic of rewarding slaves with freedom if they defended the slave system stood on its head one of the basic rationales of the war—the twisted argument that slaves preferred to be indentured rather than fend for themselves as "wage slaves" in the cruel capitalism practiced by the North.

At the end of the war, the South was as shattered as any defeated country could be. Physically, it was a land of blackened farms and cities, vacant homes, destroyed factories, rotting wharves and destitute families. The war killed a quarter of the South's white men of military age, two-fifths of the livestock, half of the farm machinery. It ruined thousands of miles of railroads and razed farms and plantations, as well as wiping out the entire system of slave labor that had undergirded the economy. According to

McPherson, two-thirds of the South's wealth, including its slaves, simply vanished in the war. Whatever advantages the North had over the South at the war's outset multiplied at the end. In 1860, the southern states held 30 percent of the nation's wealth; in 1870, it was 12 percent. In 1860, the South's per capita income, including slaves, was two-thirds that of the North. After the war, it was two-fifths.

For its fight to preserve a reactionary way of life and to be free of the exploitation of the North, the nation's South became a place of death, destruction, ruin, debt and humiliation. The South's distinctive feelings of pessimism and resentment were to continue to play a part in the nation's politics and economic revolts for many decades to come. At least a hundred years would pass before the South could recover.

CHAPTER FOUR

⌁

"There Is No Tax More Equal"
The Union Saved, and America Transformed

WITH ITS WEALTH, POWER AND IMPORTANCE AS THE financial and commercial capital of the United States, New York City had much to lose from a civil war. Its retail stores, factories and banks were dependent on the cotton trade and the production and sale of New York–made goods to the South. Small wonder that the city was an outpost of sympathy for the Confederacy.

On a campaign visit in 1860, Lincoln took time to sit for a portrait at the studio of Mathew Brady. He also gave a defining speech at Cooper Union, opposing slavery but reiterating his belief that the Union must be preserved. Most of the city's leading businessmen, bankers and merchants would oppose his election because of their fear of war and their southern sympathies. The *New York Daily News*, edited by Benjamin Wood, brother of the mayor, Fernando Wood, said that if the Republicans won, "we shall find negroes among us thicker than blackberries swarming everywhere." In November, New York City cast nearly two-thirds of its votes for other candidates, but a Republican landslide upstate put the state in Lincoln's column.

As South Carolina and other states seceded, New York's merchants issued a resolution of solidarity with the South and the right of its states to break away. The support from New York's wealthy classes did not stop the rebels from repudiating their debts to the city's banks, traders, shipping companies and other businesses. Southerners were cynical about the support, knowing that it derived from a commercial relationship that primarily benefited New York and exploited the South. As southerners fantasized that Britain and France would come to their aid to maintain the flow of cotton imports, they predicted vast unemployment in the North if the South seceded and believed that the state would act on its economic self-interest.

On the eve of war, such dire prospects for the North's economy were not unrealistic. Lincoln understood the stakes, but he had his mind on the larger problem of preserving the Union. When as President-elect he stopped in the city on his way to Washington for the inauguration in early 1861, he held a breakfast meeting at a mansion on Fifth Avenue with leading Republicans. Many favored compromise in the confrontation between the states. Someone noted that a large number of millionaires were in attendance. "Oh, indeed, is that so?" Lincoln replied tartly. "Well, that's quite right. I'm a millionaire myself. I got a minority of a million in the votes last November." Later in Washington, the financier William E. Dodge brought him an anxious message. If war erupted, grass would one day grow in the nation's great commercial centers. Lincoln tried to be reassuring but replied that the Constitution had to be "respected, obeyed, enforced, and defended, let the grass grow where it may."

In the beginning, the city's manufacturing economy shook violently. Tens of thousands of people lost their jobs as the city's shipyards, ironworks, boot and shoe factories, carriage makers and dry goods producers, even the ice makers, halted with the loss of southern markets. But before long, the Civil War turned out to be a boon to the city's economy and to the North in general. It led to the creation of wealth in the North centered on the great metropolises, as well as in the smaller industrial towns. Describing New York City at the height of this boom, Dodge wrote a friend in England in 1863: "Our streets are crowded, hotels full, the railroads and manufacturers of all kinds except cotton were never doing so well and business generally is active."

The astonishing accumulation of wealth, and the class resentments it inspired, has to be understood as the Union faced the challenge of tapping this wealth to pay for the war.

———

A new era arrived in New York City when Fort Sumter surrendered. Edwin G. Burrows and Mike Wallace, in their history of the city, *Gotham*, describe New Yorkers caught up in patriotism and setting aside their concerns about repudiated debts, trade disruption, financial bankruptcy and the potential loss of business to southern ports, where lower tariffs were likely to siphon imports previously bound for the North. The working class favored war "virtually overnight," they write. Despite warnings about what would happen in the event of war, the Stock Exchange, the Board of Currency, the Clearing House banks, the Chamber of Commerce and other leaders of the business community lined up with the fight for the Union. At Union Square, more than 100,000 New Yorkers rallied in support of the battle with bands and flags. Lincoln transferred money into New York banks to purchase arms and supplies for the Army. Quickly these banks began providing funds to charter ships, procure supplies and transport troops.

The city's traders followed suit by selling huge new quantities of wheat and corn, brought in from the Midwest aboard the Pennsylvania, Erie and New York Central railroad lines, to a hungry

Europe. British capital suddenly flowed to the North to build still more lines. With New Orleans cut off, the Great Lakes ports and the Erie Canal picked up the slack. Industry in the North sprang to life, supplying the Union's war matériel and related projects, including a gleaming new iron dome for the United States Capitol, forged in the Bronx. The Brooklyn docks teemed with men and equipment to handle the goods sent abroad.

Even cattle and lumber were brought into the city from the West; more than two hundred slaughterhouses sprang up in the city, a number exceeding Chicago. Sugar poured in as well, and new refineries were built, making sugar one of the city's largest industries and the Havemeyers one of its wealthiest families. After the discovery of oil in Pennsylvania in 1859, the city became a center for oil refineries. Shipbuilding exploded as the government ordered new gunboats and merchant ships to handle the new trade, though the nation's merchant fleet was to suffer severely from attacks by southern privateers during the war. Thousands of men were hired to work at the Brooklyn Navy Yard, where the demand was high for machinists and engine builders. The *Monitor*, the Union's proud ironclad, was built at Greenpoint in Brooklyn.

All this manufacturing continued to be protected by tariffs, part of the great Republican scheme to build America into a mighty industrial fortress, the very policy that the South had found exploitive and punitive. Workers in New York making $100 a month did not earn enough to shop at the emporiums for the wealthy, A. T. Stewart's and Lord & Taylor. But they tended to see their jobs as dependent on the protectionist system. It was the rich manufacturing families that benefited the most from the Civil War economic boom: Cooper and Hewitt in guns; Phelps and Dodge in ironworks; Squibb and Pfizer in the new industry of pharmaceuticals. Old retail merchant and department store families, such as the owners of A. T. Stewart's and Brooks Brothers, got contracts for military uniforms, sometimes distributing goods of poor quality made of rags and glue called "shoddy."

As riches accrued, so did the perception of their unequal distribution. By 1863, the city's upper 1 percent held 61 percent of the city's wealth. Before the war, the city had a few dozen millionaires. The number grew to several hundred by the end. "In celebration of their expanded or newly minted fortunes, the rich went on a shopping spree," write Burrows and Wallace. "After striking successful deals at the Astor House, speculators decked out in velvet coats, gold chains, breast pins, and rings dined at Delmonico's on partridge stuffed with truffles. The 'shoddy aristocracy' paraded down Fifth Avenue on Sundays or trotted around the new Central Park in their shiny equipages wearing thousand-dollar camel's hair shawls. Contractor parvenus gloried in liveried servants and imported luxuries. In 1862 the genteel Maria Daly was horrified to hear that 'a soldier's wife went to Tiffany and Young's . . . and ordered the greatest quantity of pearls and diamonds and plate.'"

Well before the war, the wealthy of America had begun holding a dramatically large portion of the nation's wealth. According to the economic historian Lee Soltow, 37 percent of the nation's wealth was held by 2 percent of the people, and the top 5 percent held 50 to 60 percent of the nation's wealth in the 1850s. This inequality was tolerated, according to Soltow, because the average person was gaining wealth and saw the system as making it possible to get more. (Back in the 1830s, Tocqueville had noted that the wealthy classes in America were not as despised as the chateaux-dwelling elites of Europe.) But the Civil War weakened the tolerance of ordinary people, and not simply because farms and factories emptied out so that men could fight in battle. Inflation eroded the purchasing power of all Americans. War profiteering stoked their anger. An article in Harper's entitled "The Fortunes of War" assailed the contractors, speculators and others who were getting rich off others' misery, noting that the cost of a dinner at Delmonico's could "support a soldier and his family for a good portion of the year."

In the shadows of New York City's mansions and emporiums were vast shantytowns of tenements and slums. Strikes spread among carpenters, shipbuilders, machinists and longshoremen. Workers, particularly Irish Americans, feared that employers would bring in immigrants and, even worse, African Americans from the South to take their jobs at lower wages. Uneasiness reached a peak in mid-1863 as Lee and the Army of Northern Virginia marched north through the Shenandoah Valley and into Pennsylvania. Union forces, including regiments from New York City, gathered to meet Lee's army at Gettysburg. It was in this period that the draft, which had been approved a few months earlier, went into effect, allowing men of privilege to find a substitute or hand over $300 to pay for one (nearly a year's wages for an unskilled laborer). It did not go unnoticed, according to Burrows and Wallace, that the $3,000 paid by Treasury Secretary Chase for an imported shawl for his daughter at A. T. Stewart "now represented the price of ten men's lives."

Resentment spilled over in the city in mid-July 1863, when the drawing of lots for the draft sparked rioting. Rampaging crowds, many of them Irish American immigrants, poured out of their tenements and descended on railroad stations, police precincts, Fifth Avenue mansions and an armory on Second Avenue, where they carried off guns. Mobs chased after blacks, lynching their victims and destroying their homes and stores. To suppress the insurrection, Secretary of War Stanton dispatched 6,000 federal troops from Pennsylvania, despite fears among some that Lee would try to advance again after being defeated at Gettysburg. The "draft riots" went on for four days, leaving a thousand dead and a terrible residue of race hatred. Many feared the kind of class warfare that had erupted in Paris in 1848. In Washington, Democrats from New York City began lobbying for a negotiated settlement to the war and a "peace candidate" to run against Lincoln in 1864. Led by August Belmont, representative of the Rothschild family, they settled on General George McClellan, who had been dismissed by Lincoln for his military failures.

Consumed by the demands of war, Treasury Secretary Chase did not have an easy time navigating the economic changes churning underneath the surface. Chase disliked war speculation as much as anyone. With gold prices spiking whenever there was bad news from the front, he often had to intervene by selling gold to push prices back down. "Gold, gold, gold, gold—hoarded, bartered, bought, and sold," went the financiers' cry. Asked for his opinion of the gold speculators, Lincoln was said to have banged his fist on the table and called for speculators to be punished by having their heads shot off.

The President was more solicitous of the conditions of the nation's labor force and invited workers' delegations to the White House. At a meeting with the New York Workingmen's Association, he deplored what he called "the hanging of some working people by other working people," adding, "It should never be so. The strongest bond of human sympathy, outside of the family relation, should be one uniting all working people, of all nations, and tongues, and kindreds." Lincoln spoke of need for "remunerative wages" in government contracts. And on at least two occasions, according to Gabor Boritt, a scholar of Lincoln's economic views, the President actually received the leaders of striking unions whose workers had walked off their jobs on Navy contracts. "I know the trials and woes of workingmen," he told a delegation of strikers. "I have always felt for them."

———

The issuing of the final version of the Emancipation Proclamation on New Year's Day 1863 was a moment of spiritual triumph that belied the turbulence surrounding Lincoln's presidency. The war was not going well, the Republican Party had been set back in the November elections and the cabinet was in turmoil since Chase's offer to resign. Despite his anger over Chase's insubordination, Lincoln felt he had no choice but to give him a free hand in handling the finances of a war that was costing $2 million a day. "You understand these things," he said when asked by the Secretary to deal with regulating trade with the South. "I do not."

With more greenbacks flooding the country and a sputtering effort by Jay Cooke to sell more bonds, the winter of 1862–63 was, in the words of the economic historian Sidney Ratner, "the darkest period in the financial history of the federal government." In early 1863, Chase issued another batch of greenbacks, bringing the total amount of borrowing to $900 million. In an attempt to stabilize the nation's currency, the administration won enactment of the National Banking Act, designed to eliminate the chaos of a national system dominated by state banks. Lincoln played a decisive role in the legislation's success. Under the new law, national banks were subject to federal inspection, overseen by a new position called Comptroller of the Currency, and required to invest a third of their capital in federal bonds deposited with the Treasury Department. They could then issue bank notes that could be used as legal tender because they were backed by that investment.

The effect of the act was to shore up the banking system by putting the federal government's credit on the line. By the end of the war, more than 11,500 banks had joined the national system. "All private interests, all local interests, all banking interests, the interests of individuals, everything, should be subordinate now to the interest of the Government," declared Senator John Sherman, ushering in a new era of federal power over the nation's finances.

On the military front, the year 1863 did not begin auspiciously for the Union. McClellan's ouster did nothing at first to improve the North's fortunes. In Richmond, after a great victory at Chancellorsville, President Jefferson Davis and General Robert E. Lee decided to make another attempt to invade the North, sending troops through the Shenandoah Valley and into Pennsylvania, where the southern tide was turned back. The biggest and most decisive battle of the war took place at Gettysburg. It ended with the defeat of the Army of Northern Virginia and its devastating retreat back to the Shenandoah Valley. Lincoln's spirits lifted so much that he and his wife, Mary Todd Lincoln, began going out in public more in the latter half of the year, including to the theater. In November, Lincoln attended the wedding of Treasury Secretary Chase's daughter Kate to William Sprague, former governor and now senator from Rhode Island, one of the social events of the season, although Mrs. Lincoln declined to attend. Facing election the following year, Lincoln was determined to become the first President since Andrew Jackson to win a second term. He knew it was not going to be easy.

Democratic criticism focused on the military stalemate and the financial cost of the war. The mounting attacks from Democrats, who were emboldened after their 1862 electoral victories, focused on the armed forces' standoff and the draining of national treasure. "Whence the money to carry on?" cried Clement L. Vallandigham, the leading southern sympathizer among the Democrats. "Where the men? Can you borrow? From whom? Can you tax more? Will the people bear it?"

In December, Chase gave his answer, calling for another round of tax increases and borrowing. Again the ratio was heavily weighted to issuing more debt. Writing to his friend Edward D. Mansfield, editor of the *Cincinnati Gazette*, Chase declared: "What I mean is simply that the Govt. can no longer borrow without interest to any appreciable extent. And payment of interest necessitates taxes." Chase again complained about Lincoln and others in the cabinet. "I should fear nothing if we had an Administration in the first sense of the word guided by a bold, resolute, farseeing, & active mind, guided by an honest, earnest heart," he wrote a colleague. "But this we have not. Oh! For energy & economy in the management of the War. But how can we have it with these heads?"

Rumors began spreading in 1864 that some Republicans wanted to dump the President and replace him with Chase. The Secretary was apparently orchestrating a fund-raising campaign conducted by his son-in-law, Senator William Sprague of Rhode Island, and the bond super salesman Jay Cooke. Lincoln's loyalists fought back by attacking Chase for tolerating corruption and inflation. The chosen battering ram was Representative Francis Preston Blair, Jr., of Missouri, a former Army corps commander and an imposing and athletic six-footer, who charged that Chase had presided over a "profligate administration" at Treasury and tolerated corruption and fraud in the Mississippi Valley's war supply effort. Chase once again offered to quit. Lincoln suspected that his Treasury Secretary was orchestrating complaints throughout the administration. "I suppose he will, like the bluebottle fly, lay his eggs in every rotten spot he can find," he said. But once again he declined the resignation offer.

The Treasury chief was preoccupied, in any case, with the need for further steps to increase federal revenues. Congress preferred extending and raising the small taxes on spirits, tobacco, carriages, auction sales, sugar, toll bridges, advertisements and the like over increasing the income tax. But a growing body of financial experts realized that an income tax was at least an effective means for raising the necessary funds and meeting the standards of fairness. Their views would lead to a renewed debate about how progressive the tax should be. Returns from the 1862 legislation had fallen short of Chase's goal, so the House Ways and Means Committee proposed to refine the tax, making it 5 percent on all incomes over $600, with no increases after that level. In eliminating the progressive feature of the existing law, the committee was rebuffing the advice of the new Internal Revenue Commissioner, Joseph J. Lewis, who had wanted higher rates for higher incomes. Lewis, a Pennsylvania lawyer, contended that the income tax had actually been a popular innovation "welcomed by the people in a manner that is believed elsewhere unparalleled."

The Commissioner's views turned out to have considerable support among House members, for the Ways and Means bill was attacked as soon as it got to the floor. "I think it is just, right, and proper that those having a larger amount of income shall pay a larger amount of tax," declared Representative Augustus Frank, an upstate New York Republican congressman who was also a railroad director and later a bank director in the Rochester area. "The larger tax we pay at this time, the safer we are and the better will be the securities of the government." His alternative was to keep the 5 percent tax on $600 or more income, but to raise it to 7.5 percent on income more than $10,000 and 10 percent on income more than $25,000.

Among those opposing Frank's progressive alternative was the increasingly crotchety Ways and Means chairman, Thaddeus Stevens. Stevens had reluctantly backed the existing tax in 1862 and seemed to entertain second thoughts. He deplored the "vicious" and "unjust" theory that it was all right to mete out "a punishment of the rich man because he is rich." The government might just as well seize a man's entire wealth over, say, a million dollars. Justin Morrill, chairman of the Ways and Means panel's tax-writing subcommittee, agreed. Unequal tax rates were "no less than a confiscation of property, because one man happens to have a little more money than another," he said, warning that the rich might leave the country rather than pay such a tax.

Morrill and Stevens had their own agenda. As ardent protectionists, they were arguing in favor of higher tariffs as the best way to raise revenues, unacceptable to lawmakers from farm regions. A growing band of these congressmen began to argue that the rich had to pay their "fair share" of the tax burden. Rufus P. Spalding, a respected Democrat and former state supreme court justice in Ohio, argued that higher rates of income tax should be seen as a luxury tax on those best able to sacrifice at a time of war. "Go to the Astors and Stewarts and other rich men of the country and ask them if in the midst of a war [this measure] is unreasonable," thundered Representative J. B. Grinnell, an Iowa Republican. "I could not advocate anything else in justice to the middle classes of the country."

Morrill tried mightily to stem the populist tide on the House floor, arguing with passion that the entire system of American government rested on the principle "that we make no distinction between the rich man and the poor man." A man of modest means was "just as good" as a man of wealth, he said. "It is seizing property of men for the crime of having too much!" he said. "I can speak fairly on this subject because I do not belong to this class." The new progressive rates passed with a large majority.

The mood for a more progressive tax accelerated in the Senate, where a phalanx of Republicans tried to stop it. Pitt Fessenden, the flinty chairman of the Senate Finance Committee, attempted to find a middle ground by acknowledging that while those with "very large incomes" could "better afford" to pay the income tax, an "odious and ungenerous discrimination" against the rich could destroy American prosperity. The wealthy minority, he said, should not be punished simply because "it is convenient to lay your hands upon them." Responding to that worry, a new progressive voice, Senator Lyman Trumbull of Illinois, noted that the poor had suffered the most from high tariffs while "fighting to protect the millionaires" in the war—millionaires who "can afford to pay liberally of their means."

In the end, pragmatism and the need for revenue carried the day. The Senate approved a tax rising to 10 percent on incomes of more than $15,000. The final bill called for the 10 percent rate to kick in at $10,000. The Tax Act of 1864 also raised taxes on dividends, trust companies and other businesses, and it established and extended the principle of withholding the tax at the source. It also introduced the principle of deducting for rent or its equivalent for a person's housing—an important tax break for home owners that was seen as progressive and has remained inviolate.

If the new and higher income tax rates on the wealthy represented a victory for Americans of moderate means, the impact was quickly diluted as Stevens and Morrill counterattacked. They urged higher tariffs to "shelter and protect" businesses from foreign competition. Their tariff law raised the average rate of duties from 37 to 47 percent, which meant that nearly half the value of purchases of imported goods by the American middle class was the result of artificial duties. Rammed through the Congress after only five days of debate, the higher tariffs were a gift to the wool makers, textile owners, iron and steel companies and other members of the

National Manufacturers Association. Lawmakers from farm areas were unhappy. "New England manufacturers are getting richer every day—richer and richer and richer," Representative S. S. Cox, an Ohio Democrat, warned as the legislation was being debated. "They are . . . becoming owners of this country." But his appeals failed, and the tariff law enacted in 1864 established the foundation for protectionism that would last for decades.

The new tax and tariff measures together, enacted in the spring and early summer of 1864, raised hope that the Treasury at last would have enough money to finish prosecuting the war. Chase did not agree. Noting the Union's recent gains on the battlefield, he told associates that still more money would be needed to sustain them and to pay for recently enacted bonuses to anyone who brought in new recruits to the Army. "Can we keep Grant & Sherman so furnished with men & means that they can inflict decisive blows on the rebellion?" he wrote in his journal that June.

On the heels of the revenue crisis came a burst of speculation that was driving up the price of gold, undermining the value of American currency. "Oh, for more faith & clearer sight!" Chase complained in his diary. "How stable is the City of God! How disordered is the City of Man!" Once again he would have to ask Congress for another revenue measure—"another great & painful responsibility!" The Union's financial plight was worsening. The Secretary was in near despair. "What can be done to arrest the decline of public credit? I see nothing effectual except taxation which will make excessive borrowing unnecessary & military success which will make necessary borrowing possible on reasonable terms."

Responding to the Secretary's prayers and to the fiscal emergency, Justin Morrill summoned the Ways and Means Committee to raise the income tax once again, effectively raising the tax for 1863 alone to 8 percent for income greater than $600 and 10 percent on income greater than $10,000. "As a whole, and taking it alone, there is no tax more equal than an income tax," Morrill declared, sounding a different note from the weeks before. The Senate adopted the changes because of the emergency.

As Congress debated these emergency measures, the crisis in Lincoln's cabinet over Chase and his political maneuvering finally blew up beyond repair. It began with Chase's reviving his long-standing fight with Seward, formerly governor and senator from New York, by moving to fill jobs at the Empire State's offices of the Treasury Department with his own appointees. Lincoln, seeking to placate his Secretary of State, who was a leader of the party's moderate wing, told Chase that he feared the appointments were too radical. Chase responded with another resignation, probably thinking it would once again be spurned. But this time Lincoln's patience with the maneuverings of his cabinet was running out. The Union Army was fighting some of the deadliest battles of the war, from the Wilderness campaign to Spotsylvania Court House and Cold Harbor, yet Grant and his men were still unable to destroy Lee's army or capture Richmond. Lincoln had won the Republican nomination in June, silencing those who had wanted to replace him with Chase or anyone else. It was time, he concluded, to accept Chase's resignation. "I thought I could not stand it any longer," the President told John Hay, his secretary.

On June 30, Chase held what he thought would be a routine meeting with Senator Fessenden at the Capitol to discuss gold prices and taxes. Suddenly a messenger summoned the Vermont senator out of the room. Returning, he asked his guest, "Have you resigned?" Chase, confused, said yes, as a matter of fact.

Rushing back to his office, Chase found Lincoln's acceptance on his desk. "You and I have reached a point of mutual embarrassment in our official relation which it seems can not be overcome, or longer sustained, consistently with the public service," it said. The Treasury Secretary was stunned. He bitterly complained that Lincoln had never supported him in his efforts to raise revenues for the war and that the President had embarked on a "timid & almost proslavery course" toward the Confederacy.

Lincoln, seeking to placate the man who had served him and his country with dedication, sent word that Chase would be selected as Chief Justice of the United States if a vacancy occurred. In his final reflections in office, the Treasury Secretary was philosophical about the slippery nature of his commander in chief. "I cannot sympathize with his notion more than once expressed to me & others that the best policy is to have no policy," he told his diary. "He cannot sympathize with my desires for positive & energetic action. It is best that he try somebody else."

To replace Chase, a former governor of Ohio, some of Lincoln's political advisers recommended another ex-governor of the same state, David Tod, an amiable lightweight Democrat who did not have the confidence of Republican barons on Capitol Hill. He knew "no more of finances than a post," commented the *New York Herald*. After a meeting at the White House to discuss the job, Lincoln agreed. The President then turned to William Pitt Fessenden of Maine, the respected if acerbic elder statesman of the Senate. Ailing and weak, Fessenden at first told Lincoln that he feared the crushing burdens of the job would end up killing him. "Very well," the President replied. "You cannot die better than in trying to save our country."

In the summer of 1864, Confederates fought the Union forces to a bloody stalemate in the East. The national debt had soared to $1.7 billion, with the war heading toward a cost of $3 million a day. Time was running out. The Treasury had only $19 million in cash on hand, not enough even to pay impending debt service costs or the salaries of soldiers. Jay Cooke's bond sales were also falling short of their goals. Lincoln faced these difficulties with fatalism, religious resignation and a simple determination to press on. At his request, Congress pushed for more Army recruits and abolished the $300 commutation fee for conscripts. Lincoln began to think that it was "exceedingly probable" that he would be defeated for re-election by

General McClellan, the Democratic nominee, who now favored a negotiated peace with the Confederacy. By early fall, the tide started to turn. McClellan became enmeshed in squabbling within his own camp over the terms of a possible peace agreement with the Confederacy. In September, news of General William Tecumseh Sherman's capture of Atlanta and General Philip H. Sheridan's victory at Winchester gave a new burst of confidence to the Union. Shortly after Lincoln's election victory, Sherman began his scorched-earth march from Atlanta to the sea, arriving in Savannah in December.

These favorable developments made it easier for Fessenden to raise another $200 million in notes and bonds in the last few months of 1864 and another $700 million in the first months of 1865. The Treasury determined that more taxes would be needed to finance the last big costly push toward victory. The new Secretary wanted to raise another $300 million, at least some of it from another increase in the income tax, which he no longer viewed as "oppressive or unjust." Rather, he said, the tax was an excellent way of securing "the blessings of good government" for all Americans.

In February 1865, shortly after Congress adopted the Thirteenth Amendment, abolishing slavery, Representative Morrill proposed another income tax increase, this time to 10 percent on incomes over $3,000. For many lawmakers, once again, his proposal was insufficient. Some wanted the top rate to go to 20 percent. But the bill cleared the House as Morrill proposed and went to the Senate, where Fessenden's successor as chairman of the Finance Committee, Senator John Sherman, took a somewhat different approach in defining the need for an income tax. He argued that the huge debt incurred by the federal government was enriching an entirely new class of investors who had purchased the bonds, while workers had no chance to reap the same advantage.

Sherman said it was important to avoid "the same uneasy struggle between capital and labor, between the rich and the poor, between fund-holders and property-holders, that has marked the history of Great Britain for fifty years." In its final form, the tax levied 5 percent on incomes from $600 to $5,000, and 10 percent on incomes above $5,000. To prevent evasion, the government was empowered to increase any taxpayer's estimate of income. There were to be stiff penalties, including the doubling of tax owed, if taxpayers filed a false return.

The Union now had the wealth, people and determination to bring the war to an end. In his final annual message the previous December, Lincoln had declared that the nation's sense of purpose was "unexhausted, and, we believe, inexhaustible." A million men were in uniform, and they were better equipped than ever. Immigration and the natural population increase more than made up for the 300,000 who had died in battle. Lincoln was not exaggerating when he said there were enough resources to "maintain the contest indefinitely."

In February, Fessenden, begging Lincoln to be relieved because of his failing health, resigned so that he could complete his career by representing Maine in the Senate. Lincoln replaced him with Hugh McCulloch, a conservative former Indiana bank president who was serving as Comptroller of the Currency. These were the final weeks of the war, a time of peace feelers from the Confederacy that came to naught. On the day of Lincoln's inauguration, March 4, Washington was a sea of mud after several days of torrential rain. Legend has it that the sun burst through as Lincoln took the oath of office for the second time. The man who raised his hand to swear Lincoln in was Salmon Chase, who had fought so long to sustain the nation's finances during the war and was now elevated, as Lincoln had promised, to the post of Chief Justice.

The President delivered his shocking message—that all the blood and sacrifice of the war might well have been God's way of exacting repayment after centuries of toil and death meted out to slaves—while calling for reconciliation "with malice toward none." In private, Lincoln was not above indulging in mordant humor, telling his wife that after the White House he wanted to visit California to see everyone "digging gold to pay the National debt."

Some days later, Lincoln visited the defeated Confederate capital of Richmond, where he arrived unannounced. Some black workmen were the first to recognize him. "Bless the Lord, there is the
great Messiah!" cried a man of about sixty, dropping his spade.
"Glory, Hallelujah!" As he and the others fell on their knees, trying
to kiss the President's feet, Lincoln told them, "Don't kneel to me.
That is not right." Word spread of his presence, and soon he was
surrounded by throngs of former slaves, shouting, "Bless the Lord,
Father Abraham's come." Leading Tad with his left hand, Lincoln
headed toward the Confederate White House, shedding his long
coat in the warm sun. He sat in Davis's study and then toured the
building. At the Virginia statehouse, which was a shambles, he
perused official documents and glanced at the worthless Confederate $1,000 bonds strewn across the floor.

Lincoln learned on April 9 of Lee's surrender at Appomattox.
The night of April 11, he gave a speech at the north portico of the
White House, offering thoughts about reconstruction and declaring that it was time to consider extending the vote to African
Americans, at least those who were educated or had served in the
Union Army. He presented no concrete ideas for the future of the
rebel states but said only that those loyal to the Union must be in
charge. He did not share the view of the radicals that the South's
social structure had to be eradicated, with its estates divided up
and doled out to black families. There were no other thoughts
about racial integration, interracial marriage, racial equality or
other issues gripping many Americans with anxiety. Only the
prospect of peace dominated his thinking and his talk. In the
crowd, as he had been on the occasion of Lincoln's second inaugural a month earlier, was a disgruntled twenty-six-year-old actor
with an unstable personality, probable links to the Confederate
secret service and a determination to seek revenge. On Good Friday, April 14, at Ford's Theatre, the actor John Wilkes Booth
sneaked into the presidential box, aimed his derringer and pulled
the trigger. Mary Lincoln screamed, Booth jumped to the stage and
fled, and the next morning the President was dead.

General Lee's surrender at Appomattox Court House on April 8, 1865, settled the historic issues over which the Civil War had been fought. The Union prevailed, slavery was abolished and the dominance of the industrial North was complete. But underlying the new era of Reconstruction were deepening cleavages among Americans as the federal government actively fostered and protected American industry. The barons of capitalism, in turn, not only sought out government help but also mobilized their resources to repeal the Civil War era taxes on wealth as both unjust and unhealthy. They even threatened to go to court to have the income tax declared unconstitutional. That tactic proved unnecessary. Within seven years after the Union's victory, Congress repealed both the income tax and the inheritance tax, eliminating the tax burden on the wealthiest Americans.

The Civil War had cost $5 billion for both sides and left a mountain of nearly $3 billion in Union debt that would take years to retire. There were huge additional costs to be borne in paying out Army pensions and binding up the nation's wounds. But the war had buried the old definition of the United States as a union to be preserved and replaced it with a new identity as a nation, a change traced by Lincoln's own speeches. This new nation had a new unified national currency, a federally regulated banking system, a continent-wide rail system, a program to distribute public lands in the West, a federal responsibility to charter corporations and a network of land grant colleges. Businesses learned during the war how to operate from coast to coast.

Despite the devastation in the South and the Union's debts, the American gross national product skyrocketed. Federal government spending went from 2 percent of the gross national product before the war to an average of 15 percent, close to the nearly 20 percent level of modern times. Because the newly prosperous nation was preparing to demobilize at breakneck pace—some 800,000 men left the Army in the first six months after the war, and the federal budget dropped by $1 billion in a year—it seemed possible that there would be enough money to pay for the costs of Reconstruction and also reduce at least some wartime taxes. The debate over which taxes to reduce or eliminate revived all the old antagonisms. Merchants and farmers wanted to lower tariff barriers, while industrialists and their allies in Congress went after the income tax.

Morrill, who chaired the tax subcommittee on Ways and Means, set his initial sights on abolishing the income tax's two-tiered rate structure. Always offended by the idea of taxing wealthier citizens at higher rates—he compared the concept to highway robbery—Morrill sought to make the tax uniform at 5 percent for all incomes greater than $1,000. Though the tax was paid by only a tiny percentage of Americans, it was widely criticized in the press and among influential opinion leaders on various grounds. Many argued that the revenue was no longer needed and that graduated rates were fundamentally unfair. Still others detested the publication of tax returns, calling it an invasion of privacy, and claimed that the tax was administered inefficiently. The subsequent scandals of the postbellum period gave critics ammunition because they could argue that the tax supported wasteful and corrupt spending by the government.

Opposition to Morrill's proposal was strong. It came not only from many other House members but also from President Andrew Johnson, a Democrat who had grown up in poverty in North Carolina and had served as a stalwart pro-Union wartime governor in Tennessee before his selection by Lincoln as vice president. Johnson had never opposed slavery, but he saw himself as a foe of privilege. In the postwar tax battles, he said that taxes should not fall "unduly" on the poor but tap "the accumulated wealth of the country."

Some House members wanted to make the income tax even more progressive than it was. Rejecting Morrill's appeals, the House approved an amendment by Representative Frederick A. Pike of Maine to make the tax 5 percent on income more than $5,000 and 10 percent on income more than $10,000. In the end, the Senate kept the tax at its existing level of 5 percent on income more than $600 and 10 percent on income more than $5,000. But in renewing the tax, Congress declared that it would be payable every year "until and including the year 1870 and no longer."

The election in the fall of 1866 cemented the control of Congress by radical Republicans, emboldening them not only in their punitive approach to the South but also in their drive for high tariffs and muscular government on behalf of business. Among the harshest of the Reconstruction Era steps directed at the South was the invalidation of the entire Confederate debt. Congress also ruled out any possibility of slaveholders being compensated for the loss of their slaves. Beyond the total destruction of vast swathes of Confederate farmlands and cities, these steps wiped out billions of dollars of assets held by the South's aristocracy. By contrast, in the North, everything possible was done to redeem the Union's debt.

In 1867, Morrill finally succeeded in enacting a flat rate of 5 percent on the income tax for incomes in excess of $1,000. The Senate went along and the law took effect on the historic day of March 2, 1867. On that day, Congress also enacted two laws directed at an increasingly isolated President Johnson—the Tenure of Office Act, which limited his power to remove cabinet officers, and the Reconstruction Act, which put ten Confederate states under military rule and denied them representation until they ratified the Fourteenth Amendment, which had been written to guarantee full rights to all citizens and invalidate state laws depriving anyone of life, liberty or property "without due process of law." (The Fourteenth Amendment, designed to protect former slaves, was interpreted for many decades by federal judges as a protection of corporations against attempts by Congress to regulate their activities.)

The years 1867 and 1868 brought to a boiling point a long-simmering confrontation between Congress and Johnson over policies regarding the South. Lincoln had taken many steps designed to help southern states return to self-government once the war was won. Johnson, adopting a similarly conciliatory approach to the vanquished states, wanted to let them write their own constitutions, even if that meant impairing the rights of African Americans in the old Confederacy. With most states refusing to ratify the Fourteenth Amendment, and race riots spreading in Memphis and New Orleans, Johnson blustered at his critics but seemed to have no interest at all in protecting the lives and rights of former slaves.

The Tenure of Office Act was one of Congress's many responses. It trimmed various powers of the President, including his prerogatives as commander in chief of the armed forces and his ability to replace cabinet members. Johnson responded with indignation and, in a desire to test the act, removed Secretary of War Stanton, the most prominent radical left in the cabinet. With Stanton barricading himself at the War Department, the House voted in early 1868 to impeach Johnson for "high crimes and misdemeanors in office." The "crime" was basically one of disagreeing with Congress on Reconstruction policies. It was not even clear that the Tenure of Office Act applied to Stanton. After a tumultuous trial, the Senate fell one vote short of the necessary two-thirds majority required to remove Johnson from office.

As the 1868 election approached, Johnson was not considered a serious candidate. Republicans rallied around General Ulysses S. Grant, a war hero who had no political experience and was willing to follow the path of the radicals. The Democrats struggled mightily through the presidential election to rid themselves of the taint of disloyalty to the Union, but without much success. They seized on some economic issues almost as a diversion, focusing on a demand for the restoration of easy money in the form of new "greenbacks" that would not be backed by gold. It was their perception that inflation and an eroding currency would help farmers and others burdened by debt. The Democrats' demand for cheaper money, which was to echo for the rest of the century, helped the party solidify some support. Despite a robust and confident campaign that was generously financed by bankers, manufacturers and corporations, Grant won with only 53 percent of the popular vote.

Although a brilliant general and man of action, Grant had a shy, distrustful and inarticulate manner and took office when the job required someone with extraordinary vision and generosity. Before the war, Grant had spent several years in private life and came to have a particularly keen admiration for business success. Other than civil rights for African Americans, he had little interest in social reforms and, as it turned out, little sensitivity to the corruption surrounding him. Though personally free of gross venality, the new President accepted loans from Jay Cooke and others seeking federal favors, and he appointed several cabinet members for whom bribery was a way of life. Favoritism was made possible by the federal role in rebuilding America, a task that involved vast public expenditures for private ends.

Grant's election coincided with the readmission of most of the southern states under terms dictated by the North, namely, accepting the constitutional amendments abolishing slavery and enshrining the rights of all citizens. With memories of the war fading, wealthy interests mobilized against both the income and the inheritance taxes enacted during the patriotic fervor of several years earlier. "The Income Tax is the most odious, vexatious, inquisitorial, and unequal of all our taxes," the *New York Tribune* said in 1869. The *New York Times* had supported the income tax during the war but changed its mind, in part because of its view that Washington had become a sump of wasteful and corrupt spending.

There is no indication that the tax was widely unpopular among Americans, the vast majority of whom were not affected by it. Indeed, David Wells, the Special Commissioner of Revenue, reported in 1870 that only 250,000 persons paid the tax, out of a population of 39.5 million, not enough to touch off a groundswell of popular feelings. But the drive to repeal was mounted with intensity by an array of lobbying groups, especially an organization based in New York City and Philadelphia calling itself the Anti–Income Tax Association. The other main factor against the tax was the progress made under President Johnson and then under Grant to reduce the public debt, from close to $3 billion at the end of the war to less than $2.5 billion in 1870.

Because of the federal surplus, Congress felt pressure, especially from western lawmakers, to reduce tariffs. In general, however, the tariff structure was kept at a high level. Congress even moved in 1869 and 1870 to raise tariffs on such items as copper, steel rails, marble and nickel. Indeed, many protectionist lawmakers believed that repealing the income tax and reducing federal revenues would have the beneficial effect of raising the pressure to keep tariffs high. In 1870, the House Ways and Means Committee proposed to tinker with the income tax. One of Congress's tariff kingpins, Representative William D. Kelley of Pennsylvania—known as "Pig-iron Kelley" because of his devotion to the iron industry—was in the forefront of the anti–income tax faction in Congress. Another was Representative Benjamin Butler of Massachusetts, who called the income tax "the most irritating, provocative of opposition, and imperfect of all taxes." But most House members responded to the compelling arithmetic of who paid the tax and who did not. As Representative Washington Townsend of Pennsylvania told his fellow lawmakers, opposition to the income tax did not come from "the masses of the people" but from "the men of gigantic capital," including railroad cartels, stock dealers and "men of colossal fortunes and extraordinary incomes." In 1870, the House responded to these cross pressures by maintaining the income tax but lowering the maximum rate to 3 percent and increasing the exemption to $2,000.

In the Senate, the most articulate champion of retaining the tax was John Sherman of Ohio, who had become chairman of the Senate Finance Committee. At first, the Senate voted to eliminate the income tax. Then the senators changed their mind, in part because of Sherman's persistence. He called the tax "the most just and equitable tax levied by the United States" and "the only discrimination in our tax laws that will reach wealthy men as against the poorer classes." Despite Sherman's appeals, the Senate went ahead to lower the income tax rate again. The new rate was 2.5 percent on incomes more than $2,000. Moreover, Congress extended the tax for only two more years and banned publication of all individual tax returns. The 1870 act also repealed the inheritance tax, eliminating a considerable source of revenue for the federal government that came mostly from four states—New York, Massachusetts, Pennsylvania and Ohio—where much of America's wealth was concentrated.

The drive to repeal the income tax reflected another important trend begun in the post–Civil War era, the ascendance of Congress and the eclipsing of the office of President. In perhaps the greatest of his contrasts with Lincoln, Grant espoused the view that domestic and economic policy belonged to Congress, which was at the height of its susceptibility to the influence of money. Grant's own Treasury Secretary, George S. Boutwell—who had served as Lincoln's first Internal Revenue Commissioner—remained a champion of the tax within the administration. While Grant told members of Congress that he favored repeal, Boutwell went so far as to conceal revenues coming into the Treasury in order to make Congress believe that income tax revenue could not be spared. Under the new rates enacted in 1870, fewer than 100,000 Americans paid the tax, and critics began to argue, not that it was only fair for the very richest citizens to pay, but that it was not worth the bureaucratic expense to tax such a small portion of the population.

As the election of 1872 approached, the tax and tariff issues were potent enough for Grant to take at least some action. Trying to shore up support among farmers and others, Congress approved a 10 percent reduction in tariffs on most items, including cotton and wool textiles, iron, steel, paper, glass and other items. Tariffs were also eliminated outright on coffee and tea, putting Grant in the enviable position of being able to campaign as a proponent of the "free breakfast table." But these were baby steps with marginal impact, designed to preserve the whole protectionist system.

Throughout the assault on the income tax, opponents had considered the step of going to court to challenge the tax's constitutionality. Some suits were filed, and parts of the tax were upheld by various courts, including the Supreme Court. But as the expiration of the tax approached, there did not appear much sentiment in Congress to continue it anyway. Senator Sherman fought once again to keep the tax alive. He warned in March of 1872 that if the income tax were repealed, the entire tax system would rest on taxing the consuming habits of ordinary Americans of modest means, leaving relatively untaxed the incomes of those who had vast reserves of wealth in property or private earnings. He asserted that one of the most solemn obligations of the federal government was to protect the property of Americans. It was therefore only proper "to require property to contribute to their payment."

Sherman's appeal was to no avail. Congress was more sensitive instead to the demands of the growing number of wealthy entrepreneurs, investors and tycoons, who were at their moment of maximum influence. The power of the new class of wealthy rested on newly consolidated railroads and the many large fortunes created by the Civil War. The landscape of wealth had changed. Whereas New York City had had a handful of millionaires before the conflict, there were hundreds of millionaires afterward. Their fortunes were in the tens of millions of dollars. A. T. Stewart, the dry goods magnate, was worth $50 million, and other millionaires, such as William B. Astor, Cornelius Vanderbilt and the banker Moses Taylor, were not far behind. Before Congress abolished the publication of income tax returns, it was reported that Astor had paid more than $1 million in income tax, while Vanderbilt and Taylor had paid more than $500,000. Even these amounts were believed to be underestimations. After the war, many millionaires routinely engaged in tax evasion or tricks to hide their income. What they did not bother to hide was their vast influence.

In 1869, Grant's friend Jim Fisk worked with Jay Gould to monopolize the market in gold, driving up its price so they could make a killing. Instead, on "Black Friday," September 24, 1869, a collapse in gold prices engulfed a vast number of speculators and investors. Fisk and Gould managed to bribe enough officials to avoid prosecution, and Fisk remained close to his trusting friend in the White House. Years later the Crédit Mobilier scandal revealed that a construction company owned by stockholders of the Union Pacific Railroad had ensnared many prominent members of the Grant administration and Congress.

The rampant corruption in Washington led to a reform movement within the Republican Party, which joined with Democrats to nominate Horace Greeley for a quixotic run at the White House in 1872. By then, the income tax was gone. Its abolition had one more important and lasting effect. That was to guarantee that the federal debt, which had been incurred to preserve the Union for all citizens, would now have to be retired largely by the working classes and farmers. The fact that the American debt—its bonds, notes and other forms of loans—was owned by the wealthiest Americans meant that taxpayers of modest means were working to pay off the investments of the richest taxpayers. As the tax historian Sidney Ratner notes, the Civil War debt "became one of the most powerful instruments in America for the enrichment of the rentier class, the leading capitalists." For the next forty years, farmers, workers, small merchants and other working-class Americans carried this debt burden, to the benefit of the rich.

Over the ten-year period of its existence during and after the Civil War, the income tax played a crucial role. In the first year, the amount collected was less than $3 million. But by 1866, the tax generated $73.5 million in federal revenues, then declined in the years after that. (In the ten years before it was repealed, total collections came to $376 million.) As for the proportion of the tax burden comprised by the income tax, in 1863 the income tax amounted to 7 percent of federal revenues. It grew to a peak of 24 percent in 1867, whereupon it declined until 1872. On average, then, the income tax accounted for about a fifth of federal revenues during the war. (The balance of federal revenues came from tariffs and various internal taxes on commodities and commercial activities.)

The income tax was crucial to the prosecution and winning of the Civil War. It left behind memories of many problems and myriad confusions. Distinctions between gross and net income, between what we would call earned and unearned income, and between regular income and capital gains—all these were imposed late and in a haphazard way. There were indeed sectional disparities in the tax. New York paid a third of it, followed by Pennsylvania at more than 11 percent. Other big taxpaying states included Massachusetts, Ohio, Illinois, California, New Jersey and Maryland. These were the states that would have bad memories for years to come.

As for the number of taxpayers, it reached a high of 450,000 in 1866 and dropped to 73,000 in 1872. Most historians say that the tax was never paid by more than 1 percent of the American population. But one historian and expert, W. Elliot Brownlee, says that the calculations showing a tiny percentage of taxpayers are too low because they mistakenly include Confederate families as part of the tax base. In fact, Brownlee asserts, by the end of the war, more than 10 percent of Union households were paying an income tax.

Among the Civil War era taxpayers was at least one who claimed that he had happily handed his money over to the federal government. Mark Twain reported in 1864 that he had paid an income tax of $36.82, plus a $3.12 fine for filing late. But this was all right with him, he said, because it made him feel "important" that the government was finally paying attention to him.

The Civil War and Reconstruction eras left a nearly forgotten legacy of the income tax as a symbol of the economic struggles underlying the battle over slavery and states' rights. At its root, the Civil War was caused nearly as much by the great economic changes and tensions of the era as it was by the dispute over slavery. As the Progressive Era historian Charles A. Beard argued many decades later, it was not always easy to tell "where slavery as an ethical question left off and economics—the struggle over the distribution of wealth—began."

In their seminal work *The Rise of American Civilization*, Charles and Mary Beard argued that the Civil War constituted a second

American Revolution, with the manufacturing base of the North solidifying control over the rest of the country, crushing the South militarily and wielding the economic power to take control of the West. For the Beards, the regressive tariff system was the core of this system of control, because tariffs helped to build up industry at the cost of those in the farm sector, placing the burden of government on the consuming masses rather than the capitalist and owner classes. The income tax, it must be said, was peripheral to that grand design. By the end of Reconstruction, the system of high tariffs was impregnable and the income tax but a memory.

Because the nation prospered behind its tariff walls, most everyone accepted the rationale behind the taxes on imports. Farmers and others suffered from prices that were higher than they would have been without tariffs, but most people believed that tariffs kept Americans fully employed in domestic industries. Farmers supposedly benefited because with improved access and transportation links, their crops made their way to the dining tables of the exploding working class in the cities.

Not everyone agreed. In his speeches defending the income tax from 1870 through 1872, Senator Sherman of Ohio presciently laid out the logic for the eventual overthrow of the American system of high tariffs and no income tax. He would later become a major figure in American finance, the author of the Sherman Antitrust Act and Treasury Secretary under President Rutherford Hayes. His criticism of the tax system in the years after the Civil War was to be cited decades later, when the cause of the income tax was revived. Sherman observed that the poor bore a disproportionate burden inflicted by tariffs and taxes on licenses, spirits, tobacco, beer and other items. "We tax the tea, the coffee, the sugar, the spices the poor man uses," he said in 1870. "We tax every little thing that is imported from abroad, together with the whiskey that makes him drunk and the beer that cheers him and the tobacco that consoles him. Everything that he consumes we call a luxury and tax it; yet we are afraid to touch the income of Mr. Astor. Is there any justice in that? Is there any propriety in it? Why, sir, the income tax is the only one that tends to equalize these burdens between the rich and the poor."

Addressing the argument that the income tax was inquisitorial, Sherman argued that it was no less "inquisitorial" when states like his own state of Ohio levied a property tax and sent out assessors to determine the value of every citizen's holdings. He added that the costs of the Civil War, far from disappearing, would continue for many years. There were pensions to pay for and huge debts that needed to be retired. It made no sense to him to spare the wealthiest citizens these costs.

Finally, Sherman warned of instability if the tax were rescinded. The "popular clamor" resulting from abolishing the income tax, he noted acidly, would not come from manufacturers, or the daily newspapers, or the gentlemen members of the Union League and other associations of the privileged. "You will hear clamor coming from the mass of the people who will complain of injustice and wrong," he declared, "and their voice, although not often heard in the way of petitions, when it comes to you is more mighty than the waves of the sea."

It would take another generation for those waves to roll across the political landscape. They would be stirred up by an economic crisis, the likes of which Americans had never seen.

CHAPTER FIVE

———— ⌖ ————

"The Communism of Combined Wealth"
Politics and the Panic of 1893

IT BEGAN IN THE COLD.

A freak late-winter storm cloaked the city of Washington in snow and ice on the early morning of March 4, 1893, the day of the inauguration of Stephen Grover Cleveland for a noncontiguous second term as President. Shortly after dawn, brave crowds began lining the parade route along Pennsylvania Avenue to celebrate the Democrats' recapture of the White House. They shivered in their overcoats and fur hats, stamped their feet, huddled together and gulped whiskey to keep warm. Even the ladies nipped from what the *New York Times* called "dainty little silver" pocket flasks.

By late morning, the snow eased up. Looking satisfied and prosperous with his walrus mustache and 250-pound girth, Cleveland left the Arlington Hotel for an open carriage pulled by four spirited black horses. The wind kicked up clouds of snowflakes, and soon a

light powder covered the once and future President's wide over-
coat, silk hat and long gray whiskers. At the east portico of the
executive mansion, Cleveland was greeted by President Benjamin
Harrison, the Republican he had defeated. It was a peculiar
moment, the only transfer of presidential power in which outgoing
and incoming presidents had run against each other twice, each
one losing once and winning once. "Little Ben" Harrison (he was 5
feet 6 inches) was a taciturn, colorless and unpopular President
overshadowed in office by Republican congressional kingpins. His
only real claim to the office four years earlier had been that he was
the grandson of "old Tippecanoe," William Henry Harrison, the
hero of an Indian battle whose term as the ninth American President had been cut short when he died of pneumonia right after his
inauguration.

The wind seemed colder by the time the presidential carriages
arrived at the Capitol. Inside the Senate chamber, the oath was first
administered to the new Vice President, Adlai E. Stevenson of Illinois, a populist-leaning politician (and grandfather of a future
Democratic presidential candidate) who had been put on the
Democratic ticket to try to appeal to anxious and resentful farmers
in the West. But most everyone's attention focused on Cleveland's
dark and beautiful young wife, Frances, who had captivated the
nation when she married the bachelor President in his first term.
All eyes fixed on her as she removed her storm coat to reveal a
camel's hair suit trimmed with brown chenille, a velvet brown
cape, and a bonnet of pearls and ostrich feathers. Four years earlier,
after Cleveland had won the popular vote but lost to Harrison in
the Electoral College, Frances Cleveland cheerfully assured the servants at the White House that they would be back. Now here she
was, clearly pleased to have fulfilled that promise.

From the Senate chamber, the official party repaired outside to
the inauguration platform, where fierce gusts were blowing hats,
umbrellas and snow across the expanse east of the Capitol. His
robes flapping, Chief Justice Melville Fuller administered the oath

while Harrison held his hand at his face to protect it from the cold. But the crowd cheered as Cleveland waved, and they cheered even louder when he kissed his wife.

Cleveland endured the cold that day. But his presidency was about to be hit by a different kind of storm, one of far greater intensity. The nation was headed toward the worst economic crisis in its history. The new depression, known as the Panic of '93, was the latest of many cycles in the boom-and-bust era of the nineteenth century, but this downturn was to last until the end of the century—and by some measures until 1907. As Cleveland was assembling his cabinet, banks, farms and factories were sliding into bankruptcy. Family fortunes were dissolving. In big cities and grimy factory towns, workers were struggling with long hours, layoffs and pay cuts. In the West and South, farmers were hungry and living in rags, their livelihood squeezed by falling prices for their crops and rising costs of freight, storage and payments on their debts. Many were forced to burn corn for fuel and dump their wheat because it was too expensive to get to market.

In his inaugural speech, Cleveland spoke briefly about the coming challenges, warning vaguely of the dangers of business monopolies and inflation. But his response to the misery of farmers and workers was as bleak as the weather. It was not the role of government to intervene, he said. In fact, he proclaimed, a grave danger was posed by "the prevalence of a popular disposition to expect from the operation of the government especial and direct individual advantages." Paternalism, he said, was the "bane of republican institutions and the constant peril of our government by the people." Paternalism sapped a country's strength, he lectured. "It undermines the self-reliance of our people and substitutes in its place dependence upon Government favoritism."

The new President's austere prescription for the economy conformed to the prevailing view of the time. It would take another generation for a new consensus to form in American politics. But the spirit of government intervention that would characterize the

Progressive Era and later the New Deal was germinating in the Panic of 1893, shaping the issues and dictating his responses.

The panic was the first American economic crisis that deepened sharply because of worldwide factors—a global overproduction of farm and manufactured goods, speculation in foreign markets, and weak financial and banking institutions in Europe. These causes were little understood at the time, with the result that popular blame focused primarily on the economic power of the railroads, banks and industrial cartels and the political machines that they seemed to control. The depression and the resentments flowing out of it plunged Cleveland into a vortex that would force a realignment of the Democratic and Republican Parties and sharpen a debate that persists today. New attitudes would eventually emerge on monopolies, trusts and the plight of workers and farmers. There would be new thinking about the role of government in regulating business, protecting workers and farmers and providing a safety net for victims of economic misfortune.

These changes would be produced by a combination of idealism and fear—the idealism reflected a growing sense of American community, and the fear focused on the dangers of wealth accruing to the few, the resentment of the many who were poor, and the potentially volatile mix of class hatred and instability. For now, these feelings swirled around two central issues: monetary policy (how much money and inflation to allow in the system) and taxes (who should pay them and how the burden should be shared).

From these debates came reform, and one of the principal reforms was the income tax.

In the next two years, Congress would enact an income tax, only to see it declared unconstitutional by the United States Supreme Court. The Court's decision, in turn, would produce a stormy reaction that spilled into the 1896 presidential campaign. By the end of Cleveland's second four years in office, dissidents and rebels would capture the Democratic Party and launch it on a new and progressive course.

As always, the debate was about economics but the terms were moralistic. In the battle between rich and poor, between North and South, between industry and farms, between owners and consumers, all sides felt that they—more than their political adversaries—embodied the virtues of hard work and sacrifice that formed the foundation of American society. Around the issues of gold versus silver and the income tax versus the tariff was a fight over different definitions of prosperity, democracy and fairness. It was a struggle over wealth and power and over the very character of the United States as it prepared to enter the twentieth century.

———

He was always known for saying no.

Descended from a long line of Puritan ministers and deacons, growing up in his father's Presbyterian parsonage in upstate New York, Grover Cleveland originally intended to join the ministry himself and always carried an aura of self-righteousness. After the death of his father in 1853, the teenager dropped out of school to support his family as an assistant at a school for the blind in New York City—a cold and dreary place that young Grover left to make a job-seeking trip to Cleveland, Ohio, where there was said to be a family connection to the city's founder. On the way, he stopped off in the Buffalo area to visit a great-uncle. He ended up staying. He studied law, became involved in Democratic ward politics, got himself elected Erie County Sheriff and started a private law practice. In a decision that later came back to haunt him politically, he avoided military service during the Civil War by paying someone to take his place.

While serving as County Sheriff, Cleveland fearlessly prosecuted crooked government contractors and started building his reputation as an incorruptible public servant. In 1881, he was earning a modest income as a bachelor lawyer in his forties who cut a wide swath in Buffalo's clubs and taverns while cultivating contacts in the town's working-class and immigrant communities.

It was then that a group of reformers, dismayed over a series of incompetent and corrupt administrations, tapped him to run for mayor. He won with a comfortable margin. At City Hall, he confronted an array of vested interests and became known as the "veto mayor," dismaying even some of his partisans by opposing favoritism in appointments and contracts. Two years later, Democrats saw an opportunity to capture the statehouse after a series of Republican scandals in Albany. Battered by their own corruption problems in New York City, party kingpins turned to Cleveland as a clean alternative, hoping they could control him once he got elected. After winning, however, the "veto mayor" quickly became the "veto governor." Refusing to play the spoils system game, Cleveland infuriated the Tammany party machine in New York City when he blocked legislation to lower the fare on the city's elevated trains, on the grounds that the measure violated a state contract with the companies operating the trains. When reformers picked him to run for President in 1884, Tammany Hall opposed him, but that only enhanced his reputation nationwide. "We love him most for the enemies he has made," said a delegate placing his name in nomination.

The presidential election of 1884 was a saturnalia of mud slinging. Cleveland's opponent was Senator James G. Blaine of Maine, "the plumed knight" of Republican politics, who was reviled by his detractors as a "continental liar" (as a favorite Democratic song put it). Blaine, moreover, seemed unable to overcome his own association with a corrupt railroad deal years earlier. But just as Cleveland's victory seemed assured, Republicans counterattacked by seizing on an old story that Cleveland had earlier fathered and supported an illegitimate child. "Ma! Ma! Where's My Pa?" Republicans roared out at campaign rallies. ("Gone to the White House. Ha! Ha! Ha!" Democrats replied.) Cleveland was also criticized as a draft dodger and, despite his reputation, a tool of big-city Democratic machines. As the election approached, the Republican campaign suffered a blowup of its own when a leading Protestant minister in New York City labeled the Democrats the party of "rum, Romanism and rebellion," referring to its alliance of Irish Catholic immigrants in the North and supporters of the Confederacy in the South. A voter backlash moved New York to the Democratic column, and Cleveland squeaked by with a popular vote margin of less than 30,000.

"He is a truly American type of the best kind," the poet and essayist James Russell Lowell wrote after Cleveland's inauguration in 1885. But though Cleveland could be humorous in private, in public his pompous manner came across to many as sanctimonious and unfeeling. Dogged by the old accusations of sexual misbehavior and draft dodging, he was beset by new rumors that in the White House he drank and beat his young wife. A larger problem, however, lay in the fractious coalition that made up the Democratic Party: sons of the old Confederacy, patrician aristocratic reformers in the North, big-city party machines and farm-state politicians resentful of the money and power in the Northeast.

Navigating among these interests, Cleveland had to practice compromise. He opposed patronage and favored civil service reform, for instance, but only up to a point. He vetoed bills granting military retirement benefits to individual Civil War veterans, charging that the pensions were being handed out to deserters or men who had never served in the armed forces. He may have been right, but critics felt Cleveland was actually placating the old South. The one serious economic issue of Cleveland's first term was the tariff. He sided with those seeking to lower tariffs, as demanded by many farmers, workers and consumers, but he was unable to overcome opposition in Congress, where the monopolies and trusts defending the protectionist system essentially controlled the agenda. With little accomplished in his first term, Cleveland lost the 1888 election to "Little Ben" Harrison, though he won slightly more of the popular vote.

Before leaving office, Cleveland got off a final blast at the business interests that blocked tariff reform and supported his opponent. In a remarkable message to Congress, using language no recent President had ever used, he deplored the conditions in the cities, where, he said, "wealth and luxury" jostled with "poverty and wretchedness and unremunerative toil." Corporations were "fast becoming the people's masters," he said, adding: "Communism is a hateful thing and a menace to peace and organized government. But the communism of combined wealth and capital, the outgrowth of overweening cupidity and selfishness, which insidiously undermines the justice and integrity of free institutions, is not less dangerous than the communism of oppressed poverty and toil."

Returning to private life, Cleveland moved to New York City, where his lifestyle was closer to the first brand of communism than the second. With his wife and new daughter, Ruth (known far and wide as "Baby Ruth," the inspiration for a candy bar's name), Cleveland moved to a luxurious house on Madison Avenue. He belonged to the right clubs, went to the right parties, spent his summers at a new home at Buzzards Bay in Massachusetts and joined a powerful Wall Street law firm that handled the legal affairs of J. P. Morgan's financial empire.

As the 1892 election approached, Cleveland was urged to run by his new friends on Wall Street. Many of them were concerned about Harrison's unpopularity and worried that someone hostile to their interests would seize the Democratic presidential nomination. They were pleased especially that Cleveland began to speak out more and more about the need for a strong currency. The financial community looked on terrified as a growing number of Democrats favored the introduction of silver-backed currency to expand the money supply and produce inflation, which would help farmers and others pay their debts. Cleveland's stand for "hard money" was not the only thing that got him support from financiers. They also liked his advocacy of civil service reform. Henry Villard, a railroad magnate and agent of German banks, got permission from Cleveland to promote his candidacy as "the only Democrat who could be elected" and the only one who could thwart the party's takeover by "free silver" advocates. Leading the former President's campaign was William C. Whitney, a Wall Street lawyer, speculator and business operator involved in railway franchises in New York, who had served as Secretary of the Navy in the first Cleveland term. In that post, he had entertained lavishly with his wife, Flora, who was famous in Washington for her ringing defenses of Cleveland against the charge of wife beating. Also on the team were Oscar Straus, the department store millionaire (who was to go down with his wife on the *Titanic*), and Charles Fairchild, a lawyer who had been Treasury Secretary in Cleveland's first cabinet and was now a leading New York banker.

At the Democratic convention in Chicago, Whitney lashed the party's warring factions together with a platform that was deliberately ambiguous on several issues. Though Cleveland opposed silver-backed currency, the platform pledged to establish a currency backed by gold and silver if European trading partners would go along. (Everyone knew they would not, since they opposed a weak American currency even more strongly than American businessmen did.) On the subject of the tariff, the platform also equivocated. It promised to lower barriers—but only if industry and labor were not hurt.

In truth, the Democratic platform resembled that of the Republicans. As a result, angry farmers and workers favoring "free silver" and other liberal reforms rallied around the new Populist Party. At the Populists' 1888 convention in Omaha, delegates heard speech after speech attacking the nation's elite interests, which were said to have captured both major parties and all the other institutions of power in America. "Corruption dominates the ballot-box, the legislature, the Congress, and touches even the ermine of the bench," declared the novelist and essayist Ignatius Donnelly. "The people are demoralized." He spoke further of muzzled newspapers, impoverished workers and farmers and home owners strangled by debt. The nation, Donnelly declared, was on "the verge of moral, political and material ruin" brought about by the "colossal fortunes for a few." The Populist platform included a call for unlimited coinage of silver; government ownership of railroad, telegraph and telephone systems; and direct election of senators, who were then chosen by state legislatures. Another plank called for a return of the graduated income tax that had been enacted during the Civil War.

If they succeeded at nothing else, the Populists frightened the industrial barons of the East into thinking that a revolutionary rabble was gathering at the gates. Whitney, meanwhile, resolved to have Cleveland move to the left to try to get some Populist votes. Despite his antipathy to big-city machines, the former President was hungry enough to suggest to them that he would not be averse to a little old-fashioned spoils system patronage. Whitney also beseeched Cleveland to temper his opposition to silver-backed currency by making some expressions of sympathy for farmers. "In the south the impression of you got by the people is that you do not appreciate their suffering and poverty," Whitney wrote the candidate during the campaign. Cleveland responded at a rally in Madison Square Garden: "The wants of our people arising from the deficiency or imperfect distribution of money circulation ought to be fully and honestly recognized and efficiently remedied."

Nevertheless, Whitney harvested campaign money from industries eager to keep tariff barriers high. From the sugar trust led by Henry Havemeyer came a big donation in return for pledges that Cleveland would take care of its interests. A bankers' committee headed by August Belmont, representative of the Rothschilds, also gave contributions to ensure that sound money would remain a Cleveland priority. Railroad interests seeking protection from antitrust actions were also given assurances that their concerns would be taken into account. Cleveland was probably insulated from these machinations, which ran counter to his earlier stated beliefs. "I have not been consulted at all—or scarcely at all—about the conduct of the campaign," he asserted.

Cleveland's main advantage in the campaign was the unpopularity of Harrison, a President widely seen as the tool of Republican kingpins in Congress. He had at least been candid enough to admit that he could not name his own cabinet because party chieftains "had sold out every place to pay the election expenses." During Harrison's term, Republican congressional leaders handed out fat pensions to Civil War veterans and their widows and orphans. They passed legislation to enrich premiums to bond holders, build pork-barrel projects in favored districts and even return federal taxes paid by northern states during the Civil War. The expenditures reached a peacetime record, earning the Republican majority the name the "Billion Dollar Congress." The money for these programs came from tariffs, which were raised under the leadership of Representative William McKinley, an Ohio Republican who was chairman of the House Ways and Means Committee. The general level of import duties went from 38 to nearly 50 percent of the value of goods purchased by consumers. As a sop to the western states, Congress had passed the Sherman Silver Purchase Act in 1890, calling for the Treasury to purchase a set amount of silver each month and put new silver-backed dollars into circulation. The law was intended to increase the money supply, as demanded by agrarian interests, and to halt the downward spiral of farm prices, but it had little effect. (Equally ineffective was the Sherman Antitrust Act of the same year. Though it barred monopolistic activities in theory, no administration was inclined to carry it out, and in any case, the courts interpreted its provisions so narrowly that it was useless as an enforcement tool.)

The first warning signs of discontent with Harrison and the Republican congressional leadership erupted in the 1890 election, a Democratic landslide that sent McKinley packing and swept in a new generation of Democrats, including a young Nebraskan named William Jennings Bryan. There were other signs of unrest. In mid-summer 1892, a worker uprising occurred in the grimy steel town of Homestead, Pennsylvania, offering a foretaste of the turbulence that lay ahead. In Homestead, 3,800 workers struck over working conditions and pay cuts. Henry Clay Frick, in charge of Andrew Carnegie's steel interests, sent armed Pinkerton detectives on barges up the Monongahela River to confront the strikers, who met the Pinkerton forces with a barrage of gunshots, dynamite blasts and small cannon fire. The Pinkertons surrendered, and the battle resulted in the death of three detectives and ten workers, with dozens wounded. The same summer, a Russian immigrant anarchist tried to kill Frick in his Pittsburgh office. Frick, recovering from his wound, managed to break the steel strike. Still, the Homestead incident—along with other strikes at mines in Tennessee and Idaho—spread fears nationwide that European-style class warfare was in danger of taking root on American soil.

Running hard for the White House that summer, Cleveland was scathing in his criticism of the way the Homestead strike was crushed. What remedies he had in mind were never clear. When the votes were counted on Election Day, the former President won with a wider margin than he had in 1884, carrying such Republican strongholds as New York, New Jersey and Connecticut. Still, the industrialists who had quietly helped his campaign were not displeased. "I am very sorry for President Harrison," said Frick, "but I cannot see that our interests are going to be affected one way or the other by the change in administration." Discontent was high enough, however, that the Populist candidate, the former Union general James Weaver, carried six mountain and plains states with over a million votes.

"I only wish," Cleveland wrote a friend, "God would put it in my power to make known to the Democratic Party what the last election means."

The meaning of the presidential election of 1892 became clear soon enough. A Democrat, not a Republican, would have to deal with the economic crisis that suddenly emerged. The Panic of '93 had actually begun in the final days of Harrison's term, with the failure of the Philadelphia & Reading railroad and a subsequent wave of selling on Wall Street. British and European banks that had financed the American railroads demanded payment in gold for the stocks and bonds they were unloading. Bank failures led to foreclosures on mortgages to farmers. Within two months after Cleveland's inauguration, the stock market collapsed. Within the year, bankruptcies spread to 500 banks and 15,000 businesses in a disastrous trend the *Bankers' Magazine* described as "ruin and disaster run riot over the land." The depression of 1893 reduced the national income by 10 percent, driving millions out of work and the unemployment rate to 20 percent. The collapse of prices on farms further inflamed feelings among workers in industry and mines and swelled the lines of people seeking food, shelter and clothing from charities in the large cities.

Facing the crisis, Cleveland sought to assemble a capable cabinet but ran into problems. "I cannot get the men I want to help me," he wrote a friend, adding that too many friends "expect things." In a group of conservatives with whom he felt comfortable, the most important job went to John G. Carlisle, the new Treasury Secretary, who had served as Speaker of the House and later senator from Kentucky. On Capitol Hill, he was known as a scrupulous parliamentarian with a record of sympathy for railroad interests, free trade and silver-backed currency. On currency, at least, he changed his mind, saying he would rather be right than consistent. Carlisle also had the reputation of being fond of drink. It was said that he disappeared on drinking binges for days or weeks at a time. On financial matters, Cleveland's other close adviser was Daniel Lamont, his former private secretary in Albany and the White House, appointed Secretary of War. Rounding out the prosperous and complacent inner circle was Richard Olney, the Attorney General, a former corporation lawyer from Boston who had represented New England financiers, railroads and the whiskey trust.

The depression was a time of hunger, economic contraction, confusion and blame. In the absence of a consensus over what to do, farmers blamed the banks and the exclusive reliance on gold-backed currency. Workers blamed their employers, and employers blamed the unions. Led by the House Speaker, Thomas Reed, Republicans and their business allies blamed low tariffs for allowing a flood of cheap imports that hurt American business. Banks blamed advocates of silver currency for panicking the markets and speeding the flow of gold to creditors overseas. Cleveland sympathized with the banks, and his most urgent priority was to restore gold as the sole basis for American currency.

The battle over silver versus gold currency had raged at the center of American politics since the 1870s. One of the milestones was the 1873 law known to proponents of silver currency as the "Crime of '73," which abolished—surreptitiously, the critics charged—the use of silver for coins and replaced it with currency based exclusively on gold. Following the law, there was an abundance of silver on the market. As a result, pro-silver forces campaigned to restore the coinage of silver, with the old ratio calling for sixteen times as much silver in a silver dollar as there was gold in a gold dollar. That ratio would have made a silver dollar worth less than a gold dollar, enabling farmers to pay their debts more cheaply.

In 1878, the pro-silver forces in Congress had forced passage of the Bland–Allison Act, over the veto of President Rutherford Hayes, requiring the Treasury to buy a fixed amount of silver every month and coin it into dollars. A dozen years later, in 1890, the Bland–Allison law was replaced by the Sherman Silver Purchase Act, sponsored by Senator John Sherman of Ohio, which lowered the limit on the amount of silver that could be purchased by the Treasury without banning the practice entirely. The Sherman Silver Purchase Act had little effect on inflation one way or another. But Cleveland saw any use of silver for dollars as a drag on American economic health. With silver currency being used by many Americans to pay their debts, foreign creditors were increasingly demanding to be paid in gold. As a result, American gold reserves had started eroding, from $150 million in 1891 to $110 million the next year. Only intervention from American banks at the end of 1892 had kept them from plunging below $100 million, which was generally regarded as the threshold below which the nation would approach insolvency. Cleveland was determined to turn this situation around as the first step toward economic recovery.

———

One morning in May 1893, a few months after his inauguration, Grover Cleveland discovered a rough growth on the roof of his mouth. His doctor determined it to be a malignant tumor that had to come out at once. The White House went into a frenzy, fearing that public disclosure of a threat to the President's life would send financial markets into a deeper tailspin. An operation would have to be carried out, but in secret. In July, Cleveland boarded the yacht *Oneida* on the East River in New York, propped himself up on a chair against the mast and was operated on by a clandestine team of surgeons. When the President awoke after the removal of part of his upper jaw, he looked up in a daze. "Who the hell are you?" he managed to ask through a mouth full of cotton. Cleveland recuperated while the *Oneida* cruised in Buzzards Bay, but associates said the procedure deepened his fatigue and foul temper.

The main reason for the President's sour mood in his early months was not his surgery but the difficulty he was having in restoring the gold standard. The fight over the repeal of the Sherman Silver Purchase Act had accelerated in April, when Treasury Secretary Carlisle acknowledged that gold reserves had fallen below $100 million. Despite that, lawmakers representing western states, where crop failures threatened to wipe out farmers' livelihood, were determined to maintain or extend the use of silver currency. The legislative battle took place between August and October, ending with a victory for Cleveland.

Despite the repeal of the Sherman Silver Purchase Act, the nation remained mired in its economic morass. By the end of 1893, 642 banks had closed doors, 22,500 miles of railway had gone into receivership and an estimated one-fourth of American industries were out of business. The depression also drastically reduced federal revenues, most of which came from the tariff. One of the reasons that the Democrats had won the congressional elections in 1890 and the White House in 1892 had been their successful attack on the McKinley Tariff Act of 1890. Sponsored by Representative William McKinley in the House, the law raised the effective tariff rates from 44 to 48 percent, a step widely seen by voters as protecting trusts and corporations at the expense of consumers.

After Cleveland's election to a second term, the Democrats knew they had a mandate to lower tariffs. Some believed that if tariffs were lowered, the result might actually be increased imports, with no loss—and perhaps an increase—in revenues. But despite Democratic majorities in both the House and Senate, it would not be easy to overturn the tariff. Both parties were split along regional lines, and the fight over repeal of the Sherman Silver Purchase Act had left Bryan and many others extremely bitter. On the other hand, Cleveland could not count on conservative Democrats to support him in lowering tariffs, even though he had catered to their interests on the gold standard. The tariff took a back seat to the currency battle through most of 1893, but its moment was soon to come.

———

"Cleveland's troubles," the biographer Allan Nevins writes, "never came as single spies but as battalions."

One "battalion" departed from Massillon, Ohio, on a chilly Easter Sunday in 1894, with forty newspaper reporters (Jack London among them) in tow, to carry out a march on Washington. Leading the unruly procession was a well-to-do Massillon businessman named Jacob S. Coxey, a Populist who had long advocated a federal work relief project to be financed by $500 million in Treasury borrowings. When Congress refused to consider it, Coxey turned to publicity stunts. The brainchild of the march was his partner, Carl Browne, a flamboyant former rancher, carnival barker and journalist who delivered speeches while dressed up as Buffalo Bill. With Coxey in a carriage and Browne on horseback, they made their way across Ohio to Pennsylvania and crossed over the Alleghenies into Maryland, with followers joining them along the way. Newspapers across the country chronicled their progress. A ragtag group of 500 protesters finally straggled into the nation's capital on May Day, where they were arrested, beaten and trampled by the police. Coxey and two lieutenants were arrested and jailed at the Capitol.

A more formidable "battalion" challenging Cleveland in 1894 was the strike at a factory that manufactured railroad cars in the town of Pullman, south of Chicago. Pullman was a 300-acre company town where the workers had to rent their homes and buy their food and other essentials from the company. The Panic of '93 forced the Pullman Company to lay off 3,000 workers and cut others' wages, but it continued to pay dividends to shareholders and charge workers the same for its services. After the Pullman local struck on May 11, the American Railway Union under the leadership of Eugene V. Debs stepped in, refusing to handle Pullman cars. Twenty-four railroads retaliated against the union, dismissing railway workers who joined in the job action. Strikes quickly spread to every railroad in the Midwest, disrupting the nation's entire transportation system. Debs, a fiery organizer and speaker, urged workers to be peaceful. But the workers' discipline was tested when railroad companies tried to bring in strikebreakers to handle the Pullman cars.

Responding to what had become a crisis in the nation's transportation system, Cleveland's Attorney General, Richard Olney, assigned 3,400 newly hired special deputies to keep the trains running. Olney also got a court order to end the strike, but it was ignored. At the White House, Cleveland agonized over what to do. Governor John Altgeld of Illinois, a Democrat, was sympathetic to the strikers and appealed to the President to take a conciliatory approach. Instead, on July 4, the President sent federal troops to Chicago, provoking a rampage of workers, who destroyed rail cars and burned and stole property. A dozen people were killed in the Pullman riots, but the strike was broken.

In all, some 1,400 strikes spread across the country in 1894. More than 660,000 men lost their jobs because of strikes and lock-outs, many of which deteriorated into violence. But the Pullman debacle, coming two years after the disastrous and unsuccessful Homestead strike, was a turning point for the labor movement, dividing its leadership over tactics. On the one hand was Debs, who had wanted to widen the Pullman strike; on the other hand was Samuel Gompers of the American Federation of Labor, who opposed such confrontational tactics. After the Pullman strike, Debs was convicted of engaging in a conspiracy to restrain trade in violation of the Sherman Antitrust Act. It was a painful irony for the labor movement. The Sherman act, nominally intended to curb industrial cartels, had become a battering ram against unions. Debs went to jail for six months—and became "the most popular man among the real people today," in the words of the author Henry Demarest Lloyd.

A more quiet "battalion" creeping up on Cleveland was the growing shift in public perceptions resulting from the unrest after the Panic of '93 and the findings of respected intellectuals that the United States was becoming a nation with a deep divide between rich and poor.

One of the most respected surveys came from a prominent New York City lawyer with close ties to his city's industrial elite. Thomas Shearman, founder of the law firm of Shearman & Sterling, came to the issue, ironically, after a career defending some of the major robber barons of the era, including James Fisk, Jr., and Jay Gould. Both clients were constantly sued for swindling investors in deals involving gold, railroads and other ventures. With his full beard (but no mustache), striped trousers and silk hat, Shearman was an imposing presence in the courtroom. But his preference was to settle cases out of court. Born in Birmingham, England, Shearman had worked his way up after starting as a law firm office boy. He was an energetic reformer, comfortable in both Democratic and Republican circles, who took the side of aggrieved Indians, sweatshop workers and the poor. But what brought him the most fame was his defense of his friend the Reverend Henry Ward Beecher of Brooklyn against charges of adultery in what many called the trial of the century. Beecher, charged with seducing a parishioner's wife, was acquitted.

In 1889, Shearman had published an essay in a leading magazine called *The Forum*. Entitled "The Owners of the United States," it listed the wealthiest people in America and proved to be tremendously influential. In England, he said, a thirtieth of the people own two-thirds of the wealth, but in America, wealth was concentrated on an even smaller percentage. Shearman used census data and information gleaned from contacts with the wealthy, though he asserted he would never violate anyone's confidence. The names of the wealthiest Americans cited by Shearman were familiar: Astor, Vanderbilt, Armour, Rockefeller, Flagler, Huntington, Drexel, Morgan, Marshall Field and so on—in all, seventy names representing a worth of $2.7 billion, or $7.5 million each. No other country had such a tight concentration of millionaires, he wrote. By contrast, he wrote, four-fifths of American families did not earn as much as $500 a year. He said 50,000 families owned half the nation's wealth, much of it derived from ownership of railroads, factories, oil refineries, mines and banks.

More significant than Shearman's findings were his conclusions about how wealthy men had managed to escape taxation, leaving the burden of taxes and tariffs "exclusively upon the working class." Since 1860, federal taxation had increased sixfold, yet the tax burden was primarily borne by the poor. At the same time, corporate profits had increased tenfold, much of it untaxed. It cost rich Americans 8 to 10 percent of their earnings to finance the government, while the poor paid taxes equivalent to 75 to 80 percent of their savings.

Shearman was careful not to advocate "arbitrary limitations" on wealth. But he warned that if the existing tariff and tax system were to continue for thirty years, "the United States of America will be substantially owned by less than 50,000 persons, constituting less than one in five hundred of the adult male population."

A re-examination of the tax system had been bubbling beneath the surface of American politics since at least the 1880s. Some Democratic conventions had started calling for an income tax in the early 1890s, and in late 1893, a Ways and Means tax subcommittee headed by Tennessee Democrat Benton McMillin started looking into the possibility of major changes in the law. Shearman was among those summoned as expert witnesses. It was "high time," the lawyer told the lawmakers, to reform an "unjust and unequal" tax system. An income tax of 2.5 percent, he explained, could reduce tariffs by 25 percent, yielding great benefits for the poor and for working class Americans. Such a tax system would increase the burden on wealthy people like himself, he acknowledged. "I am arguing against my own interest," he went on, "but the time has come for taking broad views of these questions."

———

In May 1893, Charles H. Jones, editor of the *St. Louis Republic*, wrote a letter to Representative William Jennings Bryan of Nebraska, a member of McMillin's tax-writing subcommittee. Jones had been following Bryan's battles against wealthy interests in Washington, and he had a suggestion. "The most effective weapon against Plutocratic policy is the graded income tax," the editor declared. The wealthy, he added, "dreaded nothing more."

Jones urged Bryan to study some of the published essays about the dangers of concentrated wealth, a problem he said an income tax could alleviate. "The income tax is one that ought to be levied at the next session of Congress," the letter said. "Some way of increasing the revenues must be found, especially if we are to redeem our pledges of tariff reform." He concluded with a kind of pledge. "I think you could do it," he said, "and if you will undertake it I will be in Washington to back you up."

Who was this man who received the fateful letter from Jones? To understand him, it helps to view the broad stretch of midwestern plains from which he came.

The geography books of the late nineteenth century described the plains of the Midwest as the Great American Desert. To early settlers, its rocky soil, arid winds and dry riverbeds made the place seem almost uninhabitable. The early pioneers' houses were made of mud and sod, though along the Platte River and its tributaries, the settlers cut down trees to build isolated log cabins. They also dug shelters in the earth, known as dugouts, to protect themselves against howling blizzards, dust storms and scorching summer droughts.

Yet in this great expanse of land, hopeful homesteaders found that if they struggled, they could cultivate wheat, corn, oats, potatoes and fruits. They could also raise farm animals. Life was anything but bucolic. Among the hazards were wild animals, disease, insects, long dry spells and attacks by Pawnee or Sioux Indians. These hardships were compounded in the 1870s by an unusual bout of heat waves, along with great swarms of grasshoppers darkening the sky and devouring entire crops in what victims saw as a kind of biblical plague. In winter, blizzards exacted their own toll, wiping out cattle herds. In the face of these hardships, many settlers retreated, often on the same prairie schooners they had arrived in with so much hope. Those who remained managed to make Nebraska a state in 1867, locating its capital in a salt marsh basin fifty miles west of the Missouri River. Named after the recently martyred President, Lincoln, Nebraska, was a frontier town populated by 40,000 souls in the 1880s. It boasted its own stockyards, mills, banks, newspapers, barbershops, clothing stores and even gaslights.

In 1888, a rangy lawyer from downstate Illinois arrived in Lincoln for a visit. Looking like an athlete with long dark hair and a wide jaw, Bryan was a formidable presence even at the age of twenty-eight. He had a resonant voice, an outgoing manner and fervent ideals and religious convictions rooted in his family of Scotch-Irish immigrants. His father had been a lawyer, farmer and Democratic state legislator who lost an election for Congress in southern Illinois in 1872. From his earliest days in prep school and college in Jacksonville, Illinois, near Springfield, Bryan had been fired up politically by free trade, monetary policy, temperance and other issues of the day. Even as an adolescent, he had developed an astonishing skill for florid oratory, studying elocution, voice modulation, gestures and rhythm of language under a favorite professor. He once wrote in an essay that "Virgil well says, 'If you would bid the tears of others flow, yourself the signs of grief must show.'"

At law school in Chicago, Bryan starred as a class politician and debater, working part-time in the law firm of former United States senator Lyman Trumbull, who had bolted the Democratic Party to support Lincoln during the Civil War. Among the lessons that Trumbull taught his protégé was to be wary of the dangers of the growing concentration of wealth. Bryan paid attention. He wrote to Mary Baird, his future wife, about his concerns that small businesses were being gobbled up by big corporations in steel, railroads and oil, and he predicted that farmers and workers would one day revolt against a system in which they created wealth enjoyed by others.

Bryan had hoped to practice law in Illinois but found it difficult to make a living. His trip to Lincoln was to collect some debts for a client, but the real payoff came when an old friend and classmate, Adolphus Talbot, invited him to team up in a law practice in Nebraska. The state had become hardened by cycles of boom and bust, particularly the Panic of 1873, which had bankrupted farmers and generated anger over the power of banks, merchants, railroads and other middlemen. Bryan immediately started speaking out against all these forces, charging also that high tariffs were protecting the wealthy manufacturers of farm equipment and other goods that farmers needed. He carried the free trade gospel to far corners of the state, working himself up so much in one address that he talked for two-and-a-half hours and left the crowd demanding more. When Bryan returned home, he woke his wife, sat on the edge of the bed and declared: "Mary, I have had a strange experience. Last night, I found that I had power over the audience. I could move them as I chose. I have more than unusual power as a speaker. I know it. God grant I may use it wisely." He then got on his knees to pray.

Running for Congress in 1890, Bryan campaigned in a state devastated by drought, blizzards and crop failures. At the same time, overproduction in other parts of the United States and the world had sent prices spiraling downward to the lowest levels since the Civil War. It was the perfect environment for Bryan's pitch that the banks were to blame for restricting the supply of money and that the way out of the fix was to expand the coinage of silver and to lower tariffs. "When you buy $1 worth of starch," he told listeners, "you pay 60 cents for the starch and 40 cents for the trust and the tariff." It was a successful formula he rode to victory and a new career in Washington.

The nation's capital in the Gilded Age was a city that rivaled New York for social excess. Many wealthy industrialists kept places in the district, where they entertained politicians and diplomats at lavish parties. The Senate was a millionaire's club. The doyenne of Washington society was Madeleine Vinton Dahlgren, daughter of a congressman, widow of a famous admiral and author in 1881 of the popular book *Etiquette of Social Life in Washington*, which advised readers on how to address a Russian count or pay a call on a minister from Queen Victoria's Britain. Among those in Washington's high society were the writer Henry Adams, the investment banker William C. Whitney, the editor Whitelaw Reid and the young Civil Service Commissioner, Theodore Roosevelt. Bankers and generals joined the Metropolitan Club, while the more scholarly flocked to the Cosmos Club. On Sunday, there were promenades near the old town houses of Georgetown and along the newer mansions on Connecticut Avenue.

Bryan, who arrived in the nation's capital riding a tide of national disgust over the administration of President Benjamin Harrison, was happy not to be invited to join the swells of polite society. With his grandiloquent manner, western boots, striped trousers, string tie and crushed hat, he was dismissed by a newspaper reporter as "one more of those hayseed Congressmen." But if Bryan felt out of place, he hardly showed it. Some colleagues saw an air of destiny about him. He was sociable and outgoing, but his favorite activities were singing hymns in church and spending time in libraries and bookstores to learn more about money, tariffs and taxes.

As Bryan took his place in Washington, feelings of disenchantment were spreading across the country. In May 1891, a great meeting occurred in Cincinnati, drawing all those dissatisfied with American economic policies. The gathering included representatives of the farmers' organizations known as the Grange and the Farmers' Alliance. There were also prohibitionists, women suffragists, antimonopolists, people favoring a restoration of greenback currency and the early workers' group known as the Knights of Labor. Their platform called for an abolition of the national banking system, free coinage of silver circulated at a ratio to gold of 16 to 1, and a graduated income tax.

At this early stage, Bryan was most deeply interested in silver. As a practical matter, however, the tariff was the issue of the day in Washington. It was also an issue he could exploit through his membership on the Ways and Means Committee. In his maiden speech, Bryan compared the tyranny of the tariff to slavery, denouncing it as a device by which "one man is authorized to collect money from his fellow man." If the tariff existed to protect workers, as some people said, why was it that American workers never saw the benefit in terms of higher wages? He mentioned that he had read about banquets in New York City costing $10 a plate, "when within a stone's throw of their banquet hall were people to whom a 10-cent meal would be a luxury." His speeches generated considerable publicity throughout the country.

Running for re-election in 1892, Bryan, despite his popularity, had to overcome a handicap because Republicans had redrawn his district to add Republicans and subtract Democrats. He also had to fight a rearguard action against the barons of his own party in Nebraska, who were less than enthusiastic about his tariff and tax policies. Challenging Bryan's stance on free trade, the Republican congressional candidate would hold up dry goods, red flannel and cutlery, saying they were made in Nebraska and needed to be protected by high tariffs. Bryan, in turn, would hold up butcher knives and dress goods, declaring that these could be purchased for 50 percent less in Mexico. He squeaked through with a margin of 140 votes. Shaken by the narrowness of his victory, Bryan at first flirted with trying to get the Nebraska legislature to send him to Washington as a senator. When he failed to secure enough votes, he threw his support to a Populist and former Republican, William V. Allen, a child of pioneers, a lawyer and a onetime activist in the Farmers' Alliance who later would become an important ally for lower tariffs and the income tax.

Once again Bryan prepared to return to Washington. This time he had a Democratic President at the head of his party, with whom he would try to make common cause. Instead, he went to war with him in 1893 over gold, helping to lead the fight against repeal of the Sherman Silver Purchase Act. In a speech on August 16, Bryan praised Cleveland as a sincere man—as sincere, in fact, as the mothers in India who (according to what he had read) threw their children into the sacred Ganges River in the deeply held belief that they would survive. Sincerity was not enough, he said. More important was the plight of farmers and others squeezed by debts and high prices. "The poor man who takes property by force is called a thief," Bryan thundered, "but the creditor who can by legislation make a debtor pay a dollar twice as large as he borrowed is lauded as the friend of a sound currency."

CHAPTER SIX

—⚬—

"Fraught with Danger . . . to Each and Every Citizen"

Enacted by the People, Rejected by the Court

PERHAPS INSPIRED BY HIS LETTER FROM CHARLES JONES, editor of the *St. Louis Republic,* William Jennings Bryan began in the fall of 1893—around the time of the battle over the gold standard—to draft a bill for a graduated income tax, to be imposed on incomes greater than $3,000 or $4,000. He had spent much of the year wading through some extremely dense materials on the subject, including scholarly papers, studies at the Treasury and State Departments and books from the Library of Congress. Although he had several allies among the western and southern members, all the Republicans on the House Ways and Means Committee were opposed, as were some key Democrats who were probusiness.

After winning the repeal of the silver standard, Cleveland was ready to turn to the tariff issue. In December 1893, he sent an annual message to Congress calling for extensive reductions. Revenues, he said he hoped, would increase as a result of lower tariffs and also from the imposition of some new taxes, including "a small tax upon incomes derived from certain corporate investments."

Later Treasury Secretary Carlisle suggested an inheritance tax and a tax on income from stocks and bonds. It was a first venture by top officials, at least rhetorically, into the tricky and controversial realm of taxing income by the federal government, and it stirred immediate opposition in the business community. Cleveland and Carlisle responded by not pushing their suggestion. From the perspective of the Keynesian economic theories accepted today, but not understood in the nineteenth and early twentieth centuries, increasing taxes at a time of recession is widely accepted as counterproductive. But Cleveland and Carlisle decided against pushing the tax package for political rather than economic reasons. They were fearful of angering business in the depths of an economic crisis.

Following the dictates of the Constitution, all revenue bills originated in the House. The pivotal figure in the tax-and-tariff battle was the chairman of the Ways and Means Committee, William L. Wilson, a West Virginia Democrat with definite populist sympathies. Courtly, compact and vigorous in his speaking style, Wilson had served in the Confederate Army—he was with Lee at Appomattox—and taught classics and served as a university president before being elected to the House. Wilson was skeptical of the income tax for an important reason. He feared that pushing for it now would undercut the chances of his main priority, lowering the tariff, especially if the two measures were tied together.

The Ways and Means subcommittee on taxation was the scene where the battle for the income tax first unfolded. Its chairman, Benton McMillin of Carthage, Tennessee, had supported reinstatement of an income tax since at least 1879. (The tax, enacted during the Civil War and repealed in 1872, had been reintroduced at least sixty-six times in Congress, usually by western or southern lawmakers.) While Wilson pushed for sweeping tariff reductions,

McMillin and Bryan persuaded their subcommittee to adopt a tax of 2 percent on incomes of $4,000 or more. At first, they proposed that the tax be considered separately from the tariff. But it was predictable that the tax and tariff changes would be considered as a whole.

The proposal by Bryan and McMillin drew fire from an array of conservative bastions, from the New York Chamber of Commerce (which labeled it "socialistic and vicious") to the *New York Times* and a string of influential papers throughout the East. On the other hand, Joseph Pulitzer's *New York World* and some other populist-leaning papers, such as the *St. Louis Republic*, lent crucial support.

The year 1894 opened in the House with Wilson's assault on the nation's high tariff walls. Caught in the middle between an alarmed business community and critics who said his bill did not go far enough, Wilson agreed to some important amendments. One of them, a ban on duties for sugar, won support from several lawmakers who were hoping that the loss of federal revenues would increase pressure for an income tax. "Vote for free sugar and an income tax," supporters said. The big break for the tax bill came when Wilson dropped his opposition to it, instead supporting it as long as it was considered separately from the tariff. In late January, McMillin rose to present the income tax bill to the House floor, which supporters said would raise $75 million. Bryan, meanwhile, filled several pages of the *Congressional Record* with information on tax laws overseas. The bill ran immediately into a congressional buzz saw of opposition.

The ensuing debate over the income tax became embroiled in the issues of a new American industrial society, particularly the growing concern among Americans over the power of the trusts. The defense of wealthy interests was not confined to the Republican Party. More dangerous to the income tax than Republican hostility was the all-out war against it by key Democrats, especially those from the wealthiest community in America—New York City. Leading the opposition was a tall, burly congressman, a master at political operating named Bourke Cockran, a Tammany Hall warrior with a heavy beard and resonant Irish brogue. Many years later Winston Churchill described Cockran as the greatest American orator he had heard.

Born in Ireland, Cockran had moved to New York as a teenager, practiced law and become a stalwart at Tammany Hall. Like his Democratic brethren in the world of patronage and corruption, he despised the sanctimonious Grover Cleveland and had tried to block Cleveland's nomination as President in 1884 and again in 1892. But to understand why the city's Democratic organization opposed the income tax, it is necessary to understand just what it represented in the New York of the 1890s under the leadership of its boss, Richard Croker. Reserved and taciturn, Croker was a shrewd, ruthless and corrupt politician who bore a striking resemblance to Ulysses S. Grant. He had come to America in steerage from Ireland in 1846 and started out by working as a court attendant to a lawyer representing the railway interests of Commodore Vanderbilt and Jim Fisk. Relentlessly vilified by educators, clergy, reformers, publishers and journalists, Croker was investigated and once in 1874 even tried for murder (the case was dismissed). But he also had plenty of raffish charm. The journalist muckraker Lincoln Steffens once said of him: "Richard Croker never said anything to me that was not true unless it was a statement for publication."

Croker consolidated his hold over Tammany in the mayoral election of 1886, in which the radical reformist author Henry George and the future President Theodore Roosevelt lost to Abram Hewitt, an industrialist and congressman who had once opposed Boss Tweed but ran this time as Boss Croker's candidate. New York City in the 1890s was engulfed by 18,000 new immigrants a month and awash in crime, prostitution, police corruption, poor sanitation and disease. But Tammany was the protector of wealthy interests, opposing those advocating a more active government for the poor, because it did not want to lessen their dependence on the Democratic Party organization for jobs and favors. The party thrived on what one of the party's sachems, George Washington Plunkitt, famously called "honest graft"—riches derived from the awarding of purchase contracts and jobs. Party shakedowns were hardly confined to street corner vegetable markets. They extended to Wall Street, where wealthy brokers either gave shares to Croker and his cronies or passed on tips so they could make money by a little bit of informed buying and selling on their own. In the 1890s, Croker was so wealthy he could afford several annual trips to Europe, seven homes and a stable of racehorses. (He was later driven from power and into exile in Britain after a police corruption scandal involving shakedowns of everyone from shoeshine boys to brothels.)

Shortly after McMillin and Bryan introduced their income tax bill on the House floor, there was a stir in the Capitol. Boss Croker, it was said, had arrived in Washington to rally his Tammany troops against the bill. Collecting his loyalists in the office of the House Speaker, he declared that opposition to the tax in New York City was so immense, even some of their safe seats were in jeopardy.

In a debate held by the Democratic caucus in the House, one of the leading opponents of the tax recruited by Tammany was a cantankerous sixty-eight-year-old New York City representative, Daniel E. Sickles, a long-retired Civil War general who had lost a leg at Gettysburg and had once shot dead a man for having designs on his wife. Propping himself up on his crutches so that he could shake both fists, Sickles demanded that his fellow Democrats tell him where in the 1892 party platform did the party call for an income tax. For all he knew, he said, Democrats had held that the tax was unconstitutional.

But, someone asked, hadn't Cleveland himself advanced the idea of a tax in his message to Congress the previous December? Sickles fumbled for a moment and replied that Cleveland was referring merely to a tax on corporations. "A tax on corporations would be better than this, because you can collect it, and you never can collect an income tax," he declared.

"On what do you base that assertion?" a colleague called out.

"On human nature," Sickles shot back, "and that is a pretty good thing to base legislation on." He went on to list all the great Democrats of New York who opposed the tax, until someone interrupted him. "Won't you add Croker?" he asked, and the place erupted in jeers. "Yes, I will," Sickles snapped, "for there isn't a better Democrat or a better citizen alive today than Richard Croker."

After their caucus debate, the Democrats as a whole voted to support the income tax and attach it to the tariff. It remained to be seen, however, whether Democratic defections from the tariff-and-tax measure would doom the overall bill. The *New York World,* which was pro-tax, trumpeted the inclusion of the measure with the headline "Income Tax Wins." But on the House floor, victory was far from certain and the atmosphere was tense. "The talk was all of the tariff, but the air was full of the income tax," the *New York World* reported. The only tactic left to Cockran and opponents was to filibuster and delay the new bill, flinging objections at every moment.

On January 29, McMillin moved in the House that the Wilson tariff bill be amended to include the income tax, as the Democrats had earlier voted to do. The arguments for and against the tax are worth summarizing because they offer a clear glimpse into the evolving attitudes toward wealth and fairness at the center of the issue.

McMillin opened the debate, charging that the concentration of wealth fostered by Republicans had driven the poor to "begging for alms" in the streets. It was now time, he added, to "impose taxes for public purposes and not private gains." The tax on corporations, the Ways and Means Committee had maintained, was justified by the "special privileges and advantages" that corporations derived from the federal government. "The Democratic Party, if it is anything, is the friend of the capitalist and the poor man alike," declared McMillin. "We would put in the lockup the law-breaking anarchist and then we would tax the capitalist. This is no assault upon wealth." The *Congressional Record* reported prolonged applause at this point. McMillin argued that an income tax, far from stirring class antagonism, would diminish it. With the government costing eight dollars per capita to run, he asked, was it not just for "a small piece" of the revenue to be derived from "accumulated wealth"? The Army, Navy and other government operations protected the nation's wealth, McMillin said. It was only fair, therefore, to shift the tax burden "from the laborer, who has nothing but his power to toil and sweat, to the man who has a fortune made or inherited."

As the Tennessee congressman ran through his arguments, applause in Congress only seemed to grow louder. Addressing questions that the tax was not collectible, McMillin pointed out that $346 million had been taken in before the Civil War tax was repealed in 1872. But his point that got the most reaction was the one supporting equity in the system. A man earning income from $50 million in bonds, he declared, paid no tax whereas tariff duties were paid by "the man who drinks one cup of sweetened coffee, the man who wears one suit of clothes, the man who wipes his face once on an imported towel." It was not as if the tax would apply to untold numbers of Americans. McMillin estimated that only about 85,000 persons would fall under its provisions.

In the debate over the tax, lawmakers added some historical stretchers to McMillin's fact-based arguments. One congressman said that "when darkness settled over Egypt" it was because 3 percent of her population owned 97 percent of the wealth. When Babylon "went down," he said, 2 percent of the population owned all the wealth. When Persia "bowed her head," 1 percent of the population owned all the land. Partisans then listed the wealthiest people in the world, who included the Emperor of Russia, the Sultan of Turkey, the Emperor of Austria, the Emperor of Germany, the King of Italy, Queen Victoria and others who, it was said, were worth less than the Rothschilds, Rockefellers, Vanderbilts and others in the United States. Was a progressive tax against the laws of nature? Some lawmakers cited St. Luke: "For unto whomsoever much is given, of him shall be much required." Was the tariff-and-tax bill an insidious example of class legislation? That could not be, when it already cost $40 for a suit of clothes that, without the tariff, could be purchased for $25, or $100 for a harness that would otherwise cost $75, or $3 for a scythe that, without the tariff, would cost only $2.25.

Democrats and Republicans from the Northeast were the main forces against the tax. An income tax, they said, was justified only by war. It discriminated against business, encouraged fraud and rewarded the South while punishing the North. They charged that it would depress real estate, erode stock values and hurt business. Many warned that it would be declared unconstitutional. They said it would encourage taxpayers to lie about their wealth, thereby fostering dishonesty.

But it was hard to argue against facts. Most instructive to the House members were the findings of the Ways and Means Committee, which used census figures from 1891 to show that more than 13 million families had an assessed wealth of more than $62 million, of which the top 70 families were worth more than $2.6 million. A tiny handful of persons owned over one-half of the wealth in the United States, while one-sixtieth owned over two-thirds of the wealth. On the lower end of the scale, the tables showed that three-quarters of American families were not worth more than $600 for all members. The tariff was seen in this context for what it was—a tax that exaggerated the basic economic inequality among Americans. The Ways and Means Committee's breakdown thus demonstrated that poor families paid taxes in the form of higher prices due to tariffs on dishes, cups, forks, clothing—indeed, "everything except water and air."

Above all, many proponents of the income tax saw it as a safety valve, a way of placating the restive lower classes who might otherwise be alienated from American society. Representative Uriel Hall, a Missouri Democrat, called it "a measure to kill anarchy and keep down socialists."

The long and dramatic debate over the income tax came down on January 30 to a showdown between its two most eloquent partisans, Bourke Cockran and William Jennings Bryan. "Like athletes on a football field," said the *New York World*, they strode into a packed House chamber with the galleries filled overhead.

With "profound regret," Cockran rose first to oppose the bill and the effort to attach it to a tariff reduction measure that he supported. The income tax, he declared, was nothing more than a "special tax" on 85,000 wealthy Americans, any of whom could evade it if they wanted to lie about their riches. "Instead of taxation it will be baksheesh," Cockran charged dismissively. Imposing taxes exclusively on the wealthy, he argued, would lead to their wielding disproportionate influence over the government. "Does any sane man believe that Democratic institutions could live under such a system," he asked, or "that a government entirely supported by a class would not ultimately be controlled by a class?" His speech thus worked itself up into portraying the tax as an assault on democracy and ultimately on the poor, who because they were not paying taxes would sink in status below "the richest and the proudest" citizens.

His own district, Cockran said, had only 2,000 taxpayers who would be subjected to the new law. But it was the poor who would feel "humiliated and degraded" by these taxpayers being elevated to first-class citizenship. The ancient empires did not fall because of inequality between rich and poor, as some in the House had declared, said the congressman. The empires of old fell because they failed to protect private property and "human industry" from government oppression. "Sir," Cockran concluded, with a magnificent flourish, "I protest against this betrayal of our ancient principles. I protest against this treason to our faith, to our platform, to our traditions, to our heroes. I protest against partial laws, whether they be intended to favor the few or the many. I demand for all men the same equality before the law which they enjoy in the sight of God. In the name of one God whom we all worship; in the name of that one party which the majority here supports I demand now, as I have always demanded, one citizenship, one country, one law, one Democratic faith, one common plane of equality for all the people, without distinction of wealth, of birth, or race, or of creed!"

A burst of applause rang through the crowded House chamber and galleries. Lawmakers rushed to congratulate Cockran but quickly shifted their attention to Bryan, who began by saluting his fellow Democrat's rhetorical gifts.

"If this were a mere contest in oratory, no one would be presumptuous enough to dispute with Mr. Cockran," he said. But the Tammany congressman, he said, was speaking for the monopolists and millionaires of America, whereas he, Bryan, was "clad in the armor of a righteous cause" and speaking for 60 million common people. One by one, he demolished Cockran's points, especially the argument that it was somehow a "badge of liberty" for the poor to pay taxes along with the rich. "If taxation is a badge of free men, the poor people of this country are covered all over with the insignia of free men," he declared. The poor did not pay the Civil War era income tax, and yet their patriotism and participation in the war were undiminished. Was he, Bryan, a demagogue? "They call that man a statesman whose ear is attuned to the slightest pulsation of the pocket book," he declared, "and they describe as a demagogue any one who dares listen to the heartbeat of humanity." Was it socialism to exempt the poor from income taxes? No, because the poor pay heavy taxes in the form of the tariff: "They weep more because fifteen millions are to be collected from the incomes of the rich than they do at the collection of three hundred millions upon the goods which the poor consume." Was the tax "inquisitorial" and intrusive? Bryan pointed out that New York collectors had long asked citizens for the value of their property in order to collect the property tax.

"But they say that the income tax invites perjury," Bryan went on, dripping with sarcasm. "Why, sirs, this Government has too much important business on hand to spend its time trying to bolster up the morality of men who cannot be trusted to swear to their incomes." Turning to his colleagues, he asked if their districts were full of perjurers. If so, he asked, why not go out and punish them? It was not undemocratic to ask the rich to pay proportionately more to support the government, he said. "Who is it most needs a navy? Is it the farmer who plods along behind the plow upon his farm, or is it the man whose property is situated in some great seaport where it could be reached by an enemy's guns?" But the Nebraskan's most withering point followed his quotation from the Savannah-born lawyer and society figure Ward McAllister, who years earlier had helped select the members of what was known as "the Four Hundred" (so called because of the number of people who could fit in Mrs. William Astor's ballroom).

In a letter in the *New York World*, McAllister had opposed the tax in a most infelicitous way. Reading from it, Bryan slyly provoked catcalls as he quoted McAllister as complaining that a tax of 2 percent on incomes exceeding $4,000 would drive "rich men to go abroad and live" where they could escape such high taxes. "But whither will these people fly?" Bryan asked, drawing peals of derisive laughter. "If their tastes are English—'quite English, you know'—and they stop in London, they will find a tax of more than 2 per cent assessed upon incomes. If they look for a place of refuge in Prussia, they will find an income tax of 4 per cent." Drawing on his prodigious research, he went through all the countries of Europe, explaining that they, too, had an income tax. "I repeat," said Bryan at the end. "Whither will they fly?" More laughter. "Are there really any such people in this country?" he went on. "Of all the mean men I have ever known, I have never known one so mean that I would be willing to say of him that his patriotism was less than 2 percent deep." If such people exist, he said, "we can afford to lose them." They shall be, he said in closing, like the condemned of the poem "The Man Without a Country," the wretched whose departure would be "unwept, unhonor'd, and unsung!"

It must have been extraordinary to hear these two rhetorical geniuses throw thunderbolts at each other, but Bryan appears to have gotten the better of the day. Cries of "Vote! Vote!" echoed through the House as he was mobbed by colleagues telling him that he had just given the speech of a lifetime. The House quickly rejected two amendments raising the income tax rate higher than the level in the bill. Then it voted overwhelmingly to attach the income tax to the tariff bill. Two days later the House took up the two measures, now in one bill, and once again the galleries were packed so tightly that the elevators could not function and women had to be carried away.

Now in the final moment, Thomas B. Reed of Maine, Republican House leader and former Speaker, led the attack against the bill. Speaker Charles Crisp of Georgia counterattacked. But neither made any reference to the income tax. Wilson, the Ways and Means chairman, addressed the tax and tariff issues together. Noting that he had originally opposed twinning the two measures, he defended the final bill as an effort to balance the weight of taxation in a fair way. The roll call, he declared, would soon be entered "not only upon the Journals of this House, it will be written in the history of this country, it will be entered in the annals of freedom throughout all time. . . . This is a roll of honor. This is a roll of freedom, and in the name of honor and in the name of freedom, I summon every Democratic member of this House to inscribe his name upon it."

When the bill in its entirety finally passed on February 1, Bryan and other elated lawmakers rushed toward Wilson, lifted him on their shoulders and paraded him around the House floor. "The Democratic hen," said the New York Daily Tribune, "has hatched a Populist chicken at last."

———

After a tough fight in the House, tariff and tax reform faced an even more uphill battle in the Senate, an institution of millionaire lawmakers with a narrow Democratic majority. Pro-tariff lobbyists were determined to get the Senate to block the House bill or cripple it with amendments.

More than their House colleagues, senators were sensitive to the special interests benefiting from protectionism. The senators from Louisiana were against the free sugar provisions. The senators from West Virginia, Maryland and Alabama were against lower duties on coal and iron ore. The foes of tariff reduction made common cause by voting for each other's pet interests, a practice known then as now as "logrolling." It was worth the political risk for Democrats to break with their President and support higher prices for all Americans—as long as they won the battle to help their own narrow constituent interests. "I can afford to oppose this bill and beat the President," said Senator Arthur Gorman of Maryland, as recounted later by Andrew Carnegie. "But I cannot afford to oppose and be beaten by him."

Pro-tariff forces pounced on the House bill as soon as it reached the Senate Finance Committee. Led by Senator Nelson Aldrich of Rhode Island, nearly all Senate Republicans were opposed to lower tariffs. What made the difference was the wavering among Democrats. The bill cleared by the Finance Committee restored moderate tariffs on an array of items. But on the Senate floor, the drive to raise tariffs back to old levels was unstoppable. Senator Gorman acted to restore high tariffs on coal and iron ore. Whiskey interests got the committee to increase duties on whiskey. Henry O. Havemeyer of the American Sugar Company, which controlled four-fifths of the sugar-refining industry, won the restoration of sugar barriers. Raw sugar, which had been declared free of tariff barriers in 1890, was now granted a tariff of 40 percent.

Havemeyer exercised considerable influence within the Cleveland administration. He had helped William Whitney, Cleveland's 1892 campaign manager, and Daniel Lamont, the War Secretary, profit from speculation in sugar stocks. Whitney and Lamont, in turn, advised Cleveland to accept some higher tariffs as a way of getting a bill through the Senate. In that spirit, Cleveland directed his allies in the Senate to "go ahead and do the best they could" to salvage the bill. Instead, the Senate adopted a grand total of 634 amendments, effectively stripping away all the tariff cuts enacted by the House.

The Senate also went through a ferocious debate on the income tax, still attached as an amendment to the bill. The chief opponent was Senator David Bennett Hill, an upstate New York Democrat who had served as Cleveland's lieutenant governor and succeeded him in the Albany executive mansion before going to the Senate. Hill had his own eye set on the White House in 1896. Taking up Bourke Cockran's cause, he offered 23 amendments to modify or defeat the income tax, declaring that it would undermine business confidence and deepen class antagonisms. The income tax, he said, was the product of "little squads of anarchists, communists and socialists" bringing their pernicious ideas from across the ocean to American shores. As a political matter, Hill warned that passing that tax would bring the greatest electoral defeat to the Democrats since the Civil War.

The income tax could not even count on support from some of its old champions in the Senate, including Justin S. Morrill of Vermont and John Sherman of Ohio, who criticized the measure for failing to differentiate between different kinds of income. But the tax remained in the bill, thanks largely to the determination of its main champion, Senator William Allen of Nebraska, the former Republican picked for the Senate when the Nebraska legislature passed over Bryan in early 1893. In defending the tax, Allen asserted that 9 percent of the families in America owned 71 percent of the wealth. In New York alone, he declared with an air of astonishment, there were 119 millionaires! He rattled off their names: Vanderbilt, Whitney, Rockefeller and so on, along with the amount of tax they would pay. The proposed amendments to lower the tax exemption level were defeated. Many senators fully expected that the income tax would eventually be declared unconstitutional anyway.

The tariff bill, with its negating amendments but with the income tax intact, passed the Senate on July 3. Encouraged by the White House, William Wilson, the House Ways and Means chairman, tried to get some of the tariff cuts restored in a House–Senate conference. He failed. In the House, Wilson read dramatically from a letter from Cleveland condemning his fellow Democrats in the

Senate. The President denounced "the methods and manipulations of trusts and combinations" that brought this result, especially in sugar, and charged that the abandonment of the cause of lower tariffs "means party perfidy and party dishonor." In one of Cleveland's more memorable phrases, he denounced the wealthy interests of "the communism of pelf"—an archaic term for ill-gotten gains.

Cleveland now faced an excruciating dilemma. He had not made a major fight over the tariff, as he had over silver. Should he now veto the bill and set up a confrontation he probably could not win? Or should he sign it, on grounds that there were some improvements in the bill—the duty on wool was removed, and some minor duties on other items were lowered—and seem utterly subservient to Congress? In the end, he let the bill become law without his signature.

The Wilson–Gorman Act, as the tax and tariff measure became known, represented a calamitous defeat for Cleveland, marking the beginning of the end of his presidency. For Bryan, however, its inclusion of the income tax represented his most important legislative accomplishment. The tax was not so much on the rich as on the very rich. Its provision for a 2 percent tax on incomes of $4,000 or more applied to only 2 percent of American taxpayers, yielding an estimated $75 million. The tax was to be levied for five years starting January 1, 1895, on corporations and individuals. It was to apply to all "gains, profits and income derived from any kind of property, rents, interest, dividends or salaries, or from any profession, trade, employment or vocation," which included inheritances and gifts. The tax was also to apply to the net profits or income above the operating and business expenses of corporations, companies and associations doing business for profit, but not partnerships. Corporations resented that they had no $4,000 exemption from the tax and that some businesses—building and loan associations, mutual savings bank and mutual insurance companies—were exempt. Also exempt were states, counties and municipalities, and charitable, religious and educational associations.

The new law's main flaw, in the view of many supporters, was that there was no mechanism to collect the tax at the source of income, from employers. Because the tax affected only a tiny minority of Americans at the top of the scale, it would be an exaggeration to call it a dramatic change in the nation's economic and political structure. From the perspective of more than a hundred years later, Americans might be able to filter the debate of the 1890s through the experience of our contemporary tax debates in the Bush and Clinton eras, which revolved around whether to increase or decrease rates for those in the same top 1 or 2 percent of the wealthiest Americans. But the 1894 law, though affecting only 2 percent of the taxpayers, was a landmark. The tax's enemies vowed never to let it survive.

———

He was not anyone's first choice.

Melville Fuller, a scholarly and versatile lawyer with a private practice in Chicago specializing in commercial and real property law, was one of the most obscure people to be elevated to Chief Justice of the United States. His one advantage was that he was an active Democrat enjoying a friendship and political association with President Grover Cleveland. Just before the end of his first term, Cleveland turned to Fuller when several other candidates were ruled out for various reasons. One possibility, for instance, had been the House Speaker, John Carlisle, recognized for his parliamentary brilliance. But Cleveland even then worried about Carlisle's drinking. "I won't appoint a man to be Chief Justice of the United States who might be picked up in the street some morning," the President told a senator pushing the Kentuckian. (Carlisle's problems did not deter Cleveland from appointing him Treasury Secretary in his second term.)

Fuller was not an imposing physical presence. He had a round face, wavy shoulder-length silver hair and a thick drooping mustache. He was a tiny man whose chair had to be elevated in order for him to be seen on the bench, where he was surrounded by men physically—and regarded as intellectually—bigger than he was. "Fuller came to a Court that wondered what this little man was going to do," Felix Frankfurter wrote later. "There were titans, giants on the bench. They were powerful men, both in experience and in force of conviction, and powerful in physique, as it happened."

As it turned out, Fuller came to be regarded as an effective Chief Justice, earning the respect of those opposed to his conservative philosophy. On a court of towering egos and conflicting ideologies, he developed a reputation for firmness, tact, humor and an ability to mediate. To keep the mood collegial, he inaugurated the practice of the justices all shaking hands with each other every morning, a practice that continues to this day. Justice Oliver Wendell Holmes, Jr., who served later with him, said upon Fuller's death in 1910: "I suspect that it would be easier to get a man who wrote as well as Marshall than to get one who would run the Court as well as Fuller."

It was Fuller's fate to adjudicate problems arising from the great shifts in American society brought about by monopolies, technological breakthroughs, migration from the countryside and overseas to the cities, and the difficulties of racial justice. To deal with these changes, Congress turned increasingly to government solutions, provoking a counterreaction in the court. Fuller was one of the court's most fervent advocates of states' rights, individualism and limits on the powers of Congress, especially when it came to regulating corporations or curbing property and individual rights. (Perhaps the most notorious of the Fuller court's decisions, upholding the constitutionality of racial segregation, was later handed down in *Plessy* v. *Ferguson* in 1896.) The Supreme Court had a long history of confronting Congress, but until the 1890s, it did not deal much with Congress's power over everyday business issues. Then the year 1895 saw a rapid fire of rulings that were among the most momentous in the high court's history.

First, in a case known as *United States* v. *E. C. Knight & Co.*, the court held that the Sherman Antitrust Act outlawing monopolies did not apply to a cartel that had virtually complete control over the manufacture of refined sugar, the so-called "sugar trust." The court accepted the sugar trust's argument that Congress had overstepped itself in seeking to regulate the manufacture, as opposed to the commerce, of sugar. The decision shocked those who looked to the government to regulate the trusts, but it was applauded by the very man who should have been in charge of defending the law, Cleveland's Attorney General, Richard Olney. Before joining the cabinet, Olney had been a lawyer for railroads and the whiskey trust who advocated the repeal of the Sherman Antitrust Act. Not succeeding in that cause, he had advanced the narrow interpretation before the court in the sugar case.

Olney, conservative in most matters, had been responsible for sending in marshals to crush Coxey's army. He had also achieved a major victory in 1895 when the Supreme Court, in the second of its conservative rulings that year, upheld the arrest and conviction of Eugene V. Debs for disobeying the court order to call off the Pullman strike. That decision ushered in an era of employers using such court orders until thirty-seven years later, when it was outlawed during Franklin Roosevelt's New Deal.

But it was the third decision, the income tax case, that produced the biggest economic earthquake of the Fuller court of 1895. The court's rejection of the income tax was one of the most fateful rulings of the era. It provoked a cry of outrage and indignation from critics, who likened it to the Dred Scott decision of 1857 rejecting the right of states to outlaw slavery. It became a major contention in the 1896 presidential campaign. It prefigured the anguished arguments in the New Deal about the "nine old men" who substituted their own conservative judgment for the will of the people as expressed by Congress. It led to eighteen more years of debate and maneuvering to get a constitutional amendment to enact a tax that could withstand legal challenge. Indeed, it can be said that along with the Knight and Debs rulings, the income tax decision laid the groundwork for the popular revolt against conservatism characterizing American politics well into the next century. Eventually that revolt would overturn all three rulings.

———

No sooner had the income tax passed the previous August than it was challenged in court in several suits by shareholders seeking to restrain corporations from paying it. Some of the suits were dismissed and others were consolidated in a case known as *Pollock* v. *Farmers' Loan and Trust Co.*, which the Supreme Court accepted in January 1895. Defending the income tax were Olney—more supportive than in the sugar trust case—and a private attorney he was glad to have on his team. He was James C. Carter, a brilliant and dramatic New York City lawyer who had represented the Continental Trust Company when it was sued by one of its shareholders to prevent it from paying the tax. Rugged, powerfully built and with a deep, resonant voice, Carter was a mesmerizing speaker who could appear both sad and stern at the same time, though he sometimes had to keep his hostility toward his adversaries in check. Carter had once been considered by Cleveland for the job of Chief Justice.

When arguments began in March, the plaintiffs focused on what they believed was the threshold issue: whether the tax was a "direct" tax as defined by Article I, Section 2, of the Constitution, which said that a "direct tax" must be "apportioned among the several States . . . according to their respective numbers." Since most of the income tax derived from a handful of states where the richest Americans lived—New York, New Jersey, Pennsylvania and Connecticut—the tax would have to be declared unconstitutional if it were defined as a "direct" tax.

Olney and Carter argued that the definition of a "direct tax" was clear and that the income tax did not fall into it. They asserted that by tradition and under prior court decisions, a direct tax was defined as a capitation (poll) tax or a tax on real estate. Among the precedents they cited was a 1796 decision in which the Supreme Court upheld a tax upon carriages. In that case, the court said the tax was not direct, making it clear that direct taxes related only to property, real or otherwise. All subsequent decisions of the Supreme Court upholding taxes on insurance companies, transfer of real estate and even the Civil War income tax followed this line of thinking, saying that the only definition of a direct tax was the one outlined in 1796.

Those challenging the income tax argued, on the other hand, that the income tax, which taxed income *derived* from property, was the functional equivalent of a property tax and therefore unconstitutional because it was not apportioned to the states based on population. They also advanced a more philosophical argument about the compact at the heart of the founding of the United States. Ratification of the Constitution, they said, came only after the more numerous poorer states agreed not to gang up on the fewer number of rich states to tax them disproportionately. In effect, the plaintiffs argued, all past definitions of direct taxes or indirect taxes were secondary to this fundamental compact.

Several of the lawyers made a separate argument. They held that even if the tax were not considered direct, it should be thrown out on the basis of the so-called uniformity clause of the Constitution, which holds that all taxes have to be "uniform" around the country. The plaintiffs' lawyers argued that although it was not precisely clear what the word *uniform* meant, a tax imposed on some kinds of income and not others, and only on the wealthy, seemed a clear violation of the uniformity concept. (The government argued that the principle of "uniformity" applied only to geographical uniformity and that other sorts of exemptions were clearly allowed.)

These were the dry legal arguments. What made the case so compelling were the issues that evoked great emotion: appeals to morality, justice, fairness, the future of democracy, the stability of the country and the question of basic rights to privacy and private property in an evolving economy. The battle before the Supreme

Court was also a theatrical event, an exercise of advocates advancing self-interest in the clothing of principle. The courtroom was filled with members of Congress, the government and lawyers from across the country, and all the major newspapers covered the arguments extensively. Challenging the law was a phalanx of distinguished corporate lawyers whose clients included the most powerful corporations in the United States.

William D. Guthrie, an ultraconservative Republican and wealthy lawyer for big corporations and propertied interests in New York City, opened the arguments, warning that "class legislation and attempts of the majority to spoliate private property would ultimately wreck the American republic." He asked the court to serve as a "bulwark of the people against their own unadvised actions, their own uninstructed will."

The second lawyer on the team, George F. Edmunds, was a former Republican senator from Vermont who was a constitutional expert and the author of a law outlawing polygamy in Utah and other territories. As a member of the Senate Judiciary Committee, he had worked closely with Fuller on legislation relieving the justices of the obligation to serve on circuit courts around the country. Bald, with a flowing white beard and an acerbic manner, Edmunds was renowned as a respected conservative elder statesman. He now demanded that the court "bring the Congress back to a true sense of the limitations of its powers," saying that the tax imposed by people who paid nothing, on a small minority who would pay a lot, would lead to "communism, anarchy, and then, the ever following despotism."

Rounding out the plaintiffs' lineup was Joseph Choate, a prominent New York Republican, club man, after-dinner speaker and foe of Tammany Hall. Representing Standard Oil and the tobacco trust, he denounced the tax in purple tones as based on "principles as communistic, socialistic—what shall I call them—populistic as ever have been addressed to any political assembly in the world." He appealed to the court emotionally to defend the interests of private property and vested interests. "I do not believe that any member of the Court ever has sat or ever will sit to hear and decide a case the consequences of which will be so far-reaching as this," he said. Head-on, he met what was surely the court's concern, which was that the legislation before them was supported by a majority of Congress and most probably a majority of Americans. But he challenged the court to exercise its wisdom "no matter what the threatened consequences may be." Four-fifths of the Civil War era tax was paid by the residents of four states—New York, Pennsylvania, Massachusetts and New Jersey—he said. Surely the justices did not want Congress to exercise the "untrammeled and uncontrollable" power to single out taxpayers so selectively. To uphold the tax, he concluded, would be to embrace "a doctrine worthy of a Jacobin Club . . . of a Czar of Russia."

In his defense of the tax, Olney, no antagonist of business, assailed wealthy and corporate interests for trying to get the court to supplant the prerogatives of Congress. He warned the court not to "overlook and overstep" its power. But it was Carter who fired the sharpest arguments. Dismissing the notion that the tax represented a new weapon in a growing class war, he said the best way to preserve private property was to relieve the masses of excessive tax burdens. "Nothing could be more unwise and dangerous— nothing more foreign to the spirit of the Constitution—than an attempt to baffle and defeat a popular determination by a judgment in a lawsuit," he warned. Carter evidently recognized that the court would wonder why the rich should be singled out for paying the tax. He argued that it was because the poor had already had to pay more than their share of consumption taxes and tariffs and that this measure was aimed at evening the balance. Finally, he argued on practical grounds that the tax was a safety valve at a time of unrest: "the only path of safety is to accept the voice of the majority as final."

In an initial decision in April, the court ruled five to three that the tax on rents or other income from real estate was indeed a direct tax and therefore unconstitutional because it was not properly apportioned among the states. The justices also threw out the tax on income from interest on municipal bonds as an infringement on states' prerogatives. The court, with eight justices sitting, was evenly divided on whether other portions of the statute were valid and also on whether the law as a whole should be thrown out because of a couple of faulty provisions. Writing for the majority, Fuller in effect adopted the plaintiffs' dubious historical and legal arguments about the definitions of a direct tax. He nimbly swept aside a Supreme Court decision in 1864 upholding part of the Civil War era income tax as not applicable to the present case because it was explicitly addressed not to the income tax on real estate but to other earnings. A tax on income from land was the equivalent of a tax on land itself, a direct tax, Fuller said. As for the argument that such taxes had to be distributed according to population, Fuller accepted the contention that this fundamental premise was part of the original compact of rich states and poor states banding together. To have a tax that took most of its revenues from a handful of wealthy states was seen in this light as undermining a historic principle of national unity.

From Fuller's argument, one could conclude that it would be impossible to have any kind of income tax on income from property. In order for such a tax to be apportioned among states according to their population, the federal government would have to impose varying rates for each state—higher rates on poorer states and lower rates on richer states—on property of the same value. It made no sense (as advocates of a nationwide direct tax had found during the Civil War). Nor was it practical.

The mood of the court is best seen not in Fuller's opinion but in the concurring opinion of the eldest member of the court, Justice Stephen Field. Unlike Fuller, Field was a renowned jurist, famous for his temper and brilliance, from a respected legal family. (As a youth, he had practiced law in New York City with his older brother, David, a prominent New York attorney who later hired

Thomas Shearman for the law firm that was to become Shearman & Sterling.) He was a world traveler who had studied the classics and many languages and had traveled in the Middle East as a young man. After practicing with his brother in New York, he ventured to California in the year of the big gold rush. There he practiced law in rough-and-tumble gold rush territory and learned to shoot from his pocket to protect himself. In the California State Legislature, Field was known as a shrewd and pragmatic lawmaker who drafted civil and criminal procedures and later rose to become a justice on the California Supreme Court.

After Field was appointed to the United States Supreme Court during the Civil War, however, he left behind his reputation for flexibility and became increasingly conservative and temperamental. He approached every case with an extremely narrow view about the function of national government, embracing the doctrine of "natural rights," in which it was accepted that property rights exist among men in their natural state—and that to protect such rights constitutions are written in the first place. Field's reputation for a hot temper went back to the gold rush days and seemed to grow over the decades. In the summer of 1889, while riding circuit in his home state of California, he apparently cast aspersions on a woman appearing before him, provoking her husband—a lawyer and former colleague of Field on the California Supreme Court—to fire a shot at him.

In 1895, Field had been on the court for thirty years. Respected as an elder statesman, he nonetheless had grown weak, cantankerous and by some accounts senile. His own nephew and colleague on the court, David Josiah Brewer, had joined with other colleagues to suggest he resign. Field did not participate in many decisions in his final years, but the income tax got his juices flowing. He said it represented a "usurpation" by Congress and an "assault upon capital." Going way beyond the issue at hand, he charged that the law "will be but the stepping stone to others, larger and more sweeping, till our political contests will become a war of the poor against the rich." The irony was that Field had himself upheld the Civil War era tax but now seemed to grow more reactionary with age, or at least to have a different standard for a peacetime tax than for a wartime tax. Clearly he was more concerned about property rights than precedent.

As is often the case, the dissents were eloquent. Edward D. White, a former Louisiana senator and plantation owner who had served in the Confederate Army and who had been appointed to the court by Cleveland, argued for upholding the entire tax. White would later become Chief Justice after Fuller's retirement. Now he warned that for the court to ignore precedent and annul its previous decisions on direct taxes and on the income tax during the Civil War was "fraught with danger to the court, to each and every citizen and to the republic."

But the case was known less for its dissents than for the confusion over the fact that the decision was partial and divided. Though the court was emphatic about its rejection of taxation of income from real property, it was either silent or in disagreement on other major questions, such as whether it was constitutional to tax income on stocks and bonds. The lawyers, as well as the public, were utterly confused. On only one issue was the court clear. It threw out all taxes on municipal bonds as an infringement on the rights of the states. But did the court's decision invalidate the entire law? Was the tax on personal property (as opposed to real estate) unconstitutional? What about the charge that the taxes were not uniform?

Because of these uncertainties, the plaintiffs asked for a rehearing and got one in May.

By now, Carter had dropped out as a defending lawyer in the case, probably because Continental Illinois, his client, was uncomfortable with his arguments. His absence proved to be a disaster for the cause. This time there were nine justices, not eight. Associate Justice Howell Jackson, a former Tennessee senator, had been sick the previous time out but was now well enough to attend. Each theme was repeated. Olney made the mistake of essentially criticizing Fuller's opinion. He also felt constrained to address the argument that the tax was some sort of communist plot. He warned that Fuller's original decision posed a danger if the country should find itself in need of revenue in a crisis or war. But he was no match for Choate, who urged that the entire tax be thrown out. Choate expanded the argument that income from personal property (including stocks and bonds) should have the same protections as real property, though he admitted there were no precedents for such a claim.

There was much speculation throughout the legal community about what the court would do. In late May 1895, it threw out the whole tax, agreeing with Choate about personal property. Again with Fuller writing the opinion, the court reasoned that although other pieces of the law might be valid, the real property part of the tax was integral to the whole, so that removing it would invalidate the entire law. Although Fuller implied that taxes on wages would be constitutional, in a clever dig at the argument that the taxes were just, he said that if taxes on wages remained, a new injustice would arise. A tax on wages but not on other forms of income should be struck down because "what was intended as a tax on capital would remain in substance a tax on occupations and labor."

What was most startling about the second decision was its creation of one of the great historic riddles of the Supreme Court, known to scholars as "the mystery of the vacillating jurist."

In the second decision, Justice Jackson—the absentee the first time around—voted in favor of upholding the other parts of the income tax law while throwing out the tax as it applied to property income. The decision was 5 to 4 to throw out the entire law, however. Logically, Jackson's vote should have dictated a 5-to-4 ruling in favor of upholding the remainder of the law, since the court had earlier been divided 4 to 4 on that question. Therefore, one judge who voted earlier to uphold the tax on income derived from sources other than property had switched his vote.

Who was that justice? The voting breakdown was secret, and published reports at the time did not disclose his identity. At first, it was widely supposed that it was George Shiras, Jr., an undistinguished Pennsylvania lawyer who had represented large steel corporations and the Baltimore and Ohio Railroad before joining the court. The intense criticism of him as the alleged vacillator was met with silence, and the charge never was proved.

Historians of the court and the income tax have focused their speculation on two other justices. One is David Josiah Brewer, a former Kansas Supreme Court Justice who was Justice Field's nephew. He shared his uncle's conservative views on due process and had once declared that "the paternal theory of government is to me odious." The other possibility is Horace Gray, a scholarly Boston lawyer with a reputation as a martinet who demanded strict decorum in the court. Like Field, he had grown more and more conservative in his later years. Perhaps, the speculation goes, he felt strongly about precedent in the first case and changed his mind in order to uphold the will of the majority of the justices. The mystery has never been solved.

———

As soon as Fuller finished reading the decision on May 20, John Harlan, once described by Justice Holmes as "the last of the tobacco-spittin' judges," gave one of the great fiery dissents in the annals of the court.

Harlan was a onetime slaveholder from Kentucky who nonetheless sided with the Union during the Civil War. Months earlier he had dissented angrily in the sugar trust case. Now, his face reddening, Harlan banged the bench, glowered at his colleagues and even shook his finger at both Fuller and Field in what *The Nation* called "the most violent political tirade ever heard in a court of last resort." He charged that in ruling against the tax, the court had decided basically that without a constitutional amendment, there could never be a tax on incomes in support of the federal government. That position, he declared, was a threat to society and a recipe for social unrest. Harlan said the court's action invested property owners "with power and influence that may be perilous to that portion of the American people upon whom rests the large part of the burdens of the government, and who ought not to be subjected to the dominion of aggregated wealth."

Justice Field, backing Fuller once again, seemed to get even more emotional the second time around. He warned in his concurring majority opinion that an income tax would unleash evil forces. He made it clear that the decision was not based on narrow grounds of what was or was not a "direct" tax, but on larger philosophical ones. "The present assault upon capital," he declared, "is but the beginning. It will be but the stepping-stone to others, larger and more sweeping, till our political contests will become a war of the poor against the rich; a war constantly growing in intensity and bitterness." The court's high purpose, he suggested, was to prevent "sure decadence" from destroying the country.

In his own brief dissent, seconding Harlan, Justice Jackson said the decision was "the most disastrous blow ever struck at the constitutional power of Congress." And Justice Henry Brown scolded the court for its obsessive fears of socialism, saying: "I hope it may not prove the first step toward the submergence of the liberties of the people in a sordid despotism of wealth." Finally, Justice Edward D. White, who had also dissented before, charged that the majority had enshrined "invested wealth" as protected by the Constitution, making the Constitution into an "engine of the most outrageous oppression and inequality the world has ever known."

A century later the controversy over the court's decision on the income tax remains a subject of debate. The court's conservatism was clearly rooted in the dogma that the government had no right to interfere with private property and freedom of contract. The most dramatic evidence for this view of the high court is not only the Pollock case but a decision ten years later—the most notorious decision of the Fuller era, *Lochner* v. *New York* (1905). The Lochner ruling threw out, as a violation of the liberty of contract, a state law placing a sixty-hour ceiling on the work week of bakery employees. It drew a stinging dissent from Associate Justice Oliver Wendell Holmes, Jr., one of many attacks on conservative supreme courts echoing throughout the modern era, especially during the New Deal.

To the court's conservatives, government regulation of private behavior violated the laws of Adam Smith. Liberal critics of such thinking argued that it was a mistake to attribute the principles of modern capitalism and classical economics to the Constitution. (Felix Frankfurter once said that some conservative judges had treated Adam Smith as though his writings "had been imparted to him on Sinai.") Conservatives assumed that certain "natural rights" pre-existed the Constitution and that the Constitution was implicitly intended to protect these rights. Their view was that these "natural rights" were instrumental to social and economic order.

Some scholars of today see the court's belief in the doctrine of property rights and liberty in the nineteenth and twentieth centuries as somewhat akin to the way the Warren court of the 1950s and 1960s expanded the right of due process to throw out segregation in public schools and uphold the right of privacy, one-person-one-vote and other measures. The Warren court, like the Fuller court, had an activist identity, striking down state and federal statutes and practices because of their alleged violation of deeply rooted principles rather than specific strictures in the Constitution.

"Each Court viewed itself as the guardian of a public morality that was anchored in and made authoritative by the Constitution," writes Owen Fiss, professor of law at Yale and an exponent of the analogy between the Fuller and Warren courts. In his history of the Supreme Court in this era, *Troubled Beginnings of the Modern State, 1888–1910,* Fiss links the Fuller court's devotion to property rights with the Warren court's devotion to human rights. Indeed, he sees the Fuller and Warren courts as "locked in a dialectic across history." Taking a position that no doubt would rankle some liberals, Fiss argues that the Fuller court needs to be understood as "an institution devoted to liberty and determined to protect that constitutional ideal from the social movements of the day."

Whatever the logic of the justices, whatever the analysis that can be applied to the court's decision, whatever the reasoning of learned people on all sides, the ruling touched off a firestorm of outrage that inflamed the country. The *New York World* called it a "triumph of selfishness" perpetrated by corporation lawyers. "Today's decision," added the *St. Louis Post-Dispatch*, "shows that the corporations and plutocrats are as securely entrenched in the Supreme Court as in the lower courts which they take such pains to control." The leading northeastern and midwestern papers exulted. "The fury of ignorant class hatred," said the *New York Tribune*, "has dashed itself in vain against the Constitution." It added: "Thanks to the court, our government is not to be dragged into communistic warfare against rights of property and the rewards of industry."

The court also had its defenders among scholars and experts, but there were many critics even in this group. The editor of the *American Law Review* charged that "some of the judges seem to have no adequate idea of the dividing line between judicial and legislative power." An article in the *Harvard Law Review* predicted that the decision might well be reversed in the future.

Well before the Pollock decision, the courts had been a target of populist anger. Farming interests often tended to see judges as servants of the wealthy elite, especially because so many farmers had been hauled into bankruptcy for failure to pay their debts. The big corporations, on the other hand, knew how to use the law to achieve their ends. Railroads, for example, were practiced hands at getting municipalities to help them by issuing bonds to pay for the building of railroads. Sometimes, however, the railroad companies simply walked away from these deals, leaving municipalities with the obligation to pay off the bondholders. In several important decisions, the Supreme Court insisted that the municipalities had to do so. There were even some cases of state officials imprisoned for refusing. The courts also blocked local governments from imposing regulations on railroads and operators of grain elevators. They threw out state attempts to regulate rates. These decisions had laid the groundwork for the three-pronged assault of 1895, including the rejection of the income tax.

Some in Congress reacted with fury, moving to sponsor a joint resolution calling for an amendment to the Constitution permitting enactment of an income tax. Another tough criticism came from Governor Altgeld of Illinois, Cleveland's nemesis in the Pullman strike. "The Supreme Court has come to the rescue of the Standard Oil kings, the Wall Street people, as well as the rich mugwumps," he said. Others called for unspecified action to nullify the court's ruling and for the impeachment of the anti-tax judges for usurpation of legislative power. It remained for these passions to play themselves out in the coming presidential election campaign.

———

On a wintry morning in early February 1895, just as the combatants over the income tax were preparing their briefs for the Supreme Court, the most powerful financier in America—in fact, the most powerful man in America—boarded a private railroad car in New York for a trip to Washington to meet with the President of the United States.

John Pierpont Morgan and two associates were traveling as the nation's financial crisis was taking another turn for the worse. Despite a series of bond issues by the United States government in the previous two years, American gold reserves were continuing to dwindle. In January of 1894, they had sunk below $62 million, well beneath the $100 million threshold of what was considered viable. To replenish the gold that was lost, Cleveland had authorized a series of borrowings to buy gold. It did not help that his banker friends were the ones urging him to do so. That only underscored who his friends actually were: such men as Henry Villard (who represented German bankers), August Belmont (the Rothschilds), James Stillman (National City Bank) and Francis Stetson, Cleveland's former law partner and now counsel for J. P. Morgan.

Morgan was fully aware that the Treasury's bond issues had been only temporary expedients. The bond sales did not deter investors and bondholders from selling their securities and demanding to be paid in gold. The government bonds may even have worsened the situation. In order to buy them, many bankers simply withdrew gold from the Treasury, and so the bond sale had no effect on gold reserves. The crisis was such that the United States was literally running out of gold to meet its obligations. Dockworkers in New York harbor were loading bullion on board ships bound for creditors in Europe as reserves dwindled at the federal vault near Wall Street. What could Cleveland do?

The answer was in the hands of the banker on the train.

With his huge girth, brooding manner, walrus mustache and bulbous nose that reddened when he lost his temper, Pierpont Morgan was an intimidating man who was said to be more obsessed with order and control than with wealth. He was the son of a rich merchant from Hartford who had established a bank in London during the Civil War. He grew up with every advantage, including study at Harvard and the University of Göttingen in Germany, and established himself in New York City in the 1870s. Morgan invented the idea of banks as the pre-eminent instrument of capitalism. By taking over one railroad after another, consolidating their debts and reorganizing them into trusts—"morganizing," as it was called—he extended his reach throughout industry. Whether aboard his huge 165-foot yacht, *Corsair,* or at his Madison Avenue home, Morgan was at the center of most major financial deals in the country. In 1885, he brokered a war between the New York Central and Pennsylvania Railroads. In the 1890s, the House of Morgan consolidated and reorganized most of the nation's railroads. Later Morgan did the same thing for the steel industry, eventually persuading Andrew Carnegie to join with other companies to form the United States Steel Corporation in 1901. His machinations led similarly to the creation of General Electric, the American Telephone and Telegraph Company and International Harvester.

When Morgan and his associates arrived in Washington, they were told at first that the President would not be available to see them. Cleveland, battered by reverses on the tariff in Congress and by an economy that seemed immune to revival, could not afford to be seen kowtowing to the likes of J. P. Morgan. Morgan was adamant. "I have come down to see the President, and I am going to stay here until I see him," he declared, whereupon he retired to a hotel and settled his nerves by playing solitaire into the night.

The next morning Cleveland summoned Morgan to the White House. As the banker impatiently stubbed his huge black cigar into an ashtray, the President blandly persisted in saying that another public bond sale might be justified. But on this day, American gold reserves plummeted to $45 million. A clerk informed Treasury Secretary Carlisle that only $9 million remained in government vaults on Wall Street. Morgan interjected that he himself knew of a $10 million charge that was about to be lodged.

"If that $10 million draft is presented, you can't meet it," he told the President, effectively warning that the United States was in danger of defaulting on its debts and ruining its credit in the eyes of the world.

"What suggestions have you to make, Mr. Morgan?" Cleveland replied.

The bailout that ensued was a greater success than the previous public bond issues because of Morgan's participation. Together with the Rothschild banking house in London, represented by their American factotum, August Belmont, Jr., Morgan collected and handed over to the United States 3.5 million ounces of gold—much of it obtained from abroad—in exchange for $65 million in thirty-year bonds at 3.75 percent. The bankers sweetened the deal by agreeing to work with European creditors to stop the demand for payments in gold. When word of the deal became known, the financial markets stabilized. "You cannot appreciate the relief to everybody's mind, for the dangers were so great scarcely anyone dared whisper them," Morgan said. On Wall Street, the bonds immediately rose in price. Not only had the banks brought the American government to its knees—they had profited handsomely in the process.

In political terms, however, the bailout was precisely the catastrophe that Cleveland feared it might be. Following so many missteps and missed opportunities on the tariff, on gold and other issues, the bailout by Morgan sped Cleveland's presidency toward its doom. And the agent of Cleveland's downfall was the man from Nebraska who had been fighting him since the beginning of his second term.

———

After winning passage of the income tax, Bryan confidently prepared to face the voters in the fall of 1894. He was in for a surprise. The sense of hopelessness over economic conditions, along with widespread impatience with Cleveland's ineffectiveness, drove many Democrats to the Populist Party, which increased its votes from 1892 by more than 40 percent. The election was a setback for the Democrats, who retained only narrow control of the Senate and lost the House to the Republicans. It was the prelude to an even bigger loss two years later, an election that would cast the party into political wilderness for nearly twenty years.

As the economic situation deteriorated, Cleveland came to symbolize everything the South and West detested. Ridiculed as "His Obstinacy" by William Allen White, reviled by Populists like "Pitchfork" Ben Tillman of South Carolina, Cleveland became a target of vitriol and mockery. "He is an old bag of beef," said Tillman in the election campaign that fall, "and I am going to Washington with a pitchfork and prod him in his old fat ribs."

The 1894 election posed a dilemma for Bryan. His first major decision was to announce his retirement from the House and to try instead for the Senate. Part of the reason was his desire to avoid having to run for re-election every two years. After all, his margin of victory back in 1892 had been wafer thin.

Under the Constitution, it was still up to the Nebraska legislature to choose the members of the Senate. But Nebraska had adopted the Progressive Era reform of holding a popular vote to advise the legislature. In his campaign, Bryan borrowed heavily from the Populist platform and could claim one of its main planks, the income tax, as a genuine accomplishment. He called for railroad regulation, public ownership of telephone lines and debt relief for farmers. He attacked Cleveland for the labor injunction that ended the Pullman strike. His Republican opponent was general counsel for the Union Pacific Railroad and a fiscal and monetary conservative. But Bryan was distrusted by the Populists of Nebraska. Its candidate drew votes away from him, and he lost the election.

At first, Bryan's wife wanted her defeated husband to give up politics. "You have asked me the impossible," he replied. Instead, he decided to write, speak and campaign with a "grand design"—as improbable as it must have seemed—to raise his sights and capture the presidency in 1896.

After the Supreme Court decision on the income tax, Bryan added the high court justices to his list of enemies. Governor John Altgeld ("Altgeld the Anarchist," his enemies called him) of Illinois, who had opposed Cleveland and compared him to Judas Iscariot for breaking the Pullman strike, asked Bryan to address a conference on silver in June of 1895. Altgeld was immensely popular but could not run for President, having been born in Germany. Bryan, now thirty-six years old, was beginning to make a national name for himself as an orator and firebrand. On tours, he greeted supporters with a big bear hug, talked of a fusion ticket with the Populists and made silver the focus of a drive to seize state convention after state convention. All the while, he publicly waved off suggestions of interest in the White House.

It is often suggested that Bryan simply seized the 1896 Democratic convention in Chicago with his "Cross of Gold" speech. In fact, he had been meticulously cultivating delegates for months, compiling lists and working to advance the concept of fusion, which led logically to him as the candidate. But there were obstacles. Altgeld, sympathetic on the issues, was suspicious of Bryan's motivations. "You are young yet," he told him. "Your time will come."

In fact, Bryan's rival candidates all lacked energy and magnetism, especially those from the party's conservative wing. Although Cleveland had not yet renounced his own interest in renomination, few politicians believed he had any chance. The President instead designated his longtime operative, William Whitney, to be his eyes and ears at the convention and to be ready in case lightning struck. The overriding objective for Cleveland and his allies in the party was to defend the gold standard, along with fiscal and monetary conservatism. Like some of the justices on the Supreme Court, the President had no trouble envisioning the possibility of a new civil war, this one along class lines.

The Democratic convention began on July 7 in the sweltering heat of the Coliseum in Chicago, the biggest permanent exhibition hall in the world, with a floor area of 5 ½ acres. The cast of characters was remarkable. There was Whitney, looking impeccably dressed with his hat tilted rakishly, calling shots behind the scene. There was Altgeld, portrayed in cartoons with a lighted fuse in his hand and a mad gleam in his eye (because he had freed three accused bomb throwers jailed after the riot by anarchists and protesters in Haymarket Square in Chicago in 1886). Pitchfork Ben Tillman, the South Carolina senator, sported a silver pitchfork lapel pin.

Bryan set his eye first on the platform, hoping to make it a vehicle for his candidacy. It was a singular rebuke to the incumbent President. It denounced Cleveland's handling of the Pullman strike and called for the usual list of liberal reforms. To all this was added a new issue, the Supreme Court's invalidation of the income tax.

The issue was to prove surprisingly contentious because, although there was widespread support for the tax, many Democrats were uneasy about saying anything to attack the court or the rule of law. The first draft of the platform denounced the Supreme Court rejection of the tax and called on Congress "to use all the constitutional power which remains after that decision . . . so that the burdens of taxation may be equally and impartially laid, to the end that wealth may bear its due proportion of the expense of the government."

The conservative press was aghast at this plank, and critics warned that the Democrats were challenging the court's independence. Senator David Hill of New York, who had fought against the tax in the Senate debate in 1894, led the fight to change the platform in its entirety.

On the eve of the platform debate, Bryan was serene at dinner with his wife and a friend. "I will make the greatest speech of my life tomorrow in reply to Senator Hill," he declared, adding that he thought he might even be chosen to lead the fight against the Republicans. When Mrs. Bryan expressed skepticism, Bryan replied: "So that you both may sleep well tonight, I am going to tell you something. I am the only man who can be nominated. I am what they call 'the logic of the situation.'"

The next day, July 9, there was such a fervid and emotional atmosphere in the hothouse convention site that one reporter compared it to an insane asylum. As predicted, Senator David Hill rose to denounce the platform and singled out its denunciation of the Supreme Court. "Why was it wise to assail the Supreme Court of your country?" he demanded. "That provision, if it means anything, means that it is the duty of Congress to reconstruct the Supreme Court of the country. It means, and such purpose was openly avowed, it means the adding of additional members to the Court, or the turning out of office and reconstructing the whole court."

Governor William Russell of Massachusetts, not Hill, was the man backed by most leading conservative Democrats to win the nomination. But Russell was frail, fatally ill at the age of forty. His bravery at the podium riveted the audience as he pleaded with the convention not to abandon its traditional principles and go down the road of easy money, radical politics and ruin. Then he sat down, a picture of disappointment and grief that seemed to break his resistance. He would be dead within a week.

Russell's appearance was a remarkable contrast to the next speaker, who strode to the platform looking all the more handsome, energetic and youthful. Eyes flashing, his jaw thrust forward, his head thrown back, Bryan grasped the lectern. In great arching oratorical flourishes, he excoriated the moneyed interests and extolled the farmers and workers as the backbone of American economic strength. "Burn down your cities and leave our farms, and your cities will spring up again as if by magic," he declared. "But destroy our farms, and the grass will grow in the streets of every city in the country." As for the Supreme Court and the income tax, Bryan declared: "They say we passed an unconstitutional law. I deny it. The income tax was not unconstitutional when it was passed. It was not unconstitutional when it went before the Supreme Court for the first time. It did not become unconstitutional until one judge changed his mind, and we cannot be expected to know when a judge will change his mind."

The speech brought forth volley after volley of cheering, foot stamping, applause and emotion. Bryan ended with the issue of gold, in one of the most extraordinary rhetorical culminations ever delivered. "Having behind us the producing masses of the nation and the world, the laboring interests and the toilers everywhere, we will answer their demand for a gold standard by saying to them: 'You shall not press down upon the brow of labor this crown of thorns—you shall not crucify mankind upon a cross of gold!'"

At first, the peroration produced a stunned silence as Bryan extended his arms as if crucified. Only after he started backing away from the platform did the place erupt with twenty-five minutes of yelling, weeping and pandemonium. The next day Bryan rejected a deal to be nominated vice president. On the fifth ballot, the convention prepared to go through another roll call when Governor Altgeld stood and announced that Illinois would cast its forty-eight votes for William Jennings Bryan of Nebraska. The floodgates opened, and the stampeding delegates nominated Bryan for President.

The nominee had his work cut out for him. He courted skeptical Democratic newspapers, especially in the East, appealing to the *New York World* that even though it was skeptical of silver, it should remember that he supported the income tax, one of the newspaper's favorite causes. Bryan's other challenge was to capture the nomination of the divided Populist Party. At their convention in St. Louis, the Populists endorsed the income tax, declaring that "we regard the recent decision of the Supreme Court relative to the income tax as a misinterpretation of the Constitution and an invasion of the rightful powers of Congress over the subject of taxation." They also called for postal savings banks, public ownership of railroads and telegraphs, public works projects and an end to labor injunctions. Many were annoyed that Bryan was making silver the dominant issue. Bryan had the job of embracing the party without scaring off moderates. It did not help that the Populist convention struck many observers as little more than an immense wild-eyed and furry rabble. (One journalist said he was convinced there was "some mysterious connection between Populism and hair.") The *New York Times,* no friend of Bryan's anyway, said it was a convention of "freaky Coxeyites" rallying around a "crank" for President.

Bryan got the Populist nomination and went on to be nominated by several other splinter parties. Throughout this period, Cleveland kept silent, vacationing off Buzzards Bay, but Whitney and other anti-Bryan Democrats formed a new National Democratic Party with its own candidate, designed to draw votes away from the party's nominee.

While Bryan's opponent, Representative William McKinley of Ohio, author of a tariff that was a high-water mark in protectionism, sat at home in Canton receiving visitors, Bryan stumped from one end of the country to the other. Indeed, his tireless cross-country campaigning marked the first such attempt by an American presidential candidate, opening a new chapter in American politics.

The issue of the income tax helped set the stage for Bryan's wobbly start. In his formal acceptance address in Madison Square Garden, he acknowledged awkwardly that he was speaking "in the heart of what now seems to be the enemy's country," a reference to the hostility of Tammany Democrats, as well as Republicans, in New York. It was no understatement. On the income tax, the New Yorkers were still vehemently opposed. In his speech, Bryan tried to reassure critics who were alarmed about his criticism of the Supreme Court. He said he did not challenge the high court's authority to throw out the tax but nonetheless believed that it had erred and hoped that it would reverse itself. Afterward, Tammany leaders boycotted his reception, and Bryan's advisers began suggesting that the Democrats write off the East, if only because he had no money to wage an uphill campaign there. While Boss Croker supported Bryan out of party loyalty, Bourke Cockran, his adversary during the income tax debate, did not.

Toward the end of the campaign, Bryan began displaying signs of fatigue, anger and bitterness. In the fall, he came back to New York, however, this time emphasizing his sympathy with labor and the income tax instead of silver, which had never resonated with the immigrants and workers of New York City. That helped, but there was residual concern about Bryan's denunciations of the Rothschilds and Jewish bankers back when Cleveland had resorted to his bond issues. Now Bryan hastened to explain that, in denouncing these moneyed interests, "we are not attacking a race" but greed and avarice. He even said that the "Hebrew race" could sympathize with the struggle of the masses "by reason of their history." But the sobriquet "Boy Orator of the Platte" was beginning to have a ring of sarcasm, and when Bryan asked his audiences to say whether they were carrying any gold on them, he only stirred fears of pickpockets.

In the final weeks of the campaign, something mysterious happened—a kind of October surprise. The price of wheat rose from 64 cents a bushel in July to 82 cents a bushel in October. Corn also rose in price. Foreign demand for American grain increased, helped by a crop failure in India and other parts of the world. As optimism grew among farmers, steamships were heading into New York harbor, this time laden with gold for deposit. Gold reserves around the world started increasing, in fact. A new cyanide processing technique was speeding the production of gold from recent discoveries in the Klondike, South Africa and Australia. In the weeks before the election, there were nearly $48 million in gold imports. It was part of a global economic turnaround.

The favorable economic news was, of course, bad for Bryan. The fact that an increased supply of gold, along with its beneficial effect on prices, had vindicated his theory of money supply was hardly to his political advantage. In the final weeks of the campaign, he was increasingly savaged in the press as being everything from insane to a frustrated actor to a bigot to someone beholden to the silver mines. Toward the end, he knew he had lost, and he arrived home in Lincoln after an unprecedented—and precedent-setting—campaign of 3,000 speeches and more than 18,000 miles of travel. The electoral vote was 271 to 176, with McKinley receiving 7,107,822 votes (50.88 percent) to Bryan's 6,511,073 (46.77 percent). It was a crushing defeat.

The defeat of Bryan by McKinley was one of the great watersheds of American political history. For one thing, Bryan succeeded as no one had in tying farmers, city workers and small businessmen together in an alliance that would serve as the springboard for Woodrow Wilson's victory sixteen years later and last for many generations after that. He invented the whole idea of the modern presidential campaign. As Mrs. Henry Cabot Lodge, wife of the Massachusetts senator, wrote to the British ambassador, the Democrats were "a disorganized mob at first, out of which there burst into sight, hearing, and force—one man, but such a man!

Alone, penniless, without backing, without money, with scarcely a paper, without speakers, that man fought such a fight that even those in the East can call him a Crusader, an inspired fanatic—a prophet!"

It was only a matter of time before Bryan's cause of using government to help farmers, workers and the struggling middle class would rise again. Accompanying that cause would be the eventual enactment of the income tax.

CHAPTER SEVEN

"A Peculiar Obligation to the State"

Theodore Roosevelt Proposes an Income Tax

FOR MANY DECADES THE UNITED STATES HAD LOOKED covetously at Cuba, the last and most prized vestige of the Spanish empire in the Western Hemisphere. Eventually the political turbulence on that island, only a short boat ride from Florida, propelled Americans into a rendezvous with global expansion, burdensome responsibilities and a debate at home over fairness, sacrifice and taxes.

Crushed by Spanish oppression, Cubans had engaged in a series of revolts culminating in wars of independence from 1868 to 1878 and again in 1895. The United States contributed to the island's impoverished conditions by imposing a tariff on raw sugar. But while cracking down on the rebels, Spanish forces destroyed the Cubans' sugar mills, sugar cane fields, homes and businesses. The most despised tactic of Spain's General Valeriano Weyler—"the Butcher," as he was called in the American press—was to force large numbers of Cubans into fortified areas, where armed guards kept them behind barbed wire and under heel. Thousands died from starvation and disease under this policy of "reconcentration."

The American press, led by the *New York Journal* under William Randolph Hearst and the *New York World* under Joseph Pulitzer, whipped American readers into a frenzy over the suffering on the island. Incensed readers began to demand that the United States intervene and annex Cuba. Although American businessmen feared that a war with Spain would be bad for trade and for their extensive investments in Cuba, they were in the minority. Others picked up the cry. Among those calling for action was a young assistant secretary of the navy under President William J. McKinley named Theodore Roosevelt.

As President Cleveland had been before him, McKinley was reluctant to be drawn into a war, in part because of the wariness of his business allies. To defuse the situation, a new government in Spain recalled General Weyler and granted the island a limited amount of self-government. In January 1898, the Navy Department dispatched the battleship *Maine* to Havana as a friendly gesture to the rebels and to protect the lives of endangered Americans. For nearly three weeks, the *Maine* remained in Havana Harbor as Spanish officials complained heatedly about the intrusion. In Washington, an increasingly agitated Roosevelt told associates that war was imminent.

On the night of February 15, the *Maine* blew up in a fiery explosion, killing 260 crew members and engulfing the harbor in smoke and flames. The cause of the explosion remains a mystery to this day, but most Americans had little doubt that Spanish authorities were the culprits. Spain denied involvement, offered to conduct an investigation with the United States and—in a last-ditch effort to head off war—agreed to end its "reconcentration" program and grant amnesty to the rebels. These and other conciliatory gestures were swiftly rejected in Washington, where war frenzy was at a fever pitch. Under pressure to act, McKinley called on Congress to recognize the insurgents. Spain reacted by declaring war, and on April 25, Congress followed with a war declaration.

The Spanish-American War was a four-month, largely agreeable adventure that ended with a great American victory and the ceding to the United States of Cuba, Puerto Rico, the Philippines and Guam—a new American empire befitting a nation that was becoming one of the most prosperous in the world.

However glorious wars are to journalists, politicians and other spectators, they must be financed. Many of the old issues regarding payment of war expenses, dating from the Civil War, returned to the forefront—but with a twist, since this time business leaders not only were opposed to their taxes being raised but were also skeptical of the need for the war itself. The same mixture of Civil War era demands for borrowing, taxing and raising tariffs suddenly crashed down on the nation's capital and its elected leaders. A renewed debate over fairness in the tax system forced lawmakers to demand sacrifices from the wealthy through new corporation and inheritance taxes. The war set the stage for another round of battles over the income tax after the turn of the century.

McKinley had campaigned for President against Bryan in 1896 in the shadow of hard times. Indeed, the Republican Party proclaimed him to be "the advance agent of prosperity"—a slogan that expressed more a hope than a guarantee. Even before the talk of war, the new President had to deal with a treasury drained of revenues and the issue of taxes to keep the nation solvent.

Reassuring in both style and policy, McKinley was a dapper, pleasant-looking, genial, plump and short man of somewhat pompous manner whose sartorial taste tended toward white linen vests and a red carnation in the buttonhole of his coat. As a former major in the Union Army who had served in the United States House of Representatives and twice as governor of Ohio, McKinley was a shrewd political operator, as well as a man of considerable substance and popularity. He entered the White House surrounded by trusted advisers, from the political operative Senator Mark Hanna of Ohio to his Treasury Secretary, Lyman Judson Gage, a former president of the First National Bank of Chicago. The three shared a belief in the gold standard and the Republican core idea of protectionism, though not for the high tariff walls advocated by the most extreme members of their party. McKinley's most immediate problem was a federal deficit created by the collapsed economy and rising expenditures for Civil War pensions, debt service and public improvements. Though few recognized it at the time, such costs were the signposts of America becoming a modern social welfare state.

The deficit led McKinley and Gage to the traditional method of raising revenue, tariffs. Led by Representative Nelson Dingley, Jr., a former governor of Maine serving as chairman of the House Ways and Means Committee, the Republican-controlled Congress ignored the protests of farmers and workers and in July of 1897 raised barriers to their highest levels since the Civil War. Duties reached an average of 57 percent, a crushing burden on the consumers of everyday items from leather, wool and woolens, silks and linens, to iron and steel products and raw sugar. They were so high that American companies developed a new concern: that tariff walls were undercutting the ability of manufacturers and farmers to sell their goods abroad. The anti-tariff argument was that for Europeans to buy American, they had to sell to America in order to earn dollars, and lower tariffs would help them do so. This new challenge to the wisdom of high tariffs spread to parts of McKinley's own Midwest, where Republicans began breaking away from the protectionist fold. The argument that lower tariffs would help, not hurt, American producers was especially popular in Wisconsin, New England and the Mississippi Valley, where it caught the attention of a young Republican Party politician, William Howard Taft.

The new tariff signed into law by McKinley, intended to produce new revenues for the deficit-ridden American government, was a failure. Indeed, it succeeded only in curbing imports, which resulted in diminished revenues. Once the war began in 1898, the drive for more federal revenues became urgent. After hiking tariffs the year before, Congress had no appetite to do so again. Instead, Representative Dingley proposed to raise $500 million from borrowing and $100 million from an array of special taxes on everything from banks to theaters, circuses, pawnbrokers, insurance policies, toilet articles, chewing gum, beer and wine. Democrats protested that these taxes fell more heavily on the poor. Led by Representatives Joseph W. Bailey of Texas, the House Democratic leader, and Benton McMillin of Tennessee, redoubtable veteran of the 1890s tax wars, Democrats still yearned for ways to circumvent or confront the Supreme Court over its rejection of the income tax. They tried to attach an income tax amendment to the tax bill, but most lawmakers wanted to avoid sending another bill to the Supreme Court, possibly inflaming public sentiment against the justices in wartime.

Faced with no possibility of an income tax, Democrats and Populists united around a proposal for an excise tax on corporate gross receipts. Republicans resisted, but a final war tax measure was approved in June taxing gross receipts over $200,000, which applied solely to sugar and petroleum-refining companies. The War Revenue Act of 1898 included one crucial innovation, an inheritance tax on "legacies" (personal property) and "successions" (real property). The tax exempted estates under $10,000 and property passing to the surviving husband or wife. The tax rate increased depending on the size of the estate or the nature of the relative. It was an important development in Americans' evolving thinking about their tax system because it was designed purely as a tax on fortunes, albeit those of the deceased.

The inheritance tax already had a distinguished history in America, going back to taxes on the probating of wills in the colonial era. A broad inheritance tax was briefly considered during the War of 1812, and during the Civil War, it passed Congress with little debate because of the widespread demand in the North for sac-

rifice, especially from the wealthy. Increased in 1864, the rates for
the Civil War inheritance tax ranged from 1 to 6 percent, depending on the value of the property and the relationship of the person
receiving the inheritance. By 1869, the tax was bringing in $2.4
million a year, but by then the war was over, and protectionist
Republicans began to fear that unless it was repealed, the surplus
in revenues might create pressure to reduce tariff barriers.
Although the inheritance tax had been established in England in
1780, in France in 1796, in Italy in 1862 (and would take effect in
Prussia in 1873), Congress repealed it in 1870, when it also
reduced rates in the income tax.

After repeal, however, the inheritance tax remained widely discussed as a concept. Articles supporting the tax appeared in many
academic and popular journals. Perhaps the most surprising figure
advocating a return to an inheritance tax was the industrialist
Andrew Carnegie, whose essay "The Gospel of Wealth" in the
North American Review in 1889 inspired popular reassessment of the
tax toward the end of the nineteenth century. The gospel according
to Andrew Carnegie developed, as he recalled it, in a memorandum
written early in his career in which he vowed that, once he made
$50,000 a year, he would stop trying to make more money and turn
his efforts to "benevolent purposes." (He did not stop trying to
make more money, but he did keep his pledge on turning to philanthropy.) Calling the accumulation of wealth "one of the worst
species of idolatry," Carnegie declared that "there is more genuine
satisfaction, a truer life, and more obtained from life in the humble
cottages of the poor than in the palaces of the rich." So fervent was
Carnegie's belief in the virtues of "honest poverty" that he even
questioned whether it was wise to eradicate poverty at all. "To
abolish honest, industrious, self-denying poverty," he declared,
"would be to destroy the soil upon which mankind produces the
virtues which enable our race to reach a still higher civilization
than it now possesses."

What was to be done with the great fortunes of the few? They could leave their estate to family members and heirs, a step harmful to the recipients, or permit the state to tax the estate away and use the money for public purposes. A third way was most appealing to Carnegie—establishing a mechanism in the form of endowments or foundations in which surplus wealth could be administered "for the common good." Philanthropy, he argued, should help those who help themselves or perhaps endow libraries, parks, recreational places, works of art and public institutes to help men "in body and mind." A man who dies possessing his wealth and leaving it to his heirs, Carnegie concluded in his essay, dies "disgraced."*

In the final years of the nineteenth century, especially after victory in the war with Spain, the United States was a nation that possessed great wealth—and it was feeling anything but disgraced. In 1860, the national wealth had been $16 billion. By 1890, it was $65 billion. By 1900, it was $88.5 billion. Per capita wealth had grown from $514 in 1860 to $1,165 in 1900. But while capital investment and output were skyrocketing, the average real income of wage earners was holding steady or falling. In railroads, iron and steel, copper, meatpacking, milling, tobacco and oil, the trend by industry of reorganizing through mergers into huge combines accelerated. At the lower rungs, the 30 million men and 8 million women in the nonfarm workforce struggled to keep up, often in unsafe and unhealthy sweatshops, with no insurance or protection from accidents, sickness, old age or sudden unemployment.

The richest 1 percent of Americans owned 47 percent of the nation's property and received 15 percent of the national product, whereas a third to a half of those in the industrial sector—including many children in the workforce—lived in poverty. Craft unions

---

*In 1901, Carnegie sold his steel works for $250 million and retired. He died in 1919, having left $350 million for philanthropic endeavors, from Carnegie Hall in New York City to the Carnegie Institution of Washington, the Carnegie Endowment for International Peace and more than 2,800 libraries.

organized by the American Federation of Labor were expanding with hundreds of thousands of new members, but workers and farmers felt overmatched by banks, middlemen and industrialists. Studies of the concentration of wealth in a handful of families continued to be read and quoted toward the end of the century, leading to a renewal of demands for taxes on income, gifts and inheritances.

An outpouring of books documenting the poverty of the cities began to stir the conscience of middle-class Americans. Inspired also by books about business abuses, American intellectuals were becoming increasingly skeptical of a political system built on slums, sweatshops and impoverished farmers. This new awakening to the injustice of the system, especially among the middle class of salaried workers and professionals, became known as Progressivism.

For many decades after the Civil War, Populism, the name for the agrarian revolt and criticism of banks, tight money and high tariffs, reflected the unrest and misery of farmers caught in a financial squeeze. By contrast, Progressivism was an urban phenomenon of the middle class and even the prosperous. As William Allen White observed, Populism was idealistic in its way, but it was also a somewhat neurotic movement, "full of hates and ebullient, evanescent enthusiasms." Progressivism was more subtle. Its adherents resisted radical reform and were generally of two minds about everything connected to the economic progress achieved under modern American capitalism. In their view, for example, corporations were a product of evolution that enriched society, as well as a potential menace to liberty and democracy. Such ambivalence extended to the meaning of wealth itself, as exemplified by Carnegie's essay. Wealth could be a goal for virtuous men, yet wealth was also something that needed to be kept under control if society were to avoid instability and disruption. Wealth strengthened society even as its excesses threatened to break it apart.

Running through people's attitudes was what the historian

Richard Hofstadter terms the "upheaval of status" that seemed to marginalize so many established families—the traditional small merchants, manufacturers, lawyers, editors, preachers and other persons of eminence in their communities. The rise of a new wealthy class threatened not only the livelihood of the poor farmers and workers of America but also the status of the middle class. But Progressivism happened, in this view, because of what Hofstadter describes as the displacing of "the old gentry, the merchants of long standing, the small manufacturers, the established professional men, the civic leaders of an earlier era." College-educated men with community roots suddenly were shocked by the ability of new wealth to corrupt the political system. This unsettled middle class had to do more than look down on the masses from an aristocratic perspective. They had to evolve a new philosophy of government that would meet the demands of the discontented without catering to them.

Today many historians challenge Hofstadter's thesis that Progressivism occurred because of the overthrow of the old gentry. Robert Wiebe, a historian wrestling with the issues defined by Hofstadter, argues that progressive reforms arose not from the old aristocracy's anxiety over being displaced but from a wider search for order in the chaos of economic change. But whatever the wellsprings of change, the end result was the same: the reform of basic institutions and a search for a tax system that was equal to the new landscape of industrial America.

The Progressive Era was a time of vast reform in the relationship between government and wealth. But the progressives' attitude toward wealth as wealth was especially instructive. Hofstadter speaks of the emergence of the concept of two types of wealth, good and bad—a difference, as he puts it, between "new" and "old" wealth, and between "the men who are getting rich and the men who *are* rich." If there was a main cause of the new inequality, in the eyes of the progressive intellectuals, it was the existence of large business consolidations—and the power they wielded over

American government policies. For some reason, however, the forces that produced this new kind of thinking did not actually come together as a nationwide movement until after 1901, Hofstadter says. Demands for reform had been gathering force for years in American cities and states. The economic crises of the 1890s—the recession, bread lines, joblessness, Coxey's army, labor militancy and fiery rhetoric—then slowly deepened the capacity of Americans to view the nation's political scene with a fresh sense of right and wrong.

The new attitudes would fall into place with the arrival of a new, accidental President who would succeed McKinley after an assassination and tap the inchoate sentiments developing under the surface.

———

Theodore Roosevelt was a man of some money and privilege who came to distrust the power of great wealth. He grew up in a household in New York City that the biographer Henry Pringle describes as "solid, respectable and a little complacent." His father, Theodore Sr., was a well-to-do glass importer whose business on Maiden Lane in New York City failed under pressures that, in a small way, reflected larger economic changes in the American industrial landscape. Domestic glassmakers were able to produce their goods more cheaply, forcing importers like the elder Roosevelt out of business. Turning to banking, Theodore Sr. was able to prosper, however. He was a charitable man, a benefactor of an orthopedic hospital and the YMCA, and a man with conservative values that he inculcated in his son, Theodore Jr., born in 1858. Among these values were faith in hard work, distrust of the complaints of the working class, and concern about threats to the stability of a newly optimistic and prosperous American society.

Little in Theodore Roosevelt, Jr.'s background and upbringing foreshadowed the transformation he would help to bring about in society and in the government and the presidency. The course of his life embodied the essentially conservative nature of the era's reforms—the fact that the reforms were carried out by Roosevelt and others in order to save American industrial capitalism from its own excesses. From the comfort of the household in which he grew up, Roosevelt developed a genuine compassion for the underclass. But as a former law-and-order police commissioner in New York City, he also worried about anarchy arising from gross economic inequality. As Edmund Morris points out in the second volume of his biography, *Theodore Rex*, Roosevelt was seen by many critics as a kind of traitor to his class simply from throwing himself into the strenuous life of a cowboy, soldier and adventurer—even more so from abandoning what could have been a life of privilege for the dirty alleyways of public service and government. He could be sanctimonious about his own higher calling. He found rich people boring, he said, not nearly as interesting as men of accomplishment in the sciences or arts.

Young Theodore's family was prosperous but not in the same league as other families in the vanguard of the new industrial era. They had enough money, however, for T.R. to travel frequently to Europe, where he was more interested in the outdoors than in musty museums. Indeed, his twin obsessions were his studies, particularly of nature, and his health. To overcome his asthma, Theodore transformed himself from a frail child into a muscular adolescent by boxing and working out with weights and exercise bars. As a teenager, he began to show some leadership skills. At Harvard, he joined important clubs but still was better known on campus for his eccentric and priggish manner than for his popularity. His refusal to smoke or drink, his flaring whiskers and his use of such favorite phrases as "By Jove!" made him seem a bit pretentious and more than a bit of a dandy. On a campus where it was fashionable to be cool, superior and aloof, Roosevelt stood out as a striver—not to make money but to make himself more virtuous and accomplished as a man of cultivation and achievement.

Roosevelt did not seem to have developed any significant political views at Harvard, except that he may have participated in a parade on campus for the Republican presidential candidate, Rutherford B. Hayes, during the 1876 campaign. Hayes was considered a moderate reformer, proponent of the civil service and foe of political bosses. The drunken rally that Roosevelt is said to have attended included appeals for "Hard Money and Soft Electives," as well as "Free Trade, Free Press and Free Beer." Indeed, Roosevelt's support of lower tariff barriers, a position then associated with the Democrats, foreshadowed some of his later political problems.

In this period, Roosevelt also started to learn what it was like to manage his own family money, and he had a typical upper-class distaste for the task. After Theodore Sr.'s death in 1880, the estate had to be divided four ways among the children. For Theodore, it provided an income of only about $7,500 to $10,000 a year—not much by the standards he apparently aspired to live by, but enough, at least initially, for him to entertain friends, take trips and buy clothes—suits, gloves, hats and shoes. Roosevelt was not adept at saving money. He helped found G. P. Putnam's Sons, the publishing company, with an investment of $20,000, but the check for that amount bounced because his bank account had only about half the cash to cover it. "He never had any idea where his money went," said his friend and partner, Major George Haven Putnam. While arduously courting the beautiful and elusive Alice Hathaway Lee before their wedding in 1880, Roosevelt showered her with $2,500 worth of brooches, necklaces and other jewelry purchased on one shopping spree in New York. Reprimanded for his extravagance by his uncle James A. Roosevelt, a banker who had helped him with loans, Theodore told a friend that he would change his ways. "I have been spending money like water these last two years," he said, "but shall economise after I am married."

After a brief time at Columbia Law School, he cast about for a role in politics. His wide circle of friends and acquaintances, assisted by the local Republican organization, made it possible for him to run and win election to the state assembly in 1881 on his first try. Arriving in Albany in January 1882, Roosevelt was once again, as he had been at Harvard, a fish out of water. He disdained the maneuvering and patronage politics that governed the place and was almost proud of "the venomous hatred with which I am regarded by the politicians who supported me." He remained a free trader but had limited sympathy for labor, despite his support of labor's position for lowering tariffs. Roosevelt dismissed a bill forbidding streetcar employees to work more than twelve hours as a misguided and "purely socialist" attempt to coddle workers and repeal the laws of supply and demand.

Much of his record was concentrated in battles against corruption in the takeover of a Manhattan elevated railroad by Jay Gould and other robber barons. Roosevelt sometimes fought on the side of New York's reform Democrat governor, Grover Cleveland, but he later regarded the future President as corrupt. His record as a legislator may have been undistinguished, but the reputation Roosevelt cultivated was not. Indeed, everything about him seemed calculated to make an impression—his eyeglasses hanging from a black silk cord, his sandy hair and flaring sideburns, his prominent flashing teeth, his habit of wearing evening dress each night and, most conspicuously, his high-pitched voice ringing out in the cavernous assembly chamber: "Mr. Speak-ah! Mr. Speak-ah!"

Roosevelt's foes tried so hard to bring him down that they once resorted to a blackmail attempt. When a woman fell to the pavement in front of him, he sent her home, declining to accompany her, apparently avoiding a trap set by several enemies who were waiting to confront him and puncture his image. Roosevelt's biggest political setback occurred when he tried unsuccessfully to be elected Speaker of the Assembly in 1883. After that failure, he decided not to seek re-election to the legislature in 1884 and instead cast his eye on the national political scene.

To advance in the Republican Party, however, Roosevelt could not continue to be a free trader, so in a foretaste of his presidency, he abandoned that position and fully embraced the party's alliance with business in the new industrial era. Despite the unsavory reputation of James Blaine, the Republican presidential candidate in 1884, Roosevelt reluctantly backed the party nominee, along with a party platform calling for a high tariff, the gold standard, railroad regulation and civil service reform. Indeed, Roosevelt, while seeing himself as a reformer, proclaimed his contempt for fuzzy-headed waverers who abandoned the G.O.P. in its hour of need.

That election year also brought the pivotal personal crisis of young Theodore's early years, the unbearable death of his beloved wife on Valentine's Day in 1884—hours after the death of his mother on a separate floor of the same house in New York City and two days after giving birth to a baby girl, later christened Alice Lee. Plunged into the deepest despair, he sought solace in the western wilderness, where by his own account he had to keep moving to keep his spirit alive. "Black care rarely sits behind a rider whose pace is fast enough," he later wrote.

Life in the Dakota Badlands proved to be a defining experience personally, as well as politically. It threw Roosevelt into contact with a rough but bracing crowd of individuals, deepened his love of nature and toughened him for the combats that lay ahead in his life. But in financial terms, his few years in the West were a disaster. According to the biographer H. W. Brands, he invested $80,000 in cattle, supplies, labor and a ranch house and other buildings at Elkhorn, only to see most of it wiped out by drought and a couple of unusually hard winters. Roosevelt loved the hard work, the stark beauty of the land and the life of the gentleman cowhand, shouting "By Godfrey!" and "Hasten forward quickly there!" to the other cowboys, even as he still refused to smoke or drink. He served as a deputy sheriff, captured cattle rustlers and was quite a picture in sombrero, fringed and beaded buckskin shirt, chaps, boots with silver spurs and a pearl-handled revolver. But within two years, he returned to New York, his family and his political ambitions.

Newly married in 1886 to a childhood friend, Edith Carow, he listened as some of his friends suggested that he run for mayor or seek appointment as president of the Board of Health. He also had reason to worry about his financial situation. It was so straitened that he had to consider selling the magnificent home he had built on Sagamore Hill, a crest overlooking the quiet Long Island inlet known as Oyster Bay.

Like many in the upper classes, Roosevelt worried in this period about social unrest, labor disruptions and violence, including the 1886 bomb explosion in the antipolice demonstration by anarchists in Haymarket Square in Chicago. Drafted by Republicans, he ran for mayor of New York in the fall of that year, coming in third after Tammany Hall's candidate, Abram Hewitt, and Henry George, the radical economic reformer whose book *Progress and Poverty* advocated a single heavy tax on the unearned appreciation in the value of land and a removal of taxes paid by consumers. In what would prove to be a classic pattern for Roosevelt's career, the Republican bosses reached out to him for help but distrusted him as unmanageable—in this case, because he was seen as too much of a reformer and free trader. The Republican calculation was both cynical and understandable. They figured that Roosevelt could win if George drew enough votes away from the Democrats. Instead, Roosevelt was trounced and had to read several versions of his own political obituary in the papers. "You are not the timber of which Presidents are made," one said.

In defeat, Roosevelt turned to literary output to make his living, writing books on life in the West, biographies of political figures and a new philosophy driven by nationalism. The presidential victory of Benjamin Harrison in 1888 led to his appointment to the United States Civil Service Commission, where he attacked the Republican barons and their spoils system. He had an active social life in Washington, but his personal finances were still suffering. His post paid him only $3,500 a year, and he didn't have time to earn the extra money he had been making from writing books.

With a new daughter joining his two sons and a daughter, Alice, from his first marriage, the family had to find a larger house in

Washington. Edith wrote him plaintive notes about bills, asking: "How many of them do you think you can pay?" She put her husband on an allowance and suggested he consider resigning from the Harvard Club. Then one of her uncles died in 1892, leaving her a bequest that tided the family over briefly. Nevertheless, Roosevelt was taken aback when told in 1893 that as a result of an error by the family's financial counselor, he had run a $2,500 deficit in his personal accounts that year. "Even my Micawber-like temperament has been unable to withstand a shock it received this week," he wrote to his sister. He scrimped, cut out champagne, curtailed his entertaining and once again thought about selling the house at Sagamore Hill. "The trouble is that my career has been a very pleasant, honorable and a useful career for a man of means; but not the right career for a man without means," he observed.

Financial pressures eased with Roosevelt's appointment in 1895 to the Police Board in New York City, where he was quickly elected president and earned $6,000 a year while overseeing a corrupt department that had once been described by the pastor of Madison Square Church as "a very hotbed of knavery, debauchery and bestiality." Prowling the streets to talk to everyone from patrolmen to prostitutes, Roosevelt was suddenly a hugely popular figure in the public eye. Seeing the grim underside of New York City up close for the first time in his life, he developed an abiding conviction that easing the misery of the lower classes was vital to public safety, as well as just. Roosevelt also befriended social reformers like the journalist Lincoln Steffens and the writer and photographer Jacob Riis, who one day asked if he might ever run for President. "Don't you dare ask me that!" Roosevelt shouted. "If I do," he added, "I'll be careful, calculating, cautious, and so . . . I'll beat myself. See?"

The campaign battle between William McKinley and William Jennings Bryan in 1896 brought out Roosevelt's innate conservatism. Like all Republicans, he opposed everything Bryan stood for. McKinley rewarded Roosevelt with an appointment as an assistant secretary of the navy, but like other party leaders, the President was disturbed by Roosevelt's bumptious qualities and growing calls for the United States to build up its military and exercise its muscle on the international stage. "The truth is, Will, Roosevelt is always in such a state of mind," McKinley complained to William Howard Taft, a rising star in his administration. In the Navy Department, Roosevelt was arguing that the time had come for war with Spain. The opportunity arrived when the *Maine* blew up in Havana Harbor. Roosevelt was contemptuous of those "commercial interests" that were resisting war, another stage in his growing doubts about the selfishness of big business. Many of his friends were astonished when he resigned and left his family behind to go off to war with the First United States Volunteer Cavalry Regiment, known as the Rough Riders, an odd organization of cowboys and onetime college athletes and polo players that Roosevelt helped recruit from the Harvard, Yale and Princeton Clubs.

On horseback, Roosevelt led the victorious charge on Kettle Hill, wearing a polka-dot scarf around his hat. Soon he returned a hero to New York, where party kingpins planned to run him for governor. There was one small problem. Roosevelt had signed two affidavits testifying that his residence was in Washington. Ever financially strapped, he evidently was trying to avoid New York taxes on Sagamore Hill and his other home on Madison Avenue. To avert political criticism, Roosevelt's supporters hastily produced letters saying that he had all along intended to remain in New York and not lose his voting rights. For good measure, Roosevelt paid $995.28 in New York City taxes in 1898.

The war was not especially popular in New York, especially among big business and financiers, and Roosevelt's run for governor was not a sure thing. There was a whispering campaign that he had not even stormed the hill in Cuba. He squeaked through the election with a small margin, after following the established pattern for campaign fund-raising in the state. Donations came in from the Mutual, Equitable and New York insurance companies and from the Metropolitan and Third Avenue railways. The party boss, Senator Thomas Platt, boasted that he had collected $10,000 from J. P. Morgan. Platt was nonetheless concerned about some of Roosevelt's earlier statements that were sympathetic to the poor, critical of trusts and questioning of "the right of a man to run his own business in his own way."

One advantage of becoming governor was that Roosevelt was now paid $10,000 a year and was ensconced in a grand Victorian mansion in Albany with a full staff to do the cooking, cleaning and serving. In the first months after his inauguration in January of 1899, Roosevelt deferred to Platt. But by April, to Platt's dismay, he was seeking a tax on corporate franchises, a measure he later termed his "most definite and important" achievement as governor. The new governor also challenged his party over patronage and civil service reforms, and he refused to appoint corrupt hacks pushed on him by Republican bosses. It was during his testy dealings with Platt that he told a friend: "I have always been fond of the West African proverb: 'Speak softly and carry a big stick, you will go far.'" Platt had a different idea of how far Roosevelt should go. He wanted to send his quarrelsome governor off in 1900 to what he hoped would be the oblivion of the vice presidency under McKinley.

At first, Mark Hanna and the Republicans around McKinley did not take kindly to Platt's idea. They were suspicious of Roosevelt's ambitions, sanctimonious manner, antibusiness leanings and zealotry. The vice presidency did not appeal to Roosevelt, who thought that his own path to the White House would be better pursued by his winning re-election as governor or serving in McKinley's cabinet as Secretary of War. But the stir was palpable in the Republican convention hall in Philadelphia when Roosevelt entered wearing a big wide-brimmed black hat obviously intended to evoke the Rough Riders. "Gentlemen," a delegate said as the convention started applauding, "that's an Acceptance Hat."

Hanna, looking down from the platform, suddenly stopped smiling as he realized that the delegates wanted to draft the New

York governor. Platt was delighted, but Hanna is said to have entertained reservations. "Don't you realize that there's only one life between this madman and the White House?" he is widely quoted to have asked an associate, though scholars say the quote is apocryphal. On the ticket, Roosevelt happily did the bulk of the campaigning while McKinley rested above the fray. Once again the Democratic nominee was Bryan, running on a platform of opposition to business combinations, to the gold standard and, this time, to American imperial ambitions over the territory seized in the victory against Spain. Roosevelt's response was to champion not only prosperity—"the full dinner pail"—but honor, decency, patriotism and global responsibilities. McKinley swept the Electoral College, taking 51.7 percent of the popular vote to Bryan's 45.5 percent.

As vice president, Roosevelt tried to prove himself a good Republican, hoping to run for President in 1904 even though no one in his job had reached the White House in recent history. To show deference to business, he gave a dinner for J. P. Morgan. "You see," Roosevelt wrote his friend and fellow New Yorker, Secretary of War Elihu Root, "it represents an effort on my part to become a conservative man in touch with the influential classes and I think I deserve encouragement."

Carrying out the main task of the number-two man, Roosevelt presided over the Senate, and with so little to do, he thought about studying law in his spare time. In September 1901, the Vice President was attending an outing of the Vermont Fish and Game League on Isle La Motte in Lake Champlain when he got a message from Buffalo, on the other side of New York State. McKinley had been shot while attending a Pan-American Exposition on the shores of Lake Erie. Roosevelt sped to Buffalo by train but, after being told on his arrival that McKinley was recovering, decided to return to his vacation. He was in the Adirondacks when another report arrived telling of McKinley's worsening condition. On board the train to Buffalo, he learned that the President was dead.

The assassination, barely six months into McKinley's second

term, sent a shock wave through Wall Street, where Roosevelt's efforts to placate the business community had failed to impress anyone. Indeed, the rumor was that upon hearing the news, J. P. Morgan cursed, staggered to his desk and grew red in the face. "That damned cowboy is President of the United States!" Hanna famously declared. After being sworn in, Roosevelt reached out to Hanna but complained privately that the party's pre-eminent boss was treating him like a child, calling him Teddy, a name he detested. When Hanna suggested that Roosevelt go slowly and avoid making any changes in McKinley's policies, the new President initially agreed. He concentrated on establishing his legitimacy and reassuring the jittery financial markets that he would continue McKinley's policies.

"It is a dreadful thing to come into the Presidency this way," he wrote Henry Cabot Lodge. "But it would be a far worse thing to be morbid about it."

———

Although Roosevelt recalled that he had not "entered the presidency with any deliberately planned and far reaching scheme of social betterment," few presidents have taken that office better prepared for the challenges he would face.

His first crisis occurred shortly after he took office in 1901. Investors fighting for control of the Northern Pacific railroad, which dominated the northwestern part of the country, agreed to the creation of a vast holding company controlling the region's transportation, called the Northern Securities Company. Among the financial leaders who forged the deal were J. P. Morgan and Company, the Rockefellers and the railroad barons James J. Hill and E. H. Harriman.

Farmers and others in the Northwest immediately feared that the powerful cartel would soon have a stranglehold over transportation in the region, raising freight rates and getting richer than ever off the monopoly. In the face of political pressure to do something, Roosevelt proceeded cautiously. The Sherman Antitrust Act had been on the books for ten years. Enacted to go after the trusts, it had never before been used successfully to prosecute a major business combination. Instead, the act had been invoked several times as a cudgel against unions. Moving to test his powers against what he later called "the tyranny of mere wealth, the tyranny of a plutocracy," the President directed his Attorney General, Philander C. Knox, to sue under the Sherman act to break up the new cartel. Wall Street was aghast.

When Morgan and Hanna appealed to the White House to ask why the lawyers could not just settle the suit, Roosevelt rebuffed them. Eventually a federal court ordered the company broken up, paving the way for government action against forty-four more corporations during his term, from the beef trust to the tobacco trust to chemical and rail trusts to the Standard Oil Company. Roosevelt became known as a "trustbuster," though he himself persistently believed that, by itself, breaking up companies was no magic solution to the nation's economic problems. Some historians judge Roosevelt's reputation as a scourge of trusts to be exaggerated, but there is no question that his approach marked a shift in government philosophy and action. In other steps, he persuaded Congress to establish a new Department of Commerce and Labor in 1902, with a Bureau of Corporations that could collect and make public information about financial arrangements.

The anthracite coal miners' strike of 1902 also helped awaken Roosevelt to the power of the underclass. For many decades, coal miners had struggled to improve their miserable existence in towns across Illinois, Ohio, Pennsylvania and other states. When 240,000 members of the United Mine Workers struck in May, the big railroads, which owned most of the mines, refused at first to negotiate. As the strike threatened to create shortages, drive up prices and force the closing of schools in New York City and elsewhere, Roosevelt declared that he would use troops if necessary to go in and produce the coal. At his negotiating sessions with the mine owners, Roosevelt, confined to a wheelchair from a leg injury in a streetcar accident, was so angry over their intransigence that he later told a friend that he felt like throwing one of them out the window. He appealed to their patriotism and to fears of "a winter fuel famine," but they responded with complaints about having to negotiate with criminals, anarchists and saboteurs.

Under public pressure, J. P. Morgan forced the operators to settle by agreeing to a commission to study the issue. The commission ended up awarding miners a 10 percent wage increase in 1903. The strike helped place Roosevelt in the extraordinary position of being a friend of both labor and business, a highly unusual reputation for a Republican. In the coal strike, he said he favored "a square deal" for both sides, and the expression stuck. The President began to understand that his own "natural allies" were less the heads of the giant industrial cartels than the farmers, small businessmen, workers and the middle class.

While trust-busting and square deals for workers may have become Roosevelt's priorities, they were not at the top of the Republican agenda in Congress. The party's leaders, instead, had been hoping since the end of the Spanish-American War to repeal the inheritance tax passed in 1898. Opponents had tried to get the tax thrown out in court but without success, though in upholding the tax in May of 1900, the Supreme Court issued a ruling that the tax historian Sidney Ratner calls "a remarkable exercise in dialectical ingenuity and judicial legislation." The high court directed that the tax rates be calculated not on the size of the entire estate but on the size of each share of an inheritance, an order that effectively lowered the rates, which were now based on smaller amounts. The ruling kept millions of dollars from being paid to the federal government, diluting the effect of its graduated rates. Conservative editorials hailed the decision as fair, while many liberals were happy that the tax at least had been upheld.

McKinley's re-election in 1901 had spurred foes of the inheritance tax to get Congress to repeal it, along with other taxes imposed to pay for the war. Roosevelt's holdover Treasury Secretary, Lyman J. Gage, also favored repeal, viewing it as affordable in light of federal surpluses that now reached $50 million. Republicans rammed the repeal through the House in early 1902, despite protests from Democrats. Again the dissenters argued that the inheritance and corporation taxes were the only means to tap into what they called "lawless and predatory wealth." But Republicans argued that they had pledged to repeal the wartime taxes as soon as the war was over. What the inheritance tax opponents ignored was any effort to reduce the tariff as well. The House passed the repeal by a vote of 288 to 0. The Senate followed with a few minor amendments, and the final act, approved on April 12, retained the excise taxes on oil and sugar companies and taxes on bankers and brokers.

For many years, Theodore Roosevelt had managed to sidestep the nearly untouchable issues of taxes and tariffs. An early free trader, he later had supported protectionism while advancing up the Republican ranks. But after Roosevelt became President, his increasing sympathies for the poor, the farmers and the working classes seemed inconsistent with support for high prices of the goods they consumed. Political pressures were changing at the same time. The agitation for reform in the late nineteenth century brought a host of new ideas about government and society in the industrial age, from worker rights to populism to William Jennings Bryan's attacks on the tariff as unfair to average Americans. The result was a development of consumer consciousness reflected in the way that politicians now talked about the needs of "the plain people," "the common man," "the taxpayer," "the man on the street" and "the American housewife." It was only natural for such talk to increase pressure for lower tariffs.

Defending the protectionist system, however, were the two most powerful leaders in Congress. The first was the Speaker of the House, Joseph ("Uncle Joe") Cannon from Illinois, whose genial, benevolent manner belied the stern hand he wielded. Cannon disdained Roosevelt's sympathies for the poor, attributing them to ignorance of the fundamentals of the modern industrial state. "Economics was a subject of which he knew nothing," the Speaker said of the President. The other protectionist leader was Senator Nelson Wilmarth Aldrich of Rhode Island, a wealthy banker whose daughter had married John D. Rockefeller, Jr. (Their son, Nelson Aldrich Rockefeller, rose to become governor of New York and vice president.) Senator Aldrich led a conservative oligarchy of colleagues, many of them millionaires.

Early in his term, Roosevelt catered to the barons of Capitol Hill, hoping to win their political support by being selective in his fights. He also focused more on regulating or breaking up the trusts than on tariffs, taxes and monetary policy, issues that— despite their enormous impact on average Americans—did not stir his blood. "My feeling about the tariff question is, of course, that it is one of expediency and not of morality," Roosevelt wrote in 1903. "There is nothing more intrinsically right or wrong in a 40 percent tariff than in a 60 percent one."

Taxes and tariff were also deemed not worth a fight with Cannon, Aldrich and the old guard as the 1904 election approached. Indeed, Roosevelt feared the conservatives might try to deny him the party's nomination. "President of the United States!" he told an acquaintance. "I'd rather be *e-lect-ed* to that office than have anything tangible of which I know." He felt especially vulnerable, he said, because he had "no machine, no faction, no money" to prevent the Republican barons from moving against him. With the death of Mark Hanna in February of 1904, however, Roosevelt's fears of a Republican revolt eased somewhat. The power vacuum in the G.O.P. led to jockeying for the job of party chairman, led by Matt Quay of Pennsylvania, whose famous comment "I will shake the plum tree" was an excellent summation of his attitude toward fund-raising and patronage. But Quay also died in 1904, giving Roosevelt a freer hand to replace Hanna. The President in the end tapped his Secretary of Commerce and Labor, George Cortelyou, who had spent the previous years supervising the very corporations he would now be turning to for campaign contributions.

At the Chicago convention, when the tariff issue had to be addressed, Roosevelt again stood by the old guard on behalf of protectionism. The Democrats this time passed over Bryan and opted for a conservative nominee, Alton Parker, chief judge of the Court of Appeals in New York and someone with ties to the New York banking world. But the Democrats still could not get much support within the business establishment. Indeed, the election looked like an easy victory for the Republicans until October, when Joseph Pulitzer published an editorial in the *New York World* charging Roosevelt with corruption.

The Bureau of Corporations in the Commerce and Labor Department, the editorial declared, had abandoned investigations into business in return for campaign donations to the Roosevelt campaign. It was a scheme for "buying protection," said the newspaper, which demanded that Roosevelt disclose how much money Cortelyou had raised from the paper trust, coal trust, sugar trust, oil trust, tobacco trust, steel trust, national banks and insurance trust and the railroads. With an almost conspiratorial glee, Democrats charged that such robber barons as Harriman and Frick had met in New York and agreed that Roosevelt's election was essential to the future of the country. Parker, the Democratic nominee, was slow to pick up the charge himself, but he eventually accused the administration of trying to blackmail corporations.

Roosevelt acknowledged that he had received campaign money from corporations but declared that it was "monstrous" and "a wicked falsehood" to suggest that extortion was involved. Corporations contributed to his campaign, he explained, because they had a "tremendous stake in the welfare of this country," which they knew "can only be secured through the continuance in power of the Republican party." As a precaution, however, when it became known that the Standard Oil trust had sent Cortelyou a check for $100,000, Roosevelt told his chairman to return it, though it is unclear whether his directive was followed.

Clearly Roosevelt's response to the Democrats' charges was disingenuous. He said he had "little to do" with his own fund-raising, but it was obvious that donors, while perhaps not getting guarantees, were at least trying to ensure their own immunity from future trust-busting actions. It took another year for Parker's charge of corporate contributions to be documented, first by a state legislative investigation and later by a congressional inquiry. The revelations persuaded Roosevelt to endorse a ban on corporate campaign contributions, which he would sign into law in 1907. But in the 1904 campaign, Parker was unable to prove his charge of a quid pro quo or even the specifics of the contributions. Roosevelt won the election on November 8 with an extraordinary 57.4 percent of the popular vote. Elated over his achievement, the President made a quick decision he came to regret. He declared immediately after winning that this would be his second and final term in office.

Despite Roosevelt's election victory, it was significant that Eugene V. Debs got more than 400,000 votes, the best showing ever by a Socialist candidate. Candidates running as progressive Republicans scored victories in the Midwest and elsewhere, promising more aggressive actions against business combines, as well as other reforms, including voter initiatives, referendums, recall petitions and direct primaries. Their success seemed to have been propelled in part by a vast proliferation of magazines, books and mass circulation newspapers featuring journalists who specialized in exposing corruption and telling lurid tales of a predatory class of elite capitalists. Among them were Lincoln Steffens and Ida Tarbell, whose history of the Standard Oil Company in *McClure's* magazine aroused public ire over the accumulation of wealth, extravagance, trusts, labor-capital conflicts and the inequities of the tax and tariff system.

Instead of slaking the public's thirst for reform, Roosevelt's actions seemed actually to raise people's hopes for more.

Taking the oath of office for another four years at the White House, Roosevelt looked a bit stouter than four years earlier, but his exuberance was undiminished. Now at last, he felt, he had a mandate to complete his robust agenda. In January of 1905, Roosevelt had addressed the Union League Club of Philadelphia and called for "an increase in the supervision exercised by the Government over business-enterprise." But no one was quite sure what form the new "supervision" would take.

The twin concerns in the business establishment were, once again, that Roosevelt would wage an assault on the tariff, the center of Republican economic philosophy, as well as seek to regulate the railroads and other businesses. But for all his fiery words and unpredictability, the President remained cautious, in this area at least. Two days after the 1904 election, Roosevelt told his friend Nicholas Murray Butler, president of Columbia University, that he had already started to try to secure tariff reform in his second term. A few weeks later other friends reported that he considered the issue dead, in large part because of the opposition of the old guard. "I shall not split with my party on the matter," the President reportedly said. In his 1905 annual message, he said there was "more need of stability than of the attempt to attain an ideal perfection in the methods of raising revenue." He told the journalist Jacob Riis that he was "up to my ears in all the fighting" on issues other than the tariff.

Roosevelt's actual goal was to use the tariff issue to frighten the party's old guard into cooperating with him on enacting legislation to control the railroads. As the historian John Morton Blum has written, tariff reform—never an issue over which his passions stirred—was "less an objective than a device" in Roosevelt's second term. The main injustice, in his view, was the railroads' persistent practice of price-gouging rivals and granting rebates to favored customers, all in an effort to extend their control over commerce. A series of court decisions had prevented local and federal efforts from curbing the railroads' collusive conduct. Yet as these predatory practices grew, farmers and many others dependent on the railroads demanded that Congress authorize the Interstate Commerce Commission to set rates and prevent price discrimination. Roosevelt determined to respond to that pressure. Once he abandoned his threat to seek tariff reductions, he was able to line up support from, first, Speaker Cannon and then from Senator Aldrich of Rhode Island to support a package of railroad reforms. The final result, known as the Hepburn Act, gave the I.C.C. the ability to establish railroad rates, subject to review by the courts (a mitigating factor that was criticized by the progressives).

The year 1906 was a productive and turbulent one for Congress and Roosevelt in other areas. Following disclosures about the dangers of patent medicines, Congress approved a pure food and drug law pushed by Roosevelt's Agriculture Department. Upton Sinclair's exposure of horrific conditions in the nation's meatpacking houses in *The Jungle* led to a presidential investigation and the passage of a federal meat inspection law. Roosevelt also proposed that Congress abolish child labor, a step that was not acted on. Indeed, labor was one area in which Roosevelt felt increasingly caught between sympathy for worker grievances, especially the use of injunctions to break strikes, and his loyalty to fellow Republicans who were antilabor. These and other struggles also reinforced Roosevelt's concerns in general about the power of entrenched corporate interests, and how to curb that power in a way that would not stifle the spirit of free enterprise. "Somehow or other," he wrote to the British historian Sir George Trevelyan, "we shall have to work out methods of controlling the big corporations without paralyzing the energies of the business community."

The signs of Roosevelt's uneasiness flowered in the spring of 1906. "I do not like the social conditions at present," he told his Secretary of War, William Howard Taft, that March. "The dull, purblind folly of the very rich men; their greed and arrogance . . . and the corruption in business and politics, have tended to produce a very unhealthy condition of excitement and irritation in the popular mind, which shows itself in the great increase in the socialistic propaganda." What he intended to do about his concerns was not clear. Then on April 14, at the laying of the cornerstone of a new office building at the House of Representatives, he delivered a proposal. Echoing an analogy he had offered a few weeks earlier at a dinner at the Gridiron Club, Roosevelt assailed all the sensationalist writers who, he said, inveighed against the evils of big corporations without seeing any of their many redeeming features. Such writers, the President said, reminded him of "the Man with the Muck-rake" in Bunyan's *Pilgrim's Progress*—the character "who was offered a celestial crown for his muck-rake, but who would neither look up nor regard the crown he was offered, but continued to rake to himself the filth of the floor."

Like *square deal*, the term *muckraker* has lived on, though it has lost its intended pejorative implication. The speech reflected once again the President's continuing attempts to define a middle ground for himself—a moderate course between two extremes that he felt were threatening American society. But the next day the *New York Times* and other papers headlined a separate part of the speech, calling for a "tax on wealth." Without endorsing any particular piece of legislation, Roosevelt had called for "a progressive tax on all fortunes" above a certain amount—a renewal of the inheritance or estate tax. The tax, he said, should be framed so as "to put it out of the power of the owner of one of these enormous fortunes to hand on more than a certain amount to any one individual." The goal should be to prevent inheritance or transfer of "those fortunes swollen beyond all healthy limits." It was not as if Roosevelt were making an extremely radical proposal. By the early 1900s, about thirty states had inheritance taxes, though only in New York and Pennsylvania did they yield more than $1 million. The tax had also been adopted by Britain, France, Austria, Canada and other countries, not to mention by the United States during the Civil War and the Spanish-American War. But the proposal hit the public like a bombshell.

Champ (James Beauchamp) Clark, Democratic leader in the House, was in the audience and described in his memoirs "the eminent Republican magnates" smiling complacently and "having the time of their lives" as Roosevelt made his way through the attacks on crusading journalists. As the President got to the part about the inheritance tax, "The Democrats were jubilant and applauded hilariously, while the smiles froze on the faces of the Republicans," Clark wrote. "The President seemed to be delighted with the sensation he had created and the consternation he had wrought among Republican statesmen. Their curses on him for that speech were not only deep, but loud." Indeed, the speech ignited a firestorm in conservative circles, where it was labeled Roosevelt's "Cure for the Disease of Wealth." The President's words, said the *Philadelphia Record*, gave "more encouragement to state socialism and centralization of government than all the frothy demagogues have accomplished in a quarter of a century of agitation of the muddy waters of discontent." The *New York Times* lamented that Roosevelt had failed to understand that great fortunes were themselves raising the standard of living of everyone else.

The following December, Roosevelt went still further in his cure of the "disease." In his annual message to Congress at the end of 1906, he said there should be a tax on income as well as inheritances. Returning to the theme of the power of personal fortunes, he warned against "the men who seek to excite a violent class hatred against all men of wealth," as well as "that other creature, equally base but no baser, who in a spirit of greed . . . seeks to exploit his fellow Americans with callous disregard to their welfare of soul and body." He suggested again that there was "every reason" for the federal government—"when next our system of taxation is revised"—to impose a "graduated inheritance tax, and, if possible, a graduated income tax."

One interesting aspect of this message was that Roosevelt was embracing an argument going back to the Civil War: the wealthy man, he said, enjoys unusual protections from government and therefore has "a peculiar obligation to the State because he derives special advantages from the mere existence of government." To discharge that obligation, he said, the rich should pay a "full and proper share of the burden of taxation" imposed "in a spirit of entire justice and moderation." Without a specific proposal in mind, he said that "in the near future" Congress should, first, adopt an inheritance tax similar to the ones adopted in 1862 and 1898, and then an income tax that could somehow get around the Supreme Court's ruling of 1895. "The question is undoubtedly very intricate, delicate and troublesome," he admitted, and he offered no path toward resolving it. The President's passivity was striking. He was essentially leaving it to Congress to take the initiative while saying that the income tax issue was deserving of "long and careful study" over a period of time in which the public could become familiar with its pros and cons. The harsh verdict of some historians is that on tax issues at least, Roosevelt was more talk than action. "In spite of many strong words," writes the tax historian Randolph Paul, "Roosevelt did little to deprive the privileged of their wealth or to discourage their malefactions."

By the last two years of his presidency, Roosevelt's record had nevertheless thoroughly dismayed the business community and their champions in Congress. In addition to regulating the railroad, meatpacking and drug industries, he had battled mining, grazing and oil interests over laws governing public lands, expanded the national park and forest systems and enacted a law selling public land and using the receipts to build dams and reclamation projects. Congress had tried to block several of his conservation initiatives, including the creation of new forest reserves. The lawmakers also passed bills granting water rights to private interests, and Roosevelt vetoed them. All these battles were seen as taking their toll in terms of lost business confidence, which in turn became a widely cited factor leading up to the Panic of 1907.

The panic had been preceded, as were most collapses of that era, by rampant speculation on Wall Street, industrial overproduction and overconfidence. Once the markets became jittery, Roosevelt tended to blame speculators and financiers, whom he called "certain malefactors of great wealth." The main cause of the panic was the weak American banking system. But business countered that Roosevelt's policies had created a crisis by undermining investors' confidence in railroads and other enterprises.

By October, prices on the New York Stock Exchange had plunged to new lows, once again causing a whiff of fear over bank failures. One spark in the mix was the failed attempt by several New York trust companies to corner the copper market, leading to a wave of bank losses. Roosevelt sent Cortelyou, now his Treasury Secretary, to New York to meet with J. P. Morgan, though he himself took no part in the tense discussions with the most powerful banker in the world, choosing instead to go on a bear hunt. Cortelyou eased the crisis somewhat by depositing $25 million in government funds in the banks, but the relief was temporary.

To stave off the panic, J. P. Morgan stepped in to pool funds from the leading New York City banks while the government watched from the sidelines. As he had in his earlier encounter with President Grover Cleveland, Morgan organized the rescue coolly and behind the scenes, sending out instructions to his operatives as he remained ensconced in a small room next to the library in his home on Madison Avenue, playing solitaire, puffing on cigars and greeting delegations of panic-stricken bankers begging for action.

One focus of the effort to shore up the banks was the financially tottering Tennessee Coal and Iron Company, which was serving as collateral for numerous loans. Morgan's proposal was for the giant United States Steel Corporation to purchase the Tennessee concern, thereby shoring up the banks dependent on its solvency. To get approval for the deal, Morgan and Henry Clay Frick of United States Steel traveled on a special train to Washington, where they sought immunization from prosecution for violations of the Sherman Antitrust Act if the acquisition proceeded. A witness later recalled that Roosevelt responded by commenting that he didn't think he would be criticized for going along. Later Roosevelt recalled that he consented because of the dangers of a bank failure, but critics charged that the President had allowed himself to be duped. Roosevelt always defended his decision. He later declared that he "never had any doubt of the wisdom of my action—not for a moment." But it was clear that the episode had shaken him, making him somewhat more reluctant to go after business cartels at the very end of his term.

The depression ushered in by the Panic of 1907 was to last for at least two years. Once again hard economic times forced cities and states throughout the country to set up public works projects to employ people thrown out of work. Relief organizations in New York City tripled their caseloads. Steel mills dismissed a third of their employees, and comparable layoffs occurred in other industries, such as breweries and machinery.

Taking note of the bad economic news and also the wave of protests they generated, Roosevelt struck a hopeful note in his annual message to Congress at the end of 1907. "In no nation are the fundamental business conditions sounder than in ours at this very moment," he declared. But, he added, "in any large body of men," there was bound to be dishonesty and "unscrupulous and reckless" conduct. As for the oft-deferred question of tariffs and taxes, Roosevelt recommitted himself to protectionism but suggested that he understood how tariffs could reflect an abuse of corporate power. Tentatively he suggested that the time had come—as it must "every dozen years or so"—to review the tariff laws to make sure they did not confer "excessive or improper benefits" on the few.

But with only a year left to his presidency, the President suggested that the issue be dealt with after the 1908 presidential election. Alongside such a tariff review, he said that an income tax and an inheritance tax should receive "the careful attention of our legislators." Once again his tone was passive on an essential pocketbook issue. The Supreme Court's rejection of the income tax as unconstitutional, he acknowledged, made him speak "diffidently." But, he said, there was no question that a graduated income tax would be a "desirable feature of Federal taxation, and it is to be hoped that one may be devised which the Supreme Court will declare constitutional."

In hindsight, it is possible to see that, in his attitude toward wealth, Roosevelt had evolved from his early posture of indifference to one of heightened concern about the power that the wealthy wielded in society. No doubt this was due in part to his background of privilege, in which the trappings of the rich in society failed to impress him. "I am simply unable to understand the value placed by so many people upon great wealth," he wrote to a friend in the spring of 1908. His statements also clearly reflect what he saw as the dangers posed to society of concentrated wealth and power. But as the historian John Morton Blum points out, it is easy to remember Roosevelt strictly as a legendary personality, champion of reform and larger-than-life actor on the world stage, and to forget his essential pragmatism on many issues. Blum notes that Roosevelt was first and foremost "a professional Republican politician" grappling all his working life with the business of government, politics—and compromise. His desire was to preserve order in society, not tear it apart. The income tax was clearly a cause for which he was prepared to take a stand, but not to stake his presidency.

To see Roosevelt as a soothing, moderating political figure seems at odds with his combustible personality. Contemporaries did certainly not see him that way. One old friend, Nicholas Murray Butler of Columbia University, wrote to Roosevelt at the end of his presidency to convey his "grief and sorrow" over the President's business bashing. It was not so much his programs that troubled Butler, but the lack of "dignity" and "restraint" of his remarks.

One of the ironies of Roosevelt's presidency is that his successor, a President of vastly more "dignity" and "restraint," became the one to drive the income tax toward enactment.

CHAPTER EIGHT

"The Congress
Shall Have Power . . ."

The Sixteenth Amendment Is Launched

WILLIAM HOWARD TAFT DID NOT RELISH RUNNING
for President. Indeed, he did not savor much about public life. "I
am not a politician and I dislike politics," Taft complained as the
1908 election campaign got under way. Yet his four years in office
proved to be a pivotal turning point for the politics of the Progressive Era and for the income tax.

After choosing not to run for another term, and then regretting
the decision, Roosevelt had to select which of his protégés should
succeed him at the White House. He cast his eye on two cabinet
members who were his closest confidants. Taft, the Secretary of
War, was valued by the President as a stouthearted comrade-in-
arms. Elihu Root, the Secretary of State, shared Roosevelt's activist
approach to world affairs and his roots in Republican politics in
New York State.

Roosevelt and his two close aides sometimes liked to think of themselves as the Three Musketeers. The President had urged Root, a prominent Wall Street lawyer, to run for governor of New York in 1904, which might have positioned him for the nomination, had he won. Roosevelt could also have chosen the progressive governor of New York, Charles Evans Hughes, to succeed him, since Hughes had a record of reforming the state's insurance industry and regulating public utilities and water power. But Hughes was too distant and unappealing a personality for Roosevelt's taste.

Caution led him to designate Taft, whose performance as a viceroy in the Philippines before joining the cabinet had been well received among the citizens of the newest outpost of the American empire. It might have occurred to Roosevelt that the record of achievements compiled by Taft related primarily to distant lands and distant problems. But Taft plainly subscribed to Roosevelt's domestic policies, even though he had little to do with bringing them about and had commented that Roosevelt might have been more careful and respectful of legalities in implementing them. Above all, Taft had nothing approaching Roosevelt's zest for political combat. "A national campaign for the Presidency to me is a nightmare," he said.

For all the President's hopes, there was little in Taft's background to suggest that he would continue Roosevelt's radical agenda. He was a low-key, considerate and erudite man who began his career deciding cases against the interests of labor as a judge in Ohio. In one decision, he ruled against a boycott of goods produced by plants being struck. A federal judge by the age of thirty-four, he always nurtured the ambition to become Chief Justice of the United States—a feat he would achieve in 1921. Roosevelt respected Taft's accomplishments and was convinced that he shared the goals of the Square Deal. If Taft was cautious and slow, an impression reinforced by his huge girth—he weighed 350 pounds at the height of his career—people took this quality to be the product of his careful and judicious mind and temperament.

But he was hardly one for eloquence. When he got the nomination, he declared: "I haven't a word to say. To tell you the truth, I can't find the words. They won't come. But I don't need to tell you that I'm very proud and happy."

The ominous signs of future problems for Taft and the progressive agenda were evident at the 1908 Republican convention. Despite the convention's progressive facade, the old guard, not Roosevelt, was in charge. In the platform, an attempt by Taft and Roosevelt to put in some measures sympathetic to labor were first blocked and then diluted by supporters of the National Association of Manufacturers. Labor leaders who had been grateful to Roosevelt migrated back to the Democrats. Taft easily got the support of business leaders like Rockefeller, Morgan (who said, "Good! Good!" when Taft was nominated) and Carnegie. It turned out that he was less successful at fund-raising than Roosevelt had been in 1904, however. He campaigned as a champion of small business, not big business. One result of that support was that Taft felt somewhat more strongly than Roosevelt that tariffs needed to be lowered for the sake of consumers and small businesses alike. Indeed, 40 percent of the N.A.M., which was then a small-business-oriented organization, favored lower tariffs, as did farmers, city dwellers and progressives.

On the Democratic side, Bryan, defeated in 1896 and 1900 and yielding to the "gold Democrat" Alton Parker in 1904, had remained a leader of the Democrats and free silver Populists. After his defeat in 1900, he had founded a weekly journal called *The Commoner* and continued pressing for a variety of favorite causes, as well as for a single term for President and the popular election of senators. He also kept up his crusade against corporate contributions to political campaigns. Bryan supported primary elections, municipal ownership of utilities, stricter pure food laws, a ban on child labor and self-government for the Philippines and other overseas dependencies newly acquired by the United States. After 1900, he spoke little about free silver. He also became more religious, drawn to a fundamentalist faith and high moral standards while heatedly assailing the materialism of the age and the bastions of privilege. After having taunted Roosevelt to embrace genuine progressive reform, he saw Roosevelt do just that. But as Democrats moved to the right themselves in 1904, Bryan got caught fighting the conservatives in his own party, as well as the Republicans. Nevertheless, the defeat of Alton Parker that year led to demands for Bryan's return as party standard-bearer.

Taft frankly envied Bryan's crowds and his skills as an orator, but despite his self-proclaimed aversion to politics, he was shrewd enough to realize that the passions stirred by the Great Commoner might frighten Republicans and bring them to the polls. Taft and Roosevelt nevertheless worried that because of recent economic hard times, 1908 might not be a good year for Republicans, especially since the shadow of the Panic of 1907 had not lifted and the party was left divided by Roosevelt's performance. Indeed, Roosevelt was seen to have moved so far to the left that some in the press spoke of a "Roosevelt–Bryan merger" in which the outgoing President's supporters might feel more comfortable voting for the Democrat as his successor.

Roosevelt had once viewed Bryan as a dangerous demagogue with "silly and wicked" ideas. He came to see him toward the end of his presidency as "a kindly, well-meaning, emotional man." Bryan had something else going for him: as a candidate, he was learning how to sound more conservative, even to the point of criticizing socialism. To prepare for his third run for the White House, Bryan also took a world tour and impressed the King of England as "agreeable and intelligent but a little gaseous, you know." He easily captured the party's nomination in the summer of 1908.

On the important issues of tariffs and taxes, the 1908 campaign was notable for the evolution it marked within the Republican Party and the nation as a whole. Responding to the public's anxiety over hard economic times, the G.O.P. platform of 1908 called for more spending on public improvements (which, of course, was not deemed socialist) and immediate "revision of the tariff" by the next President. But as many historians have noted, the word *downward* was omitted next to *revision*, even though the public was encouraged to believe that *downward* was the word intended. As a concession to Republican hard-liners, the platform also embraced protectionism as a principle, noting that it was necessary to help industry compete with cheaper production costs overseas and also provide a "reasonable profit" to American industries.

Even more important, Taft followed Roosevelt's lead and suggested that he favored a graduated income tax, both to make the tax burden more fair and to provide revenue for the government, now that deficits had returned as a result of the recession following the Panic of 1907. He had earlier been on record as agreeing with critics of the tax that it was inquisitorial and that it would encourage perjury. On the other hand, Taft had at times suggested that an income tax might be needed one day to make up for lost revenues in the federal budget. Most important, he had also declared firmly that he was opposed to a constitutional amendment establishing an income tax. "In my judgment an amendment to the constitution for an income tax is not necessary," he said. "I believe that an income tax, when the protective system of customs shall not furnish income enough for individual needs, can and should be devised which, under the decisions of the Supreme Court, will conform to the constitution."

As for the Democrats, the income tax issue had become less prominent since 1896. Now that the political climate had changed and Roosevelt had embraced the idea, the Democrats were ready to reintroduce it enthusiastically as a main plank in their platform. Bryan put a new twist on it, however. No longer did he talk about reintroducing the tax as a bill, challenging the judges on the Supreme Court. The platform declared its support for "a constitutional amendment specifically authorizing congress to levy and collect a tax upon individual and corporate incomes, to the end that wealth may bear its proportionate share of the burdens of the federal government." And Bryan defended the tax as a moderate, not radical, step. Reprising his speeches from the early 1890s, he noted that "the most conservative countries in the old world" had adopted it. If a tax bill could be drafted as Taft had proposed, in a way that could be accepted by the Supreme Court, "well and good, but that is uncertain," Bryan declared. Otherwise, he asserted, surely Taft would not oppose an amendment to achieve it.

The tariff was no doubt a more compelling issue to voters in 1908 than the income tax. That was probably because lower tariffs would affect all voters, whereas the income tax previously had been directed almost exclusively at the tiny percentage of wealthy tax-payers. But the presidential campaign was notable for the implied consensus in the income tax's favor. The tax was also supported, for example, by such minor-party candidates as William Randolph Hearst, the quixotic publisher who had first tried to wrest the Democratic nomination from Bryan and then ran as an independent. The Socialist candidate, Eugene V. Debs, traveling on a train known as the "Red Special," called for a more radical agenda of public ownership of land, transportation, distribution and means of production and "the unconditional surrender of the capitalist class." He and the Socialists also, and once again, called for a graduated inheritance and income tax.

For all of Bryan's attempts to portray himself as a moderate, his third attempt to win the presidency failed to convince the voters. The issue for him was "Shall the People Rule?" He barnstormed the country, speaking on single issues in various cities: the tariff in Des Moines, trusts in Indianapolis, guarantees for bank deposits in Topeka. The problem was that he had no paramount, overriding rationale for his candidacy. Roosevelt had succeeded in defusing so many issues that Taft did not seem to be the enemy of change that Bryan portrayed him as being. The Democrats tried to accuse Taft of allowing "favor-seeking corporations" to buy the election with campaign donations, but the charges did not stick. Taft was so convinced that he would be able to glide into the White House because of Roosevelt's popularity that he backed away from attacking Bryan too harshly. Indeed, Roosevelt felt his protégé was overly inclined to wage another front porch campaign. "Do not *answer* Bryan, attack him!" he told the candidate. "Don't let him make the issues. . . . Hit them hard, old man!"

On November 4, Taft returned to Cincinnati, confident of a victory—more confident than he should have been. He won with only 51.6 percent of the popular vote, doing well in the urban states but falling short of Roosevelt's electoral achievement in others. Bryan, though still feared and reviled by business as a socialist, turned out to be more appealing to the Democrats than Parker had been four years earlier. His long years of riding the lecture circuits in remote areas had endeared him to many voters. He ended up capturing three states that had voted for Roosevelt, and he picked up votes from rural and urban areas that were economically distressed. In another blow to Taft, several midwestern states elected Democratic governors in 1908. Farmers, workers and small businessmen clearly distrusted Taft, and organized labor worked for the Democrats rather than the Socialists. The electoral vote was 321 to 162.

Although Taft had managed to align himself with the nation's prosperity and to convince voters that while he was not an inspiring choice, he was the best guarantor for restoring the nation to economic health, the election revealed cleavages within the Republican base that would prove fateful for his agenda. The party now had three main divisions: the old guard eastern industrial establishment, the urban progressives and the western agrarians. The political wind was shifting. It was Bryan's platform that would be enacted in the years to come.

———

Taft's inauguration on March 4, 1909, was enveloped by another blizzard that blanketed the capital with snow and ice, cutting off communication to the outside world and reducing crowds along the parade route to a handful. For the first time in sixty-three years, bad weather forced a new President to take the oath of office inside the Senate chamber.

For his part, Roosevelt was relinquishing the White House in a cloud of regrets and resentments over perceived slights from Taft, large and small. ("I knew there would be a blizzard when I went out," he joked, hours before he was to become a former President.) Among the presumed insults was Taft's decision to replace the frock-coated white ushers at the front door with liveried Negroes and to order some of these changes before the Roosevelts even moved out. Roosevelt told an associate that in office, Taft would do his best, "but he's weak." In a gesture of friendship, the Roosevelts invited the Tafts to dine with them at the White House on the eve of the inauguration and to spend the night. But the dinner was not a festive one. Taft noticed that Mrs. Roosevelt seemed depressed and later referred to the dinner as "that funeral."

The new President arrived with a fair amount of hope from both reformers and conservatives. Some progressives were even optimistic that the drive for reform could benefit from a new, more sedate atmosphere at the White House. "Roosevelt has cut enough hay," they said. "Taft is the man to put it into the barn." Conservatives were also hopeful, now that they had gotten rid of that "mad messiah," Roosevelt.

In his inaugural address, Taft promised to continue the successful policies of the previous twelve years. He made no reference to an income tax but pledged to combat "the lawlessness and abuses of power of the great combinations of capital" controlling railroads and business. In an encouraging development for progressives, he vowed to press for some tariff reductions, as well as a graduated inheritance tax to make up for lost revenues. He labeled such a tax "correct in principle and as certain and easy of collection."

Once installed at the White House, however, Taft felt no more comfortable occupying the office than he had in campaigning for it. He wrote to Roosevelt that when he was addressed as Mr. President, "I turn to see whether you are not at my elbow." Among associates, he kept referring to Roosevelt as "the President," even after Mrs. Taft asked him to try to stop. "He will always be the President to me, and I can never think of him as anything else," Taft confessed.

Although Taft's own mandate was not as sweeping as his predecessor's had been in 1904, the Republicans returned to Washington with a solid grip on Congress, a 214-to-175 margin in the House and a 60-to-32 one in the Senate. It was thus not going to be easy to bring about any changes in the tariff. A first sign of trouble over the iron control of the old guard in Congress came as Uncle Joe Cannon sought re-election as House Speaker. At least thirty Republicans were agitating to defeat him, and along with the Democrats, they could claim a majority to change the House rules to at least reduce the Speaker's powers. To the insurgents' dismay, Taft offered no support for such a change. The new President had no love for Cannon, but he hoped that by supporting him for Speaker, he might be able to work with him, as well as with Nelson Aldrich in the Senate. "What a fool I would be if I joined, or permitted myself to countenance, the yelping and snarling at Cannon and Aldrich," Taft said, explaining that the only way to make progress was to deal with the powers that be. But Taft's tactics, however defensible, were only the first sign of what would grow into an estrangement between him and the progressives.

Cannon was a wily practitioner of politics described by Taft's biographer, Henry Pringle, as part fraud and part genius. His public image was that of a crude, cracker-barrel philosopher who liked to spit tobacco, quote the Bible and tell off-color stories. Tall, erect and gray, he had the disconcerting habit of rolling his own big black cigars and chewing on them, leaving his lips smeared with tobacco shreds while trying to make a point with listeners. But there has probably never been a greater servant of the nation's corporate elite than Cannon as Speaker. Over the years, he managed to keep his troops in line through his control of committee memberships, including the all-powerful Rules Committee. Taft clearly disliked

Cannon but tried to keep his opinion to himself. "I have not said anything for publication," the President wrote Root, "but I am willing to have it understood that my attitude is one of hostility toward Cannon and the whole crowd unless they are coming in to do the square thing."

Taft's efforts to build a friendship with Aldrich were no less energetic. The Rhode Island Senator was sixty-eight years old, an imposing six-footer with penetrating, icy eyes, a reputation for discretion, an ironic sense of humor and a taste for luxurious surroundings and fine art. He had brazenly used his position as chairman of the Senate Finance Committee to enhance and expand his holdings in the banking, sugar, rubber, gas and electricity industries, all of which benefited from his firm stance in favor of protectionism. After serving in the Union Army and rising to the position of Speaker of the House in the Rhode Island legislature, he came to Washington and immediately joined a small coterie that ran the Senate's business and acquired power and wealth through a canny understanding of Senate rules. Using his unmatched skill at party fund-raising, Aldrich reaped contributions for himself and other senators by pushing legislation favorable to donors' interests, particularly the tariff bills of 1890, 1894 and 1897. His success fortified him in the belief that on tariff reduction, he could rebuff a President, not to mention popular will and the protests of a vocal minority in Congress. It was this formidable senator that Taft naively felt he could trust as a friend, "a man with whom I don't always agree, but whose effectiveness, straightforwardness and clearheadedness, and whose command of men everybody . . . must recognize."

Whereas Roosevelt had been at least somewhat skillful in dealing with the congressional barons, and certainly in the art of generating public pressure by use of the bully pulpit, Taft was an amateur. As Archie Butt, the President's military aide, wrote in his letters, many things about Taft could be explained by his "complacency." He shrank from Roosevelt's attempts to expand the powers of the presidency. He was suspicious of reformers and comfortable with the very wealthy men Roosevelt had found obnoxious. "He believes that many things left to themselves will bring about the same result as if he took a hand himself in their settlement," Butt observed later. "He acts with promptness and vigor when he has got to act, but he would rather delay trouble than seek it." Taft's innate conservatism compelled him to fill his cabinet with trusted corporation lawyers, another action that raised the ire of progressives. He replaced Roosevelt's aggressive Interior Secretary, James R. Garfield, with Richard Ballinger, a lawyer and former mayor of Seattle with an expertise in laws affecting mines. The new Secretary immediately became the focus of complaints that he was impeding an investigation into the allegedly corrupt awarding of coal-mining rights on public lands in Alaska.

Taft's greatest virtue, perhaps, was that he understood his limitations. He told Roosevelt in these early days that he hoped both Cannon and Aldrich would "stand by the party platform and follow my lead" in bringing about progressive change but admitted that he lacked the ability to educate the public on such issues. "I fear that a large part of the public will feel as if I had fallen away from your ideals," he concluded. "But you know me better and will understand that I am still working away on the same old plan."

Even Roosevelt would have had trouble enacting the "same old plan" himself, particularly tariff revision. The lingering recession had left the federal government with a $100 million budget deficit, the largest since the Civil War. Taft felt the deficit was an excellent argument in favor of lowering tariffs, since doing so would increase imports and bring in more revenue. In addition, since the turn of the century, the cost of living had risen significantly. Americans were increasingly putting the blame for the high cost of living on business cartels and their ability to keep cheaper imports out. "I believe the people are with me, and before I get through I think I will have downed Cannon and Aldrich too," he wrote in January of 1909, before taking office. Aldrich was not persuaded. Indeed, he questioned whether the party had ever made a commitment to do so. "Where did we ever make the statement that we would revise the tariff downward?" Aldrich asked, a comment Taft labeled "most unfortunate."

Much as Taft said he favored change, it was not his style to make demands. He quickly discovered that Representative Sereno Payne, the upstate New Yorker who served as chairman of the House Ways and Means Committee, owed everything to Cannon, not the new President. The tariff bill proposed by Payne actually increased tariffs on some goods (certain cotton fabrics, gloves, hosiery, plate glass and fruit) and imposed new duties on others. Taft was stunned by Payne's devotion to industry. He complained that the bill amounted to a tax on the breakfast table, on clothing and on other necessities of the middle class. As a form of mild pressure, he suggested that if tariffs were not lowered, Congress might wish to revive the idea of a corporate tax, but Payne rejected that step as harmful to the economy. The Ways and Means chairman made one important concession to progressive doctrine, however. He introduced the idea of an inheritance tax, designed to bring in $20 million for the federal treasury, on top of the $30 million estimated yield of the tariff changes. Modeled on a similar tax in New York, Payne's proposal provided for a tax of 1 to 5 percent, depending on the size of the bequest and the relationship of the heir to the deceased.

Dissatisfied with Payne's concession, progressives in the House opened their own drive for an income tax, hoping to attach it to the tariff legislation. One of their new arguments focused on the federal deficit. But a separate factor reflected the changing role of public expectations in a new century. The government over the decades had expanded to take on new responsibilities and new expenditures, ranging from pensions and debt costs from the Spanish-American War to such new federal activities as rural free delivery of mail, land reclamation and construction of the Panama Canal. New taxes of some kind were clearly needed for a new era. Leading the new effort was Representative Cordell Hull, a Tennessee Democrat and protégé of Benton McMillin, an author of the original income tax bill in 1894. Hull allied himself with the House minority leader, Kentucky Democrat Champ Clark, the lawyer and former newspaper editor who had earlier so enjoyed seeing the Republicans squirm when Theodore Roosevelt lectured them about the "wealth tax" on inheritances.

Both Hull and Clark knew they could not get their bill passed in the House, but they hoped to bring publicity to the cause and educate voters in the process. In his speeches, Hull, for example, referred to income tax laws passed in England, Prussia, Switzerland, Norway and Sweden. He argued in favor of re-enactment of the old 1894 law, minus the tax on state and municipal bonds, the one provision that the Supreme Court had decisively ruled as an unconstitutional infringement on state governments. A constitutional amendment was cumbersome and unrealistic, Hull warned. The existing tax system, he asserted, amounted to an "infamous system of class legislation" that burdened the average person while "virtually exempting the Carnegies, the Vanderbilts, the Morgans, and the Rockefellers, with their aggregated billions of hoarded wealth."

Hull's advocacy of the income tax came after several years of growing support for the idea in academic journals. In 1906 in the *North American Review,* for example, the tax was supported by Wayne MacVeagh, a former Attorney General in the Garfield administration, who argued that it was a mark of "singular stupidity" for capitalists to resist "every attempt to impose upon them their proper share of the public burdens." It was hardly revolutionary, he said, "to adopt a system of taxation which has been accepted by the most aristocratic and conservative legislative assemblage in the world—the House of Lords of Great Britain." At the University of Wisconsin, an economics professor named Delos O. Kinsman wrote an influential article in an academic journal in 1909 noting that there was a "spirit of reform now sweeping the country," with several states studying or setting up commissions to establish their own income taxes. Finally, Edward B. Whitney, a former assistant attorney general, argued in the *Harvard Law Review* in 1907 that while the Pollock decision of 1895 was deeply flawed, it would be better to adopt a constitutional amendment than to make another try at passing a law.

Proponents argued further that the tax would accomplish beneficial social purposes. The government, they noted, had expanded to take on new responsibilities and new expenditures. Financing the government was a newly urgent imperative. There would be other benefits to the tax. Even the fact that individuals would open their books to federal revenue inspection would lead to good behavior on the part of citizens, they said.

But as Hull and Clark had anticipated, Speaker Cannon blocked their efforts to attach the income tax to the tariff bill, which had evolved into a model of the legislative corruption that tended to surround tariff considerations in Congress. A typical example was the way that Representative Lucius N. Littauer of New York, a glove manufacturer, had managed to get Cannon to include a tariff on hosiery and gloves in the bill as a payoff for his earlier support for Cannon's re-election as Speaker. Taft nevertheless hoped that he could persuade Aldrich to accept the bill, which had only modest reductions on some goods, as it came out of the House.

Even those limited hopes were immediately dashed. Instead of going along with even the moderate lower tariffs of the Payne bill, as Taft had hoped, Aldrich moved to increase duties on everything from iron ore to raw flax, coal, print paper, iron and steel goods, lead products, lumber, fruits and silks. In all, he added no fewer than 847 tariff amendments, ending up with a bill that, by some measures, actually raised tariff rates overall from the all-time highs of the Dingley law enacted during the Spanish-American War. Where in the record, Aldrich again demanded to know, had the Republican Party ever committed itself to aiding the consumer as opposed to the big corporations that employed hardworking Americans? "I ask, who are the consumers?" he demanded further. "Is there any class except a very limited one that consumes and does not produce? And why are they entitled to greater consideration?" He rejected all suggestions to add either an income tax or a corporation tax and even deleted the inheritance tax that had been appended in the House.

But Aldrich underestimated the strength of the anti-tariff forces. He had dismissed opposition to high tariffs as rooted in a handful of states represented by demagogues. In fact, they were an extremely effective group.

The noisiest and most emotional of the progressives in the Senate lineup was Robert ("Fighting Bob") La Follette, former governor of Wisconsin, who had arrived in the Senate in 1906. Descended from French Huguenots, La Follette grew up on the family farm in Wisconsin and studied and practiced law in Madison, where his resonant voice, tall, thin frame and shock of dark hair made him a famous figure. He had ambitions to be an actor and had once won an interstate oratorical contest by reciting a speech by Iago in *Othello*. After election as district attorney in Dane County, La Follette went on to serve in the United States House of Representatives from 1885 to 1891 and won as the Republican candidate for governor in 1900. At the statehouse and later in the Senate, his speaking ability was legendary. It was routine for him to go on for hours, reciting reams of statistics to criticize unfair taxation and railroad rates and the strangling of the little people. While filibustering in the Senate to stop an emergency currency measure supported by Roosevelt, he began talking at noon and ended at seven o'clock the next morning, pausing only once to rush to the bathroom, exclaiming that he had had an attack of diarrhea. (He lost the fight, and Roosevelt called his theatrics "pointless and stupid.")

In 1908, La Follette had tried and failed to wrest the party's presidential nomination from Taft. Thereafter he set his sights on succeeding Taft in 1912. Clearly, in 1909, he had to oppose what

was now called the Payne–Aldrich tariff bill with its 847 amendments. He was joined in the fight by an impressive array of insurgent senators, many from the Midwest, who were responsive to
complaints from farmers about high prices. Among them were
Joseph Bristow of Kansas, Albert Cummins of Iowa, William E.
Borah of Idaho and some converts like Jonathan Dolliver of Iowa,
Moses Clapp of Minnesota and Albert J. Beveridge of Indiana.

With the help of Democrats, they divided Aldrich's bill into different parts and assigned one of their team to master each in preparation for the floor debate. La Follette produced tables to indicate
that in its entirety the bill raised tariffs by 1.5 percent, from what
was effectively a 40.21 percent tax on consumer goods to a new tax
that amounted to 41.77 percent. He and others advanced a new
argument as well, that free trade was good for the environment
because imports would reduce American exploitation of natural
resources by the oil, coal, lumber, iron and lead industries. "We are
not sovereign here," La Follette lectured the senators. "We are but
servants. The sovereigns are in the workshops, on the farms, in the
factories, in the stores and counting rooms. It is the average interests of the whole people we should serve, not certain special interests."

Throughout the Senate's deliberations, La Follette and the
other Republican progressives tried vainly to enlist Taft in their
cause. Reports circulated in Congress that Taft would veto the
Payne–Aldrich tariff and then that he would not. Senator Beveridge
of Indiana visited Taft in the White House and reported back that it
was useless to try to get Taft to oppose the bill. Talking to the President, he said, was like talking to a refrigerator. Later his hopes
lifted and he wrote his wife, "Saw Taft—he is with us." Still later he
realized that Taft was not going to intervene and that "the administration is doomed." For his part, Taft viewed Beveridge as a "selfish
pig" and remained of the opinion that the other rabble-rousers in
the progressive movement were demagogues.

The Senate, like the House, was also the scene of a renewed

drive to attach the income tax to the tariff. Leading that charge was Joseph Bailey of Texas, who had recently moved over to the Senate from the House. Bailey was a tall, powerfully built, free silver Democrat who borrowed heavily from Hull's research on the history of the income tax and also adopted the theme that an income tax was a sound alternative to the tariff as a vehicle to raise revenues. Bailey had a fierce style, melodious voice and a bit of a shady reputation. There were many stories about his past help for a subsidiary of Standard Oil in return for a $3,300 loan and his efforts as an attorney to a Texas lumber and oil baron for whom he helped secure the right to drill and cut trees on Indian territory.

Radicals also suspected Bailey of sabotaging Roosevelt's pure food bill of 1906, but Bailey was also an extremely effective debater on behalf of the tax. Arguing that the $60 million to be raised by the tax was needed to close the $100 million deficit, he proposed a 3 percent tax on incomes in excess of $5,000, exempting income from bonds issued by states and local governments, hoping (as Hull had hoped) to circumvent the Supreme Court's constitutional objections fourteen years earlier. The job of government, Bailey argued, was to protect property and maintain order, both of which benefited the rich perhaps more immediately than others. "If I were counsel for the rich," Bailey said, "the first advice that I would tender them would be to advocate a law like this." An income tax, he concluded, "would do more to silence the envious voice of anarchy than all the benefactions and the charities which they can do."

In a memorandum to the economic historians Roy G. Blakey and Gladys C. Blakey, Cordell Hull later praised Bailey's presentation as "a remarkable speech of two hours and a half, with the floor and galleries completely filled every moment of the time. . . . After his speech the income tax movement flared up noticeably throughout the Nation." But Hull also noted that support for the tax derived from growing anxiety in the South and West over the high cost of living, trusts and business combinations, high tariffs and other pressures on the middle class. For lawmakers from those regions, taxing wealth was a way of redressing the balance by spreading sacrifice to the fortunes in the Northeast.

Bailey's arguments for the tax were joined by an equally persuasive presentation from Senator Borah. Newly elected but nationally famous for having prosecuted "Big Bill" Heywood and other radical labor leaders in the murder of former Governor Frank Steunenberg in Idaho, Borah argued forcefully that the Supreme Court had been incorrect in defining the income tax as a direct tax in the Pollock case. He called for the tax to be resubmitted to a new court.

Recalling that Senator John Sherman had predicted in the 1870s that an income tax would eventually become necessary because of the growth of American wealth, Borah said sarcastically that Sherman was hardly someone "given to radicalism [or] socialism." At stake, he declared, was not simply the need to raise "a little revenue for the Government for the next few years" but a principle that government could raise the necessary resources for its own survival. The framers of the Constitution, he asserted, never intended that the tax burden fall "upon the backs of those who toil" while exempting "the great accumulated wealth of the Nation" from federal taxes. "This cannot be true," the senator concluded. "It was never so intended; it was a republic they were building, where all men were to be equal and bear equally the burdens of government, and not an oligarchy, for that must a government be, in the end, which exempts property and wealth from all taxes."

As support grew for the Bailey income tax bill, Senator Albert Cummins of Iowa—another tall, energetic and magnetic personality—advanced a rival approach calling for a graduated tax on individual, not corporate, income, with a rate rising to 6 percent on earnings over $100,000. Putting aside their egos for the sake of the cause, he and Bailey agreed in May to join forces on a bill to tax both corporate and individual incomes over $5,000 at a flat rate of either 2 or 3 percent. There was to be a rebate to prevent double taxation for individual income from corporations. Bailey at first threatened to shut down the Senate if a time were not set for consideration of his bill, proposed as an amendment to the tariff.

Playing for time, Aldrich moved to put it off to June, hoping to send it to the Finance Committee for a suitable burial. Despite complaints by Bailey about "postponement after postponement," Aldrich's motion carried. Cummins was furious, since he had earlier warned Bailey against premature action. "The two income tax leaders looked across at each other with flushed faces and lowering brows," said the New York World on May 28.

The tax debate soon became even more complicated, thanks to a new factor introduced by Senator Norris Brown of Nebraska. To overcome objections that the income tax bill was unconstitutional, he proposed a resolution calling for a constitutional amendment permitting an income tax rather than a change in the law. Brown's proposal had one advantage for income tax foes: it would consign the bill to an uphill struggle to win approval in three-quarters of the state legislatures. Aldrich, however, was unimpressed. He remained fearful that the drive to lower tariffs and attach an income tax was gathering strength. The real threat, in his view, was that an income tax would raise enough revenues to support the federal government and lead to the destruction of the protective system altogether.

To Aldrich, the twin evils of lowering the tariff and enacting the income tax raised the specter of machinery stopping, iron furnaces being snuffed out and industries lying prostrate. In the words of Senator Chauncey Depew of New York, chairman of the New York Central board, the tax was "the most direct possible attack upon the protective system," unjustified except in times of war.

Having fought against lower tariffs, Aldrich now found himself fighting on another front, against the income tax, which he declared "was supported by the Socialist party, by the Populist party, and by the Democratic party with a few honorable exceptions, simply as a means for redistribution of wealth." Protectionism was good, not bad, for workers, he declared. But the Rhode

Island senator was also increasingly hammered by criticism that he had overplayed his hand by adding 847 amendments to the tariff bill. "The protectionist ship is a pretty staunch old craft," said the *New York Times*. "But, really, Senator Aldrich is steering her straight upon the rocks."

At the White House, Taft was unsure about how to respond to the fracas in the Senate. The swirl of pressures around him was made all the harder by the health of his wife, Nellie. The Tafts often retreated from the White House for rides on the Potomac River and vacations in Beverly, Massachusetts, on the North Shore. On May 17, Mrs. Taft suffered an abrupt stroke on board the presidential yacht, *Sylph*, on the Potomac. The Attorney General, George Wickersham, was talking with her when suddenly she fainted. Archie Butt, the President's military aide, recalled later that Taft went "deathly pale" and "looked like a great stricken animal." She spent several months recovering.

Taft had to decide which of the five separate proposals on taxes and tariffs in the Senate he should support. They were the Payne tariff bill passed by the House, which revised the tariff system moderately downward; the Aldrich version of the Payne bill, with its 847 amendments; the Bailey income tax bill; the Bailey–Cummins compromise income tax bill; and Senator Brown's joint resolution for a constitutional amendment for an income tax.

The balance of power in the Senate was clearly shifting. Although Aldrich might have been able to stop tariff reduction, the income tax seemed to be gaining ground. Senator Henry Cabot Lodge wrote to Theodore Roosevelt that proponents of the tax "had the votes" to pass it. That assessment reached the White House when Cummins and Borah informed Taft that they had the votes of at least nineteen Republicans who, with all the Democrats, could pass a bill. Alarmed that Taft might yield and support the tax legislation, Aldrich rushed to the White House on May 24, along with Lodge and Senator W. Murray Crane of Massachusetts, to beg for help in blocking the tax. As Taft later recalled, the three senators "came to appeal to me to save them from that situation." It was a "rude awakening" for the President, said the *New York World*.

What happened next is not clear. The only certainty is that both Taft and Aldrich emerged from the meeting with a decision to investigate the possibility of a corporation tax as a possible alternative to the income tax. Taft's biographer, Henry Pringle, describes the President's manner as "suave" as he proposed the corporation tax as a compromise. Other accounts suggest that it was Aldrich's idea. Their plan was to persuade the hard-line Republican senators to agree to a corporation tax and convince supporters of the income tax to press for a constitutional amendment rather than tax legislation that would force the Supreme Court to rule.

The compromise had the advantage of addressing Taft's desire not to challenge the Supreme Court and create a potential crisis regarding the legitimacy of an institution he revered and still hoped to join someday as a justice. Taft had earlier thought that an income tax could be drafted in a way that would meet the court's objections, but he changed his mind when presented with an opportunity to avoid another rebuff like the 1895 Pollock ruling. "Nothing has ever injured the prestige of the Supreme Court more than that last decision," the President told an associate, adding that "many of the most violent advocates of the income tax" would be glad to avoid its repetition.

Taft was fortified in this view by Senator Root, who warned that if popular pressure made the Supreme Court change its mind on the income tax, the court's reputation for integrity would be damaged in the public's eyes. If, on the other hand, the court reiterated its rejection of the income tax, he added, popular anger would undermine "the independence, the dignity, the respect, the sacredness of that great tribunal."

Although Aldrich suspected that a constitutional amendment would fail to win ratification, he made a last-ditch effort to dilute the agreement by limiting the corporation tax to two years. Taft, however, "was enjoying the sweet sensation—it would be all too brief—of being in the saddle," Pringle writes. The President simply noted that Aldrich's proposal would not stop the nineteen Republicans from voting for the income tax. The next day Aldrich withdrew his objection. Taft wrote to his brother Horace, "The situation is not one of my yielding to Aldrich, but of Aldrich yielding to me."

In early June, the heat in Washington was torrid and the air was heavy with humidity in the Senate chamber. Rumors were flying about the discussions between the Senate and the White House. Taft sent a message to Congress on June 16, explaining that the corporation excise tax would be imposed on "the privilege of doing business as an artificial entity," with a potential yield of $25 million. Warning of the dangers of budget deficits, he said the only safe way of imposing an income tax was to enact a constitutional amendment. The 2 percent corporate tax, however, had the additional advantage of preventing "a further abuse of power" by corporations because of government "supervisory control" through the tax system.

Taft's message provoked an inevitable outcry in conservative quarters, with the *Hartford Times* warning that it was "a hook in the nose of every big corporation in the country" and tantamount to the sort of "drastic power" that had been advocated by both Roosevelt and Bryan. Conservatives managed to get a few provisions cut back so that the bill exempted small corporations, savings banks and some holding companies. But at a White House dinner with reluctant members of the Senate Finance Committee, both Taft and Aldrich explained bluntly that the corporation tax was the only way of preventing something worse.

"This is the very distressing and embarrassing alternative and there is no other," said one senator.

"Yes, that is exactly it," replied Aldrich.

Yet in spite of the genius of the Aldrich–Taft compromise, it would not be easy to get the pro–income tax forces to agree to the corporate tax. Democratic supporters of the income tax were "madder than hornets," said the *New York World*. Republicans and progressives like Borah, Cummins and La Follette said that while they would support the route of a constitutional amendment, they would not back off their drive to enact an income tax by passing a law. "A tax upon the net income of corporations alone will very imperfectly reach the desired result," they said in a statement. "It will tax tens of thousands of stockholders whose total incomes are very small, and will exempt in large measure the immense personal incomes of the country." Their principal argument was that corporations would simply shift the cost to consumers by charging higher prices. As for the compromise on the income tax, Borah also warned that it would take only twelve states to block ratification of the constitutional amendment.

Historians have generally described President Taft as an aloof, if not bumbling, chief executive. On this issue, at least, he actively lobbied to get the compromise passed. As Aldrich took wavering senators on long evening rides through Rock Creek Park, Taft invited them for golf games, leisurely walks, car drives and dinner on the White House terrace. To senators, he argued that the compromise before the Senate was the only way to heal the Republican Party rift, and to business lobbyists unreconciled to the tax, he stressed that popular sentiment could no longer be ignored. Congress, he explained, faced a choice over which kind of tax to impose, not whether there should be any tax at all. The President's military aide, Archie Butt, described a meeting between Elihu Root, now a senator from New York, and Taft's Attorney General, George Wickersham, on the drafting of the tax proposal.

"Well, George," said Root, "for a man who has always eschewed politics of all kinds, you certainly have got knee deep in it."

Wickersham replied that Taft was the one who was knee deep. With some satisfaction, he observed that it had been "a long time since Congress has come to the White House for its advice."

Still fearing that Senator Bailey would try to get an income tax law passed in the Senate, Aldrich sought a delay to build up support for the Taft-backed alternative. Then when Bailey was absent, he let Lodge introduce an innocuous amendment on the tariff. Without warning, he quickly substituted that amendment with one drafted at the Justice Department under Wickersham's supervision, calling for a special excise tax of 2 percent on net incomes over $5,000 for corporations. His purpose was to force a vote approving the corporation tax before Bailey could introduce his income tax proposal. He succeeded; Bailey was outfoxed.

"I shall vote for a corporation tax as a means to defeat the income tax," Aldrich told the Senate, perhaps stating the obvious. He said he was "willing to accept" something he disliked rather than adopt "a great evil" that would "destroy the protective system."

Senator Root acknowledged that many critics would accuse him of voting for the corporation tax as the lesser of two evils. "I care not," he declared. "I am for the corporation tax because I think it is better policy, better patriotism, higher wisdom than the general income tax at this time and under these circumstances."

In the end, the Senate passed the Aldrich tariff with the corporate tax on July 7, voting 45 to 34. Bailey's alternative of an income tax was now all but dead.

When the tariff and corporation tax bill reached the House–Senate Conference Committee, its 847 Senate amendments met with furious objections by House members who had advocated lower tariffs. In addition, Representative Payne expressed distaste for the corporation tax and got it reduced from 2 to 1 percent. Taft hoped that the conferees would at least eliminate some of the higher tariffs added by the Senate but picked his targets with caution, concentrating on trying to get a few reductions on scattered items like hides, gloves, hosiery and lumber. "I am not a high-tariff man, I am a low-tariff man," the President insisted to a friend.

But Cannon refused to budge, in what Taft called "the greatest exhibition of tyranny that I have known." A standoff between Speaker and President over this handful of reductions led Cannon briefly to threaten an adjournment. Calling his bluff for once, Taft threatened to summon the House back. He then went off to play golf and join some friends for dinner. When the news arrived that the conferees had indeed agreed to lower duties on lumber and gloves as he had requested, Taft told his dinner companions, "Well, good friends, this makes me happy." But these concessions to Taft were almost absurdly minor.

In retrospect, Taft's biggest mistake in these maneuverings was not pressing his advantage further with Aldrich and Cannon to get them to accept further tariff reductions. After all, the conservatives were on the defensive. But Taft, for all his self-satisfaction on the tax issue, was too much of a trusting amateur when it came to dealing with Aldrich and Cannon and their allies on the tariff. He regarded it as inappropriate for a President to interfere excessively with the legislative process. He was also clearly uncomfortable allying himself with the Republican insurgents, with their blend of radicalism and fiery personalities. When someone suggested that he threaten to veto the bill, Taft dismissed the idea as "cheap publicity" that would wreck the party and "leave us in a mess out of which I do not see how we could get." He needed the Republican congressional leadership for too many other things, and besides, the measure did contain some tariff reductions and, of course, the corporation tax.

The House approved the final bill on July 31 by a relatively narrow vote, 195 to 183, with Speaker Cannon corralling uncertain Republicans. In the Senate, Bailey warned that the measure was an attempt by business "to rob and plunder industrious consumers." But Aldrich prevailed in the Senate in August, as Cannon had in the House.

In signing the bill, Taft asserted that the measure represented "a sincere effort on the part of the Republican party to make a downward revision." He said further that it lowered rates on goods valued at $5 billion a year and increased them on goods worth $600 million a year, half of which were luxury goods. Some estimates of its schedules did suggest that it brought rates down to an average of 37 percent ad valorem, compared to 40.21 percent for the Dingley tariff and the 41.77 that La Follette had said was the original cost of the bill. But progressive Republicans, Democrats and many neutral economists disputed the idea that the new law did anything to reduce tariffs. Instead, there was considerable credibility to the charge that the increases in tariffs far outweighed the reductions. Champ Clark, the House Democratic leader, estimated that the average increase on tariffs overall was 1.7 percent. Some pro-tariff Republicans actually agreed and, in fact, argued that the tariff hike was even higher than Clark's estimate.

Politically, the tariff bill was a bitter pill for Taft. But there is no question that the twin legacies of 1909—the corporation tax and the beginning of the drive to amend the constitution for an income tax—were of far-reaching consequence. Except in the Civil War, there had never been a broadly applied federal tax on corporate profits. The 1894 income tax, which had a provision for taxing corporations, was declared unconstitutional before it could get implemented. During the Spanish-American War, Congress had enacted a minuscule tax on gross receipts for oil-refining and sugar companies, a tax the Supreme Court upheld. That decision guided the drafters of the new tax.

The new tax of 1 percent on net income applied to corporations, joint stock companies or associations and insurance companies. Although its aim was to tax income, it was characterized in the law as an excise tax on the privilege of doing business as a corporation. The purpose of that language was to avoid any possibility of the Supreme Court declaring it unconstitutional on the same grounds that it had cited regarding the 1894 income tax. The tax also exempted nonprofit organizations, such as labor and farm organizations, domestic building and loan associations and charitable and religious units. Net income was reckoned to be what was left after the deduction of operating expenses, losses, interest payments, dividend income from other corporations that paid the tax and federal and local taxes. Corporations had to file a return by March 1 of each year for the previous year, containing a great variety of information about debt, income, expenses, losses, depreciation, taxes and other payments to be deducted. Penalties would be imposed for false returns. Returns filed with the Internal Revenue Bureau were also open for public inspection.

Though it set an important precedent, the tax itself was a sop to prevent more radical action. Taft was pleased with it, and the tax did help reduce the federal deficit as hoped, yielding almost $21 million in 1909. Until the corporation tax was included in the income tax act of 1913, it produced from 3.4 percent to 5.1 percent of total federal revenues a year. Had the income tax passed, its revenues would have brought in considerably more.

Nevertheless, those paying the corporation tax were anything but reconciled to it. They especially did not like the reporting requirements, the penalties for false statements and public access to their income statements. Taft's Treasury Secretary, Franklin MacVeagh, was sympathetic to their complaints, asking Taft at one point whether the President would not resent opening his own books to the government if he were a small businessman.

"I would not mind in the least," replied Taft. "Would you?"

"I certainly would," said the Treasury Secretary, "and I would do all I could to evade the law."

"Mr. MacVeagh," Taft replied, "I am in favor of letting the law work out as it was framed to do."

Subsequently, Taft agreed to restrict public disclosure of tax returns but stood firmly behind the tax. That was important. Businesses campaigned for repeal of the tax, filing lawsuits and attacking it in every forum. Republicans, though seizing on the corporate tax as a safe harbor against the income tax, hoped to repeal it eventually or try to get it declared unconstitutional. In March 1911, however, the Supreme Court upheld the law, declaring it not an income tax but an excise tax on the privilege of doing business in a corporate capacity. The court also dismissed objections that the open inspection of tax returns violated the Fourth Amendment's ban on "unreasonable searches and seizures."

Historians seem less impressed with the logic of the court than with the simple fact that its makeup had changed since the rejection of the income tax in 1895, along with popular sentiment and the overall balance of power in the United States. In their ruling, the justices seemed quite aware that the country was now demanding measures to advance the principles of equity and welfare—and that even conservatives like President Taft favored steps to prevent social discord.

As for the proposed constitutional route toward approval of an income tax, the congressional resolution calling for an amendment passed with much less discussion. There had been various proposals on its wording. Senator Norris Brown's resolution said that Congress "shall have the power to lay and collect direct taxes on income without apportionment among the several States according to population." Responding to fears that the court might find some kind of loophole and reject the tax, the Finance Committee simplified the language to read: "The Congress shall have power to lay and collect taxes on incomes, from whatever source derived, without apportionment among the several States, and without regard to any census or enumeration."

Anticipating problems down the road, Senator Bailey of Texas proposed that the amendment be approved in state conventions, as the Constitution permits, rather than by state legislatures, many of which were gerrymandered and dominated by political machines that could be bought off by wealthy interests. He also wanted the amendment to make it clear that graduated rates would be permitted. Both initiatives were defeated, and the Finance Committee's language passed the Senate by a vote of 77 to 0, with 15 abstentions, and in the House by 318 to 14.

The adoption of what would become the Sixteenth Amendment to the Constitution in 1913 was anything but a moment of celebration for tax proponents. Among the most pessimistic of the lawmakers was Senator La Follette, who declared, "The success of any given amendment is very improbable."

———

Following the enactment of the excise tax and the constitutional amendment procedure, Taft came under increasing political pressure from the antiprotectionist forces in his party. In response, he set up a Tariff Board to collect data on production costs at home and abroad and determine whether foreign manufacturers had unfair competitive advantages over their American counterparts. But he was dealing with forces larger than he could control. The entire tariff battle had widened the cleavage between the progressives and the old guard, the wing that Taft was identified with. Despite his solid record in prosecuting trusts and business collusion, including the tobacco and Standard Oil combines, the public was not to give Taft credit.

A new flood of problems for Taft began when he signed the tariff and tax legislation into law, particularly because of his assertion that the measure represented "a downward revision" in the tariff. The public did not experience any decline in the cost of living. Much of the criticism focused on "Schedule K," which kept high tariffs, and high prices, on wool and other vital commodities, lending credence to the charge that the Republicans were responsible for the high cost of clothing. The letter K became an evil symbol in editorial cartoons. In fact, the duties on wool were not really increased by the Payne–Aldrich Act, but Representative Sereno Payne himself complained that clothing store advertisements were asserting that their prices were going up 20 to 50 percent because of the bill. Taft soon admitted that the wool tariff was one of the bill's biggest defects.

Taft also got into a politically damaging debate with the newspapers, which wanted a lower tariff on imported paper. Many newspapers imported paper from Canada, and the failure to reduce their costs was portrayed by them as a deadly blow. Publishers went on the warpath, depicting the President as an enemy of the working class. Their anger grew even louder when Taft proposed increases in newspaper postal rates in 1909. The political storm would have been tough for any politician to handle, but was especially difficult for someone with Taft's awkwardness.

Traveling the country to try to sell his policies at the end of his first year in office, Taft strove manfully to convince skeptics that the new tariff was an improvement. But his tour was filled with almost comical errors. In New York, he was criticized for taking time out to have dinner with Henry Clay Frick, the steel magnate. In Boston, he was ridiculed for his praise of Aldrich as one of the "ablest statesmen in financial matters in either House." In Wisconsin, he never bothered to praise the popular senator, La Follette. Then in Winona, Minnesota, lacking a prepared text, Taft asserted in a speech at the local opera house that, contrary to popular perception, the Republicans had never actually promised to lower tariffs. "On the whole, however," he added, "I am bound to say that I think the Payne bill is the best bill that the Republican Party ever passed."

Eight or nine newspaper correspondents flashed the news, producing headlines across the country that Taft had proclaimed the new law the "best tariff in history." A couple of years later, Taft rued his words, and at the time the public reaction was calamitous. In retrospect, there is almost something endearing about Taft's oaflike manner. In Colorado, a welcoming committee that included representatives of the Woman's Christian Temperance Union gave him a dish of trout. Taft jokingly asked if the fish could make someone drunk, shocking the ladies and prompting Taft to complain later that "the good women who head the temperance movement are usually totally devoid of humor." In another town, he was presented a special huge bathtub but declined the invitation to put on a bathing suit and use it in front of the public. Taft had begun his long trip on September 14, traveled to the West Coast and ended up back in Washington on November 10—259 speeches and many, many meals later. (Observers noted that if anything, he appeared even stouter than before.)

"I cannot be mistaken in finding that the people are very friendly to me," he wrote. "I venture to think that our friends, the insurgents, will find this fact more and more apparent as the campaign for the next Congress comes on."

Once again, Taft failed to see the changes unfolding around him.

CHAPTER NINE

—⁓—

"It Will Lighten the Burdens of the Poor"

The Sixteenth Amendment Is Ratified

AFTER HIS AFRICAN SAFARI AND A FLAMBOYANT tour of speechmaking and visits with royalty in Europe, Theodore Roosevelt returned to the United States in the summer of 1910. More than a year had passed since he left office, and the former President was nearly desperate to break his silence on what he viewed as the feckless performance of his successor. Taft had "totally misunderstood the character of the movement which we now have to face in American life," he told Henry Cabot Lodge. When he got to Washington, Roosevelt drove the point home. He snubbed the President by turning down an invitation to the White House.

Taft's blunders on conservation incensed Roosevelt the most. In his view, the President's clumsiest mistake was replacing Roosevelt's Interior Secretary, James Garfield, with Richard Ballinger, who had promptly become a central figure in a scandal over favoritism shown to the Morgan–Guggenheim coal syndicate in Alaska. Taft not only backed the Secretary but also removed the legendary chief of the Forest Service, Gifford Pinchot, for siding with Ballinger's accusers. Roosevelt had met with his friend Pinchot in Portugal before his return to the United States and was alarmed by the reports of Taft's perfidy. Eventually the coal deal was canceled, but the political damage remained.

Roosevelt was also upset over Taft's failure to back the Republican reformers in the House trying to clip the wings of Speaker Cannon. He had other complaints about Taft's removal of some of his friends in the administration, but for all these grievances, Roosevelt managed to overlook an inconvenient fact: Taft had actually accomplished many things that he had not. Seeking to placate the party's dissidents, Taft included many progressives in his administration, extended the Civil Service to cover more positions, reformed the federal budget process, selected decent federal judges, established a savings system for small deposits through the postal service and created the Customs Court and the Bureau of Mines. More significant, and contrary to some popular perceptions, Taft had prosecuted trusts at least as aggressively as Roosevelt, as measured by suits filed and judgments won.

What had thrown Taft's presidency and the Republican Party into disarray was his inept maneuvering over the tariff and the income tax. In this crucial area, Taft's record was no better than Roosevelt's, but it was also no worse. Despite Roosevelt's sympathy for reformers in Congress, as President he had never taken on Speaker Cannon, Senator Aldrich and the other guardians of high tariff barriers in Congress. He, too, had advocated an income tax but had done nothing to achieve it. It was Taft who finally won the adoption of the corporation tax and—while trying to please the old guard on customs duties—backed the passage in Congress of a resolution calling for adoption of the Sixteenth Amendment, which allowed the enactment of an income tax.

In style, Taft was as different from Roosevelt as a politician could be. He talked repeatedly about how much he admired the man who had chosen him for public service and helped elevate him to the office he now held. But Taft also wanted to achieve a record of his own by working within the party's structure. It just so happened that this very structure was crumbling under the weight of the progressive revolt over the trust, tariff and tax issues. Whenever Taft tried to placate one group or another, his actions always seemed to backfire.

After the debacle of the Payne–Aldrich tariff, Taft tried to correct the perception that he supported high customs duties, and therefore high prices, by negotiating a reciprocal trade agreement with Canada. But that step only angered the corn and wheat growers who favored lower tariffs on consumer goods but not on farm products that would compete with what they were producing. Free traders in Congress tried again in 1911 to remove the duties on a hundred articles bought by farmers. They also attempted to lower the duties on wool, which even Taft admitted was overly protected, and to reduce the tariffs on cotton goods, chemicals, iron and steel. All these efforts died in Congress or were vetoed by Taft.

As Roosevelt watched Taft's problems increase, he thought at first that he could work his personal magic and reunite the Republicans under his own leadership. The former President decided to tour the country in 1910, just as the congressional election was heating up, to put forward some ideas—many of them advocated by Herbert Croly in his book *The Promise of American Life*, published the previous year—around which Republicans might rally.

In Ossawatomie, Kansas, on September 1, Roosevelt delivered a seminal speech on "The New Nationalism," setting forth what amounted to a revolutionary thesis. Attacking the Supreme Court for its probusiness decisions, Roosevelt called for the federal government to elevate "human welfare" over property rights. "Every man," said Roosevelt, "holds his property subject to the general right of the community to regulate its use to whatever degree the public welfare may require it." He called for protection of workers, regulation of corporations and, as he had many times as President, the graduated income tax. But far from uniting the G.O.P., the speech threw Taft and other Republicans into a state of shock and panic. What had happened to the former President while he was shooting wild game in Africa? Senator Henry Cabot Lodge told Roosevelt, his old friend, that intentionally or not, he was coming across in Washington as "little short of a revolutionist."

But Roosevelt was riding a tide of changing public sentiment. A great wave of progressive thought developing for a decade crested in the 1910 midterm elections, which delivered a devastating repudiation to Taft and the party establishment. Democrats captured control of the House and won most of the gubernatorial races. Republican progressives returned to Washington with more strength than ever. They included Senators Robert La Follette of Wisconsin, Jonathan Dolliver and Albert Cummins of Iowa, Albert Beveridge of Indiana, Moses Clapp of Minnesota, Joseph Bristow of Kansas and William Borah of Idaho. La Follette led them to form a National Progressive Republican League and plan to challenge Taft for the party's presidential nomination in 1912.

Despite these positive signs, Roosevelt was depressed because he could not see a clear path for himself for a comeback to the White House. At times, he seemed to prefer that Taft run again and be defeated, making it possible for him to capture the nomination in 1916. Other times he worried about the Democrats winning and bringing radical policies to Washington. He looked on La Follette and the progressive Republicans as not "big enough" for "national scale" politics. Taft handed Roosevelt a final excuse to run, but it was an ironic one. The President authorized his Justice Department in late 1911 to challenge United States Steel over its earlier acquisition of the Tennessee Coal and Iron Company—the very step that Roosevelt had approved to secure Morgan's help in the Panic of 1907. It was an obvious rebuke of the former President. Within a month, Roosevelt was encouraging friends to explore the chances of his wresting the G.O.P. nomination from Taft in 1912. They presented a petition for him to run, but it had actually been crafted at Oyster Bay. Then in Ohio in February 1912, Roosevelt announced, "My hat is in the ring."

The election year was enlivened by another factor that worked against Taft—mounting public anxiety over the concentration of power in the banking world. The new focus of progressive anger was the supposed depredations of the "money trust," uncovered during 1912 by the House Committee on Banking and Currency, led by Representative Arsene P. Pujo of Louisiana and his brilliant counsel, Samuel Untermyer. Their probe showed how a handful of banks—particularly the House of Morgan, First National Bank, National City Bank and the Bankers and Guaranty Trust Companies—held at least 341 directorships in 112 corporations in banking, railroads, utilities and other businesses, "a vast and growing concentration of control of money and credit in the hands of a comparatively few men." Voters tended to look on this concentration not as a remote abstract power but, along with high tariffs, as another force responsible for the rising cost of living that Taft was unwilling or unable to do anything about.

Fighting back against Roosevelt's challenge, however, Taft sprang into uncharacteristic action. He wielded the levers of power, patronage and party loyalty to defend himself at the party convention. Roosevelt's strategy was to win a number of primaries and thereby convince party leaders that, while they might be more sympathetic philosophically to Taft, he himself was the only Republican who could retain the White House. He did win several primaries in 1912—in Illinois, Pennsylvania and even Taft's home state of Ohio. But in the process, his campaign grew more strident, which frightened many of his old comrades, including Lodge and Elihu Root, who stuck with Taft. Mirroring the party's civil war around the country, the Republican convention in Chicago in July collapsed several times into fistfights, screaming matches, delegate challenges, lockouts and disruptions, as well as charges by Roosevelt that the party was seating fraudulent delegates. Taft, in control of the delegates if not the popular sentiments of Republicans, won the nomination easily.

On paper, the Taft Republican platform tried to sound progressive, with calls for labor laws, workmen's compensation and conservation. It favored high tariffs as vital to industry and to the preservation of jobs, but it also advocated a federal trade commission to police the marketplace. The problem was that the party's rotund standard-bearer himself was the issue for too many voters. True, the country was still prosperous and the G.O.P. had settled in as the party of government. It had not lost a presidential election in twenty years. But Taft, as a passive conservative leading a nation that was yearning for action and becoming more reformist, seemed to recognize that his party's time was up. So did the G.O.P.'s traditional backers, who scraped together less than $1 million in campaign funds, half the normal amount.

Roosevelt, meanwhile, resolved immediately after his walkout from the Republican convention to take the nomination of the National Progressive Party, which also met in Chicago—though conspicuously without La Follette, who was furious over what he viewed as the hijacking of his cause and coalition by the former President. At a wild gathering that was more revival meeting than convention, the Progressives gave Roosevelt a thundering ovation of fifty-two minutes when he first appeared and an even louder one for his closing peroration: "We stand at Armageddon and we battle for the Lord." Roosevelt's acceptance speech was an astonishing vision of the welfare state that would not be put forward again until another Roosevelt captured the White House two decades later.

Among the reformers in the hall were Jane Addams of Hull House and Harold L. Ickes, a young urban Progressive and later New Dealer. There were some who felt that Roosevelt, a wild-animal-slaying war hero, was a little out of place with all those earlier-day flower children, but his self-righteous tone was in perfect harmony with their high-minded hopes. He endorsed all the reforms in the Progressive platform and assailed the Democratic and Republican Parties as favoring government of "the rich few." The platform called for referendums on laws declared unconstitutional by state courts and curbs on injunctions against strikes, as well as for "strong national regulation" of corporations, securities, the farming sector and public health.

On other issues, however, Roosevelt's policies differed from those of the reformers. Progressives tended to favor breaking up the trusts. The former President favored allowing them to exist but with strict government regulation. With this semitolerant attitude, he retained the support of many in the financial world, particularly those who feared that a Democratic President would wage war on capitalism. Indeed, some of Roosevelt's Wall Street backers, such as George W. Perkins, a partner of J. P. Morgan, thought the former President was more sympathetic toward trusts than Taft, and he persuaded Roosevelt to soft-pedal his talk on the subject. (In return, Perkins and other corporate backers brought in campaign donations from their business friends.)

Roosevelt was also conflicted over the tariff. Like the Republicans, he linked the need for some tariffs with the preservation of jobs in American factories, another position at variance with progressive orthodoxy. But on one issue the former President was clear: the source of the revenues needed for the muscular new government he envisioned. Reaching back to his philosophy as President, and to his distrust of the power of excessive wealth, Roosevelt again embraced the idea of taxing wealth—specifically, taxing incomes and inheritances.

On the campaign trail, Roosevelt looked heavier than he had some years earlier but no less feisty, with his high-pitched voice, flashing smile, thrust-out jaw and stabbing gestures. Declaring himself as fit as a bull moose, he once again came up with an enduring nickname, this time for the party. Though some, like La Follette, remained unreconciled to his takeover of the progressive movement and unwilling to support him, Roosevelt had a formula with solid appeal, not only in the urban East but in the farming West, among women (who had gained the right to vote in several states) and in the newly emerging class of consumers, workers, small businessmen and professionals. But his only realistic hope for victory was for the Democrats to nominate a weak candidate or one too far to the left for the centrist vote. It was up to the Democrats, then, to seize the moment presented by the Republican fratricide.

———

One sure way for the Democrats to squander their opportunity was to nominate William Jennings Bryan as their presidential candidate for the fourth time since 1896. Luckily for them, the bombastic Great Commoner, whose every word seemed to rattle the teeth of moderates, decided to lay down his lance this time around.

The Democrats still had to surmount their own factional divisions. With a conservative, moderately probusiness establishment pitted against reformers, populists from the South and West and the old but increasingly left-leaning political machines of the big cities, the party desperately needed someone who had a foot in all its camps. In Baltimore, where the Democrats met for their convention in the summer of 1912, four candidates were in contention: the down-home House Speaker, Champ Clark of Missouri; the conservative governor of Ohio, Judson Harmon; Representative Oscar W. Underwood of Alabama, a one-time populist who had moved to the right; and the most intriguing, an articulate but frosty-looking former president of Princeton University elected two years earlier as the reform governor of New Jersey, Woodrow Wilson.

Wilson had eyed the nomination for some time, stumping the country and giving speeches denouncing special privilege and calling for a new day in Washington. His record as a lecturer, scholar and cogent analyst of American politics brought something new to the table. He also had a reputation as a sharp moralizer and an executive sympathetic but not beholden to the vested powers of the party. With a father and grandfather on his mother's side who were Presbyterian preachers, he had grown up in an atmosphere of religious instruction, worship and desire to serve. No President since Lincoln was to identify himself more fervently as on the side of God, though he did not flinch from wily maneuvering and alliances with political bosses to get what he wanted.

Another factor in Wilson's favor as a candidate was that as the son of a preacher who had moved from place to place in the South, he regarded himself as a southerner and was indeed steeped in nostalgia for the Confederacy. Courtly, indifferent to the injustices suffered by blacks, gracious and capable of kind gestures, Wilson traveled easily among the party's southern populists. After studying at Davidson College in North Carolina and at Princeton, then a Presbyterian school called the College of New Jersey, Wilson toyed with going into the ministry but fell in love with debating, speech making and political discourse in the tradition of such British intellectuals as the political philosopher Edmund Burke and Walter Bagehot, editor of the *Economist*. Wilson studied law at the University of Virginia but set on the idea of pursuing power through the academic study of history, politics and economics. As a graduate student at Johns Hopkins University, he met Ellen Axson, another child of a Presbyterian minister, with whom he fell passionately in love, writing her fervent letters displaying the romanticism that lay underneath his cold appearance.

Wilson's 1885 book, *Congressional Government*, was a work of great influence but one, tellingly, that he researched without ever setting foot in the Capitol. In it he famously—and ironically, in view of his later political experience—described the system of a weak President and strong Congress as less responsive and efficient than the British parliamentary system. To support his family, he churned out books for large advances, including a five-volume *History of the American People* and a biography of George Washington. He left Bryn Mawr, where he taught history and political economy, at least in part because he feared that teaching women trivial-ized his academic credentials, for Wesleyan in Connecticut and later Princeton, where he taught jurisprudence and political econ-omy until he became president of the university in 1902.

Wilson was a popular professor and academic leader, famous for his acerbic wit and wry mimicry. But his years at Princeton, in a way, foreshadowed both his future political successes and difficul-ties. As president, he required Princeton students to study in each of four divisions, limiting the latitude enjoyed by students at other prestigious universities such as Harvard, and established a system of tutors, or precepts, to live on campus and guide undergraduates, as at Oxford and Cambridge in England.

But Princeton was an elite and hierarchical institution not always suited to its professorial "prime minister." Wilson disliked the eating-club system that established a two-tiered society among undergraduates, and he tried to install a plan of residential com-munities where all undergraduates would live and eat together, similar to the one adopted later by Harvard and Yale. Alumni and some faculty within the university blocked him, making Wilson bit-ter and wrecking some of his closest friendships. A second fight centered on a plan by wealthy alumni donors to locate the graduate school away from the central campus. Wilson, in opposing their proposal, believed the graduate school should be an integral part of the living and studying quarters of the students. Fighting an uphill battle, he campaigned among alumni in various cities, foreshadow-ing his future tactics at the White House.

Indeed, in 1910, on one of these trips to garner alumni support, Wilson voiced a classic progressive belief reiterated many times by Roosevelt, that attempts by elites to suppress the voice of the com-mon people would breed anger, instability and their own ruin. "The great voice of America," Wilson declared, "does not come from the seats of learning but in a murmur from the hills and the woods and the farms and the factories and the mills, rolling on and gaining volume until it comes to us the voice from the homes of the common man." Failure to heed these voices, he said, would force America to "stagger like France through fields of blood before she finds peace and prosperity under the leadership of men who understand her needs."

Wilson was so angry over his defeat on the graduate school issue that he was ready to resign. It was then, in 1910, that he came under the gaze, from across the Hudson River, of one Colonel George Harvey, a former editor of the *New York World* who had gone on to make a fortune on Wall Street and take over two influential national publications, the *North American Review* and *Harper's Weekly*. With his ties to Democratic bosses and financiers on both sides of the Hudson River, Harvey arranged for Wilson to be offered the party's gubernatorial nomination in New Jersey. Even at this early date, he and others were so impressed with Wilson's leadership abilities that they considered him to be potential White House material. Campaigning for governor, Wilson declared repeatedly that he was no tool of the bosses. He was as good as his word. Corporate wealth and political machines had long dominated New Jersey government.

As governor, Wilson acted against both, earning himself the label of "ingrate." He supported anticorruption laws and other election reforms, as well as workmen's compensation and a public utilities commission to regulate railroads and utilities. Under the guidance of his secretary, Joseph Tumulty, he learned how to thank and flatter people—up to a point. More than ever, Wilson sounded, looked and acted like a president: a square-jawed reform governor with a record of progressive accomplishment and an image of intelligence and incorruptibility, a man who could have the backing of the bosses and their allies in big business without seeming to dirty himself. Wilson's somewhat conservative approach to public policy was clearly an asset. It was soothing to business that he was not especially sympathetic to unions or immigrants, and he opposed child labor laws and denounced the idea of making poor people "wards" of the state.

At the start of the Democrats' 1912 convention in Baltimore, no candidate had a majority of the delegates. The initial front-runner was Speaker Champ Clark, who arrived in Baltimore with a wide coalition of backers from the South and the most populous states. He got a majority on ballot after ballot, falling short of the two-thirds vote needed to secure the nomination. Wilson courted Bryan assiduously, but the old warrior waited until the fourteenth ballot to endorse the New Jersey governor. Finally on the forty-sixth ballot, the delegates swung to Wilson in a swirl of backroom dealing.

That fall, the nominee barnstormed the country like a preacher and a scourge, asserting that America's destiny came from God and that "we are chosen to show the way to the nations of the world how they shall walk in the paths of liberty." He mesmerized crowds and seemed even to hypnotize himself with the high purpose he articulated, telling one startled associate, "God ordained that I should be the next president of the United States." Determined that his campaign would be free of charges of corruption, Wilson proudly boasted that he would rely not on corporate moneymen but on campaign donations of less than $100 from average Americans across the country. In the end, though, only about a third of his $1.1 million campaign fund came from small contributors. Much of the rest flowed in from wealthy Princeton friends and some big businessmen who wanted to keep him in line.

Wilson's presidential campaign was a model of reform and populist ideas. He supported lower tariffs and the income tax and assailed business monopolies. But the main theme was something called the "New Freedom," a phrase coined to counter Roosevelt's "New Nationalism" and appeal, as the former President was trying to do, to a new cadre of voters that included small businessmen, workers, farmers, professionals and consumers across America.

On trusts and business combinations, for example, Wilson was no radical, but his approach differed philosophically from that of

Roosevelt. The former President's view was that economic consolidation into trusts and cartels was inevitable and even healthy, as long as government could regulate it while promoting welfare programs for the people. By contrast, Wilson argued that economic concentration was inherently inefficient, dangerous and corrupting. Inspired in part by Louis D. Brandeis, an activist public interest lawyer from Boston who favored the breakup and prosecution of big corporations, Wilson dismissed as unworkable Roosevelt's notion of a "partnership between the government and the trusts." He preferred "regulated competition" over "regulated monopoly." Roosevelt dismissed Wilson's romantic view of freedom enshrined by small business, middle-class and small-town values as "rural Toryism."

As Wilson and Roosevelt battled for the hearts and minds of progressives in both major parties, Taft took what he considered to be a more dignified approach. He basically declined to campaign. Instead, he wrote letters for publication outlining his views. It did not work. Wilson shrewdly reached out to Bryan and Clark for help and even tried to treat Taft with respect, dropping in on him for a chat when the two found themselves in the same hotel in Boston. Taft avoided attacking Roosevelt directly and discerned his main foe to be Wilson, whom he assailed mostly on the tariff issue. As for Roosevelt, his failure to get much Republican support forced him increasingly to the left. "I've been growing more radical instead of less radical, I'm even going further than the platform," he told crowds.

There was one other challenger of note in the presidential race, Socialist Party candidate Eugene V. Debs, a tall, lean and charismatic labor organizer from Terre Haute, Indiana, who had worked his way up to national prominence in the railroad unions. The Socialists had made a strong showing in 1908 but were hampered four years later by their own divisions between moderates and radicals. Debs was in the second category, a fiery orator who began his campaign by invoking the spirit of Karl Marx and ridiculing Wilson, Roosevelt and Taft as tools of capitalism.

In the end, Wilson won an impressive victory, forging a coalition of big-city machines, northern and western progressives and southern conservatives and populists that would form some of the building blocks in the Democratic coalition that would stay together for many decades. All that Roosevelt accomplished was to pull Republican votes from Taft. Wilson's electoral victory was lopsided—435 votes to 88 for Roosevelt and 8 for Taft. No less important were the new Democratic majorities in the Senate and House, the first time since the Civil War that Democrats controlled both houses of Congress. The Democrats also won 21 out of 35 gubernatorial races. Quite decisively, the Republican reign that had begun in 1896 was repudiated.

Yet Wilson and his operatives were smart enough to realize that he had won fewer popular votes than Bryan had in each of his three tries for the presidency: 6.3 million votes to 4.1 million for Roosevelt and 3.5 million for Taft. Wilson's victory margin—41.8 percent of the popular vote—was also the lowest since Lincoln's 39.9 percent in 1860. The majority of voters had supported Wilson's opponents, leading to widespread predictions that he would be a cautious and conservative President.

Surely he had no mandate, many people said, to turn the country upside down.

———

The toppling of the Republican order in Washington took place as a separate but less noticed struggle unfolded in the states over ratification of the Sixteenth Amendment allowing the income tax.

Congressional approval of the amendment in 1909 had been both a gesture toward, and a challenge to, pro-tax warriors. Passage of the amendment was a sop to the reformers who had lost the battle to lower tariff barriers. By 1912, seventeen years had passed since the Supreme Court declared the income tax unconstitutional and lawmakers took decisive steps toward reversing the court's verdict.

Supporters of the income tax had little reason for optimism over the next obstacle—getting three-quarters of the state legislatures to approve amending the Constitution for the first time since 1870. One supporter, Democratic Senator Joseph Bailey of Texas, spoke for many when he warned in 1909 that the path toward ratification would be "fraught with extreme danger." He tried to require that the amendment be considered by specially elected state conventions rather than the legislatures, which he knew were too easily controlled by wealthy interests. His proposal failed. On the Republican side, it was hardly a secret that Senator Aldrich of Rhode Island, arch foe of the tax, had gone along with the amendment because he reckoned it would die quietly in the states.

The national arithmetic was obviously daunting. The drive for the tax got under way in the populist South and West, its base of support. Alabama became the first state to ratify the amendment in the summer of 1909, followed by Georgia, Illinois, Kentucky, Maryland, Mississippi, Oklahoma and Texas. But all that was needed to block the amendment was twelve states. If the northeastern and mid-Atlantic states, which were the wealthiest, banded together, the tax could be defeated.

A good example of the regional dynamics was New York, where at the behest of John D. Rockefeller, Standard Oil's chief attorney, John Milburn, edited and distributed a diatribe against the tax to all the legislators in Albany. The lead writer was Joseph Choate, one of the original attorneys in the Pollock case of 1895 that had thrown out the tax. With five other lawyers from the banking and business sector, he charged that if the tax were adopted, ten or twelve states would be paying 90 percent of the tax bill. Enactment, Choate predicted, would lead to western states demanding more federal money for irrigation, highways, canals and "other innumerable fads and schemes." The lawyers seemed to fear the very forces of democracy at work as they invoked the frightening specter of such a big issue being decided by "the wishes and interests of the electorate" and, even worse, by party bosses "competing for the votes of very poor and very ignorant men." A cartoon in the magazine *Puck* showed Uncle Sam pouring buckets of cash from the income tax into a grinding machine that produced bills labeled "pork barrel," "graft," and "needless public building."

Nationwide, the sentiment was more muted. A survey of newspaper articles and editorials by the historian Robert Stanley shows that most seemed to favor the tax and that the tone of the opposition was less hysterical than it had been in the 1890s. The tax was seen as unlikely to redistribute income on a significant scale. But the *New York World* and other pro-Populist papers thundered in favor of the tax as one step toward economic justice—and toward averting a possible revolt of the lower-income classes.

As Senator Borah had put it in the *North American Review* in June of 1910, the rich needed to understand that a more equitable tax system would protect their own livelihoods against the dangers of class resentment. "Every time wealth invades equal opportunity," he said, "it is undermining its own stability." Some business leaders agreed—among them Joseph Fels, the soap magnate. More typical was the pronouncement of Rockefeller, who advanced the remarkable principle that the government had no right to extend its taxing powers to private fortunes. "When a man has accumulated a sum of money within the law, that is to say, in the legally correct way, the people no longer have any right to share in the earnings resulting from the accumulation," he said.

Perhaps the most significant early attack on the amendment came in 1909 from an unusual source: Associate Justice Stephen Brewer of the Supreme Court, one of only two justices still serving who had voted to declare the tax unconstitutional in 1895. He had clearly become more open about his biases, now attacking proponents of the income tax as demagogues and revolutionaries. "If once you give the power to the nation to tax all the incomes," he declared, "you give them the power to tax the states, not out of their existence, but out of their vitality." Such comments made clear what all along had been obvious, that his earlier invalidation of the tax was based more on conservative ideology than on law. Indeed, Justice Brewer's intemperate attack was denounced as a violation of the justices' supposed neutrality on political matters.

What saved the amendment was something opponents of the income tax had not foreseen in 1909: the Taft–Roosevelt split, which led voters in the elections of 1910 and 1912 to overthrow the established order in state after state, just as they did in Washington. In his study of the ratification fight, the historian John D. Buenker found that the "hard-core" opposition to the tax amendment came from states with the wealthiest, most highly industrialized and most urbanized populations, and that these states were also the ones with the strongest Republican machines, built on alliances with small and big businesses. But the hurricane of voter sentiment—responding to the sinking economy, inflation, trusts, tariffs and widening economic inequality—pushed Republicans off the ramparts from which they had expected to block ratification.

Another factor was that some states were enacting their own inheritance and income tax laws. States traditionally relied on property taxes for revenue, but many were now finding that they needed more money to meet public demands for expenditures in education, public services and state police. Experimentation with the income tax yielded mixed results at first. Virginia enacted a tax in 1909, but many citizens refused to pay it. After some tax agents sent to rural areas were never heard from again, Virginia repealed the tax, having collected less than $100,000.

Wisconsin adopted the first permanent income tax in 1911, after approving a change in its constitution allowing the tax in 1908. After Wisconsin, the income tax was adopted by New York, Massachusetts, Missouri, North and South Carolina and Oklahoma. The rates were insignificant, usually not more than 1 percent (above an income of $800 for an individual or $1,200 for a married couple in Wisconsin). What was significant was that the courts upheld the taxes because the argument that the federal tax violated constitutional requirements for uniformity of tax payments did not hold for the states. Even the Pollock decision outlawing the federal income tax had said that the states had the power to levy one. As the Wisconsin Supreme Court declared, income taxes were "in successful operation in practically all of the great nations of the civilized world, except the United States." It is noteworthy that the court was suggesting that if an income tax had been approved "by many of the most enlightened governments of the world, and has the sanction of many thoughtful economists," it could not be considered an extreme step.

Another powerful indication of the states' attitude toward taxing wealth was the growing popularity of the inheritance tax. By 1890, six states had inheritance taxes, including New York. By 1903, the number had grown to twenty-seven states. By 1913, thirty-five states had inheritance taxes, though they accounted for only 7 percent of state revenues.

The impact of all these state actions was subtle but clear. For many years, the country had been debating whether the income tax and the inheritance tax would destroy society, incite a class war or lead to the confiscation of the wealth of the few by the many. As the historian Robert Stanley notes, the states were resolving the issue by enacting taxes, preparing a climate that would permit ratification of a constitutional amendment.

The changes in the political climate across the country were such that six states that had initially defeated ratification of the amendment or deferred consideration of it reversed themselves after voters altered the makeup of their legislatures or installed new governors in their statehouses in 1910. Defying all predictions, thirteen of the sixteen northeastern states eventually ratified it. By no coincidence, the three holdouts—Rhode Island (where Senator Nelson Aldrich was still king), Pennsylvania and Connecticut—were states in which the Republican machine was powerful enough to survive the assault of the votes in the 1910 and 1912 elections.

The most pivotal state in the battle, and the one that best illustrates the fortunes of the tax, was New York.

The Empire State—home of the wealthiest corporations, the most millionaires, and the nation's highest per capita income—was probably also the state in which the rich had the most influence in politics. Financed and beholden to the state's corporations, the G.O.P. was not the only bulwark against the tax. For many years, Tammany Hall had been too. The Democratic machine commanded the loyalty of New York City's working-class and immigrant voters in return for jobs, food and protection from the police. But for decades, Tammany was also in bed with the big corporations every bit as much as the Republicans. From the Civil War era to the tax wars of the 1890s, the city's party bosses had demanded that Democratic lawmakers in Washington oppose the income tax. On the eve of the ratification battle, opponents of the federal income tax argued that four states—New York, New Jersey, Pennsylvania and Massachusetts—had paid four-fifths of the Civil War era income tax, even though they represented less than a quarter of the population. As the *New York Times* put it, the widespread fear was that a federal income tax would allow "the Populistic States to exempt themselves and make a few Eastern States pay all, or nearly all, the tax."

Overlooked by those who hoped that New York would vote "no" was that the state was changing just as surely as the nation. While New York had the most wealth, it also had the most citizens of lesser means who would benefit from lower tariffs and from more of the tax burden being placed on the rich. Upstate residents voted Republican, of course, but these farmers and small-town residents hardly identified with the corporations that controlled and financed the party machinery. They were also among the most loyal constituents of the progressive Theodore Roosevelt.

Another factor was New York's expanding social welfare programs, which had to be paid for somehow. The state already had its own corporate income tax. An inheritance tax enacted in 1885 had been raised again and again until rich people started fleeing New York to establish official residences in other states. By 1910, Tammany and the New York Democratic machine were changing their minds about the tax. It was a pivotal moment in which the Democratic Party turned from being driven simply by patronage and party politics to being the party of liberalism and the welfare state. Two prominent New York City Democrats were among the income tax's biggest supporters: Alfred E. Smith, a pugnacious assemblyman from the Lower East Side, and State Senator Robert F. Wagner of Manhattan, who declared that "unlike our high Republican tariff, this is a tax on plenty instead of necessity" and that "it will lighten the burdens of the poor."

Initial hopes for getting the amendment adopted in New York rested with the state's patrician and progressive Republican governor, Charles Evans Hughes. Son of an evangelical Baptist minister, Hughes had a bushy beard, imperious manner and impeccable crusading credentials. As a young lawyer, he had led a state legislative investigation into overcharging and adulteration by gas companies and a later inquiry into the life insurance business that exposed secret campaign gifts to the Republican Party and its standard-bearer, Theodore Roosevelt.

With his superb political instincts, Roosevelt had embraced the disclosures and got Congress to ban corporate donations to presidential and congressional candidates in 1907. He had also urged Hughes to run for governor in 1906, in part to block the ambitious publisher William Randolph Hearst. Hughes won, though not with the enthusiasm of Republican bosses. In Albany, he had a modest prolabor record and favored the regulation of business, the direct primary and other progressive reforms. But his sanctimonious opposition to racetrack gambling, as well as his stand on other issues, was not popular with voters. Disliking Hughes's self-righteousness, Roosevelt passed over him in favor of Taft for the G.O.P. presidential nomination in 1908.

No one was sure where Hughes would come down on the amendment. After giving the matter much thought, in January 1910 he told the legislature that while he favored an income tax amendment in principle, the version before the lawmakers troubled him. In particular, he cited what he said was its implicit provision permitting the federal government to tax income derived from state and municipal bonds. Putting the borrowing ability of local governments "at the mercy of the Federal taxing power," he declared, would impair states' rights. He also declared that the amendment should have allowed the tax to be levied only during emergencies.

Hughes's message was widely publicized throughout the country, handing conservatives more ammunition to oppose the tax. The *New York Times* and other papers trumpeted Hughes's opposition, giving noticeably less coverage to his endorsement of the tax in principle. "Governor Hughes has furnished the opponents of the income tax amendment the one thing they have been seeking—a plausible argument from a highly respected source," wrote the *New York World*.

Soon the governors of North and South Dakota and Connecticut lined up with Hughes. So did a legislative committee in Massachusetts. Indeed, it seemed as if the Hughes argument would carry the day until several senators who had voted for the tax in Congress rebutted it. They argued that the amendment would not grant the federal government the taxing power feared by Hughes and other state representatives. The most powerful dissent came from Hughes's main rival for control of the New York Republican Party, U.S. Senator Elihu Root, the corporation lawyer and longtime ally of Theodore Roosevelt.

To embarrass Hughes, State Senator Wagner tried to invite Root to address the legislature with his arguments but had to settle for a letter read out loud in the ornate marble and red velvet State Senate chamber in 1910. It asserted that, contrary to what the governor maintained, Congress had intended only to circumvent the apportionment clause in the Constitution, not to violate the "well settled rule which restrains the national government from taxing state securities." The letter added that "it would be cause for regret if the amendment were rejected by the legislature of New York." As citizens of the wealthiest state, Root declared, New Yorkers should "share the burdens of the national government in the same proportion as we share its benefits."

A more cogent and acerbic answer to Hughes came from a celebrated New York economist, Professor Edwin R. A. Seligman of Columbia University. The federal government, Seligman asserted, had never taxed income from local securities, and there was no reason to think it wanted to do so now. Seligman, son of a wealthy German Jewish banking family, was a respected authority on the theory and history of the income tax, as well as a prominent figure in progressive political circles. His opinion was widely circulated, especially because it included a jab at Hughes, with whom he had studied law and maintained a friendship over the years. Professor Seligman said he would have flunked a student who had shown as little knowledge as the governor of New York had on the tax issue.

Opponents of the tax in New York invoked many other high-flown arguments about protecting states' rights, but their real concern was that the tax would threaten New York's wealth. Moralists could rail against the tax as a threat to "industry and thrift," as one Albany lawmaker put it. But as Stuyvesant Fish, a prominent banker, claimed, the tax was a device to destroy New York's industrial base. The tax was "a dangerous and unwarranted attack on wealth," in the words of Josiah Newcomb, a New York City corporate lawyer and supporter of Hughes.

To drive home the point, the *Times* even depicted the tax as hurting the poor by making it harder for the rich to give to charity. A cartoon in the paper showed a wealthy and prosperous-looking man with a top hat and banker's coat being held up at gunpoint by a masked robber labeled "Income Tax." Behind the banker stood an impoverished and pathetic-looking hooded figure labeled "Charity" with his empty hand stretched out. It is not known how many of these deserving poor read the *Times* or were moved by its concern that their condition would be so damaged by an income tax on the rich.

To marshal these arguments, an army of lobbyists, bankers, financiers, chambers of commerce officials and businessmen descended on the French gothic state capitol overlooking Albany and the Hudson River below. Rarely had the statehouse's shadowy and vaulting corridors seen such a throng. The *Albany Evening Journal*, a Republican mouthpiece, argued that the tax would "divide the population into two classes, the class which contributes to the support of the Government, and the class which does not contribute." It was an absurd comment, given that the class that supposedly "does not contribute" was actually paying most of the revenues in the federal treasury as customs duties and excise taxes.

The paper also stoked the embers of sectional resentment, citing a statement attributed to an Alabama politician asserting that New York would pay a hundred dollars for every dollar paid in his home state. Soon it became repeated in other places as a thousand to one and then a million to one. Edwin Merritt, the Republican majority leader of the Assembly, warned that New York was being delivered bound hand and foot to other states. Democrats and a handful of Republicans tried to warn lawmakers that defeating the amendment would bring retribution from the voters in November. But the Assembly and Senate rejected the amendment in April and May of 1910. The measure got more "yes" than "no" votes, but in each case the votes in favor fell short of a majority of the total number of members elected to that chamber. Ratification nationally seemed doomed.

Soon after the legislature's action, Governor Hughes decided against running for another term in 1910 and instead resigned to accept an appointment by President Taft to the United States Supreme Court. To retain the statehouse, the Republicans selected Henry Stimson, a New York City corporate lawyer and former law partner of Elihu Root who had served as United States Attorney under Theodore Roosevelt.

The Democrats nominated John Alden Dix, a political neophyte and wealthy upstate industrialist whose businesses included banking and lumber, pulp and paper (his campaign claimed, however, that not one tree on his 17,000 acres of forest was cut down without another being planted in its place). Dix preceded his run with a listening tour of the state "to learn intimately political conditions in every county." After hearing the voices of New Yorkers from one end of the state to the other, he proclaimed his devotion to lower tariffs, lower prices, lower taxes, conservation of natural resources and honesty and efficiency in government.

Dix and the Democrats tried to make their support of the income tax amendment an issue in the gubernatorial campaign, but they got more voter response with attacks on what Dix called "the extortionate and indefensible exaction of the tariff and its natural offspring—the trusts and combinations—which have increased the cost of the necessities of life." Against these charges, Stimson tried to portray himself as a battler against privilege and Dix as a puppet of Tammany Hall. As a prosecutor, Stimson had in fact gone after the railroad, paper and sugar trusts, but his appeals did not work. On election day, a freak snowstorm blanketed much of upstate, preventing many voters from going to the polls in reliably Republican districts.

But the Democrats won an impressive victory on the issues, not the weather. Helped by a whopping margin in New York City, Dix triumphed over Stimson by more than 70,000 votes. More important, Democrats swept to a 23-vote advantage in the Assembly and a 30-to-21 advantage in the Senate. The new Democratic leaders in the Albany Assembly and Senate were Al Smith and Robert F. Wagner, respectively. Both would go on to national stardom, along with one newly elected young Democrat who captured a State Senate seat in Dutchess County, the home of his family's Hudson River estate: Franklin D. Roosevelt, a cousin of the former Republican President, who won his first election victory that year.

Once in control, the Democrats wasted no time in pressing for ratification of the income tax amendment. The Tammany-controlled mayor of New York, William J. Gaynor, who had survived an assassination attempt in August of 1910, renewed the city's appeal that the income tax was antithetical to the city's interests. But Democrats in the legislature ignored his pleas, as well as the appeals of another wave of lobbyists, and ratified the amendment in July of 1911. The Senate approved it 35 to 16. The vote in the Assembly was even more lopsided, 91 to 42, as many legislators reversed their previous votes upon hearing the verdict of the electorate. One lawmaker explained his change of heart by noting that his earlier "no" vote had "met with the extreme disapproval of my constituents."

Many progressive Republicans in New York voted for the amendment, but Democrats from New York City put it over the top. The New York Democrats' support showed that the days of Boss Tweed and Boss Croker doing the bidding of big business at Tammany Hall had faded considerably. This time New York City Democrats had invited William Jennings Bryan to testify in Albany in favor of the tax. By contrast, back in 1896, the Great Commoner had got a cold shoulder from Tammany Hall when he tried to defend his support for the tax during his first presidential campaign.

———

In 1911, the year that New York ratified the tax amendment, forty of the nation's forty-six legislatures were to meet. Proponents of the tax had been hoping that they would be influenced by a Supreme Court decision in March upholding the constitutionality of the corporate excise tax law enacted in 1909. The ruling gave a certain legitimacy to the ratification drive, which began when the corporate tax was enacted. But an even bigger boost to the amendment resulted from the legislature's action in Albany in the summer. If the heart of eastern money could change its mind, proponents believed, so could politicians in other states.

Nevertheless, several states held out against the tax for various reasons. Senator Joseph W. Bailey of Texas traveled to Richmond to tell Virginia's House of Delegates that passage of the amendment would make tariff reform easier. But lawmakers were more swayed by the traditional states' rights arguments of their speaker, Richard E. Byrd (father of Senator Harry Byrd and Admiral Richard Byrd), who called the tax an assault on individual freedom. Approval, he charged, would be tantamount to Virginia inviting Washington "to invade its territory, to oust its jurisdiction and to establish a Federal dominion" within the Commonwealth. "A hand from Washington will be stretched out and placed upon every man's business," he went on. "The eye of the Federal inspector will be in every man's counting house." He predicted a future of Americans being hauled into courts, suffering from fines imposed by "distant and unfamiliar tribunals," and "an army of Federal inspectors, spies and detectives" descending on every household.

Rejection of the amendment in Rhode Island reflected the handiwork of Senator Nelson Aldrich—who had consigned the amendment to its expected burial in the states—working in tandem with the state's powerful G.O.P. boss, Charles Brayton. Brayton was a wily railroad lobbyist and an Aldrich business partner whose stock in trade was patronage, party loyalty and, when these tools did not work, bribery, though he did not admit to the latter. He just helped people get elected, he said, and "when they are in a position to repay me they are glad to do so." The Republican machine's control of the legislature rested in part on a typical peculiarity of its makeup. The State Senate members were apportioned to each of the state's thirty-nine towns, regardless of their population. This meant that the twenty smallest towns, with 7.5 percent of the population, were able to vote the amendment down at Aldrich's and Brayton's behest. When the amendment died in 1910, Brayton telegraphed Aldrich in Washington with the good news.

A similar outcome occurred in Connecticut, where sparsely populated counties, small towns and rural interests dominated the legislature, shutting out the big-city immigrant populations that favored the tax. Even the state's Democratic governor appealed to the legislature to heed the advice of his neighbor Charles Evans

Hughes, to reject the amendment. As Stiles Judson, a Republican leader in the legislature, warned businessmen, the tax would drain the state's resources to finance "billion-dollar projects of the west." Another Republican senator said that "it would be a different question if Connecticut got the benefit from the tax."

The last of the three holdouts in the Northeast was Pennsylvania, where the Republican organization and its anti-tax sentiments had roots going back to Thaddeus Stevens in the Civil War. Led by Boies Penrose—a boss who ruled Pennsylvania "as absolutely as the Sultan of Sulu ruled his distant domain and with almost as much tender regard for the interests of his subjects," according to the *Philadelphia Public Ledger*—the G.O.P. party machine employed patronage and bribery to keep its dominance. Legislators representing the Democratic machines in Philadelphia and Pittsburgh voted for ratification, but the Republicans managed to bury the amendment in a special judiciary committee in the State Senate, which reported to the legislature that this "reckless and foolish" measure would endanger the tariff system and treat the state's wealthiest citizens like "criminals." In the statehouse, the committee was known appropriately as "the morgue."

Democratic routs of previously Republican legislatures in other states in 1910 turned the tide, however. Other states that had rejected the amendment first and later ratified it were Arkansas, Massachusetts, New Hampshire and New Jersey, where Wilson had been elected governor in the 1910 landslide. In all, twenty states ratified it in 1911. Except for Maine, North Carolina and Tennessee, all were in the West. Even a thoroughly Republican state like Maine, where the party had ruled pretty much without challenge since the Civil War, drawing funds from the timber, textile and shoe industries and the loyalty of Yankee farmers and small businessmen, turned Democratic in 1910 and ratified the amendment.

Another G.O.P. stronghold, Ohio, saw a Democratic sweep in 1910 despite the presence of a native son, Taft, in the White House. The new Democratic governor, Judson Harmon, led the drive for ratification in 1911, hoping that his progressive stance would get him the party's presidential nomination in 1912. But he got an assist from Taft himself, who wrote to the speaker of the State Assembly that ratification "would be a help to us." Of course, the President continued to maintain that the tax was something he would use only in an emergency.

In New Jersey, where the Republicans reigned in the south and the Democrats ruled the big urban counties of the north, elements in both parties initially opposed the income tax, as Tammany had in New York. But the election of Wilson as governor brought a new cadre of middle-class reformers to the state capital in Trenton and a realization by some of the big-city machines that the income tax was a popular issue. Once in office, Wilson urged the legislature to overturn the Supreme Court's rejection of the income tax in 1895, calling it a case of "erroneous economic reasoning." But even with Wilson in the statehouse, the Republicans still controlled the State Senate, and the amendment was doomed. It was not until Wilson's election as President that Democrats gained control of both houses and approved the amendment. The same happened in Massachusetts, which also did not ratify until Democrats gained control of both legislative houses in 1913.

Arizona, Louisiana, Minnesota and South Dakota ratified the amendment in 1912. Eight more states, five of them in the East, ratified it in the first two months of 1913. On February 3, 1913, Wyoming became the thirty-sixth state to ratify the Sixteenth Amendment, reaching the constitutional requirement that three-fourths of the states must adopt an amendment to make it law. The final tally was 42 in favor, 6 against—or 88 percent of the states. The states that approved the amendment generally did so by overwhelming margins. On February 25, 1913, Secretary of State Philander C. Knox applied the Great Seal of the United States to the Sixteenth Amendment to the Constitution and, in so doing, overturned the Supreme Court's rejection of the tax, consigning it to a footnote of American history.

Supporters of the tax amendment hailed its ratification as the dawn of a new day. But it would be up to the man taking the oath of office on the Capitol's eastern steps less than two weeks later to enact the tax into law. That man, Woodrow Wilson, had a lot of other things on his agenda.

CHAPTER TEN

"Here at Last Was Fruition . . ."

The Income Tax Is Enacted

AFTER NEARLY SIXTEEN YEARS IN THE WILDERNESS, Democrats eagerly seized control of Congress and the White House, with Woodrow Wilson as their leader. To their disappointment, however, the new President asked for the celebrations to be kept to a minimum. He delivered a brief inaugural address on March 4, canceled the inaugural ball and reviewed the inaugural parade with stoic forbearance. "This is not a day of triumph," the new President declared at the Capitol. "It is a day of dedication. Here we muster, not the forces of party, but the forces of humanity." Promising "to cleanse, to reconsider, to restore" after many years of misrule, Wilson was effectively offering a foretaste of what the historian John Morton Blum has called "the politics of morality" that would characterize his presidency, from its brilliant launch to its eventual crash landing.

Wilson's "New Freedom" was to produce the greatest outpouring of social legislation Americans had ever experienced, during a brief interval in which, as Wilson the political scientist once put it, the ruling class of America would use Hamiltonian means of a strong central government to bring about Jeffersonian ideals of egalitarianism. His presidency would transform the American banking and currency system, create new industrial and farm policies and expand the protection of American natural resources. But the first of its accomplishments was lowering the tariff and enacting an income tax, reforms aimed directly at American middle-class pocketbooks.

More than Roosevelt, Wilson and his associates believed, and were able to act on their beliefs, that the federal government needed to serve as a counterweight to corporate wealth and as an aggressive agent to help ordinary men and women. Wilson's legacy is cited even by conservatives as a fateful turning point at which "do-gooders" harnessed the income tax not only to raise revenues for a growing government but also to redistribute the wealth of Americans in a way they deemed to be more fair. Yet at the outset of the New Freedom, no one could foresee that war, not social justice, would drive the tax upward in the Wilson years.

The strictly economic themes of Wilson's inspirational inaugural address offered a bracing taste of the moral absolutism he would bring to the job. Proud of American industrial achievement, he nonetheless implored listeners to ponder "the human cost" of economic power on workers, men and women and children whose "groans and agony" could be heard in American mines, factories and homes. "The great government we loved has too often been made use of for private and selfish purposes, and those who used it had forgotten the people," he declared, pledging to lift Americans up to a new light and a new day. The new President's first priority was to create a level playing field economically—to make sure that government did not favor giant cartels over workers, ordinary entrepreneurs and "the man on the make" struggling up from the lower rungs of the economic ladder. Wilson viewed these smaller people and businesses, not monopolies, as the engines of American prosperity.

In the tight circle of Wilson's loyal advisers, the most powerful was a man without cabinet portfolio, Colonel Edward M. House, a shrewd and subtle Texan who was said to be able to "walk on dead leaves and make no more noise than a tiger." House served as Wilson's principal liaison with the business community, domestic politicians and later with European leaders. He first met the future President on one of Wilson's visits to New York City in 1910 and established an immediate friendship. The political skills of the Colonel (an honorary title) were a good match for Wilson's grand philosophizing. The President called him "my second personality" and "my independent self" until their association broke apart during peace negotiations at the end of the war, when after his stroke Wilson's wife all but hijacked his presidency.

The other important figures in the kitchen cabinet were Joseph Tumulty, Wilson's secretary, and Captain Cary T. Grayson, a ship's doctor who became Wilson's attending physician, close adviser and personal friend. A sign of trouble in the new President's inner circle flared over his falling out with William McCombs, his presidential campaign manager and a man the new President did not want around as a reminder of his closeness to the old political bosses. As McCombs later recalled, Wilson told him immediately after the election, "I wish it clearly understood that I owe you nothing." And he delivered on what he felt he owed.

In the cabinet were William Jennings Bryan as Secretary of State, rewarded for his pivotal role in swinging the Democratic nomination to Wilson, and several other political loyalists. For the crucial job of Treasury Secretary, Wilson chose William Gibbs McAdoo, a Tennessee-born stock trader, entrepreneur, builder of rail tunnels and energetic New York City buccaneer who had been Wilson's biggest supporter from big business during the campaign. Upon being tapped for the job, McAdoo at first demurred, saying

he was not qualified because he was neither a banker nor a financier. "I don't want a banker or financier," Wilson shot back. "The
Treasury is not a bank." What Wilson wanted was someone smart
enough to work with Congress to create a new federally regulated
banking system, enact a new tariff, impose an income tax and
establish an aggressive new policy on business collusion.

The day after his inauguration, Wilson called Congress into an
extraordinary session for a historic assault on the tariff system,
which he had said in his inaugural address "cuts us off from our
proper part in the commerce of the world, violates the just principles of taxation, and makes the government a facile instrument in
the hands of private interests." Indeed, Wilson underscored the
urgency of rolling back the tariffs by delivering his message personally in the first presidential appearance inside the Capitol since the
days of Jefferson. He knew that despite the new Democratic majorities, it was going to be a challenge to get around the conservative
committee barons who still dominated Congress and who had had
quite a lot to do with his own nomination and electoral success.
"My head is with the progressives in the Democratic party," he told
his secretary, Joseph Tumulty, "but my heart, because of the way
they stood by me, is with the so-called Old Guard. They stand
without hitching."

The President's firmest advocate for tariff reform was McAdoo,
who later wrote in his memoirs that the system of high trade barriers had been appropriate for the era of Alexander Hamilton, when
it protected "young and weak industries," but was not for the current era. "It is a general tax on the entire population for the benefit
of private industry," he argued. The tariff did not affect just
imports. When a duty on watches raised the price of watches, it
gave license to every American watchmaker to raise his price to
that level or just below it. McAdoo argued against the theory that
tariffs protect high wages. On the contrary, he said, millions of
workers get no benefit at all from it. A cotton farmer might benefit
by a penny a pound from higher prices for cotton because of tariffs,

but that same farmer had to pay higher prices for shoes, plows, pots, pans, clothes and glass for his windows.

The drive for changes in the tariff system had actually begun after Wilson's election, when Representative Oscar W. Underwood of Alabama, chairman of the Ways and Means Committee, approved and sent to the House the most extensive downward revision of the tariff since the Civil War era. Wilson now set about to get it enacted. Underwood was the scion of a Kentucky political family who had grown up in the frontier outpost of St. Paul, Minnesota, and set out to build a political career in Birmingham, Alabama. From the start, he said he supported the tariff for revenue but not for protection, a stand that pitted him against both Taft and the growing iron and steel industry of his hometown. Once a rival of Wilson's for the presidential nomination, he proved himself one of the President's most reliable allies in Congress, first in the House and later in the Senate.

The main Democratic aims for tariff reform were to keep duties high on luxury goods, to lower the rates on goods produced domestically by trusts and to remove tariffs altogether on "necessities" and raw materials. The battle over Underwood's tariff bill drew an army of lobbyists to Capitol Hill representing wool and sugar producers, cotton manufacturers, paper makers, fruit producers in California, mills in Minnesota, and Texas ranchers—so many influence peddlers that Wilson noted "a brick couldn't be thrown without hitting one of them." But the bill passed the House by a vote of 281 to 139 on May 8, a little more than two months after Wilson took office. It was an extraordinary achievement for a new President.

Then the bill went to the Senate, the traditional burial ground of tariff legislation. Despite the fact that Democrats were in control by a margin of 51 to 45, the Senate, as the smaller and cozier body of lawmakers, remained extremely susceptible to lobbying by powerful business interests. Although the Seventeenth Amendment was ratified in early 1913, requiring the direct election of senators, the Senate remained an American House of Lords, or at least a

House of Millionaires. The first hurdle was the Senate Finance Committee, whose senior Democrat, Furnifold McLendel Simmons of North Carolina, was an ultraconservative, anti-Populist white supremacist—and foe of lowering tariffs. But in return for Wilson's support in his quest to become chairman of the Finance Committee, Simmons backed his changes in the tariff. While denouncing the lobbyists as an "industrious and insidious" force, Wilson joined forces with La Follette and a handful of other progressive Republicans to get what he wanted.

By September, the Senate passed what had become known as the Underwood–Simmons tariff bill. After differences were ironed out with the House, the bill won final passage in October. It marked the first time a tariff bill was enacted to serve the interests of American consumers, as well as those of American industrialists and owners. It did so by dramatically lowering the cost of living for Americans, reducing the added cost of goods from about 40 percent to 27 to 29 percent. Also of benefit to Americans of modest means, the highest tariffs were reserved for luxury products, and several day-to-day commodities and industrial necessities were placed on the so-called "free list," including raw wool (down from 44 percent), iron ore, steel rails, farm implements, coal, lumber, wood pulp, leather boots and shoes, paper and such farm products as meat, eggs and milk. Suddenly food, clothing and other necessities were cheaper as a result of the new law.

To make up for the lost revenue, Congress embarked on a road no less dramatic, one that its leading proponent, Representative Cordell Hull, had long dreamed of.

Born in a log cabin in the foothills of the Cumberland Mountains of central Tennessee, Hull drew from a background that mixed populism with a life of hard work in the backwoods of his home state. He was the son of a farmer, logger, whiskey still operator and merchandiser who was shot and almost killed by Yankee bushwhackers during the Civil War, and who after the war tracked down one of the gunmen in Kentucky and shot him dead. Young

Cordell (named after a respected county judge) was the middle child in a family of five brothers, proud later in life of his homespun clothes and modest upbringing. He did chores on the farm, feeding livestock and milking cows, and later helped his father with hauling logs to the river, putting them on rafts and running them downriver to a mill. In winter, he studied under a tutor hired by his father and read by candlelight at night.

A pivotal moment came early in this bucolic life, when Hull joined a school debating society as a teenager and discovered that he loved researching historical references as much as refining his arguments. His father sent his loquacious son to school twelve miles away at an institute where he studied under Professor Joe S. McMillin, who happened to be the brother of Congressman Benton McMillin, chairman of the House Ways and Means Committee and an advocate of the income tax. Under the McMillin brothers' tutelage, Hull delved into everything from English literature to military history, resolving to study law in Nashville—which he had to get to by a five-day raft trip down the Cumberland River.

After law school in Nashville, Hull opened a law practice at the age of twenty-one and quickly won a seat in the state legislature. Slender and gawky at nearly six feet tall, Hull arrived at the statehouse in 1893 in a long striped coat and broad-brimmed hat, every inch the country politician. He traveled with a delegation of Tennessee residents to visit the White House, where he was impressed with Grover Cleveland's clarity of purpose and focus. But Hull's heart was with populism and his new hero, William Jennings Bryan. After serving for a time as a tough law-and-order judge, he ran for Congress and won in 1906.

Hoping to tap into the momentous changes under Teddy Roosevelt, Hull saw what he said was an opportunity to overthrow the dominance of privilege vested since the Civil War. As he later wrote, "the great middle class—the backbone of any democracy—was borne down along with the working class under the weight of discriminatory government policies." Within three weeks of the opening session of Congress, he introduced an income tax bill, noting in his memoirs that this was in defiance of the conventional view that the tax was dead because of its rejection by the Supreme Court in 1895. Hull recalled that the Republicans in Washington had declared in a campaign book that any attempt to impose such a tax would bring "odium" upon its sponsor. "Prepare for the funeral of the political party which imposes such a burden," the handbook declared. "I was willing to risk both the odium and the funeral," Hull said. Indeed, he had studied the history of the tax battles, going back to the Civil War and to the fights in the early 1890s led by Bryan and Benton McMillin. Hull hoped that if Congress could somehow pass a new income tax bill, the court, with at least one new member, would be more responsive to public opinion than it had been in 1895. "It was inconceivable to me that we had a Constitution that would shelter the chief portion of the wealth of the country from the only effective method of reaching it for its fair share of taxes," he wrote in his memoirs. Like Bryan ten years earlier, Hull demanded that the State Department research the income tax laws overseas. He then put the information in the *Congressional Record*. But as a young congressman, he got nowhere, despite numerous speeches and lobbying among his colleagues. He later recalled moments in his obsessive pursuit of the tax when Democratic leaders sympathetic to his views "would turn and walk in another direction when they saw me approaching" to press them on the subject.

It was a frustrating time to be in the House, where the Republican Speaker, "Uncle Joe" Cannon, had complete control. Hull even had a tough time retaining his House seat in 1908 as Taft swept into the White House. Returning to Washington, he tried once again to pass an income tax. "I have no disposition to tax wealth unnecessarily or unjustly," he said, "but I do believe that the wealth of the country should bear its just share of the burden of taxation and that it should not be permitted to shirk that duty." The time had come, he declared, for the nation to leave behind a system in which the burdens of government were borne "by those least able to bear them, while accumulated wealth has enjoyed the protection and other blessings of the Government and thus escaped most of its accompanying burdens." This time events worked a little more in his favor, as Taft acceded to a constitutional amendment in order to push his tariff bill through a balky Senate. Although Hull continued to favor legislation, not a constitutional amendment, as the best means to get the tax, he was satisfied that his own sometimes obnoxious lobbying had played a part in the result. Even as the ratification process proceeded, however, he continued to press for legislation, warning that the tax might be needed in case of war. "We cannot expect always to be at peace," Hull declared. War would cut off imports and tariff revenues, leaving America "helpless to prosecute that war or any other war of great magnitude without taxing the wealth of the country in the form of incomes."

The Democratic sweep of 1910 suddenly put Hull in a position of power and influence. Champ Clark was now the Democrats' Speaker of the House, and Underwood chairman of Ways and Means, which functioned as a kind of Democratic policy steering committee. Immediately they put the Republicans on the defensive with a series of "popgun bills" to lower tariffs. The whole purpose was to send them to Taft to veto, which he did. Worried about the constitutional amendment's ratification process in the states, Hull persisted in pushing a bill to enact an income tax, attempting to attach such a bill to a tariff measure in 1912, before the election. The bill died amid squabbling in a House–Senate conference committee. Nevertheless, he credited it with hastening ratification of the Sixteenth Amendment.

Two big boosts to Hull's cause came soon enough. First was the election of Woodrow Wilson, which Hull later described as "for me the opening of a new era." He was even more excited when he joined Champ Clark for a meeting with the President-elect at the Jersey shore. Second, of course, was the ratification of the Sixteenth Amendment. "Here at last was fruition to my work and study of twenty years," he later wrote.

In April, supporters agreed to attach an income tax bill to the Underwood–Simmons tariff measure making its way through Congress. The drafters reckoned that $100 million would be needed to plug the hole left by the loss of revenues from tariff cutbacks. Hull fretted that a tax with graduated rates might invite another court challenge, but other Democrats, notably Representative John ("Cactus Jack") Garner of Texas—who later became Franklin Roosevelt's first Vice President—argued that the tax had to be stepped up on the wealthy.

The Wilson administration worried nervously that overly high rates might backfire politically, though the President told one senator that he understood "individual judgments will naturally differ" on which rates would be seen as fair. In the end, Hull proposed a bill with rates starting at 1 percent on incomes over $4,000, with an additional 1 percent on income exceeding $20,000, an additional 2 percent on income exceeding $50,000 and an additional 3 percent on the amount over $100,000. In a cautious step to avoid another potential constitutional problem, Hull exempted the salaries of state and local government officials and federal officeholders, including the President and federal judges, as well as the interest on state and local bonds. The bill also called for taxes to be withheld by employers, as they were in England. As for corporations, a tax of 1 percent was to be imposed on their net incomes, without exemptions. Hull said that the tax would apply to capital gains only for purchases and sales within the same year, and it provided for deductions for business expenses and losses, interest costs, state and local taxes, depreciation and bad debts.

When it came time to debate the tax measure on the House floor, Hull delivered a sweeping address that surveyed the long struggle to adopt an income tax in the face of conservative and judicial opposition. Once again showing his high school debater's talent for prodigious research, he cited reams of historical precedents and declared that it was nothing less than economic justice to fix tax rates according to the taxpayers' ability to pay. And for those who feared that the tax would encourage federal spending,

Hull argued that the opposite was the case. The tax, he declared, would encourage budget restraint because lawmakers would recognize they were spending money directly taxed from Americans. As for the graduated rates, he repeated the basic argument that citizens should support the state proportionate to their income, which was in effect protected by the state. Quoting Prime Minister David Lloyd George in England, who called the tax the "center and sheet anchor" of the British financial system, Hull went over the British experience example by example, especially its adoption of the principle of withholding, known as "stoppage at the source." One advantage of this system, he noted, was that it would reduce taxpayers' annoyance over having to pay the tax directly themselves.

The tax had been heading toward eventual enactment for some time, but that did not stop conservative papers like the *New York Sun, Tribune* and *Journal of Commerce,* as well as the *Brooklyn Eagle,* from expressing outrage. The critics argued that an income tax was repugnant except in times of great national emergency, and there was no emergency in sight. Some found it especially unfair to turn employers into tax collectors. The *New York Sun,* in a typical comment, charged that the bill amounted to "taxation of the few for the benefit of the many." For all these objections, there was little debate in the Democratic-controlled House now about the principle of the tax or even about the principle of progressive tax rates. Instead, proponents tried to increase the various graduated rates— to as high as 68 percent—though their proposed amendments to do so were defeated. Also rejected was a proposal to raise the exemption to $6,000 for married men and to provide exemptions for children. So was another proposal to lower the exemption level to below $4,000—clear evidence that supporters of the tax did not want it to reach into the pockets of the average worker, whose income was only $500 a year.

As Representative William H. Murray, a Democrat from Kansas, put it, the tax was intended not as a way to burden people of modest means but as a way to tap "the surplus" of income of rich Americans "over and above that amount necessary for good living." The tax debate in the House lasted only two days, in part because lawmakers considered the issue settled with the ratification of the Sixteenth Amendment.

On May 8, 1913, the House approved with surprisingly little controversy the first income tax law that would actually take effect since 1872, when the Civil War era taxes were repealed. There was not even a roll call. But votes for the tax obviously came from the South and West among Democrats, populists and progressives. Historic as the House action was, it was hardly a radical step. Taxing incomes of more than $4,000 meant that the tax would affect only the wealthiest 3 percent of the population. The *New York Times* asserted that there were only 100 Americans with incomes of more than $1 million, and that in its entirety the tax would reach only about 425,000 individuals, raising $70 million. The *Literary Digest* noted that whereas an average American family making $1,000 would pay no tax, John D. Rockefeller would pay just under $2 million and Andrew Carnegie just under $600,000.

When the bill got over to the other side of the Capitol, there were predictions that, true to its conservative nature, the Senate would water down the income tax. Instead, a subcommittee headed by Senator John Sharp Williams of Mississippi made the tax tougher. A new consideration arose, this time over the principle of protecting the American family, which prompted the Senate to lower the exemption from taxes to $3,000 but allow an additional $1,000 exemption for married taxpayers and up to another $500 for each dependent child. Was this to be a tax, some newspapers asked, on bachelors? Eventually the Senate limited the dependents' exemptions to two children.

Once again the big fight was not over the principle of an income tax, but over how progressive to make the rates. Senators Williams and Simmons, the conservative and probusiness Democratic leaders of the Finance Committee, had their hands full trying to fend off attempts by La Follette, Borah and other western insurgent Republicans to raise tax rates on the wealthy—to as high as 20 percent for millionaires. Senator Henry Cabot Lodge of Massachusetts, the leader of the Republican establishment and a man of considerable wealth himself, dismissed their initiatives as "confiscation of property under the guise of taxation" and "the pillage of a class." But even Senator Williams agreed with the point. "No honest man can make war upon great fortunes per se," he said. "The Democratic Party never has done it; and when the Democratic Party begins to do it, it will cease to be the Democratic Party and become the socialistic party of the United States; or, better expressed, the communistic party, or quasi communistic party, of the United States." Simmons even managed to enlist Secretary of State William Jennings Bryan to support the notion that it would be "much safer to begin upon somewhat moderate lines" on the tax legislation.

As a result, the Senate rejected the attempts to hike the tax rates, but that created a new problem. The Democrats were clearly shaken by the charges from La Follette and others that the tax was too soft on the very rich. At least twenty-five Democrats threatened to bolt from the bill and back higher tax rates if some new compromise were not crafted. At a hastily called Senate caucus of Democrats on September 5, it was agreed to raise the tax rate to 6 percent on incomes over $500,000—a step that won Wilson's approval.

Lacking the votes to block the tax bill outright, Republicans tried many ways to delay its consideration on the Senate floor or to derail it by adding objectionable amendments. Some Republican senators, for example, voted for higher rates or lower exemptions in the hope that making millions of additional taxpayers susceptible to the tax would erode its support. As it stood, the tax would apply only to about 3 percent of the population. Other Republicans backed the idea of taxing state and local government salaries and income from municipal bonds, hoping that such a provision would compel the courts to strike down the entire bill. Still others tried to get the tax to be collected only by members of the Civil Service system, which might delay the collection process by a factor of several years.

Senator Elihu Root, the New York Republican who had supported the income tax amendment but felt that the tax should be imposed only in case of emergencies, was appalled at what Congress was about to do with no emergency or war in sight. "What these people want to do is to take away the money of the rich," he told an associate, "and then to pass laws distributing it among their people at home." When a friend wrote to him asking what would happen if he lied on his tax form, the senator replied, "I guess you will have to go to jail." He added: "If that is the result of the income tax law, I will meet you there. We will have a merry, merry time for all of our friends will be there."

The Senate had numerous colloquies about what constituted earned and unearned income and how depreciation would be calculated and what sort of deductions could be allowed for costs on capital gains. Various businesses also asked for special consideration. Holding companies, for example, complained that their shareholders would have to pay double taxation—a tax on the company and an individual income tax. Life insurance companies wanted exemptions on dividends earned but not distributed to policyholders. Mutual insurance companies argued for exemptions based on their supposed nonprofit status. Real estate corporations wanted to deduct the cost of interest on debt. Most businesses hated the collection-at-the source system because of the burden it would place on employers. The same demands in the House had led Hull to snap that it was "utterly impossible to write provisions in general law that would apply specifically and govern every phase of the hundreds of thousands of business transactions in the country."

Finally, on September 7, the Senate passed its version of the Underwood–Simmons tariff bill, with the income tax bill attached to it. There was no separate vote on the tax itself. The House–Senate conferees adopted the Senate version of the higher rates on the incomes of the very rich, along with the effectively higher tax rates on bachelors, and Wilson signed the final tax and tariff bill on October 3, 1913.

What had Congress wrought?

In terms of rates, the tax was less severe than the Union's tax during the Civil War and the tax in place in Great Britain. The average working American was unaffected by it. Fewer than 4 percent of Americans were estimated to be vulnerable. The law imposed a 1 percent tax on net incomes, with all taxpayers getting a $3,000 exemption and married couples getting an additional exemption of $1,000. The House's provision for exempting dependent children was dropped. Also exempted were the President of the United States and federal judges, out of respect for the separation of powers, and income from government (federal, state and local) debt, as well as state and local government salaries. On top of that 1 percent base, additional tax rates were as follows:

Rate (percent)	Income		
1	$20,000	to	$50,000
2	$50,000	to	$75,000
3	$75,000	to	$100,000
4	$100,000	to	$250,000
5	$250,000	to	$500,000
6	$500,000	and	above

Thus, the highest rate was 7 percent.

In addition to the tax on personal income, the 1913 law called for a flat 1 percent tax on the net income of corporations, joint stock companies or associations, and insurance companies. This provision superseded the 1909 law and used many of the same definitions and exemptions—for example, for nonprofit organizations. Corporations could deduct business expenses, losses and depreciation, some interest on debt and all other federal, state and foreign taxes. Many of the deductions for business expenses put in the bill have lasted until today: direct business expenses, interest on debt, taxes, losses from fire and other disasters, bad debts, depreciation and dividends paid out.

The definition of income was broad, including "salaries, wages, or compensation for personal services . . . or from professions, vocations, businesses, trade, commerce, or sales or dealings in property, whether real or personal." Also to be included were interest and dividend income and income from business transactions, including profits and sales, except for proceeds from life insurance policies. Gifts and inheritances were not included because Congress planned for separate legislation to cover them. Like businesses, individuals could deduct some business expenses, interest paid on personal debts, taxes, losses uncompensated by insurance, bad debts, some depreciation of property and income that had already been taxed as a corporation tax. Withholding, or collection at the source, survived in the final law. Tax returns had to be filed by March 1 for the preceding year's income.

Once the law was enacted, it took a while for dissemination of the rules—including a four-page form—and the creation of a whole new bureaucracy at the federal level to collect the tax. The form was given a number: 1040. ("Don't get excited," the *New York Times* advised readers, referring to the form. If read carefully, taxpayers would be guided easily to "the fateful entry of your taxable income.") Excited or not, Treasury Secretary McAdoo later said the transition was "intricate and difficult" because the new law was "so far-reaching in its effects and so complicated in its operation." The collection-at-the-source provision, for example, was especially tough on employers because the date of effectiveness of the tax was only a month after it was signed, although the tax did not have to be paid until March 1, 1914. Businesses had to increase their workforce to handle the paperwork and accounting.

Congress appropriated $800,000 to collect the tax, and the Bureau of Internal Revenue employed 30 people just to handle the letters and telegrams asking about the tax. Thirty-four field agents were paid up to $5 a day (plus $3 for subsistence) to examine the returns. It took another year to expand the bureaucracy to 350 tax collectors. Taxpayers were supposed to calculate net income themselves, and if they did so fraudulently, they could be fined up to $1,000 and receive a year's prison sentence.

All the delays resulted in a considerable shortfall in the revenues the tax was expected to yield. Congress had also underestimated the number of taxpayers who would be affected—not surprisingly, perhaps, since there was so little information on which to make projections. Only 368,000 returns were filed the first year, compared to the 425,000 estimated by the Ways and Means Committee. The revenue yield for the income tax, projected at $70 million the first year, brought in only $28 million. Thereafter the yield ran ahead of expectation. And while only a small percentage of American families earned more than the $3,000 that qualified them for paying the tax, these same families had seen their incomes double over the previous two decades.

Despite the care that had gone into wording the constitutional amendment and crafting the income tax law, including observance of the rights of states and the separation of powers, wealthy taxpayers brought two cases to the Supreme Court to get the tax struck down. It took nearly three years for the legal battling to make its way to the Supreme Court, which threw out both suits in 1916. In both *Brushaber* v. *Union Pacific Railroad Co.* and *Stanton* v. *Baltic Mining Co.*, stockholders tried to block their companies from paying the tax. But the court was unmoved by the arguments that the tax was arbitrary, confiscatory, unjust and a violation of due process.

Chief Justice Edward D. White, who had been a dissenter in the 1895 decision, now wrote the opinion for a unanimous court. Taxpayers might believe the tax "to be wanting in wisdom," he said, but it was not in the power of the courts to correct "mistaken or unwise exertions" by Congress. The decision, however, was carefully written to invite further decisions down the road that indeed would restrict Congress's power of taxation. For instance, it appeared to bar Congress's ability to tax income from state, county and municipal bonds. Nevertheless, the decision was a dramatic moment for the court. It effectively reduced the Pollock decision rejecting the income tax in 1895 to the status of a historic footnote.

———

The year 1913, the Wilson era's most productive period, was to be one of still more accomplishments. In December, Congress passed the Federal Reserve Act, a bill no less sweeping in its impact on the American economy than the income tax and tariff changes. As a presidential candidate, Wilson had railed against the "money monopoly" and "money trust" uncovered by the Pujo committee in the House—principally, the finding that a tenth of the nation's wealth was controlled by the Morgan and Rockefeller empires. Nelson Aldrich and the Republican establishment had favored creation of a central bank to be kept under the bankers' control.

Wilson, with the support of Bryan, insisted on government control, and he won with the creation of the Federal Reserve Board, which would regulate interest rates and control the money supply, and twelve regional banks, each to serve and be owned by the banks in its district. Members of the Federal Reserve were to be chosen by the President, and to assuage suspicions in the banking community, Wilson made sure to appoint conservatives to the board. Eventually the new system achieved the goal of helping banks in rural areas provide more credit, as well as credit in periods of economic recession.

Along with the income tax and tariff reduction, creation of the Federal Reserve system spread discomfort throughout the American business establishment. In a widely disseminated editorial on January 3, 1914, the *Commercial and Financial Chronicle* saw a series of "disturbing incidents and events" that "marked the advent to control of the Federal government of a most radical Administration—an Administration, too, that was determined to emphasize and to flaunt its adherence to radical doctrines."

Wall Street was especially distrustful of McAdoo. The Treasury Secretary returned the compliment, showing disdain for the investment bankers he had dealt with as a businessman in New York and declaring his determination to maintain an "absolute divorce of the Treasury from Wall Street." McAdoo, for instance, got rid of the practice of the Treasury making non-interest-bearing deposits in favored banks—such deposits had long been dispensed as patronage.

In his memoirs, McAdoo praised and damned Wall Street, calling it "the last refuge in America of the romantic spirit" because its leaders still dreamed of a "pot of gold at the foot of every rainbow," but also a place of greed and callousness toward average Americans. McAdoo was determined not to let Wall Street blame the nation's mounting economic troubles on the "Wilson panic," as some were already doing. In fact, the nation in 1913 hovered between prosperity and depression, with trade and loans increasing, farm production and construction dropping, and inflation on the increase.

Still the President kept up his assault on unbridled capitalism. In January 1914, only a month after passage of the Federal Reserve Act, Wilson again appeared before Congress and asked for antimonopoly legislation to prohibit interlocking directorates, to separate banks from the railroad industry, to tighten the Sherman Antitrust Act and to set up a Federal Trade Commission to punish antitrust violations. The Federal Trade Commission Act and the Clayton Act both passed the following October. The Clayton Act, though seemingly riddled with loopholes, was interpreted as a victory for organized labor because it sought to exempt unions and farm organizations from antitrust laws when engaged in legal activities and curbed the power of courts to issue injunctions against strikes.

But these steps only accelerated complaints that the economic downturn spreading in 1914 resulted from the administration's lowering of tariffs and what some called Wilson's "crusade against business." The president of the American Bar Association, Arthur Reynolds, accused the Democrats of "seeking to turn back the tide

of progress" and "plunge us into the sea of socialism." Other business spokesmen declared that Wilson and McAdoo looked upon
businessmen as criminals. "What the country needs more now
than anything else," said Simmons Hardware Company in a circu-
lar, "is a quiet time—and absolute rest from the agitation of politics, and assaults upon business." The National Association of
Manufacturers distributed stickers that said: "Political Turmoil
Means Industrial Depression" and "Free Business from Political
Persecution" and "The Country is Suffering from *Too Much Law.*"

Wilson responded to these attacks by slowing down the pace of
his reforms. For instance, he opposed creation of federally backed
land banks for farmers and child labor laws, issues he would support later on. As he grew more cautious, progressive Democrats
grew more restive. Their willingness to confront Wilson was not
itself a threat, but the Progressive Party was disintegrating, and
there was a danger of the Republicans reuniting. These factors
caused Wilson to change course again and pursue legislation for
various reforms, such as the Adamson Act of 1916, which stopped
a nationwide railroad strike by providing for an eight-hour day for
workers. The federal government would also grant subsidies to
states for various programs, such as agriculture education, voca-
tional courses in secondary schools and road building. Since these
subsidies were to be backed by the income tax, the effect was to
take money from the wealthy Northeast and send it to projects in
the South and West, which foes of the income tax labeled as pork
barrel spending. In sum, Wilson's presidency brought an array of
reforms never before seen in history, with an income tax fueling a
newly muscular federal government.

———

After only two years in office, Wilson was growing impatient and
feeling unappreciated. There was criticism from businessmen who
thought he was wrecking the free enterprise system, the rich who
hated the income tax, bankers who resented the Federal Reserve,

legislators angry over what they regarded as his heavy-handed demands on Congress, and reformers disappointed that he hadn't done more. Feeling besieged, he entertained a fantasy of putting on a false beard and sneaking out of the prison of the White House. And he joked about putting a sign in front of his office saying: "Don't shoot. He's doing his damndest." But Wilson also developed a fastidious style in the White House—doing paperwork in the morning after a breakfast of two raw eggs, oatmeal and coffee, receiving visitors until lunch, then taking a car ride or sometimes playing golf in the afternoon. He favored spats and elegant suits and tended to lecture rather than persuade—and to assume that when he was right, everyone else should recognize it. "He was the best judge of measures and the poorest of men I ever knew," observed Senator Williams.

In Congress, one of the members who was proudest of what had been accomplished in Wilson's first year and a half was Cordell Hull. As taxpayers began to file their returns in 1914, the congressman got a note from Treasury Secretary McAdoo, "just a line to congratulate you on the results of the income tax law." The law was perhaps unpopular "in some quarters," wrote McAdoo, but "not one-tenth as unpopular as partisan papers represent it and certainly not nearly so unpopular as the average man expected it to be."

Around the time of the McAdoo letter, Hull ventured to New York City to speak at a meeting of the New York State Bar Association, which he characterized as "the territory of greatest opposition to the tax." With great respect, he told the lawyers that he sympathized with their feeling punished by the tax's provisions, but that New York, as "the great center of commerce of the nation," had to understand that its power and wealth resulted from the industry of all Americans and that it was wrong for the wealthy to "segregate" themselves from their "fair share of taxes."

Many years later Hull recalled the period of early 1914 as a time when he and other reformers began planning to build on their accomplishments. "We were observing and studying the lower tariffs and the income tax in operation," Hull wrote. "We were preparing further legislation and steadily enacting a long list of wholesome measures." Hull was especially proud of the teamwork he and his colleagues in Congress had developed with the White House.

"And then in June," he wrote, "a shot rang out at Sarajevo!"

CHAPTER ELEVEN

"What Did We Do? What Did We Do?"

Woodrow Wilson Raises Revenue for an Impending War

THE ASSASSINATION OF ARCHDUKE FRANZ FERDINAND of Austria by a Serbian nationalist in Sarajevo on June 28, 1914, did not register with Americans at first as a momentous event. Then, in swift succession, Austria-Hungary declared war on Serbia; Russia countered with support for its fellow Slavs, the Serbs; France backed Russia; and finally Germany allied itself with Austria against Russia and France. Soon France, its ally Britain, and Russia were at war with Germany and Austria-Hungary, triggering the awful conflict that would devastate Europe and pave the way for unending tragedy in the twentieth century.

Looking on from across the ocean, Americans were not only unprepared for the explosion but confused by the distant and senseless rivalries, alliances and hatreds that consumed the combatants. As late as 1916, Wilson spoke for many when he referred to the war as "a drunken brawl in a public house." When Wilson's offer of mediation in 1914 was ignored, he appealed to Americans to avoid taking sides, but that was hard to do. Many Americans of German and Irish ancestry, as well as others still thankful for Prussian support of the Union during the Civil War, were pulled toward the Central Powers. But most felt stronger ties with Britain and France, especially after the German invasion of Belgium. Certainly the President of the United States harbored those sympathies.

Few wars have transformed the belligerent countries as extensively as World War I. It overturned the social, economic and cultural orders in Europe, Russia and beyond. It also transformed the American economic system, bringing the income tax to the central role it was to play for the rest of the century.

The reason was the cost of war. World War I would eventually cost the United States $50 billion. The federal budget grew from $742 million in 1916 to nearly $14 billion in 1918. The income tax was needed to finance that explosion in spending. Before World War I, more than 90 percent of federal revenues came from excise taxes and tariffs, but their importance was quickly eclipsed by the income tax.

Taxing the rich was logical and attractive at several levels. First, the wealthiest Americans had become more and more wealthy during the previous two decades of prosperity. A study published in 1915 by Dr. Willford Isbell King, entitled "The Wealth and Income of the People of the United States," showed that the 1.6 percent of American families who were the richest nearly doubled their share of the national income from 1895 to 1910, ending up with 19 percent.* By contrast, the 88 percent of families who earned 65 percent of the nation's income in 1890 earned only 62 percent by 1910. The poor kept their meager share of the nation's wealth

---

*Not much has changed in this respect. In 1999, the Treasury Department found that the top 1 percent received roughly 21 percent of the nation's income.

about the same. There was a strong perception among Americans that the wealthy had benefited far more from the boom years than the middle and lower classes. War would only accelerate the trend. A study of the nation's total wealth showed that in 1900, it stood at $192 billion, half of which was possessed by 2 percent of the population; by 1929, the nation's wealth would be $362 billion, with 60 percent of it held by 2 percent of the population.

At the outset of the conflict in Europe, Wilson's first priority was to defend American neutrality as the best means to preserve his New Freedom reforms. At first, the administration barred loans from any private source to the combatants, but in 1915 private loans were authorized as a means to spur exports. Despite Wilson's stance, the spillover of the fighting and the blockades on the high seas threatened economic hardship for the United States. Britain, waging "total war," forced the diversion of American ships bound for Germany and even confiscated American cargo. By 1916, trade with Germany had fallen to less than 1 percent of its value of a couple of years earlier. Later, exports to the Allies—financed by American loans—more than made up for the initial downturn. But at first, the American economy suffered as European and other investors sold off their stocks, pulling out money and lowering American gold reserves. The stock market tumbled and had to suspend operations for a brief period. The business community was in a near panic, not yet realizing what a bonanza the war would eventually become for exporters, lenders and producers of war goods.

The initial impact of the outbreak of war was on American trade. A sharp falloff in imports, and consequently in tariff revenues, plunged federal finances into the red. On August 6, 1914, Wilson's wife, Ellen, died after a long battle with kidney disease. Wilson got the bad news about the budget deficit after returning from her funeral in Georgia in mid-August. At the same time, Treasury Secretary McAdoo urged the President to adopt "some form of well distributed internal revenue taxation" to meet a possible deficit of $100 million that fiscal year. McAdoo's instinct was not to raise the income tax but to impose excise taxes on specific items, such as stamps, telephone calls and bank checks. Wilson summoned the tax-writing chairmen of Congress, Underwood and Simmons, to lay out the situation and endorse the call for new taxes. "Conditions have arisen which no man foresaw," he declared to the lawmakers, reading at the session from small sheets of typed paper. "They affect the whole world of commerce and economic production; and they must be faced and dealt with."

At this point, the politics of the South, along with its main source of wealth, entered the political debate with fateful consequences. The entire nation was hurt by the drop in trade resulting from the outbreak of war in Europe, but the South was especially hard hit. The region's economic difficulties brought an echo of the disaster resulting from the Union's blockade during the Civil War. This time, however, problems related to King Cotton, still the single biggest source of wealth in the region, were a factor in the raising of income tax rates. The 1913 cotton crop had been a near record of 14 million bales, which had fetched near record prices. Another big crop was expected in 1914, nearly two-thirds of it destined for shipment overseas. With war, the bottom fell out. Prices plummeted, costing the South hundreds of millions of dollars in income.

Southern leaders beseeched Wilson, McAdoo, Agriculture Secretary David Houston and congressional leaders for emergency cotton loans, and insisted on establishing cotton as collateral at a high price. McAdoo dismissed their request as unworkable but acknowledged that he had spent "more sleepless nights thinking about cotton than anything else" since becoming Treasury Secretary. As fear of bankruptcies and farm failures spread, the Farmers' Union came up with another idea, urging that the Federal Reserve banks purchase 3 to 4 million bales of cotton. The Fed would be paid back the next year by a tax on the crop of 1915. Again the administration demurred. "It is not a question of sympathy—the cotton growers have the sympathy of the whole world in their distress—but a question of sound business and good government," replied Houston.

The confrontation between the administration and the cotton farmers in 1914 was a bitter irony for a President who had campaigned stressing his southern heritage. Wilson often liked to say that "the only place in the world where nothing has to be explained to me is the South." Yet on this issue, at least, the southern growers despaired of getting a chance to explain their plight. So members of Congress from cotton-growing states formed a bloc with tobacco interests that threatened to vote against Wilson's $100 million revenue package. Wilson needed no explanation about that sort of discontent eating at a vital part of his political base. He met with lawmakers from the region but still opposed any measures not "within the limitations of economic law and safe finance." He could feel their pain, he said—the South's distress was "the thing that is giving us the greatest concern just now," he wrote in a letter—but he was not sure how to address it.

A possible solution was offered in the form of a proposal to have private bankers create a fund of $150 million, administered by the Federal Reserve, to lend to farmers until they could sell their cotton a year later. Colonel House urged Wilson to accept it, asserting that "the ordinary technicalities and niceties should not be allowed to stand in the way." Wilson went along, hoping that it would put the South "on the high road to real recovery." But the cotton-fund project quickly failed. The banks set their loan rates too high for the farmers to be able to repay. Southerners long sympathetic to the President began suspecting him of "jollying the South" while maintaining cozy ties to Yankee banks. "The President stood in the road and condemned the South, which made him, to heavier loss and more widespread misery than it has known in three generations," declared Governor Oliver Colquitt of Texas.

———

While the efforts to help the South sputtered, lawmakers from cotton-producing states were waging a separate campaign against Wilson's proposed $100 million revenue package. They took their concerns to Underwood and Simmons, leaders of Congress's two tax-writing committees, saying that while their region was suffering, the industrial North and grain-producing Midwest were poised to profit from goods sold to the war combatants. Under pressure from their southern colleagues, Underwood and Simmons agreed that at least a third of the revenue from the new tax package would be raised through the income tax.

The President feared that the income tax could not raise revenues quickly enough for his needs, however. He summoned Underwood and Simmons to the White House and asked that increases in the income tax be stricken from the bill—not as a matter of principle but strictly because of the timing. "We will have to start all over again," Underwood told reporters as he left the White House session.

The final tax bill produced by the Ways and Means Committee in late 1914 was a mixture of taxes on beer, wine, tobacco, gasoline, bankers and brokers and a stamp tax on bonds, mortgages and various types of documents. It passed, with southerners either dissenting or going along with a mind to bringing the income tax issue up again. In the Senate, the bill was changed to placate farm interests (by removing the gasoline tax) and raise tobacco and liquor taxes. It also added taxes on patent medicines, cosmetics, perfumes and amusements. With some more refinements, the bill was approved in conference and President Wilson rushed back from the golf course to the Capitol to sign it on October 22, 1914.

Far from American shores, Europe in these early months of war was bleeding from vast stalemates on the Russian front and in western-front trenches extending from the North Sea to Switzerland. Germany, desperate to break loose from the British naval blockade, moved to destroy it and simultaneously disrupt shipments to Britain. Flouting international rules against the sinking of neutral merchant ships, Germany launched savage submarine attacks, beginning in February of 1915. As passenger vessels sank, sometimes with Americans on board, the United States protested even while trying to avoid a confrontation with Berlin.

Then, on May 7, a German submarine sank the Cunard liner *Lusitania* as it steamed slowly off the coast of Ireland, drowning 1,198 passengers, including 94 children and 128 Americans. Americans reeled in shock, and Wilson denounced the attack—which followed by only a couple of weeks the German use of poison gas in France—as "illegal and inhuman" (though he had to concede that the *Lusitania* was carrying some armaments on board). He insisted that the attacks were a violation of international law, made worse by the refusal, or inability, of the small German submarines to rescue the victims. To avoid future provocations, the United States also tried—unsuccessfully—to get Britain to stop placing arms aboard its merchant and passenger ships.

Despite their horror over the *Lusitania* and similar episodes, Americans remained reluctant to join the war. As Wilson said on May 10, 1915, "There is such a thing as a nation being so right that it does not need to convince others by force that it is right." Yet the President's protests were too strong for many, including his Secretary of State, William Jennings Bryan, who resigned out of concern that the United States was showing too much bias toward the Allies. Robert Lansing, the State Department's counselor and an expert on international law, replaced him. In any case, the protests to Germany had little effect. The sinkings continued through August, forcing Wilson to escalate his threats with a vow to sever diplomatic relations if they did not stop. Eventually the Germans briefly backed down, but they resumed the attacks after several months.

Along with the British blockade, the horrific trench warfare and the submarine attacks came the first demands for American loans by the Allies. When private banks could not satisfy the Allies' needs, Wilson went along with a recommendation by McAdoo, Lansing and Colonel House to extend government credit paid for by bonds sold to the public. Inevitably, he had to start thinking about the unthinkable, however. What would happen if the Allies were defeated and the United States had to enter the war? Wilson confided to an associate that it was not in the United States' interest for one power to dominate in Europe and that "we are bound to intervene" to prevent that from happening. "Pacifist that I am, world peace is vital," he said. He was also feeling pressure from various organizations (including one led by Teddy Roosevelt) that were demanding measures to make America ready for war. The logic for military preparedness was driven not only by German belligerence but also by a civil war in Mexico, where Wilson had dispatched American troops to capture the revolutionary Pancho Villa after he had raided American border towns.

Responding to circumstances at the end of 1915, Wilson continued to proclaim his desire to avoid involvement in the war in Europe but also recommended to Congress a five-year naval buildup at a cost of $100 million a year and a similar program to purchase or build merchant ships. He vowed to stump the country "to explain this matter to the country and summon its support." The question was how to pay for it all. That challenge fell first to Treasury Secretary McAdoo, an improbable progressive with a Wall Street background who would become a crucial figure in making the income tax the core of Wilson's war-financing efforts.

"I was like a sea captain who finds himself standing on the deck of a ship that he has never seen before," McAdoo later wrote of his term as Treasury Secretary, during which he created the Federal Reserve system and saw the tariff reformed and the income tax pass, all in his first year in office. Blunt, forceful and calm at the center of the war turmoil at the Treasury Department, McAdoo, an affable and rangy six-foot-two-inch former business tycoon from New York, took up his post in Washington shortly after his wife's death in 1912. During the mourning period, he escaped many of the capital's social obligations and remained at his desk, working so hard that Wilson's confidant and personal doctor, Captain Grayson, began to fear he was heading toward a breakdown. Soon, however, he was cutting a wide social swath in Washington. The capital's society was atwitter over his dancing the fox-trot in public.

McAdoo also liked to go horseback riding, sometimes with Captain Grayson and occasionally with Wilson's attractive youngest daughter, Eleanor Randolph Wilson, who was also the President's favorite. By March of 1914, his friendship with Nell Wilson had blossomed into an engagement. "Isn't it wonderful?" McAdoo wrote Colonel House. "The days of miracles are not yet over or she never would have accepted me." But not everyone swooned along with him. McAdoo was fifty-one years old and the father of six children. Nell was twenty-five. Fearing that the marriage would embarrass the administration and stir resentment among other cabinet members, McAdoo offered Wilson his resignation.

Instead, the President gave his blessing. The two were married in a glittering ceremony in the White House Blue Room in May 1914. Losing his youngest daughter—"the only delightful part of me"—Wilson said he was pleased that "she has married a noble man, who I feel sure will make her happy and proud, too." But the marriage did not bring the President closer to his cabinet Secretary. In the view of Colonel House, McAdoo and the other cabinet members all felt marginalized, as if they "were nothing but clerks." Wilson was said by some to be annoyed at the way McAdoo had opinions about everything, including the business before other departments. But McAdoo was also regarded as a brilliant foil to Wilson's sermonizing seriousness. Once at a White House luncheon, Wilson asked him, "Mac, will you ask the blessing?" McAdoo, who never went to church, arose and, for once at a loss for words, muttered "Jesus" and sat down.

The Treasury Secretary also played an odd role in Wilson's own romantic life after the death of his wife, Ellen, in 1914. "Oh, my God, what am I to do?" the President cried out in despair after the doctor pronounced her dead. But then in the spring of 1915, a mere eight months after Ellen's death, Wilson met an attractive forty-two-year-old widow of a Washington jeweler, Edith Bolling Galt, at a White House tea. Smitten, he was soon writing to her every day, calling her "my perfect playmate, with whom everything that is gay and mirthful and imaginative in me is at its best." Their passion was so obvious that a joke went around Washington that when Wilson proposed to her in 1915, she was so excited she fell out of bed. Not everyone thought it was funny. After a British diplomat repeated the line at a dinner party, word got back to the White House, which demanded that the joke-telling envoy be recalled to London.

With the President distracted and in love, his aides fretted about the relationship and its political impact. Colonel House complained that the President had become, as he wrote in his journal, "wholly absorbed in this love affair and is neglecting everything else." Besides, Congress seemed on its way to granting women the right to vote—the Nineteenth Amendment would be ratified in 1920—and no one knew for sure what the impact would be from a presidential romance. It was agreed among several Wilson associates that McAdoo, the only one having a family tie to the President, should at least try to get him to consider postponing the wedding.

McAdoo is said to have devised a fictitious story that one of Wilson's earlier lady friends, Mary Hulbert Peck—whom he had met during his years at Princeton while vacationing without his wife in Bermuda—was passing around old love letters and threatening to expose him, possibly by selling the letters. Whispers about Mrs. Peck had dogged Wilson for years. Indeed, he had been sending her checks to help with her financial misfortunes. McAdoo's story, far from persuading the President to break off his romance, only stiffened his resolve to marry Mrs. Galt. He told her of his friendship with Mrs. Peck (now known as Mrs. Hulbert), begged forgiveness and won her lasting faith, love and trust. They were married December 18, 1915.

McAdoo's advice to the President carried more weight on matters of finance and budgets. He never developed the kind of warm relationship that might have resulted from his ties to the President. In his memoirs, McAdoo observed that the President often seemed, even to intimates like himself, in his own world. "I knew his mental habits," he wrote. "I saw clearly the general pattern of his thought and life. But in another sense I hardly knew him at all. There were wide and fertile ranges of his spirit that were closed to me; and, I think, to everyone else except the first Mrs. Wilson."

In professional terms, McAdoo had an extraordinary background that served Wilson and the administration well. Born in Tennessee and reared in Georgia (where his mother's family plantation was destroyed in Sherman's march to the sea), McAdoo was a southerner who cherished what he felt was objectivity about the region of his upbringing. The South, he often declared, needed to be "grateful" that defeat had destroyed the backward plantation aristocracy that had impoverished its people. (Not everything about the South was disdained. At Treasury, McAdoo kept federal offices, shops, rest rooms and lunchrooms racially segregated. Wilson went along, saying that African Americans would surely find these arrangements more comfortable.)

McAdoo remembered a childhood of poverty, family debts and hard work in Georgia, where he had split wood, milked cows, picked wild plums and blackberries and gone barefoot wearing cast-off clothes. But he had scraped his way up the ladder, getting a law degree and becoming president of a local coal company in Knoxville, Tennessee. McAdoo burned with social and political ambitions, which were not easy to fulfill in Republican eastern Tennessee. His first big business venture was a horse-drawn streetcar enterprise in Knoxville, which he wanted to convert to an electrical line. The business failed rather spectacularly, and McAdoo headed to New York City, where he arrived just as Wall Street crashed in the Panic of 1893. Living in squalor in a fifth-floor walk-up apartment on the Upper West Side, the family suffered another blow when his wife got rheumatoid arthritis and became an invalid. "The poverty, the struggle, and the anxiety of this period are indescribable," McAdoo later wrote. He became depressed and his weight dropped to 135 pounds. Still he persevered. "For the thing that is worth doing, a man must not hesitate to DO AND DARE— DO OR DIE," he later wrote.

Ambitious as he was, McAdoo developed an antipathy toward the "robber barons" of capitalism and the "trickle-down" theory that the prosperity of those at the top would automatically benefit those at the bottom. Somehow his hard work in New York paid off, and he was able to make money by buying and selling securities, investing in business and practicing law. Meanwhile, he still toyed with the idea of running for Congress or mayor of Yonkers (his new home).

After the turn of the century, McAdoo's good fortune turned up in the muck of the Hudson River. Back in the 1870s, workmen had started to build a brick-lined railway tunnel from New Jersey to Manhattan, only to be disrupted by disaster in 1880 when twenty men died in a cave-in, halting the project but not the dream of its eventual completion. Later the technology of hydraulic jacks, compressed air and cast-iron rings for the tunnel would bring the project back to life. McAdoo, who observed the decrepit docks and ferries as he crossed the river many times and who had done business over the years with railroad investors, raised money among the largest bankers and companies in New York to complete the tunnel. It was a scary project, with the twenty men entombed in the river, and workers who lowered themselves into the depths frequently coming up in agony from the bends. McAdoo kept up morale by venturing into the tunnel project himself, even while mapping plans for a second tunnel to the south. Eventually two more tunnels were planned and built.

During all these years, McAdoo negotiated and tangled with railroad companies, ferryboat operators and politicians while rallying public opinion, newspaper editorial support and backing from bankers like J. P. Morgan. He even persuaded Teddy Roosevelt to press a button at the White House that started the first train rolling to New Jersey, where his tunnel project soon helped to transform the area near the Hudson River into several popular suburban communities.

As a kind of celebrity businessman—the Donald Trump of his day—McAdoo distributed complaint forms for users of his terminals and went on well-publicized inspection tours. He introduced "hen cars" for ladies only and welcomed regulation by the New York Public Service Commission. He favored higher wages and workmen's compensation and pensions. In short, he was a peculiar phenomenon of the Progressive Era, a businessman reformer, a rags-to-riches story personified, and a dashing figure with his black suits, derby hats, long and slicked black hair, jutting chin and deep-set blue eyes—"the hero of life in New York," the *Boston Herald* called him. Indeed, McAdoo was a man who had everything except a political career. It awaited him in 1909 on a New Jersey rail platform, where he happened to meet the restless and controversial president of Princeton University.

The two men got along immediately, and McAdoo eagerly supported Wilson's run for governor in 1910. By 1912, with the presidential campaign approaching, McAdoo switched from his earlier support of the man who had launched his tunnel train. He thought Roosevelt was too soft on trusts. He was also proud to join with a fellow southern transplant and soon helped raise money for Wilson. In early 1912, he campaigned for Wilson in Tennessee and other southern states, returning home just as his wife, Sarah, died suddenly. Once Wilson was elected, McAdoo was an obvious choice for Treasury, despite his lingering reputation as a self-promoting huckster. He quickly became "the most ambitious, aggressive, and domineering member of the Wilson circle," in the words of the Wilson biographer Arthur S. Link.

McAdoo had played a significant role in negotiating with Congress over the enactment of the tax bills of 1913 and 1914. But it was not until the second half of 1915, when Wilson began his program of military preparedness and moved to sell it in speeches across the country, that the Treasury Secretary swung fully into action to raise large amounts of revenue for the federal government. McAdoo had carefully studied the sorry record of his predecessor, Salmon Chase, during the Civil War and was determined not to follow the Union's example of ruinous inflation fueled by debt. "For my part I am strongly in favor of preparedness," McAdoo said, "and I am strongly in favor of raising by taxation the necessary revenues to pay for it." Wilson agreed. "Borrowing money is short-sighted finance," the President declared in one of his budget messages. "We should pay as we go." It was a matter of generational fairness as well, he said, that "the industry of this generation should pay the bills of this generation" and not saddle its children with the debts in the future.

In December 1915, Wilson, with the need to prepare for war in mind, proposed another broad array of tax increases. The most politically distasteful of his proposals involved lowering the minimum levels of income eligible to be taxed at various rates, placing more of a burden on many more taxpayers than before. He also asked for a renewal of the tariff on sugar and a raft of new excise taxes on gasoline, automobiles, bank checks and on iron and steel. These taxes landed in Congress like a bomb. The explosion produced business demands for higher tariffs (an idea Wilson dismissed as "nonsense") and protests by every group affected by the other individual levies. Farmers mobilized against the tax on autos and gasoline. The tax on bank checks was reviled as something that would cause every American to curse as he wrote a check or licked a stamp. The taxes on pig iron and steel were attacked as unfair to the industry that was needed to make America prepared for war. The *New York World* portrayed the jockeying among Democratic critics as having "the character of ward politics in a small town."

But the biggest uproar came from those now suddenly demanding the alternative to a higher income tax, an inheritance tax and a tax on the arms industry companies making huge profits on goods sold to combatants in the war. The trade-off they were demanding was clear. If Congress were to accede to the idea of expanding the base of income taxpayers from approximately 500,000 to 3.5 million, the administration would have to accept inheritance taxes and surtaxes on wealth that were far more progressive than it had originally endorsed. If Wilson wanted a war preparation measure, it had to be financed in a progressive fashion. One tax historian, W.

Elliot Brownlee, calls this trade-off "the single most important financial decision of the war."

The principal advocate of a more progressive tax system was the new chairman of the House Ways and Means Committee, Representative Claude Kitchin of North Carolina, who succeeded to the panel's leadership post after Oscar Underwood was elected to the Senate. Son of a congressman from North Carolina, Kitchin was heir to all of the South's resentment of the powers and privileges of the North and had climbed his way up in politics by allying himself with white supremacists. He was also a masterful debater and a foe of tariffs and privilege. In the 1912 presidential campaign, he had actively campaigned for Wilson. Now he was a leading critic of involvement in the European war. He would later oppose the declaration of war in 1917, asserting: "My conscience and judgment, after mature thought and fervent prayer for rightful guidance, have marked out clearly the path of my duty and I have made up my mind to walk it, if I go barefooted and alone." Yet once war was declared, he would support it, and he worked so tirelessly that when he died of a cerebral hemorrhage in 1920, a colleague declared that he "fell as truly a casualty of the war as if he had died leading the charge upon the crimson fields of France." Wilson respected Kitchin as a wily adversary and ally: "I never knew a man who could state his position more lucidly or state yours more fairly."

The overarching charge made by the reformers, populists and progressives was that the preparedness drive was "a rich man's scare," as one Democrat put it. Kitchin's view was that "if the people really knew the facts" about the spending increases in the offing and "the danger to our country and its institutions," not one in a hundred would favor it, according to the *New York World*.

Kitchin had another ulterior motive for prodding Wilson to expand the income tax, which was that it might erode support for preparedness among those who would have to pay the tax, in New York and elsewhere. Even if that gambit failed, the progressives and populists argued, since it was the wealthy who were demanding preparedness, they were the ones who should pay for it. "Preparedness is demanded by wealth for its protection," said Senator Benjamin ("Pitchfork Ben") Tillman of South Carolina, adding, "The poor people throughout the country who have the votes are watching to see if the Party is going to call on these millionaires to pay for this preparation for the defense of the country, or even their just share of it." Wilson responded to Tillman that he understood such views but would leave it up to Kitchin and McAdoo to work out the tax.

Kitchin was most fearful of voter backlash against a tax increase, a possibility that might be limited if the increase were restricted to the very rich or to war profits. There was no question that war profits were piling up. American exports jumped from $691 million in 1913 to $4.3 billion in 1916 and $6.3 billion in 1917. Companies that supplied these goods soared in value. Bethlehem Steel stock went from 46 ¼ in January 1915 to 700 in November of 1916. Other big steel and chemical concerns expanded their output to supply everything from trucks to cotton, generators and howitzers. Millionaires seemed to be proliferating overnight.

On the other hand, despite enactment of the income tax, the system had not yet caught up with the reality of the new war-driven fortunes. Taxes continued to be borne by lower- and middle-class Americans. Of $735 million in federal revenues in 1914, $300 million came from customs paid by consumers and another $300 million from taxes on tobacco, liquor, wine and beer. Individuals and corporations paid only $71 million in income taxes. Kitchin and others knew that this imbalance had to be corrected for a tax package to pass muster on Capitol Hill. Some other lawmakers were even more radical in their approach. One representative, Warren Worth Bailey, a Pennsylvania Democrat and "radical," proposed a tax levy of up to 50 percent on top-level incomes. "If the forces of big business are to plunge this country into a saturnalia of extravagance for war purposes in time of peace," he declared, "it is my notion that the forces of big business should put up the money."

Uneasy with these demands, McAdoo at first tried to lobby the dissidents over what he called "speed-up dinners" and in other meetings. Then on January 23, 1916, he agreed to drop some of the special taxes advocated by Wilson and instead increase the income surtax, lower exemptions and retain sugar duties. By coincidence, the Supreme Court upheld the 1913 income tax law the very next day, prompting Democrats to intensify their effort to raise the tax as a solution to the spending problem. "The Supreme Court's decision has unfettered the income tax," declared Cordell Hull, ever the tireless champion of taxing the rich. "All doubt is removed and Congress is left much freer to act." As Hull was to write later, "The income-tax law had been enacted in the nick of time for the demands of the war."

With the cost of war preparations growing, in part because of the war in Mexico, the Ways and Means Committee under Kitchin wrote a substantially more liberal tax program than the one sought by McAdoo. When the bill came to the House floor in July, Kitchin declared it a product of "the best labor and best thought and judgment of the Committee." Speaking for three hours, Kitchin called it a nonpartisan bill, noting that the Democrats, with Wilson's approval, had even adopted the Republican proposal for a commission to study the possibility of raising tariffs, which had been earlier dismissed with disdain at the White House. Yet the bill also had so many tax increases on the middle class that Kitchin himself described them as bitter pills to be swallowed.

The bill had four parts: raising the income tax, reinstituting an estate tax, taxing war munitions and retaining and adjusting taxes in place on beer, wine, tobacco and other things. The income tax portion—designed to raise $100 million—proposed to increase the "normal" rate from 1 to 2 percent and increase the surtax on incomes greater than $50,000. The maximum rate, on incomes of more than $500,000, would now be 10 percent instead of 7 percent.

The munitions tax called for arms makers earning more than 10 percent profit to be taxed on gross receipts at rates varying from

1 to 8 percent, with the highest rates on gunpowder and explosives. The bill added or increased taxes on beer and wine, tobacco companies, bankers, brokers and owners of "amusement places."

As for the inheritance tax, the bill revived a levy that had died after the Spanish-American War. Hull, who led the charge for it this time, helped draft the bill after once again studying the estate and inheritance tax laws of other nations, just as he had studied their income tax laws earlier. The proposed tax would levy 1 percent on estates valued above $50,000, ranging up to 6 percent on estates of more than $450,000. By now the inheritance tax was no longer a radical notion: at least thirty-three states had adopted one. As one expert, Daniel C. Roper, wrote in the *North American Review,* the tax reflected the belief that "something must be done to discourage rapidly growing fortunes" and that "some limit must be placed upon the possibility of a few individuals acquiring so much money that the Government itself is menaced by the power it brings them."

The bill was a neatly put-together package that had something for most parties but put conservatives in a quandary, especially those who opposed taxing the rich but also favored spending to prepare for possible entry into the war. Among those with mixed views was an increasingly prominent Republican, Representative Nicholas Longworth, wealthy scion of a prominent Cincinnati family who had been a champion of protectionism and a foe of the income tax—but an advocate of getting ready to go to war, in the tradition of his father-in-law, Teddy Roosevelt. Against his criticisms, both Hull and Speaker Champ Clark defended Kitchin's bill as the fairest way to pay for the nation's security needs. "An irrepressible conflict has been raging for a thousand years between the strong and the weak," declared Hull, "and the former always trying to heap the chief tax burdens upon the latter. That conflict still continues." The bill passed in the House on July 10 by a vote of 238 to 142, with many Republicans going along.

Once again as the Senate digested the House bill, it ended up making it even more radical, in part because the need for funds was growing at a fast clip. After a month of deliberations, the Finance Committee raised the income surtax to 13 percent (which meant that the top rate was now 15 percent). The committee also raised the tax rates on millionaire-level estates and munitions profits, and it called for a new tax on corporations based on their capital, surpluses and undistributed profits. The establishment of a new commission to study the value of tariffs, accepted reluctantly by some Democrats as a price to get Republican support for the bill, was kept in by the Senate—despite the best efforts of the new senator from Alabama, Oscar W. Underwood, veteran of the tariff and tax wars as former chairman of the House Ways and Means Committee.*

The Senate passed the bill on September 6 by 42 to 16 votes, with the support of five dissident Republicans, including progressives La Follette and George S. Norris of Nebraska. In conference, the Senate won most of the votes, including the provision that pushed the top surtax rate on the income tax to 13 percent on incomes over $1 million, agreeing with the House that the top rate would be 15 percent. (Personal exemptions remained at $3,000 for a single person and $4,000 for a married couple.) The law retained the old exemptions on salaries of federal, state and local officials and on income from government bonds. The corporate income tax went from 1 to 2 percent. The tax also did not distinguish between earned and unearned incomes. In what amounted to another clear triumph of the progressive and agrarian Democrats over the misgivings of Wilson and McAdoo, the President signed the bill into law on September 8.

The most memorable footnote of the new law was that Congress and the President had at last decreed that income could be taxed "from any business," eliminating the word *lawful*. Bootleg-

---

*In the Senate, his colleagues urged him to join the Senate Finance Committee, but he said he could not stomach having to lead more battles over trade barriers. The senator was reminded of a story about a cobbler in Kentucky who inherited a fortune, closed his shop and used up all the money in a life of "wild dissipation." Returning to his shop a poor man, he suddenly inherited another large fortune. "My God!" he said, looking up from his bench. "Must I go through all that again?" Said Underwood: "And that's the way I would feel about another tariff bill."

gers, illegal gamblers and others who might be engaging in criminal activity were on notice that they had to pay taxes too, though at this stage there was no language in the bill suggesting how the taxes would be collected from them. Far more important, however, the bill marked the first time that the income tax was raised significantly, for a specific purpose, war, and with the intention of quickly yielding large sums of revenue. "The principle of income tax was now permanently established," Cordell Hull later wrote. In his memoirs, he said that by raising tens of billions of dollars over the following several years, this bill "laid the cornerstone for the structure of Government financing the first World War, the peace period following, and the Second World War." The law established the first permanent estate tax—after a $50,000 exemption, the rate rose from 1 to 10 percent on the amount over $5 million—and the first tax on munitions production and corporate capital stock.

The enactment of this tax was one of the significant accomplishments of Woodrow Wilson. In just a few years of his presidency, he had used the crisis of war to turn away from decades of Republican tariff philosophy and protection of corporate wealth. By taxing corporate profits and wealth, the government was on its way to the next step of taxing "excess profits"—profits above a certain percentage of invested capital. Yet an unusual aspect of the tax increase furor was the low-key role of the President himself. The Wilson biographer Arthur Link said that during these negotiations, Wilson was so preoccupied with the war that he did not involve himself very much in the haggling over the details of the tax legislation of 1916, one of the most significant achievements of the cause of progressive taxation.

In historic terms, the unanswered question is whether these progressive steps would have been taken without the war. Certainly the case is strong that only something as dire as war would have made the new high rates acceptable to the public. The record shows that the war and its sister issue of preparedness—what might today be called national security—was consistently evoked by proponents of all the taxes, especially the tax on inheritances. Estate and inheritance taxes had been raised during the Civil War and the Spanish-American War and repealed when the wars were over.

Besides war, there were clearly other factors at work in the enactment of these taxes. The rising cost of living, for example, made the public more wary of higher taxes on consumption. Equally important were the public's distrust of big business and its antipathy, or at least uneasiness, toward great wealth, along with the constant fear of social unrest centered on huge economic inequalities among Americans. There was now another proliferation of studies by economists, political scientists and research groups analyzing the distribution of wealth in the United States and suggesting that the income tax and the inheritance tax could become instruments of reform.

One study, by an independent group of academics, union leaders and some business representatives called the Industrial Relations Commission, endorsed the view that labor unrest stemmed from the unequal distribution of American wealth. It cited the fact that forty-four families earned an aggregate income of $55 million, whereas factory and mine workers earned less than $10 a week. Basil M. Manly, the commission's research director, spoke of the "industrial feudalism" of the Rockefellers, Morgans, Vanderbilts and Astors. He urged an inheritance tax limiting inheritances from any estate to $1 million. But the five nonlabor members of the commission endorsed a less radical proposal for an estate tax, written by Professor John R. Commons. Unions, small businessmen and farmers agreed with Manly's conclusions, but the New York Sun called them "plain outright robbery."

The logic of the munitions tax was based more obviously on the war emergency and the need to act against profits made from it. Such countries as Denmark, Sweden, Canada, France, Germany, Britain and Italy were models. The hope among some American officials was that the tax would yield a third of needed revenues (about $200 million) by taxing the profits of firms that manufactured gunpowder, explosives, arms, motorboats and submarines at a rate of 12.5 percent. Raw materials were deducted along with other expenses.

The tax was controversial. Some said it was unfair to tax industries that were helping to fill a need. Why punish the very companies that were helping their country prepare for a possible war? The public, on the other hand, still felt that big firms such as du Pont, which manufactured chemicals and synthetic materials, were making such huge profits that they might actually try to encourage war fever.

———

The 1916 election was two months away. It would be the first presidential election in American history to be affected so heavily by world events. Wilson, though he had been voted into office as a minority President, with 42 percent of the vote, had reason for some confidence, figuring that most voters who had supported Teddy Roosevelt in 1912 were now likely to be happy with his progressive record. But the main issue was not the creation of the Federal Reserve, a lower tariff, the income tax and other achievements. It was Wilson's efforts to keep the United States out of war.

At the Democratic convention in St. Louis in June, the keynote speaker, Governor Martin Glynn of New York, delivered a peroration on actions that might have provoked the President into belligerence, each time getting the cheering crowd to call out, "What did we do? What did we do?" Each time, Glynn responded: "We didn't go to war!" From that exchange came the slogan (which Wilson never used and did not really like) "He kept us out of war." Wilson was in fact too preoccupied with the situation in Europe to think much about the campaign, though he found time to draw up the platform mostly by himself, favoring an expansion of federal powers at home and a duty to secure "peace and justice" overseas.

On the Republican side, party operatives harbored a genuine hope of taking back the White House. They had reduced the

Democrats' majorities in the 1914 congressional election and could not stop thinking of Wilson as an accidental President who could be unseated with a strong nominee. But G.O.P. operatives knew they had to have a candidate who appealed to progressives. Roosevelt was not wanted. ("The people as a whole are heartily tired of me and of my views," the former President confessed.) Taft favored Senator Elihu Root of New York or the former New York governor Charles Evans Hughes, whom he had appointed to the Supreme Court.

The hopeful Republicans gathered in June in Chicago, where they heard Senator Warren G. Harding of Ohio appeal for unity in his keynote speech. The party platform attacked Wilson's foreign policies and supported limited military preparedness and some social programs. After Hughes won the nomination on the third ballot, he submitted his resignation to Wilson to run against him and got a curt acceptance. ("I am in receipt of your letter of resignation and feel constrained to yield to your desire," the President wrote.) Hughes was a candidate with a distinguished résumé and an even more distinguished appearance, with his splendid beard, but he was a lackluster and distant campaigner. Roosevelt supported him but dismissed him privately as a "bearded iceberg."

Hughes criticized Wilson as weak on foreign affairs, too friendly to labor, too anti-tariff and too much of a straddler on the war. But though he had had a solid progressive record as governor of New York, he came across in his campaign as reflexively pro-tariff, anti-labor and probusiness.

Opening his drive against Wilson at Carnegie Hall in New York City, Hughes laid out his case for Wilson as a vacillating, uncertain leader. The speech ran an hour and a half, taxing the patience even of his most loyal supporters. He tried to be folksy in the campaign. He went to a baseball game in Detroit and chatted with Ty Cobb. He descended into a Montana copper mine, kissed babies and climbed mountains. But he equivocated on war preparedness, prompting Roosevelt to dismiss him as a "bearded lady" for not being strong enough on the issue. Comments like these nudged Hughes toward a tougher stance, but his caution was obvious.

Citing the old political rule "never to murder a man who is committing suicide," Wilson ignored his Republican opponent for much of the early part of the campaign. He had his hands full with work. Among his concerns were the military intervention in Mexico, a possible nationwide railroad strike, and strains with Britain over its seizure of American mail on the high seas.

On domestic issues, Wilson determined that he had to move to the left to sew up the progressive vote. In a shift, he supported bills for workmen's compensation for federal employees and for banning child labor. In the summer, railroad workers across the country had threatened to walk out if they did not get an eight-hour day with no reduction in wages. Failing in an effort to mediate, the President sided with the unions and secured legislation to impose an eight-hour day and establish a commission to study the problem. That startling presidential intervention in a labor dispute was a high-water mark for unions. But it drove financiers to Hughes's side and breathed life into his campaign. (Republicans raised $2.5 million from industrialists such as Pierre S. du Pont, the Rockefellers and J. P. Morgan, while the Democrats got some of their $1.6 million from the munitions industry and from 170,000 small donors.)

In the fall, it suddenly seemed possible that for all his earlier troubles, Hughes could win. Indeed, Wilson was pessimistic enough to privately devise a plan for a swift succession in the event of a Hughes victory. He would appoint him Secretary of State, which office the Constitution decreed was third in the line of succession, and then resign with his Vice President, allowing Hughes to become President without an interregnum.

On election day, early returns from the Northeast and Midwest indicated that Hughes had won. Wilson went to bed in his house on the Jersey shore thinking that he might have to execute his bizarre succession plan. But during the night, the counting started to reverse as returns came in from the West. The next day Wilson golfed with friends as the returns showed him pulling ahead in electoral votes. After another day of agonizing counts, he got his electoral majority. It was the closest presidential race since the Hayes–Tilden contest of 1876, and for the first time since Andrew Jackson's re-election in 1832, a Democrat would serve a second consecutive term. In popular votes, Wilson won narrowly, with 9.1 million to 8.5 million for Hughes, improving on his and Bryan's earlier totals. He had built a Democratic victory out of a coalition of workers, big-city machines, small businessmen and southerners that would serve the party for most of the century, until it broke apart in the 1970s. It was enough for the Democrats in 1916 to secure the White House and their majorities in Congress as well.

Most of all, Wilson won the election because he was the candidate of progressive policies—and of peace. A few months later he was inaugurated in an atmosphere of mounting anxiety about war.

CHAPTER TWELVE

"The Dawn of a Day
of Righteousness"

The Income Tax, the Great War
and the Counterreaction

WILSON'S CLOSE AND PRECARIOUS RE-ELECTION victory left little time for euphoria. Fearful that the flames spreading in Europe would soon engulf his antiwar campaign, the President immediately made another futile offer to negotiate a settlement. This time he laid out his grand vision for "peace without victory," which included a League of Nations, freedom of the seas and equality among all nations and peoples. In return for peace, however, the increasingly confident Germans demanded large swathes of Belgium, France, Luxembourg, the Baltic region and colonial Africa. Within months, they resumed their submarine warfare, forcing Wilson to break off diplomatic ties.

The cost of preparing for war was mounting, and early in 1917, Wilson sent another new revenue measure to Congress, where once again it landed in the hands of Claude Kitchin and others skeptical, if not hostile, to the idea. As the *New York Times* put it, increasing the income tax would "bring home to the minds of a great number of new voters the fact that the defense of this nation is going to cost them something." The emerging alternative to raising the personal income tax was to capture resources from the American industrial arsenal. At least fifteen countries had adopted an "excess profits" tax on corporations, taxing profits above a certain percentage of invested capital. Britain had raised such taxes to a rate of 60 percent. Kitchin proposed a similar tax of 8 percent on corporate net income after an exemption of $5,000, and a separate tax of 8 percent of a company's invested capital.

The ensuing arguments reflected Americans' ambivalent feelings about business. On the one hand, business was seen as the engine of military might; on the other, as a predator trying to squeeze profits out of the suffering of war. For Kitchin, an advantage of taxing business profits was that it would hit the industrial North, where war business was booming. "You can tell your people that practically all of this will go north of Mason and Dixon's line," he told members of the Ways and Means Committee. "The preparedness agitation has its hot bed in such cities as New York." With Republicans denouncing the measure as "Kitchinism," the House passed it on February 1, sending the bill to the Senate just as the Germans sank two American ships.

The submarine attacks only stiffened the resistance of the Senate pacifists, led by La Follette, who protested that they were being asked to consider the measure under duress. They accused Wilson of stampeding the country into granting him "dictatorial powers." But with Germany moving lethally on the high seas, La Follette's arguments had little chance of swaying the Senate, which passed the bill and sent it to Wilson for his signature on March 3.

Shortly thereafter, the coup de grâce for those hoping to avoid war came with the disclosure of the so-called Zimmermann telegram, an intercepted message from the German Foreign Secretary, Arthur Zimmermann, proposing that Mexico attack the

United States in the event of war. Wilson sought to tap American outrage over the Zimmermann note by asking Congress for authority to arm American merchant ships. When the lawmakers refused, he denounced them as a "little group of willful men" and assumed the authority himself. German U-boats responded by sinking three more American ships. But as war drew closer, Wilson seemed to sink into an ever deeper cloud of gloom—"a mysterious, a rather Olympian personage . . . shrouded in darkness from which issue occasional thunderbolts," as Henry Adams put it.

His brooding was understandable. Wilson was afraid not only that war would waste American lives and treasure but also that it would destroy his beloved New Freedom program, with all its progressive gains. "Every reform we have won will be lost if we go into this war," he told an associate in 1917. "We have been making a fight on special privilege. We have got new tariff and currency and trust legislation. We don't know yet how they will work. They are not thoroughly set." His fear was that war mobilization would empower the elites that he had battled for years. "War means autocracy," Wilson said privately. "The people we have unhorsed will inevitably come into the control of the country for we shall be dependent upon the steel, oil and financial magnates. They will run the nation."

———

On the evening of April 2, 1917, Wilson drove through a drizzle to the Capitol to deliver his war declaration. He had been refining it for days, and in the antechamber, he took a long look in a mirror over a mantel to compose himself. Addressing a somber House chamber, he called on Congress not to win the war but to "make the world safe for democracy." His highest ideals permeated the speech. "It is a fearful thing to lead this great peaceful people into war," Wilson declared. "But the right is more precious than peace, and we shall fight for the things which we have always carried nearest our hearts."

As the President spoke, Senator La Follette was chewing gum and not wearing the American flag pin sported by other senators. Afterward, "Fighting Bob" refused to stand. In the ensuing two-day debate over the war resolution, he attacked what he called the "irresponsible and war-crazed press" for fanning American passions, and he argued that Germany had been more patient than provocative in its conduct. The Senate approved the war resolution on April 4, with the House following on April 6. It was the beginning of the end of La Follette's reputation. Reviled as a coward and, worse, as a traitor—"a knave or a fool," as Senator Williams put it—La Follette did little good for his cause of a more progressive income tax system to pay for the war.

In the end, war transformed Wilson and his presidency no less than the country. Beforehand, even Colonel House had worried that the President, with his intellectual approach, "was not well fitted" to lead his country into combat. "I thought he was too refined, too civilized, too intellectual, too cultivated, not to see the incongruity and absurdity of war," House later wrote. It turned out that Wilson proved himself resolute and brilliant in war. He succeeded especially in transforming American ambivalence about involvement in the fighting into enthusiasm for a "great crusade."

If Wilson and his administration were to succeed in preserving their progressive approach to governing, they would have to establish a firm government hand over the mobilization in order to head off the private abuse of power, and also institute a fair policy of taxation to pay for the war.

On the mobilization side, Wilson created an array of 5,000 war agencies to exercise greater control and regimentation of American life and business than anything seen in the past. The most intrusive was the Selective Service, or draft, which registered 9 million men in 1917 and 24 million by the end of the war in November 1918. But for all the years and expense in preparing for the war, the United States was not prepared when war was declared in early April.

Indeed, G.O.P. lawmakers, after complaining about Wilson's earlier slowness, proposed after passage of the war declaration that a special coalition war cabinet be set up to run the war. Wilson rejected the idea, instead persuading Congress to grant him extraordinary powers to meet the emergency with limited price controls, rationing and oversight of food production, allocation of raw materials and labor relations. As chairman of the War Industries Board, Bernard Baruch, who as a stock trader and investor had amassed a fortune of $1 million by the age of thirty and gone on to serve on the board of the New York Stock Exchange, wielded power over manufacturing. Herbert Hoover, an American mining engineer, set goals for food production, established prices and made purchases through a government-owned corporation chartered in Delaware. McAdoo set up a Capital Issues Committee of the Federal Reserve Board and a War Finance Corporation to borrow at low interest rates for war production. He also headed the Railroad Administration.

Separate boards oversaw the drive to build, buy and borrow vessels, some seized from the enemy, for a so-called "bridge of ships" to get men, goods and war equipment to Europe. An Aircraft Production Board produced bombers and fighters. A National War Labor Board served as an arbiter to settle worker disputes without strikes, establishing an eight-hour day and equal pay for women. The creation of these boards was in many ways the product of years of agitation by progressives and reformers for greater government control over private business. Their success would legitimize government in many eyes as a crucial player in the economy. Indeed, Wilson's agencies served as a model for what would become the New Deal. The War Finance Corporation, for example, was a forerunner of Roosevelt's Reconstruction Finance Corporation.

But the truly revolutionary development behind these boards and the expanded role of government they reflected was their marriage to a progressive approach to financing the war. The Bureau of Internal Revenue at Treasury expanded from 4,000 to 15,800 employees between 1913 and 1920 and churned out dozens of different taxpayer forms that were printed and distributed in spite of paper shortages. The Treasury had to hire accountants, lawyers and economists to pore over the volumes of reports from corporations on salaries, dividends and interest payments. The tax system was on its way to becoming an integral part of the "welfare state."

Taxes did not get much of a mention in Wilson's speech declaring war on April 2. But he did call for extending loans to the Allies and borrowing for immediate expenses, with the debts to be repaid in the future "by well-conceived taxation." Warning against saddling future generations with debt, he urged Congress to "protect our people so far as we may against the very serious hardships and evils" of inflation arising from excessive loans. This was McAdoo's view, but not everyone in Congress agreed, at least initially.

Senator Furnifold M. Simmons, chairman of the Finance Committee, argued that paying bills by bond issues was the longtime custom for war, "and I see no reason for a change in that policy." His statement sent "a little shiver of premonitory dread over those who are familiar with the financial history of the past wars in which this country has been engaged," said the *New Republic*. The magazine was, clearly, referring to the inflation caused by excessive borrowing during the Civil War.

McAdoo, of course, had studied the Civil War experience, with its ruinous inflation and worthless currency in the North and especially the South. The mistakes of his illustrious predecessor, Treasury Secretary Salmon P. Chase, gave him what he said was "a pretty clear idea of what not to do." In his view, Chase had relied on "a hodge-podge of unrelated expedients," including the issuing of nearly worthless greenbacks, to avoid confronting citizens of the Union with the need to pay taxes. Chase's biggest missed opportunity, McAdoo thought, was that he never mobilized popular opinion to support the financing of the war. He was determined not to repeat that error.

To establish a proper ratio of taxing to borrowing, McAdoo consulted a range of bankers, industrialists and political leaders. All feared that his plans for $3 billion in loans would be excessive. J. P. Morgan, the patriarch's son, warned that only $1 billion at a time should be attempted—and that the government should avoid a tax program that would fall "unjustly upon the investing class of the country," lest these worthy investors have no money left to buy bonds. Haughty and self-serving as this advice was, McAdoo was not without sympathy. "If you take the whole of a man's surplus income through taxes," he later wrote, "you cannot expect him to buy bonds, nor can you expect industry to expand and prosper."

On the other hand, progressives argued that selling bonds to rich Americans would merely fatten their bank accounts. They favored financing the war entirely by taxes, preferably an income tax with high rates on the wealthy. Senator Hiram Johnson of California belittled "the skin-deep dollar patriotism of some of those who have been loudest in declamations on war in their demands for blood." La Follette, even more bellicose, though with greatly diminished influence, declared that failure to tax the wealthy would be "nothing short of the economic crime of all the ages."

The debate over borrowing versus taxing raged throughout the country. Generally, professional economists warned against excessive borrowing. In testimony before Congress, Professors O.M.W. Sprague of Harvard, Irving Fisher of Yale and E. Dana Durand of Minnesota counseled that overreliance on bonds would produce inflation, higher interest rates and diminished profits. In the end, McAdoo split the difference, setting a loan-to-tax goal of 3 to 1. Accounting records for the war vary, but historians seem to agree that in the end he basically achieved his objective.

McAdoo got even more conflicting advice on which taxes to impose. The academic trio of Sprague, Fisher and Durand advanced a crucial justification of the income tax from both an economic and a social perspective. They argued that because the draft was, in effect, a kind of tax, depriving conscripts of the ability to earn an income for their families, it was logical to tax the incomes of Americans not drafted or otherwise serving in the military. Then came the professional economic view of how high these taxes should be. Many economists said that taxes must not be so high as to stifle investment and work, an argument that would echo across the century in tax debates. Among them were supporters of a basic progressive income tax, including E.R.A. Seligman and R. M. Haig of Columbia and Charles J. Bullock of Harvard. Seligman estimated that the recently declared war would easily cost $10 billion a year for the foreseeable future. Interest and amortization alone, he said, might require $1.5 billion in new taxes a year.

Since "the wealthier classes" would be lending the money, and repayment of debt would be borne by "the community as a whole," Seligman said that basic fairness required the repayment to be made by those most able to pay. Just as the war conscripted men into service, he said, so it should conscript wealth. Indeed, the phrase "conscription of wealth" became a popular one in the national debate.

"Patriotism," said Seligman, "can often be translated into dollars and cents—in fact, the material side of patriotism is often quite as important as the spiritual side." Moreover, he noted, war makes most businessmen and workers wealthier. It pushes up profits and wages alike, so taxes are not as high as they would otherwise seem. He also dismissed concerns about diminishing capital investment, since war would dampen such investment anyway. "From every point of view, therefore, as much money ought to be raised during the war by taxation as is economically wise," he said. If Americans were taxed at the same rate as the British, it would yield $2.5 billion a year.

Another powerful argument for raising the income tax, marshaled by Professor O.M.W. Sprague of Harvard in the New Republic, claimed that taxing the wealthy was the surest way of preventing rich people from spending money on luxuries that society could no longer afford to produce. High income taxes were also needed to keep control over resentment of the rich among the masses. In

England, Sprague said, "the large gains and extravagance of a few have caused serious discontent in labor circles." He was returning to the old argument that high taxes on the rich help keep society stable.

Sprague went so far as to propose that the government take 95 percent of all income earned in excess of the average income of the two years before the war. The theory was that at times of war, "ordinary income should be taxed 'to the bone'" without depriving the rich of their "customary standard of life." The overriding goal of a wartime tax system, he said, was to "place all citizens upon an equal footing in so far as war conditions will permit." The ideal tax system could ease "the danger that class antagonism might develop even to the point of revolutionary outbreaks."

———

For all the talk of taxing, there was no escaping the need to borrow. Indeed, the first financial act of Congress after the declaration of war in April was to authorize $5 billion in bonds—"the greatest single bond issue in the history of the world," McAdoo called it— and another $2 billion in short-term debt certificates. These sums would help meet the cost of McAdoo's first "war budget" of $8.5 billion in the coming fiscal year. At the same time, Congress authorized $3 billion in loans to the Allies, who were making increasingly desperate appeals for loans because they simply could not pay for the war goods they needed. McAdoo recounted years later that the delegations from Europe seeking loans were frequently "war weary, jangled, nervous . . . on the edge of hysteria." He recalled that one English supplicant came into his office and broke down and wept, saying, "You must forgive me—overstrain."

As in the Civil War, there were complaints that issuing bonds provided a profitable tax shelter for the rich. McAdoo had a response: the Liberty Loan. His aim was to get ordinary Americans to buy bonds so that they could profit just as the investing class had always done. The bonds would be paid back by taxes on the wealthiest Americans and corporations. He was trying to turn the long-standing class dynamics of public finance upside down, reversing the Civil War regime of bonds issued to the rich and paid off through a tariff-driven tax structure borne by consumers.

Using sophisticated marketing techniques, the federal government placed loans deeper into the middle class than had been the case during the Civil War or was the case in Europe for this war. Eventually at least a half of American families subscribed, with Americans of moderate incomes (under $2,000 a year) purchasing nearly a third of the bonds.

To reach their audience, some bond appeals were blatant and racist, picturing grotesque fat Huns dragging young women off into the night with slogans like "Remember Belgium" and "That Liberty Shall Not Perish from the Earth" and "If you don't come across, the Kaiser will." And at least some appeals to farmers were based on both patriotism and fear. "Let the Allied Army break down, and an invasion is a certainty," farmers were warned in one pamphlet. McAdoo was proud of what proved to be a brilliant innovation. "We went direct to the people; and that means to everybody—to business men, workmen, farmers, bankers, millionaires, school-teachers, laborers," he later proudly wrote in his memoirs. "We capitalized on the profound impulse called patriotism. It is the quality of coherence that holds a nation together; it is one of the deepest and most powerful of human motives."

The First Liberty Loan of $2 billion in May of 1917—tax-exempt, despite the desire of many progressives—was a smashing success, with 4 million people signing up, far in excess of the goal. The second issue, for $3 billion, came in October and was subject this time to some income, excess-profits and war-profits taxes, as well as estate and inheritance taxes, in deference to criticism that many Americans were using the bonds to shelter their income from taxes. It was even more successful, oversubscribed again this time by more than 50 percent.

As for taxes, though Americans seemed ready and willing to

sacrifice, there was no consensus on what constituted genuine economic justice. Once again, the debate flared over whether to broaden the tax to reach more taxpayers of modest means, as proposed by the "moderates" led by McAdoo and endorsed by some Republicans, such as Nicholas Longworth, or to raise the top rates on the wealthiest taxpayers, as favored by many Democrats, some of whom wanted outright confiscation of any individual income over $100,000.

Trying to strike a balance, House Ways and Means Committee Chairman Kitchin proposed a $1.8 billion tax bill that would reduce the exemption (making more taxpayers pay), increase rates at the high end on both corporate and individual incomes (to make the rich pay more) and increase a range of excise taxes and duties.

In a five-hour speech to the House, Kitchin admitted that his committee members had come up with a messy compromise but that, by and large, they had done so in a selfless spirit. "Not one man," he claimed, "even hinted that this or that tax would bring disaster to his district or his State or to the industries of his State or district and therefore should not be imposed." But that was a polite exaggeration—or testimony to the ability of lawmakers to make arguments on purely abstract and philosophical grounds, disguising the naked self-interest at stake.

Representative Joseph W. Fordney, a Michigan Republican and guardian of his state's most powerful industry, acknowledged, for instance, that he had valiantly opposed taxing automobile sales. "I quarreled and fought and sometimes came near using profanity," he told the House, no doubt hoping his words would echo in the boardrooms and factory floors back home. "I am black and blue from my head to my heels by the punishment the Committee has inflicted on me." But Fordney later voted for the bill as an act of patriotism. "We need the money," he explained.

In the Senate, conservative members of the Finance Committee at first thought they might whittle the entire package down to $1.25 billion, or two-thirds of what McAdoo had sought. They were living in a dream world. The cost of the war was mounting by the day. In France, where the German onslaught was crushing Allied defenses, General John J. Pershing, commander of the American Expeditionary Force, was trying to assemble a force of a million Americans by the end of 1917.

McAdoo sent word to Capitol Hill that the Treasury now needed $2.245 billion, not $1.8 billion, and certainly not the $1.25 billion being considered in the Senate. The tax package would have to be even higher than that, since wartime prohibition was draining the Treasury of liquor revenues. Never before had lawmakers been asked to contemplate a sacrifice on that scale. "It is the greatest burden ever put upon any people," said the New York Times (August 1917), employing a bit of exaggeration, considering the sacrifice of men and wealth in the nations of Europe. "These burdens would have been thought incredible, unendurable, but for the education through which the world has passed under German compulsion."

The debate in both chambers now centered on whether to tax "war profits" or "excess profits." It was more than a semantic quibble. Kitchin favored "excess profits," similar to a provision in the law enacted in March. In the new bill, he would raise rates to 16 percent on profits in excess of $5,000, plus 8 percent on so-called invested capital. But the concept of taxing a business's capitalization—with the government effectively deciding what should constitute an appropriate profit—seemed to many businessmen and editorial writers, and to Wilson and McAdoo, as antithetical to the tenets of capitalism.

With the encouragement of the President and his Treasury Secretary, the Senate took a somewhat different approach. Staff economists of the Senate Finance Committee argued first that calculating a company's "invested capital" was problematical—capital could easily be watered down, for example—and unlikely to yield enough money. Instead, they proposed to tax "war profits," the specific windfall earned by businesses simply from the advent of war. Rather than imposing an arbitrary tax on capital, why not reckon what a company made before the war, then during the war, and tax the difference at graduated rates? Philosophically, this argument was persuasive to many. Yet the irony was that southerners were the most opposed. In large part because of government purchases for uniforms, the cotton industry had miraculously recovered in the three years since prices collapsed at the beginning of the war, and now plantation owners were upset at being singled out for their success.

Nevertheless, the Senate proposed to tax profits that were in excess of the average profits earned in 1911, 1912 and 1913. Instead of Kitchin's flat rate of 16 percent, the Senate graduated the rate from 12 percent (on profits more than 15 percent above pre-war levels) to 50 percent (on profits more than two-and-a-half times prewar levels). Now there were new objections. Kitchin pointed out that such an approach would allow companies that had earned huge profits *before* the war to escape taxes.

In the end, in a compromise, House and Senate tax writers agreed to incorporate some of both elements. There would be a tax on "war profits," calculated on the difference between profits before the war and at present, as well as a tax on "excess" profits— that is, profits above a certain percentage of "actual invested capital." The administration, still concerned about panicking industry, hoped to keep the "excess profits" provision out of the bill, but Wilson and McAdoo were unable to dissuade Kitchin. Once again the populist-radicals achieved a significant victory. After three weeks of haggling in the House–Senate conference, Congress produced the first wartime tax measure, a complicated and nearly incomprehensible bill aimed at yielding $2.5 billion.

The War Revenue Act signed by Wilson on October 3, 1917— exactly four years after he had signed the first income tax law—was historic in almost every way, especially for how it taxed incomes, capitalization and windfall profits. Professor Seligman at Columbia called it "the most gigantic fiscal enactment in history," and many other economists praised it as a courageous step. Of course, the crowd favoring "conscription of income" proclaimed themselves uneasy with the ratio of $15 billion in loans versus $4 billion in taxation for war costs so far.

From across the ocean, a prominent young British economist named John Maynard Keynes, an adviser to the British treasury, noted in an article that for all its radical steps, the American tax effort had not reached the level of taxation on the rich or on corporate profits enacted in Britain. But what was most striking was the tax bill's burden on the upper brackets. The tax historian Sidney Ratner estimates that nearly three-quarters of the law comprised taxes on wealth (estates, high incomes and excess profits), with another 13 percent in taxes on luxuries such as jewelry and amusements or "sin taxes" on tobacco, alcohol and the like.

More specifically, the new wartime income tax established new levels of "normal" taxes and "emergency" surtaxes. Any unmarried person with an income more than $1,000 or a married couple with an income more than $2,000 had to pay some income tax, a provision that added 5 million more Americans to the tax rolls. Balanced against that expansion, however, was a drastic increase in the rates at the higher levels. From an existing top tax rate of 13 percent, the government set a new maximum rate of 63 percent on incomes greater than $1 million and 67 percent on incomes of more than $2 million.

"This is the high water mark thus far reached in the history of taxation," declared Professor Seligman. "Never before, in the annals of civilization, has an attempt been made to take as much as two thirds of a man's income by taxation." Another important feature of the law dropped the obligation of businesses to withhold taxes. Instead, employers were required to file information to the government on wages, gains and profits, leaving the responsibility to file with the individual taxpayer. As a practical matter, the filing requirements in the law gave the government enough information to monitor tax evasion just as effectively as before.

The "war profits" and "excess profits" features applied to corporations, partnerships and individuals. They taxed profits exceeding the average profits of 1911–13, as well as profits exceeding a certain rate of "invested capital," including cash holdings, tangible property and investment assets. Rates were graduated from 20 to 60 percent. In addition, the 1917 act beefed up the inheritance tax while taking care to exempt estates left by anyone killed in the war. The remainder of the tax package raised sin taxes and imposed new taxes on transportation, communication, insurance, automobiles and motorcycles, phonographs, jewelry, cosmetics, club dues, amusements and the like.

It was sobering for Americans to contemplate that more money was being raised for the war in Europe than had been spent by the federal government in all the years since 1791. Even more startling was the drastic redistribution of the tax burden. Corporations were among those most alarmed. Many viewed their survival as threatened. Some of Wilson's business supporters, such as Bernard Baruch and the financier Jacob Schiff, broke with the administration over taxes.

Wilson may have been sympathetic to them at one level, but he also understood the hard political realities. His basic views are not easily determined from the public record. But it seems obvious that the President accepted a more radical tax package than was perhaps necessary because of his own view that the state had to be a counterweight to the power of corporate and personal wealth. Had he not felt this way, the historian Elliot Brownlee argues, Wilson and McAdoo might just as easily have struck an alliance with Republicans and conservative Democrats to impose broad-based consumption taxes on the middle class and poor to finance the war. Doing so would have fractured the Democrats and betrayed the principles for which Wilson stood when he tore down the tariff walls. On taxes, at least, Wilson was in the end loyal to his southern, western and populist and progressive base—and perhaps to his ideals as well.

Just as the 1917 tax package was enacted, the war plunged through another spiral of momentous developments. The Bolshevik revolution in the fall led to Russia suing for peace while the Austrians and Germans overran Italy and hammered the British and French lines on the western front. Pershing had wanted more time to train his troops before sending them into battle, but the need for them was too great for delay. In December, fewer than 200,000 Americans had arrived in France. The following summer Pershing reached his goal of a million, a prelude to the 2 million that would be "over there" the next November.

Germany undertook a renewed offensive in early 1918, hoping to gain ground or even win before the Americans arrived in large numbers. The German assault extended from Flanders in the north to the Somme, just fifty miles north of Paris, throwing the Allies off balance and forcing Pershing to accelerate his dispatch of men to the front. Almost as soon as Wilson signed the loans and revenues authorized in October, it became obvious that the package was insufficient. Another deficit loomed, this time more than $6 billion. But at the beginning of 1918, the political terrain was slightly different. Now Congress was thinking about an election.

McAdoo was out stumping the country for the latest Liberty Loan in the spring of 1918 when press reports quoted him as saying that a new tax bill was needed. On Capitol Hill, Kitchin and Simmons knew that any such package would take months to draft, bringing its passage right up to election day and easily costing the Democrats their majorities in Congress. As the New York Times reported, McAdoo's need for more taxes "has caused more dismay than anything that has happened since the Government came into the hands of the Democratic Party."

Republicans were already assailing Wilson for the hemorrhaging costs of the European conflict as "characteristic of the want of foresight and preparedness which has marked our policy toward the war," as one put it. Kitchin and Simmons suggested that the tax bill be deferred until after November. McAdoo said no, but Wilson was not so sure. Then Cordell Hull wrote Wilson that if Congress passed another round of taxes on war profits, Americans would accept them "without complaint." Wilson replied the next day, judiciously complimenting Hull for his "very weighty argument indeed."

The letter leaked to reporters, who burst into Hull's office demanding to know if Wilson was now on board for another tax increase. But Wilson was clearly torn. He agreed with McAdoo that it would be risky to put off the tax request, but he understood the political jeopardy. His suggestion that new taxes be deferred, accompanied by a promise to enact a bill the following February, was rejected by the Republicans. There seemed to be no alternative to immediate action. On May 27, President Wilson addressed both houses of Congress with eloquent fervor, in the hope that another round of sacrifice would not be subjected to partisan political jockeying. He put it this way:

> We are not only in the midst of the war, we are at the very peak and crisis of it. Hundreds of thousands of our men, carrying our hearts with them and our fortunes, are in the field, and ships are crowding faster and faster to the ports of France and England with regiment after regiment, thousand after thousand, to join them until the enemy shall be beaten and brought to a reckoning with mankind. . . . The volume of our might must steadily and rapidly be augmented until there can be no question of resisting it. If that is to be accomplished, gentlemen, money must sustain it to the utmost. Our financial program must no more be left in doubt or suffered to lag more than our ordnance program or our ship program or our munitions program or our program for making millions of men ready. These others are not programs, indeed, but mere plans upon paper, unless there is to be an unquestionable supply of money.

It was one of Wilson's great orations, best remembered for his emotional appeal to an audience of politicians to become something more than what they were. The challenges ahead, he said, must be met "without selfishness or fear of consequences." And then came the famous peroration, or perhaps an expression of resignation by a President prepared to accept the political consequences of his actions, whatever they might be. "Politics is adjourned," he declared. "The elections will go to those who think least of it; to those who go to the constituencies without explanations or excuses, with a plain record of duty faithfully and disinterestedly performed."

With regard to the specifics of the tax package, the President laid out several crucial principles. The "intense and pitiless light" of publicity from then on would expose any attempt by lobbyists to persuade Congress not to tax war profits, he asserted. He said the lawmakers would be able to act "on this matter of taxation" because they understood the need and their duty no less than the soldiers in the trenches of Europe. Americans, he added, were not simply ready to send their men to possible death overseas. They were willing to "bear any burden and undergo any sacrifice" to win the war, including taxes. "We need not be afraid to tax them, if we lay taxes justly," he declared. "They know that the war must be paid for and that it is they who must pay for it, and if the burden is justly distributed and the sacrifice made the common sacrifice from which none escapes who can bear it at all, they will carry it cheerfully and with a sort of solemn pride." He ended his speech with the hope that when Americans saw the noble uses "for which their wealth has been piled up," they would rejoice to "see the dawn of a day of righteousness and justice and peace."

Wilson made it sound almost as if Americans were actually seeking a tax increase in order to feel the joy of sacrificing their hard-earned money for a righteous cause.

But of course, Congress was weary, exceedingly so. Kitchin was "unhappy, disgruntled, querulous," said the New York Times, and many lawmakers openly expressed doubt that the money was truly needed. McAdoo's sanctimonious lecturing of the Ways and Means Committee about "the evil consequences" of borrowing and inflation rankled the lawmakers. Kitchin, moreover, still favored taxing "excess profits" over "war profits," and he accused the Treasury of slowness in supplying information about company finances. To press his point, he cited the large prewar profits made by Henry Ford, whose company was paying no war-profits tax. The same situation, the congressman asserted, applied to Eastman Kodak, National Cash Register, Standard Oil of Indiana, American Tobacco and many other corporate giants. "We insist that these corporations, who were wonderfully prosperous before the war and equally so now, pay a part of the increased taxes," he said.

Exhausted and overworked, McAdoo asked Wilson to prod Kitchin to be more cooperative. Kitchin's insistence on taxing "excess" profits (at a fixed percentage above a certain level for business) was, in the Secretary's view, unworkable, intrusive and offensive—"a function of taxation to bring all profits down to one level" for all businesses, sapping them of "industry, foresight, and sagacity of their fruits." Finally Kitchin agreed to reduce the proposed rates on excess profits, telling the House that his differences with the Treasury Secretary were now resolved "in the most pleasant way."

The committee's bill was designed to raise $8.2 billion with a new maximum income tax rate of 65 percent and increases in taxes on corporations, war profits (with a high rate of 80 percent) and excess profits. The usual liberal papers defended the package, but the criticism was sounding more and more hysterical. Conservative papers warned that the new tax bill was socialist and a burden on "the rich and well-to-do classes." The New York Globe declared that "in view of the contents of this tax bill, we shall no more hear the nonsense that this is a 'capitalistic' war, waged for the benefit of men of capital. It is a poor man's war, waged at the expense of capital, and one of its collateral effects will be to diffuse wealth."

As the bill passed the House in September, Hull declared that "next to fighting in the front lines," there was no better test of patriotism than a willingness to pay taxes for the war. Not surprisingly, many senators failed to see it that way. Leading the assault, Senator Henry Cabot Lodge warned that the package might "reduce profits to a point which will dry up the sources" of the income tax and the ability of Americans to buy Liberty bonds. He and others pushed amendments to scale the whole package back by scrapping the provision to increase the tax on incomes and corporate excess profits and war profits.

Failing to complete the bill on November 1, the Senate went into recess. They did so as Americans could see the war situation changing drastically, and for the better. The German drive toward Paris had stalled and been repulsed by a powerful counterforce that included Americans. By the summer, the Allies had begun pushing the Germans back as Pershing made his first offensive near Verdun. In November, Americans, numbering 2 million in France alone, were helping to drive Germans back all along the western front.

The midterm elections of 1918 approached in a nation shaken and transformed in ways most Americans could scarcely understand. Though most people supported the war, the Justice Department under Attorney General Mitchell Palmer cracked down ruthlessly on disloyalty, sedition and what it viewed to be unruly dissent. Authorities banned German books and music while condoning vigilante actions against Americans of German origin. Underneath the nation's surface prosperity, millions of blacks migrated to the North, and rural Americans migrated to the cities to find work. The cost of living had increased 20 percent between 1914 and 1916, but the cost of food, fuel, energy, clothing and other goods was up by more than 50 percent.

Despite all the talk of taxing excess profits and the rich, the prosperity of the few served as a focus of resentment for many Americans, especially those whose sons had fallen in Europe's battlefields. Much of the anger centered on profiteering by companies with government contracts. McAdoo tried to combat the problem by denunciation. He charged that in the coal industry, profits were a thousand percent of costs and that Bethlehem Steel's profits were

800 percent higher than before the war. Du Pont's stock had risen so much that its executives were getting fat bonuses. "The law of supply and demand has been replaced by the law of selfishness," said Herbert Hoover. Increasingly weary of the war, high prices, sacrifices and scarcities, many Americans were ready for a change. They found it easy to blame an administration that had presided over a federal budget that had increased nearly 2,500 percent and a federal debt that had ballooned tenfold.

Wilson pleaded for support in the congressional election, declaring at one point that America's allies would see a Republican victory as "a repudiation of my leadership." Republicans recoiled at this assertion, perceiving it as a betrayal of his "politics-is-adjourned" pledge. With the Democrats also split over a variety of issues, not least the harsh austerity measures and tax hikes, the party was heading for disaster. Its base was fracturing by the week. Western wheat farmers resented the government's preference for price supports for cotton growers. Voters in the cities resented prohibition, which was being pushed by conservatives in the South. Northern liberals were upset by the crackdown on civil liberties. Many Americans opposed women's suffrage, which was being debated in Congress. Finally, the Northeast was angry over the philosophy of "Kitchinism" that had imposed high income and corporate taxes on people and businesses in that region.

And so, despite the extraordinary military success that American troops were experiencing in Europe, the electorate delivered a stinging defeat to the Democrats. Republicans captured both houses of Congress in a convincing display of renewed strength. One of the great historical questions remains, however, whether the result would have been the same if the war had been won a few days before the election instead of a few days afterward.

The armistice, with extremely harsh terms for Germany, was declared on November 11. Victory arrived at a staggering cost: 112,000 American servicemen killed (a number that didn't come close to the 1.4 million French and 900,000 British dead, representing an entire generation nearly wiped out). As for the financial cost, a calculation in 1924 held that all the warring countries incurred $82 billion to wage the Great War, with the United States spending about a fifth of that figure.

———

With the armistice and an imminent change in the political leadership of Congress, work on the unfinished tax package stalled. McAdoo scaled back his budget request, and Wilson warned that while war costs would diminish, they would not disappear altogether. In his annual message in December, he spoke of the need to prepare for the postwar "industrial readjustment" that lay ahead.

But now a new issue was emerging in the Senate: objections to Wilson's trip to the Versailles peace negotiations and to the peace terms that he was pursuing with the victors. Wilson's grand vision of a "peace without victory" and the right of European nationalities to have their own nations was his and almost his alone.

Early on in the fighting, the President had been shocked to discover an array of secret treaties among the Allies, some of them publicized after the Bolsheviks came to power in Russia in the fall of 1917. The President had outlined his own high-minded war aims that year with an enunciation of his Fourteen Points. Five were general, relating to open agreements between nations, freedom of the seas, equal economic opportunity, arms reductions and adjusting colonial claims. The fourteenth was a League of Nations, a popular proposal among the idealists and internationalists and perhaps among ordinary working people and soldiers fighting in the war, but not necessarily among the Allies or even the leadership of Congress.

Another change came with the departure of McAdoo from the Wilson cabinet. Exhausted and disappointed that Wilson had done nothing to promote him as a possible successor in the White House, McAdoo eventually moved to California, hoping to establish a political base. He was later to campaign unsuccessfully for the 1924 presidential nomination, and in the 1930s he was divorced from Wilson's daughter and served Franklin Roosevelt loyally as a California senator from 1933 to 1939. Postwar finances fell to McAdoo's successor, Carter Glass, a Virginia congressman who had served as chairman of the House Banking Committee. The Republican congressional leaders waiting to assume command after the first of the year immediately rejected his spending projections.

Determined to resist any tax package that would lock in rates for more than a year, they began laying out their own approach. It started with the reintroduction of the tariff. On the other hand, they were loath to repeal taxes across the board because they knew that the government would need the revenue, even if, as they began to assume, a Republican were in the White House after the next presidential election.

During the interregnum before the new Congress convened, the Democrats remained in control of the Senate Finance Committee, still led by Senator Furnifold M. Simmons, who went along with demands to pare back the tax hike passed by the House in the fall. Despite a torrent of criticism from Republicans, the Senate passed the bill just before Christmas without even a roll call. After the holidays, a Conference Committee churned through the House and Senate versions for more than a month. The new Revenue Act of 1918 passed on February 13, 1919, just as Wilson returned from his first trip to France with a proposal to create a new League of Nations to prevent war from ever occurring again.

The new tax law was the fourth and last big revenue measure of the Wilson years. Once again its progressive nature was its singular feature. About four-fifths of the $6 billion package was to come from taxes on incomes, war profits, excess profits and estates. Under the new law, the normal and surtax rate for the income tax went up to an astounding 77 percent—10 percent higher than the 1917 law, which Seligman had earlier labeled the highest tax rate "in the annals of civilization." It also raised rates on the excess and war profits taxes, and it included a provision taxing anyone who employed child labor, which was an attempt to ban child labor through taxation (after the Supreme Court invalidated a law banning such labor). The excess profits tax was on a scale going up to 65 percent of the amount in excess of 20 percent of invested capital.

———

With the dawning of 1919, Wilson redoubled his efforts to salvage a victory for his ideals in Europe in the face of demands from the Allies for a tough program of reparations and annexations from the defeated powers. But Wilson's uneasiness with reparations was undercut by a simple fact. The Allies had borrowed so heavily from the United States—nearly $10 billion by McAdoo's calculation—that reparations seemed the only way they could pay off the loans.

It took a threat by Wilson to negotiate a separate peace with Germany to bring the Allies around on at least some matters. In the end, what was negotiated bore little resemblance to Wilson's dream of a "peace without victory." Naively, he had underestimated the Allies' desire to punish Germany. He also blundered famously by failing to take any prominent Republicans with him to the peace negotiations in Paris. Seeing himself as the guarantor of humanity's interests after the war, Wilson brought the treaty home in February of 1919 and asked the Senate to accept it in its entirety, including its call for a new League of Nations. "I have found that you get nothing in this world that is worth-while without fighting for it," Wilson told Colonel House.

Ready to join the battle was the formidable Henry Cabot Lodge, the Brahmin chairman of the Senate Foreign Relations Committee, who had first met Wilson when he was president of Princeton and immediately distrusted him as dangerously left leaning in his politics. To Lodge, Wilson was an opportunist with "no intellectual integrity at all." His venom extended to disdain for Wilson's quick remarriage a few years earlier. "I never expected to hate anyone in politics with the hatred I feel towards Wilson," the senator wrote Theodore Roosevelt.

In substance, Lodge's main objection to the League was the treaty article calling for American military participation in any action that the member nations should authorize against an aggressor. Though Wilson got some concessions on this clause during his second trip to Paris in the summer of 1919, he was clearly already suffering under physical and mental strain from the pressures bearing down on him.

In Paris, Wilson expressed fears that he was being spied on by the French and muttered about the arrangement of the furniture in his hotel room. The final treaty contained some features that Wilson had fought for, including the establishment of new boundaries for the nations of Europe and the call for self-determination in some cases. But the treaty rejected his plea against war reparations. Returning home to the United States in July, Wilson said that Senate defeat of the treaty was unthinkable. "Dare we reject it and break the heart of the world?" he asked. To associates, he expressed certainty that it would be ratified.

Wilson's overconfidence no doubt reflected his weakening constitution. Sick, exhausted, suffering from hardening of the arteries, he may have had a stroke in Paris in early 1919. Lodge hoped to dissipate whatever public support there was for the treaty by delaying a vote as long as he could. He had the treaty read out loud in committee for two weeks and held public hearings for six.

Senator Elihu Root came up with the suggestion of a "reservation," as opposed to an amendment, which would not necessarily have required renegotiating the treaty. The main reservation, drafted by Lodge, said that any treaty obligation had to be consistent with Congress's sole power to declare war. But Wilson refused to go along with what he saw as a ploy. "Never! Never!" he declared. "I'll appeal to the country!"

Despite the warnings of his doctor, Wilson went on a cross-country speaking tour, traveling 8,000 miles and giving 36 speeches in 22 days while his strength ebbed away. In late September, his train pulled into Wichita, where Wilson's loyal secretary, Joe Tumulty, told the crowd that the President was suffering from "nervous exhaustion" and could not speak. The train immediately returned to Washington.

Complaining of headaches, the President had suffered a transient ischemic attack, a prelude to the stroke that struck him on October 1, sending him collapsing to the bathroom floor. With the President nearly comatose, Wilson's wife, Edith, and Admiral Cary Grayson, his doctor, refused to discuss the nature of his condition and laid him out on the Lincoln bed, where visitors were not allowed at first to see him. To aides beseeching her for access to the ailing chief executive, Mrs. Wilson was regally impatient. "I am not interested in the President of the United States," she told officials trying to see him. "I am interested in my husband and his health."

After some weeks, Wilson reappeared in a wheelchair or propped up in bed as visitors tried to engage him in conversation. During one such session, Senator Albert Fall, a Nebraska Republican and foe of the treaty, told Wilson as he left: "We've been praying for you, sir." Wilson was alert enough to reply: "Which way, Senator?" During Wilson's incapacitation, it was Edith Wilson who met with the cabinet, sometimes shuttling back and forth between its members and the President with word of his decisions. Some historians have concluded that she was effectively running the government.

It was in this period that the Senate passed fourteen reservations to the treaty. Wilson rejected them, even though many experts think they would not have damaged the treaty's purposes. Had he accepted them, history might well have been very different. The Senate rejected the treaty, without the reservations, in an initial vote in November of 1919. Four months later, in March, the treaty with fifteen reservations attached fell seven votes shy of the two-thirds majority needed for passage. Many historians argue that if Wilson had accepted that version of the pact, he could have won the Senate's approval.

But as his presidency wound down, the President was a changed man: petulant, self-pitying and helpless rather than incisive and thoughtful. He was also alone, cut off from his closest advisers, including Colonel House, who called his final estrangement from the man he had served for so long "a tragic mystery, a mystery that now can never be dispelled, for its explanation lies buried with him."

Along with rejecting Wilson's most important foreign policy initiative, Congress quickly began dismantling the government and tax structures that he had created to run and finance the war. The War Industries Board shuttered its doors so rapidly that Baruch had to pay the fares home for its workers out of his own pocket. As war contracts got canceled and price controls were eased, there were new fears of inflation and unemployment. Wilson recovered enough to propose setting up public works programs and farm irrigation projects to ease the transition, but the climate for a muscular federal government had disappeared with the war. America was embarking on a period of reaction against liberal reforms. Uneasiness about the future spread as workers—longshoremen, printers, clothing workers, textile workers, telephone workers—launched a wave of strikes in 1919 and Americans responded with a distinct lack of sympathy for them. Indeed, the public cheered when United States Steel broke a nationwide strike by hundreds of thousands of workers in 1920. A police strike in 1919 in Boston prompted Governor Calvin Coolidge of Massachusetts to send out state troops. His declaration that "there is no right to strike against the public safety, anywhere, anytime" drew a congratulatory letter from Wilson and made Coolidge a national figure.

In another sign of the times, Attorney General A. Mitchell Palmer responded to the Red Scare over Bolshevik agitation in Europe by making war on labor and radicals, rounding up thousands of suspects and deporting hundreds of alleged Communists. A wave of intolerance extended to immigrants, Catholics, Jews and African Americans. While this tide of reaction set in, Congress strove to phase out the excess and war profits taxes, along with the high rates of the income tax. After the ratification of the Eighteenth Amendment outlawing "intoxicating liquors" in January of 1919, Congress passed the Volstead Act, enforcing the ban over President Wilson's veto on October 27. Prohibition, a colossally misbegotten attempt at social engineering, took effect on January 16, 1920, with the side effect of draining off federal revenues.

Wilson's dream that he could turn the 1920 election into a public referendum on the League of Nations, never realistic, was quickly dashed as the Democrats, gathering in San Francisco at the end of June, all but collapsed in disarray. Against all logic, an ailing President Wilson seemed, for a time, actually to expect that his party would renominate him. Declining to designate a successor, he let two of his cabinet members battle each other—McAdoo, the disappointed son-in-law, and Palmer, the red-bashing Attorney General. In the end, the party nominated the Governor of Ohio, James M. Cox, for President and—in a gesture to the internationalists of the Northeast—selected Wilson's assistant secretary of the Navy, a promising young New Yorker from a famous family, Franklin D. Roosevelt, as his running mate.

The Republicans had every reason to be complacent. They had passed over the popular Herbert Hoover and had no interest in the progressive senator and former governor of California, Hiram Johnson, or the hero of the Spanish-American War and champion of war preparedness, General Leonard Wood, who had built up a sizable campaign war chest. Instead, in the famous smoke-filled room, a group of party power brokers coalesced around the undistinguished, pleasant but impressive-looking senator from Ohio, Warren G. Harding, and—in a gesture to sentiment outside the convention hall—they tapped the popular strike-breaking governor of Massachusetts, Calvin Coolidge, as his running mate.

The Democrats did try on occasion to revive the issue of the League, but Harding parried by declaring that he, too, favored the League, though with reservations. He won the election with a famous formulation of the nation's yearnings. "America's present need," he said, "is not heroics but healing, not nostrums but normalcy, not revolution but restoration." McAdoo memorably described Harding's speeches as "an army of pompous phrases moving across the landscape in search of an idea." In the landslide of 1920, Harding won with 61 percent of the popular vote and carried every state outside the South, becoming the most conservative and probusiness President in a generation.

Blissfully ordinary, and far more comfortable playing poker with his cronies than presiding over the affairs of state, Harding was in many ways a man of his time. Though he chose well in several cabinet posts—Charles Evans Hughes as Secretary of State, Hoover at Commerce, Henry Wallace as Secretary of Agriculture and the tax-cut advocate Andrew Mellon at Treasury—others in the inner circle betrayed him, particularly Interior Secretary and former Senator Albert Fall, an arch foe of conservation who later was convicted of bribery in the leasing of the naval oil reserves at Teapot Dome, Wyoming. The "normalcy" would last less than a decade. Before it came crashing down in 1929, the prosperity of the 1920s enabled Congress to enact five separate tax cuts, in 1921, 1924, 1926, 1928 and 1929, in spite of the need for revenue to help retire the war debt. With Harding emphasizing the need to put "our public household in order," and Mellon eager to repeal the most hated of the levies, the tax cuts included the elimination of the war profits tax, a sharp reduction of the excess profits tax and cuts in the rates of the corporate and personal income taxes.

The new era did not entirely banish suspicion among Americans toward monopolies and wealth, particularly in the labor movement and among farmers and others in the South and West, where it was still popular to favor a progressive tax system and continuing government regulation of railroads, oil leasing, energy and a few other sectors of the economy. Yet the heroes of the decade were to be the business giants lionized as the agents of what looked like permanent prosperity to the American political landscape. Wilson's

New Freedom was all but forgotten. Whereas in 1912 the nation had turned drastically to the left, perhaps without realizing it, eight years later it turned drastically to the right.

It is easy to see Wilson's achievements getting lost or trampled by the conservative policies that swept the nation in the 1920s. But the legacy he left was gigantic. Although he failed to forge a new consensus in America in favor of federal control over the economy, as Lincoln had done during the Civil War, Wilson proved that the federal government could mobilize the nation's resources to fight a global war. It could build popular support for such an undertaking through a progressive tax system and the sale of bonds to the public.

All these steps would, in twelve short years, serve as a model for financing the modern welfare state enacted in the New Deal and preserved for the rest of the century.

With regard to taxes, Wilson's legacy lay in his administration's successful financing of the war through a progressive system that took into account the wealth accumulated before and during the war itself. One of the architects of the wartime structure, Cordell Hull, proudly noted that excluding the loans to Allies, taxes paid for about a third of the cost of the war—a vast improvement over the ratio of the Civil War. Indeed, taxes made up a larger part of total revenues in the American war effort than any other country in the war.

In addition, as Treasury Secretary McAdoo long maintained after the war, the borrowing system aimed at selling bonds to the middle class was more fair and just than had been the case in the Civil War, and a more progressive tax system existed to retire the war debt. In addition, for better or worse, except for a brief period before the Great Depression with the passage of the Smoot–Hawley tariff of 1930, the war-era taxes effectively sealed the beginning of the end of the tariff and excise tax as the dominant source of revenue for the United States. From then on, it would be clear that the income tax was a far more potent and fast-acting way of raising revenue. It side-

lined the ongoing American debate over tariffs that pitted consumers (workers, farmers, small businessmen) against producers
(and the unions that sided with them in the trade wars).

Equally important, the advent of the income tax during World
War I cemented the philosophy that has guided American tax politics since then that taxes ought to be borne according to the ability
to pay. Of course, even during the war, the tax was more symbolic
than extensive. In 1920, out of a population of 106 million Americans and a workforce of 41.7 million, only 5.5 million income tax
returns were filed. Only a fraction of the wealthiest of these
accounted for a majority of the revenue received.

It is possible to view the enactment and expansion of the
income tax as merely a kind of palliative, a salve to ease American
concern about the privileges of the rich, a protection against instability—but far short of a device redistributing income among
Americans. As the tax historian John F. Witte argues, the wartime
taxes were "class legislation" in the sense that they were enacted
not to change society in any fundamental way but to make the public feel that something was being done about war profiteers and the
few who were profiting from the hardship suffered by the many.

The war transformed the attitude of Americans toward their
entire government. It became acceptable, at least in a time of crisis,
to harness the private sector under the authority of a vast government bureaucracy and to mobilize billions of dollars in public
expenditures in pursuit of an overriding goal. Government
resources, in turn, helped speed the arrival of whole new industries
in such areas as communications and transportation.

The tax structure that supported these changes was no less
transformed. In 1913, nearly half of federal revenues came from
customs duties, and almost all the rest came from tobacco and
liquor taxes. This meant that nearly 95 percent of federal revenues came from the purchase of commodities, which were paid
disproportionately by families of modest means. By 1930, by contrast, even after the tax reductions following the end of the war,

two-thirds of federal revenues came from income and corporate taxes.

Did this change result from deep progressive yearnings among Americans at a fixed point in history? It is true that for many decades the populists first, and then the progressives, demanded some kind of system that would make the sacrifice of paying for government more equitable. But the fervor for such economic justice was only one factor that brought about the changes in the tax system itself. The other factors included sectional divisions in the country, and the fact that some parts, especially the farm belts of the West and the cotton-producing South, had long been poorer and therefore bore more than their share of the tax burden through the regime of consumption taxes and tariffs that had existed for many decades. The growing reaction against the tariff, and the desire to change the basic federal financing structure, led to the most votes being cast for the two most progressive presidential candidates in 1912 and to an overwhelmingly Democratic and progressive Congress.

But the tax structure would not have occurred without the war. One of the ironies of history was that out of the devastation of civilization as it was known came the dramatic creation of a vibrant tax and economic system that Americans live with today. Only a war could drive tax rates, even for a tiny minority, from an extremely modest 7 percent at the outset of the conflict to the astounding level of 77 percent on the wealthiest Americans.

The sacrifice and dislocations demanded no less. It was not the intention of American leaders to redistribute income on a grand scale, and that is not what Americans did. But war unleashed the American willingness to use the tax system for aggressive social as well as economic ends. Once it was possible to see a great revenue engine financing a gigantic conflict, taxing the wealthiest Americans at high rates, it was more possible to contemplate such an engine supporting a welfare state. The consensus for such a state was not yet in place when Americans established their new tax system. It did not come for a dozen years, in the New Deal. The decades of debate since then have rewritten the tax code many times and in many ways.

But the system that survives intact is a product of sixty years of turmoil, from the Civil War to World War I. That turmoil leaves a legacy that survived and strengthened the nation for the rest of one century and into the next.

Epilogue

⁓

FROM 1860 TO 1920, THE ERA OF THE GREAT TAX WARS resounded with arguments over two definitions of fairness.

The first held that it was fair for society to tax income at graduated rates, according to the ability to pay, because of a need to establish some level of social equity and to curb the power of great wealth over government. Neglecting that challenge, income tax proponents argued, perpetuated and deepened the unequal distribution of the nation's riches and ultimately jeopardized the stability of American society.

But the second definition held that it was not only fair but also vital to the spirit of free enterprise to allow citizens to keep the wealth they earned. In this formulation, taxing wealth wrecks the incentives that have fueled the engine of American prosperity and enabled the nation to shoulder its responsibilities for more than a century.

Throughout history, American attitudes toward the income tax have been influenced considerably by their opinions with respect to wealth itself. It has been an especially appealing tax for those who tend to see wealth as a product of good luck, exploitation of others, political favoritism and predatory conduct toward rivals. It has been an objectionable tax for those who tend to see wealth as the logical reward for hard work, thrift, ingenuity and other admirable forms of behavior.

Any objective rendering of the narrative in this book suggests that most Americans have embodied some of both views and generally tried to find a balance between them. The anguished search for that balance has continued through the rest of the twentieth century and into the twenty-first. The one difference between the last eighty years and the sixty described in *The Great Tax Wars* is that after 1920, at least, the income tax has become largely accepted as an obligation to be shouldered by most Americans. Americans may fight about its particulars, but few mainstream leaders challenge the fundamental legitimacy of taxing wealth somewhat proportionate to the amount of wealth each American possesses. That legitimacy has been maintained while the United States has grown, prospered and survived a Great Depression, the Second World War, a cold war, postwar booms, inflation and stagnation and more wars in Asia and against terrorism in distant trouble spots.

The consensus supporting the income tax's legitimacy has never precluded fierce arguments over the proper level of the tax. Such arguments are certain to continue into the future. But before applying the lessons of the tax wars of the past to the debates today, it is worth looking at the history since the end of World War I.

Ironically, it was one of the fathers of the income tax, Woodrow Wilson, who had second thoughts about whether tax rates had gone too high. He invited Congress to consider whether taxes had not become "destructive of business activity and productive of waste and inefficiency." But it was Andrew Mellon—Treasury Secretary under Presidents Warren Harding, Calvin Coolidge and Herbert Hoover—who aggressively carried out the tax-cutting in the 1920s that Wilson had spoken of in theory. Mellon was the greatest tax-cutter until Ronald Reagan. He was a wealthy financier, industrialist and bank president from Pittsburgh whose influence was so extensive that there was a standing joke that three presidents served under him.

Mellon provided the philosophical underpinnings for the revolt against taxes, arguing that stratospheric tax rates led to evasion and drove American investments away from equities and into tax-exempt bonds, weakening the stock market. When initiative is "crippled" by high taxes, he declared, an individual "will no longer exert himself and the country will be deprived of the energy on which its continued greatness depends." In his book *Taxation: The People's Business,* Mellon declared in 1924 that taxes ought not to be "a means of confiscating wealth" but rather solely for the purpose of "raising necessary revenues for the Government." It was repugnant, he argued, to tax a man's wealth simply because in the view of some Americans "he seems to have more money than he needs."

By the end of Mellon's term, in 1932, the top marginal income tax rate was reduced from a high of 77 percent during World War I to 24 percent. But the basic concept of a progressive tax structure based on the ability to pay was maintained. In addition, in 1924, Congress adopted a differentiation between "unearned" and "earned" income, in which income generated by investments was taxed at higher rates than income taxes on wages and salaries. That fundamental principle of progressivity won Mellon's wholehearted support. "The fairness of taxing more lightly incomes from wages, salaries or from investments is beyond question," he declared. On the other hand, Congress enacted several laws in this period granting preferential tax treatment to certain kinds of activities, such as oil and gas investments. It was the beginning of another important trend in the tax area: loopholes catering to influential special interests.

The 1929 crash and the Great Depression brought changes in

thinking about taxes in Washington. When the economic collapse led to government deficits, President Hoover engaged in what was then conventional thinking about budgets. Instead of accepting deficits as necessary to stimulate the economy, Hoover did what politicians did in the 1890s and after the 1907 Panic—he called for tax increases to close the budget gap, including a general sales tax. Some Democrats revolted, protesting the hardship on taxpayers. The Revenue Act of 1932, approved by a Congress in which progressive Democrats and Republicans were in control, was the largest peacetime tax increase in American history. It raised the top income tax rate to 55 percent and increased the corporate tax to 14 percent, making the system more progressive than it had been since the Wilson era. But the result was that the tax increases, combined with tight money, only deepened the Depression.

Running for President, Franklin D. Roosevelt also embraced the conventional wisdom of the time and came out in favor of balanced budgets. He endorsed the concept of a progressive tax system, but as President he feared that raising taxes on the wealthy and on corporations might undermine support for the New Deal in the business community. Nevertheless, in 1933, he embraced several tax increases, again making the system more of a burden on the "ability to pay" of the wealthiest taxpayers. Because of other steps taken by Roosevelt, including an increase in spending, the Depression began to ease in the first part of Roosevelt's term. With the end of Prohibition, revenues from taxes on liquor flowed to the Treasury, shoring up federal solvency. In the mid-1930s, Roosevelt shifted gears politically, moving toward ever more vehement attacks on wealth and privilege, proposing a graduated tax on corporations and a higher tax on dividends, inheritance and estate taxes and raising the maximum income tax rates. The Congress gave him much of what he wanted in 1935, raising the top income tax rate to 75 percent on incomes more than $500,000—close to the levels of World War I. The entire system was more progressive, with one exception. The new payroll taxes to finance the Social Security retirement system were regressive because they did not rise according to the person's income. On the other hand, Social Security as a program was very beneficial to those at the lower end of the economic spectrum. Its benefits were fixed according to income, but as a practical matter they constituted a larger portion of a person's income at the bottom end of the scale.

After a period of New Deal optimism, an economic downturn struck the nation in 1937, caused by a contraction in public spending and the supply of money. The renewed recession, as well as Roosevelt's attempt to expand and pack the Supreme Court because of its rejection of key pieces of New Deal legislation, brought a torrent of criticism of the President. His sudden encounter with dissatisfaction in the public encouraged conservative Democrats to break with the White House and demand tax cuts, forcing Roosevelt to adopt them. These years also brought a new willingness to accept deficits. John Maynard Keynes, the British economist and advocate of deficit spending in a recession, was beginning to exercise some influence in Washington in the mid-1930s. Keynes had met with Roosevelt in 1934 and had come away puzzled by the President's lack of understanding of his economic theories. Yet by the latter part of the decade, Roosevelt became a Keynesian in spite of himself. Increasingly surrounded by economists who believed that deficit spending would boost the economy, he went along for political reasons—he did not want to raise taxes or cut spending.

The outbreak of World War II reopened the issue of war finance that the nation had experienced in the Civil War and World War I. Faced with unprecedented new demands for war mobilization, both Democrats and Republicans accepted the need for tax increases. As they had in the First World War, Democrats focused on taxing excess profits, corporations and the wealthy. "In this time of grave national danger, when all excess income should go to win the war, no American citizen ought to have a net income, after he has paid his taxes, of more than $25,000," Roosevelt told Congress in 1942, after Pearl Harbor. But countering the view of steep taxes on the rich was another view that taxes should be broad-based, applying to every American. There was also opposition to raising taxes on corporations from business leaders, who said it would hamper their ability to gear up for the war. The war years saw a steady increase in taxes of all kinds, and for the first time the income tax became a mass-based phenomenon. The worst global conflict in history made America a nation of income tax payers. According to the tax expert and historian W. Elliot Brownlee, the number of income tax payers grew from 3.9 million in 1939 to 42.6 million in 1945, and income tax collections rose from $2.2 billion to $35.1 billion. At the end of the war, nearly 90 percent of the workforce filed returns, and 60 percent paid income taxes. Income taxes accounted for 40 percent of federal revenues, with corporate taxes providing a third.

Americans accepted high taxes because they accepted their purpose: victory in the war. (The Treasury Department could not help but reinforce the sentiment with a little bit of propaganda. It even commissioned Irving Berlin to write a patriotic song, "I Paid My Income Tax Today.") Wartime taxes were high enough to accomplish a near miracle that would have been the envy of Treasury Secretaries Salmon Chase in the Civil War and William Gibbs McAdoo in World War I: keeping inflation under control.

Immediately after the end of the war, Congress moved to reduce taxes, including excess profits, excise and income taxes. What did not happen, however, was a wholesale attack on the wartime tax structure as Andrew Mellon had attempted after World War I. President Harry Truman opposed such an effort. The outbreak, first, of the Korean War, and the onset of the Cold War, along with a postwar expansion of domestic social programs, kept the need for tax revenues high.

Following their victory in the 1946 congressional elections, Republicans moved to cut income taxes across the board. A series of tax cuts were passed but vetoed by Truman, who denounced the G.O.P. lawmakers for what he said was catering to the rich. Congress upheld all the vetoes in 1947 and early 1948, though in some cases narrowly and in a fashion that embittered many lawmakers and inspired predictions that Truman could never win the 1948 presidential election. As the election approached, Congress passed yet another tax cut, lowering the rate for all brackets but concentrated especially on lower- and middle-income taxpayers. Because the bill applied to taxpayers of more modest means, it attracted significantly greater support in Congress. Truman vetoed the bill, but lawmakers overrode him. The President then campaigned against the tax cut in the 1948 election. Following his upset victory, Truman turned right around and asked the Congress for tax increases on corporations, estates and gifts and on upper-income taxpayers. The rationale was to raise money for defense and such social expenses as housing, health care and education. Congress did not buy it. No tax increase was passed.

When the Korean War started in 1950, however, Congress acted to restore excess profits taxes and raise individual income tax rates and corporate taxes. Then in 1952, Dwight D. Eisenhower was elected—the first Republican to win the White House in twenty-four years. In theory, the Eisenhower era should have been accompanied by a return to tax cutting. But Ike, it turned out, resisted tax reductions almost as much as Truman had, on the ground that deficits needed to be kept under control to curb the dangers of inflation. Not until the 1960s—and ironically, not by Republicans but Democrats—did tax cuts become a major objective of the government. This time, as Keynesian economics came to be increasingly accepted, the goal of economists was to do what was best for the economy rather than the federal budget.

Soon after taking office in 1961, President John F. Kennedy proposed a tax credit and other incentives to encourage business investment. When he signed his business-oriented tax breaks into law the following year, he called them "a good start" on the road to what he envisioned as further tax cuts for individuals and business. It was the beginning of the Democrats' interest in tax policies that would soften their longstanding reputation as antibusiness. In 1963, Kennedy proposed to take the next step with legislation for "an across the board, top to bottom cut in both corporate and personal income taxes." The President declared that the existing tax system was "a drag on economic recovery and economic growth." Kennedy's economic policies, by now, "could almost have been written by Andrew Mellon," observes the tax scholar John Witte. After two years of deliberation, the law—enacted with bipartisan support in 1964—cut income taxes across the board 20 to 30 percent. The new top rate was 70 percent instead of 91 percent. The law also contained an array of special provisions on health, capital gains, royalties, iron ore and other activities—provisions that had been designed to build support for the legislation in Congress. The law also helped solidify the electoral support in 1964 for President Lyndon Johnson, who succeeded to the presidency after Kennedy's assassination on November 22, 1963.

Johnson largely ignored tax policy until the costs of the Vietnam War began to rise. In 1968, he turned to Congress to try to raise taxes. Antiwar lawmakers opposed what they viewed as a "war tax" and conservatives opposed taxes to pay for the Great Society. Many in the business community favored tax increases, however, because of fears of inflation, and so a small, temporary surcharge on corporate and individual taxes was enacted in late 1968. But inflation continued to have a decisive effect on taxes. For one thing, rising wages and salaries were pushing taxpayers into higher and higher brackets. This trend made the income tax increasingly progressive in nature, and it fed the federal revenue stream. During the peak of World War II, federal tax receipts accounted for 22 percent of the United States gross domestic product. They dipped to 15 percent in 1950, but the cost of military defenses and modern social programs, particularly retirement benefits, pushed the level back up to 20 percent by the 1970s, where it has hovered ever since. (State and local taxes, about 5 percent of the economy after World War II, have been about 10 percent since about 1980.)

Starting in the 1970s, the debate over taxes shifted to the question of "reform" of tax breaks. These so-called "tax expenditures"—so-called because they amounted to subsidies for specific business activities—cost the federal government 21 percent of regular federal expenditures by 1967, and 35 percent by 1984. Inflation and rising tax revenues enabled President Richard Nixon to propose and eventually win approval of tax cuts in 1971, the same year that he and his Treasury Secretary, John Connally, advocated a freeze on wages and dividends, spending cuts and a cost-of-living council to oversee rising prices and worker pay. Nixon promoted another tax cut in 1975. Generally, the tax cuts of the 1970s involved tinkering with investment credits and other tax credits to promote savings and investment and capital formation and credits for retirement and child care.

In the 1976 presidential campaign, Jimmy Carter called attention to the myriad tax breaks and supposed inequities in the federal income tax system, declaring that the entire system was "a disgrace to the human race." He promised to make taxes broader and more progressive and to eliminate tax deductions for the two-martini lunch. Congress responded by passing more tax breaks to business to encourage investment, including capital gains tax reductions, in a package that President Carter signed into law in 1978.

Meanwhile, a revolt against high tax rates was gathering steam around the country. Senator William Roth of Delaware and Representative Jack Kemp of New York advocated a new philosophy of "supply-side" economics, holding that lower tax rates were needed to channel revenues into productive investment for the economy. Their approach was not new. Rather, it was an echo of Andrew Mellon's philosophy but in a new formulation. "By re-creating the incentive to work, save, invest and take economic risks by reducing the percentage of reward for that economic activity taken by the federal government in the form of taxes," said Kemp, "we will have more investment and more economic risk taking. That will expand the total economic activity, expanding the tax base from which federal tax revenues are drawn, providing additional revenues with which to offset federal budget deficits."

The tax revolt of the 1970s was something that many experts had not foreseen, but it had clear roots. Polls showed an erosion of support of the tax system, particularly the income tax, in the 1970s. It may have been driven in part by the Vietnam War, civil strife, Watergate and unpopular presidents and other leaders. Inflation was perhaps the biggest factor, because it meant that families struggling to make more money to stay even with higher prices were pushed into higher and higher tax brackets—the so-called "bracket creep" phenomenon experienced by Americans as a tax increase. Congress needed to make adjustments just to let Americans keep pace. The problem was that congressional actions in the 1970s did not help middle- and lower-income taxpayers. Rather Congress cut business taxes and gave tax breaks to special interests.

Then came the 1980 election, a political earthquake in which a brilliantly eloquent Republican presidential candidate, Ronald Reagan, won 44 states and 51 percent of the popular vote—defeating Carter and a third-party candidate, John Anderson—with a promise to lower taxes, increase military spending and restore American pride. Along with his victory came the first Republican Senate in twenty-six years and a House that was only nominally controlled by the Democrats. Reagan had endorsed the across-the-board tax cut proposed by Representative Kemp and Senator Roth, and he also favored reducing corporate taxes. Congress passed the legislation he wanted, and Reagan signed the biggest tax cut in history in mid-1981. It consisted of a three-year staged reduction in individual tax rates, plus an array of new corporate tax breaks. The bill phased an income tax cut of 5 percent the first year, then 10 percent the next and another 10 percent in the next year. Added together, they represented a total reduction of about 23 percent over three years.

What was unusual about the Reagan tax cut was its size, its multiyear commitment and its being weighted to business and upper-income Americans, who were the ones deemed as best able to "save" their tax money. Even in the 1920s, according to John Witte, tax cuts were more balanced toward all income groups. Moreover, the 1920s tax cuts were a response to budget surpluses. Reagan's tax cuts were different because they passed at a time of deficits and—along with the drop in revenues from the recession and increased military spending—contributed to even bigger deficits. Another significant aspect of these cuts was that they "reduced the role of the income tax in the nation's revenue system for the first time since the Great Depression," according to Brownlee. By the end of the decade, income tax revenues as a share of all federal taxes declined from 63 percent to 57 percent. A major factor was "indexing" of taxes, so that rates were kept even with inflation, and middle-class taxpayers would not be pushed up to higher tax rates by inflation alone.

The debate over Reagan's tax cuts continues to be vigorous. Many Democrats hold that their purpose was to deprive the Treasury of revenues and force Congress to change its profligate ways. If that was the rationale, it can be said that it worked and did not work. The tax cuts contributed to deficits rather than drastically reduced spending. On the other hand, they ushered in a period in which Republicans and many Democrats could push hard for cuts in domestic programs and succeed to some extent. Another purpose of the tax cut was to try to achieve what supporters said they wanted—an increase in saving and investment, resulting in economic growth. The creation of forty million new jobs since 1982 is widely viewed by Republicans as a product of the 1981 tax cut. For example, Lawrence Lindsey, President George W. Bush's economic adviser, has called the 1981 tax cut the centerpiece of the greatest economic revolution since the 1930s.

But the supreme rationale of the Reagan tax cut was more in keeping with the familiar argument between morality and fairness. There was a feeling by the 1980s, even among some Americans of modest means, that tax rates had simply become too high and overly punitive.

A personal note from the author might be relevant here. When I was a reporter covering the Reagan White House, David Stockman told me he believed that Reagan felt as strongly as he did about high taxes, not from any theories, but from his personal experience as a motion picture actor after World War II, when personal income tax rates were in the range of 90 percent. Reagan, his budget director said, once recalled that as soon as he reached the highest marginal tax rate—the tax rate for the additional income he was earning—he simply stopped making movies and relaxed for the rest of the year, knowing that almost all of whatever more he made for the year would be transferred to the government. It was Reagan's belief that high taxes stifled the hard work that he believed the United States needed to restore economic health. Indeed, Stockman told William Greider of the *Washington Post* that the 1981 across-the-board tax reduction was "always a Trojan horse to bring down" the rates on the wealthiest taxpayers.

After Reagan's re-election in 1984, his administration took another important step by proposing to eliminate loopholes and try to rationalize the system in order to improve incentives for private enterprise. Treasury Secretary Donald Regan argued that the tax system had become so complex that millionaires really didn't have to pay taxes because they could take advantage of various tax shelters. The resulting 1986 tax reform bill was passed with the help of Treasury Secretary James A. Baker III and such key Democrats as Representative Daniel Rostenkowski of Illinois, chairman of the House Ways and Means Committee, and Senator Bill Bradley of New Jersey.

One perhaps unintended consequence of simplifying the income tax structure was that it made more attractive the avenue of raising the income tax to help close the continuing federal deficits. In the 1980s, Democrats began demanding that in return for acceptance of spending restraint in social programs valued by their constituents, Republicans would have to agree to increased taxes on the wealthiest taxpayers. Without realizing it, perhaps, they were following a variation of the demand for sacrifice and fairness that characterized the Great Tax Wars of 1860–1920.

Such thinking guided tax and spending policies in the presidencies of the first George Bush and then Bill Clinton. In 1990, for example, Bush and the Democratic-controlled Congress agreed to a package of spending cuts. But in return, Bush had to accept some tax increases, unleashing a torrent of passion among Americans when he reneged on his memorable and notorious campaign pledge of 1988: "Read my lips—no new taxes." Specifically, the President went along with an income tax rate increase for the wealthiest taxpayers and, for those at the lower end of the economic scale, an increase in the tax rebate called the Earned Income Tax Credit. Many economists credit the Bush accord as a major step in reducing the federal deficit, but Bush paid for it dearly. Despite his impressive handling of the war against Iraq in 1991, he lost the 1992 election to Governor Clinton of Arkansas.

Under President Clinton, the Democrats returned to their traditional demand for a more progressive tax system. Candidate Clinton had called for tax cuts for the middle class and tax increases on the highest incomes. As President, he abandoned the middle-class tax cut because of his new concern about the deficit, urged by his chief economic adviser, investment banker Robert Rubin, who later became Treasury Secretary. The tax-increase package of 1993 contained $500 billion in taxes and spending cuts to be spread out over five years. Clinton asserted that 80 percent of the new tax revenues would fall on families that earned more than $200,000, and that only the wealthiest 1 percent of taxpayers would be affected by higher rates. It passed only after the Senate voted 50–50 and Vice President Al Gore broke the tie. Republicans declared that the tax increase was unfair, dangerous to the economy and, incidentally, likely to destroy Clinton's chances for re-election. Instead, it was followed by the creation of more than twenty-three million jobs in the 1990s.

The Clinton tax bill raised the top income tax rate from 31 percent to 36 percent for single taxpayers on incomes from $115,000 to $250,000 and for couples with taxable incomes from $140,000 to $250,000. Incomes above $250,000 were subject to a 39.6 percent rate. According to the *New York Times,* a taxable income of $140,000 normally means a total income of about $180,000, and a taxable income of $250,000 implies a total income of over $300,000. The other provisions of the tax bill were a 4.3-cent increase in the federal gasoline tax, an increase from 34 percent to 35 percent in the corporate income tax and another expansion of the Earned Income Tax Credit.

On the spending side, the Clinton package called for reductions of more than $250 billion over the next five years, particularly in defense and Medicare, the federal health program for retirees. Regular federal programs subject to annual appropriations—what is known as discretionary spending—were to be frozen, with any increase in one program offset by spending cuts in others. With the exception of his administration's defeated health care initiative, Clinton kept away from big spending proposals for most of his presidency.

Like the Bush tax increase and spending restraint package of 1990, the Clinton package is widely credited for having reduced the federal deficit. Many economists echo Rubin's view that deficit reduction paved the way for the economic growth of the mid- and late 1990s. Nonetheless, popular dismay over Clinton's tax policies contributed to the Republicans taking control of the House in 1994 for the first time in half a century. House Speaker Newt Gingrich, leading the "Contract With America" Republicans, proposed tax cuts for middle- and upper-income families and tax incentives for special savings accounts for housing, medical expenses and retirement—all of which tended to benefit taxpayers in the highest brackets. These proposals were so sweeping that many moderate Republicans—heirs to the "deficit hawks" of the Reagan and Bush era—objected. With the help of such Republicans in the Senate, Gingrich's proposals died.

Instead, the Gingrich era on Capitol Hill brought forth a multitude of new ideas to reform taxes, particularly by granting new
incentives for business investments. A popular idea among some
Republicans was a flat tax to replace the entire system of graduated
rates in the income tax. According to one proposal, everyone would
pay a flat tax rate, starting at 20 percent and declining to 17 percent, but have little or no ability to take deductions. Some advocates of this scheme held out the possibility of taxpayers being able
to file their returns on a postcard-sized form, virtually abolishing
the Internal Revenue Service. Many Republican candidates for
President in 1996 jumped on the flat-tax bandwagon. Clinton
responded with his own specific tax cuts in the form of child care
credits, credits for retirement investment accounts and credits for
unemployment benefits and the cost of care for an ill parent, job
training and college tuition for low-income students. Thwarted by
Republicans in his attempts to spend more money on the poor and
working class, he tried to use the tax system to benefit lower-
income taxpayers by helping them pay for activities that would
help them advance up the economic ladder.

The battle between the President and Congress on tax cuts in
Clinton's second term recapitulated arguments that have taken
place on Capitol Hill since the Civil War. This time, however, the
years of economic growth, combined with the higher tax rates
enacted in 1990 and 1993, filled the Treasury with new revenues
and led to surprising new projections of a federal surplus. It was
ironic that the tax increases at the highest levels were a major factor in this phenomenon. Though many had feared that increasing
the highest income tax rates and taxes on capital gains would
wreck the economy, it had the opposite effect; it brought in a
bounty of revenues because of the large expansion in the number of
people who paid income taxes at the highest rate due to the economy's expansion. This time, taxpayers entered higher tax brackets
not because of "bracket creep" but because they were actually earning more money in real terms. Their profits from the booming

stock market were also supplying revenue to the Treasury because of the capital gains tax. It was not surprising, then, that lawmakers would seek to reduce taxes on these wealthiest taxpayers after they had done their share—more than their share, in the opinion of Republicans—in reducing the federal deficit.

In the summer of 1999, just as the 2000 presidential election was getting under way, Congress passed a $792 billion tax cut that would have been the biggest such tax cut since the Reagan era. The G.O.P. ran into immediate criticism that it was lavishing most of its benefits on the rich. Their defense was that the rich pay the most taxes and thus should get the most out of a tax cut.

True enough, Americans of modest means were paying only a small portion of the federal tax bite. But since the 1930s, these tax-payers had paid heavy payroll taxes for Social Security, and since the 1960s, for Medicare. Both programs are perennially described as facing difficulties and in danger of running deficits in their trust funds when the first of the baby boomers retire in another ten years or so. The debate over the 1999 Republican tax cut was essentially over how progressive a tax system Americans desired. There was little doubt that the tax cut would make it less progressive. According to the Treasury Department, the wealthiest 20 percent of taxpayers earned 49 percent of the nation's total income and paid 59 percent of federal taxes in 1999. That top tier of earners, however, would have received 78 percent of the benefits of the tax cut. Similarly, the top 1 percent of Americans, who earned 14 percent of the nation's income and paid 19 percent of the taxes, would have gotten 24 percent of the tax cut money.

In 2000, Republican presidential candidates repeated the traditional attacks on the income tax system as stifling energy, hard work and risk-taking—virtuous behavior that, when rewarded, would produce greater wealth for all Americans. Candidate George Bush of Texas added to the argument by promoting his own across-the-board tax cut, which recalled the Reagan tax cut of twenty years earlier, and by declaring that the revenue collected by the government "belongs" to the taxpayers and should be returned to them when there is a budget surplus. Bush's election victory, like Reagan's, led to swift approval of his proposals on Capitol Hill. The tax cut was estimated to cost $1.35 trillion over ten years, but its actual cost was probably closer to at least $1.7 trillion, because it contained various provisions calling for early expiration of certain tax cuts in order to make the price tag look smaller.

The Bush tax cut, which is to be phased in over the next decade, guarantees that the argument over progressive taxes, a feature of American politics for 150 years, will remain lively well into the first decade of the twenty-first century. The likelihood of more strife over taxes has been reinforced by new economic projections showing that the projected federal surplus of more than $5 trillion over ten years has nearly disappeared because of the tax cut and the decline in projected revenues caused by the latest economic downturn.

The debate over distribution of the tax burden is also certain to continue. In 2001, for example, Citizens for Tax Justice, a liberal group with generally respected computer models, determined that the top one percent of taxpayers earn 19.2 percent of pretax income but pay 26.3 percent of all federal taxes. Yet the Bush tax bill enacted in 2001 awarded them 37.6 percent of the total of the tax cut in the form of cuts in the income and estate taxes. The next 4 percent of earners make 14.4 percent of all pretax income, pay 15.8 percent of federal taxes but got 9.5 percent of the benefit of the tax cut. In all, the top 20 percent of the wealthiest taxpayers, who make 58.7 percent of pretax income, and pay 67.7 percent of federal taxes, got 70.8 percent of the tax cut benefits.

In part because of President Bush's current political popularity, Democrats have been reluctant to recommend what many of their most activist members are urging: a rescinding of the tax cut, or at least the parts of it due to take effect starting in 2004. The tax cuts due to lower rates for the wealthiest taxpayers will take effect, for the most part, in the later years. They could become ripe for reconsideration, especially if there is an economic or military crisis—hardly an impossible turn of events, especially in light of the terrorist attacks of September 11, 2001. Another scenario that could cause a review of the tax reductions for those at the higher income levels would be a repetition of the events that led to the tax increases of 1990 and 1993—as parts of bipartisan deals that include pledges to restrain spending, or possibly to set aside the money for some specific purpose, such as rescuing or reforming the Social Security and Medicare systems, which are due to run deficits as the baby boom generation retires.

Economic crises and wars helped create a consensus for an income tax that falls most heavily on the wealthiest taxpayers. The consensus was forged in the period of 1860 to 1920 and has deepened in the years since then. There is no reason to think that future crises will not reinforce the basic desire of Americans for a tax system that is progressive in nature while being sensitive to the need to preserve incentives for hard work, savings, investment and other activities producing economic growth.

In the era of the Great Tax Wars, the debates over taxes were about what kind of society Americans wanted. What I have tried to show is that the search for the right balance is an endless process in which, like the riders of F. Scott Fitzgerald's boats against the current, we push forward but are borne ceaselessly back to the past. The consensus supporting the legitimacy of the income tax is likely to remain undisturbed. But its progressive nature will always be debated as long as we care about reconciling the competing demands of social equity, economic incentives and the need to pay for an expanding government.

The mixture of these demands is a function of the times. As I write this, two emergencies have appeared on the horizon. The first is the possibility of greater military involvement in the global war against terrorism and other threats in the Middle East, South Asia, the Far East or some other part of the world. The second is the danger that the vast social safety net built up since the New Deal and

Great Society—in particular Social Security and Medicare—will need to be refinanced as a new generation approaches and reaches the age of retirement. Together, these two potential crises pose a great challenge in the twenty-first century. To meet them, government will have to borrow money, raise taxes or cut spending, or some combination of all these steps, just as it has in every crisis of the past. And if there is a widely perceived desire to make tax increases a part of the answer to these emergencies, the historical record tells us that there will be a demand to impose those higher taxes especially on the wealthiest, who can bear them with the least amount of pain.

A long time has passed since the Civil War, when Representative Justin Morrill compared the enactment of the income tax to Adam and Eve being expelled from their "untaxed garden" and forced to make their solitary way in the world. We may yearn to return to the Garden of Eden, but we have learned that taxes are the price we pay to live in the real world, cope with its dangers and meet the needs of a modern nation. Even to establish Paradise on earth, we will have to pay the way.

NOTES

Chapter 1: "Circumstances Most Unpropitious and Forbidding"

Like the other chapters encompassing the Civil War, this chapter draws heavily from *Lincoln*, the magisterial biography by David H. Donald, and *The Battle Cry of Freedom*, by James M. McPherson. McPherson's opening section provides the single best summary of the economic differences between North and South on the eve of the war. Gabor S. Boritt's *Lincoln and the Economics of the American Dream* is a cogent, original presentation of Lincoln's economic philosophy and significance. Heather Cox Richardson's *The Greatest Nation of the Earth* is a valuable contribution to the understanding of the economic legacy of the Union. Another excellent book describing the economic and industrial superiority of the North is *The Causes of the Civil War*, an anthology of essays edited by Kenneth M. Stampp. Edward Pessen's *Class and Power: America Before the Civil War* was also useful in describing the economic landscape on the eve of the conflict.

Taxes are a subject of controversy even when they are being studied in the past. Many of the best books written from earlier eras see the enactment of the federal income tax as a milestone in the long march toward progress and equality. That point of view is especially reflected in Sidney Ratner's *The Federal Income Tax* and E.R.A. Seligman's *The Income Tax: A Study of the History, Theory, and Practice of Income Taxation at Home and Abroad*. They are among the most valuable sources for anyone studying the enactment of the tax during the Civil War. Other valuable books were published a generation or more ago, and I have drawn from them extensively in this chapter and others. These include *The Federal Income Tax*, by Roy G. and Gladys C. Blakey; *A Financial History of the United States*, by Margaret G. Myers; *Taxation in the United States*, by Randolph E. Paul; and *Financial History of the United States*, by Paul Studenski and Herman E. Kroos.

Three excellent books written more recently and bringing the perspective of today's politics to the debates of the past are *The Politics and Development of the Federal Income Tax*, by John F. Witte; *Federal Taxation in America*, by W. Elliot Brownlee; and *Dimensions of Law in the Service of*

Order, by Robert Stanley. Of these, Stanley argues the most forcefully that the income tax was a palliative to reinforce the power of the wealthy and conservative political establishment. His study, and the evidence he cites, is provocative and forcefully argued, although almost any incremental reform in American history can be labeled an instrument of the status quo as well as an instrument for change.

Page

9 *"Money!"*: Donald, *Lincoln*, p. 346. The portrait of Lincoln in this chapter and throughout the Civil War section draws heavily from this book.
9 *"two or three months at the furthest"*: Ibid., p. 295.
10 *the gold-producing regions of the West*: Ratner, *American Taxation*, p. 61.
11 *side of the Confederacy?*: Niven, *Salmon Chase*, p. 265.
11 *"No!" Chase fired back*: Ibid., p. 266.
13 *Exports grew*: Ratner, p. 57.
14 *92 percent of its revenues*: Stanley, *Dimensions of Law in the Service of Order*, p. 25.
15 *"Go to the Astors and Stewarts"*: Ibid., p. 33.
16 *suddenly growing a beard*: Donald, *Lincoln*, p. 258.
16 *quality defined by Keats*: Ibid., p. 15.
16 *as a classic self-made man*: Boritt, *Lincoln and the Economics of the American Dream*, p. 110.
16 *representing railroads and other powerful interests*: Donald, *Lincoln*, p. 245.
17 *"as though possessed by a dream"*: Boritt, p. 36.
18 *flat tax with the same rate for rich and poor*: Donald, *Lincoln*, p. 76.
18 *comfortable income for $2,000 a year*: Ibid., p. 149.
19 *"one and inseparable"*: Ibid., p. 292.
19 *"a moral, social and political wrong"*: Blum et al., *The National Experience*, p. 328.
20 *embodiment of the spirit of individual enterprise*: Donald, *Lincoln*, p. 234.
20 *"another new beginner to help him"*: Richardson, *The Greatest Nation of the Earth*, p. 21.
20 *"in the condition of a hired laborer"*: McPherson, *Battle Cry of Freedom*, p. 28.
23 *Lincoln left Springfield*: Donald, *Lincoln*, p. 273.
24 *The Panic of 1857*: Ratner, p. 61.
26 *in effect a dual-currency system*: Described in Studenski and Kroos, *Financial History of the United States*, pp. 176ff.; see also Hammond, *Banks and Politics in America*, and Richards.
26 *deficit projections as far as the eye could see*: Studenski and Kroos, p. 62.
26 *"even to pay Members of Congress"*: Sherman, *John Sherman's Recollections of Forty Years in the House, Senate, and Cabinet*, p. 251.
26 *"circumstances most unpropitious and forbidding"*: Ratner, p. 62.
27 *"to any other man's hundred"*: Donald, *Lincoln*, p. 264.
27 *$75 million in debts*: Studenski and Kroos, p. 75.
27 *traded at "ruinous" discounts*: Niven, *Salmon Chase*, p. 251.
27 *"His hope was to use cash on hand"*: Ibid. Also Donald, *Lincoln*, p. 301.

Chapter 2: "Chase Has No Money . . ."

29 *"Why don't they come!"*: Donald, *Lincoln*, p. 298.

30 *"Our Army is defeated, and my brother is killed"*: Sherman, *John Sherman's Recollections*, p. 261.

30 *Chase's daughter Nettie woke up*: Described by Niven, *Salmon Chase*, p. 258.

31 *Actually, it was only $20 million*: The financial consequences of Bull Run described in Ratner, *American Taxation*, pp. 64ff.

32 *"I cannot go home"*: Cited by Seligman, *The Income Tax*, p. 431.

33 *"Why should we stickle about terms?"*: Ratner, p. 65.

34 *"from our untaxed garden"*: Blakey and Blakey, *The Federal Income Tax*, p. 4.

34 *"on those who are able to bear them"*: Ratner, p. 66.

34 *"millionaires like Mr. W. B. Astor"*: Ibid., p. 67.

35 *Jay Cooke did not behave*: Cooke's relationship to Chase described in Niven, *Salmon Chase*, pp. 263ff.

36 *Lincoln was growing impatient with*: Donald, *Lincoln*, p. 325.

36 *A New York banker even told the President*: Ibid.

36 *"Chase has no money"*: Ibid., p. 330.

36 *He regarded the President's famous pragmatism as "idiotic"*: Ibid., p. 332.

36 *"generally delegated to Mr. C"*: Ibid., p. 346.

37 *waste and corruption in the War Department*: Niven, *Salmon Chase*, p. 282.

38 *shut himself in a room, weeping alone*: Donald, *Lincoln*, p. 336.

38 *Shakespeare and the Bible, and to prayer*: Ibid., p. 334.

38 *The beginning of 1862 also brought*: Chase's reluctance to raise taxes discussed and criticized by Seligman, *The Income Tax*, p. 436.

39 *"Ought not men, too, with large incomes"*: Ratner, p. 70.

39 *"Conscience, hell!"*: Korngold, *Thaddeus Stevens*. Stevens's contempt for Chase also documented and discussed in two other biographies, by Fawn Brodie and James Woodburn.

40 *"their due proportion of the burden"*: Richardson, *The Greatest Nation* p. 120.

40 *Americans of "small means" should not have to pay*: Ratner, p. 71.

40 *But the pivotal figure in the tax debate*: The description of William Pitt Fessenden is drawn primarily from his biographer, Charles Jellison, in *Fessenden of Maine, Civil War Senator*. The author attributes his cantankerousness to a secret he kept all his life: that he was illegitimate. Fessenden's father, Samuel, a student and law partner of Daniel Webster, had an affair and then took the son away and raised him. Pitt Fessenden (named after William Pitt) never saw his mother after infancy, despite repeated attempts. His illegitimacy, Jellison asserts, "fastened itself forever upon him and proceeded to gnaw away mercilessly at his sensitivity and self-esteem" (p. 5). Fessenden later became a loyal father. When one of his sons was killed at Bull Run, Fessenden wanted to go behind enemy lines to retrieve the body but was dissuaded by friends.

41 *"the very best men in New York"*: Stanley, *Dimensions of Law*, p. 29.

41 *"It will be odious, of course"*: Fessenden, *Life and Public Services of William Pitt Fessenden*, p. 191.

41 *"from any source whatever"*: Seligman, *The Income Tax*, p. 437–38.

42 *The law established the Internal Revenue Bureau:* Details in IRS official history, p. 4, Acosta, *IRS Service,* p. 33, and Blakey and Blakey, p. 5.

42 *"the goose that lays the golden egg":* Ratner, p. 78.

43 *Boutwell set up shop:* Boutwell, *Reminiscences of Sixty Years in Public Affairs,* p. 303.

43 *"My only exercise was a ride":* Ibid., p. 309.

43 *"Any news, Mr. President?":* Ibid., p. 311.

44 *homage, drawn from the New Testament:* Ibid., p. 312.

44 *would expand to 3,882 employees:* Ratner, p. 75.

44 *"no serious complaint in its administration":* Quoted by Seligman, *The Income Tax,* p. 439. Boutwell's memoirs speak fervently of Lincoln's indecisiveness and Chase's bitterness over feeling mistreated by the President.

46 *slavery might even have been preserved:* McPherson offers this view in *Battle Cry of Freedom.*

46 *"The hills were dotted with tents":* Boutwell, pp. 310ff.

46 *"I think the time has come now":* Donald, *Lincoln,* p. 375.

47 *"Will you pardon me for asking":* Ibid., p. 389.

48 *"a disastrous and disgraceful termination":* Ibid., pp. 398–99.

48 *On top of all these problems, Lincoln's cabinet:* The account of Chase's rivalry with Seward and difficulties with Lincoln drawn from Niven, *Salmon Chase,* and from McPherson, *Battle Cry of Freedom.*

49 *"I am more than half disposed to gratify them.":* McPherson, *Battle Cry of Freedom,* p. 575.

50 *"This cuts the Gordian knot":* Donald, *Lincoln,* pp. 404–5.

50 *costing $2 million a day:* Ratner, p. 80.

50 *"Lincoln still had much to learn":* Donald, *Lincoln,* p. 409.

Chapter 3: "Every Man's Duty to Contribute"

Accounts of Confederate finances are not nearly as complete or numerous as the dramatic accounts of Confederate military strategy and heroism on the battlefield. If the South was more fortunate in its generals than in its financiers and financial experts, it was also more fortunate in military and political narratives than in financial ones. The most valuable books used in this chapter are *The Confederate States of America, 1861–1865,* by E. Merton Coulter, which is volume 7 of the ten-volume series *A History of the South,* edited by Wendell Holmes Stephenson and E. Merton Coulter; John Schwab's *The Confederate States of America, 1861–1865: A Financial and Industrial History of the South During the Civil War;* the chapter "The South During the War (1861–1865)," in *The Cambridge Modern History,* volume 7, edited by A. W. Ward et al.; Richard C. Todd's *Confederate Finance;* and *The Life and Times of C. G. Memminger* by Henry D. Capers, who served the Confederate treasury secretary as private secretary. This chapter draws heavily on these studies and also on discussions of the problems of the South's finances in Ratner and McPherson.

51 *The sleepy city of Montgomery:* Nevins, *The Ordeal of the Union,* vol. 1, p. 98.

53 *"we are more enslaved than Negroes"*: This section is heavily drawn from McPherson, *Battle Cry of Freedom* pp. 6–46.

53 *"Who can doubt, that has looked at recent events, that cotton is supreme?"*: Ibid., p. 196.

54 *He paid for the office furniture:* Nevins, *Ordeal*, vol. 1, p. 99.

54 *The new Treasury chief moved quickly:* Ibid., p. 100

55 *He shut down the mints by June:* Coulter, *The Confederate States of America, 1861–1865* p. 152. Also Nevins, *Ordeal*, vol. 4, p. 230.

55 *The problem was the Union blockade:* Ratner, *American Taxation*, p. 102; Schwab, *The Confederate States of America, 1861–1865*, pp. 284–312.

55 *"it might well have made King Cotton an early source of credit"*: Coulter, p. 167.

56 *"it would have required a fleet of four thousand ships"*: Capers, *The Life and Times of C. G. Memminger*, p. 349.

56 *"The cards are in our hands"*: McPherson, *Battle Cry of Freedom*, p. 383.

57 *Karl Marx, then living in England:* Ibid., p. 550.

57 *embargo "virtually enforced itself"*: Ibid., pp. 380–382.

57 *the North's tremendous economic and military advantages:* Coulter, p. 167. Schwab (p. 293) writes that the Confederacy's mistake in borrowing rather than taxing was the notion "that posterity would reap the advantages of the war and should properly bear its burdens, a familiar excuse always offered for adopting a loan instead of a tax policy with a view to lightening the burden of the living generation, who are said to be bearing their proper share of the war's burdens in the direct loss of life and property."

58 *wealth was estimated at $4.6 billion:* Schwab, p. 285; Ratner, pp. 100ff.

59 *"We want Jeff Davis!"*: Nevins, *Ordeal*, vol. 1, p. 102.

59 *down the hall from the office of:* Office described in Todd, *Confederate Finance*, pp. 7ff.

59 *Memminger himself did not think that the signing scheme would work:* Coulter, p. 151.

59 *"the willing and of the unwilling, if there be any such"*: Todd, p. 130.

60 *"There is not an artisan in brass"*: Toombs speech of March 4, 1858, found in Stampp, *The Causes of the Civil War*, pp. 86–88.

60 *Memminger proposed duties:* Ward et al., eds., "The South During the War," in *The Cambridge Modern History*, vol. 7, *The United States*, p. 606.

61 *They tried to sell it abroad:* Ibid., p. 611.

61 *the blockade . . . strangled most of these early financing efforts:* Coulter, p. 165.

62 *"This Government belongs to the people"*: Ibid., p. 175.

62 *these backdoor borrowing practices:* Cited by Ratner, p. 103, and Coulter, p. 175.

62 *The notes were like scrip:* Ward et al., p. 611.

63 *"Great God what a people"*: Coulter, p. 154.

63 *Inflation meant ruinous prices:* Ibid., pp. 157ff.

63 *shoes from strong cloth rather than leather:* Ward et al., p. 617.

64 *"An oak leaf will be worth just as much"*: Coulter, p. 154.

64 *"For God's sake tax us"*: Ibid., p. 176.

64 *a symbol of the privileges of wealth and property in the South:* Ward et al. p. 610. The authors portray a South riven along class lines, accentuating

"the natural antagonism between those districts of the South where slaveholding predominated and those where slaves, for industrial reasons, did not exist in large numbers."

64 *"Never did a law meet"*: McPherson, *Battle Cry of Freedom*, p. 612.
64 *progressive taxation to alleviate class discontent*: Ibid., p. 615.
66 *Memminger reasoned that the in-kind tax*: Ratner, p. 103.
66 *for eventual use by the Army*: Ibid., pp. 103–4.
66 *Not surprisingly, it was the in-kind tithe that reinforced*: Ibid., p. 105.
66 *"We are in favor of a just and equitable system"*: Schwab, p. 296.
67 *"unjust and tyrannical"*: Ratner, p. 105.
67 *an effective legal challenge*: Schwab, p. 294.
67 *For all its problems, however, the in-kind tax ended up yielding*: Coulter, pp. 179–80. See also Ratner, p. 105.
68 *"Bread! Bread! Our children are starving"*: McPherson, *Battle Cry for Freedom*, p. 618.
68 *Reports of robberies and vagabond gangs*: Nevins, *Ordeal*, vol. 4, p. 234.
68 *"no moral right to amass fortunes"*: Ratner, p. 105.
69 *"the very property for which they were contending"*: Coulter, p. 180.
69 *almost nothing was really added*: Ratner, p. 106.
69 *"Memminger's Mammoth Skunk Cabbage"*: Coulter, p. 158.
70 *"never more than an officer executing the will"*: Capers, p. 347.
70 *letter of resignation*: Todd, 79; see also Capers, pp. 365–66.
70 *the new Secretary immediately renewed*: Coulter, p. 163.
70 *"Our finances are now a wreck"*: Ibid., p. 162.
71 *He made the gesture of donating*: Ibid., p. 171.
71 *But before these taxes could be implemented*: Ratner, p. 107.
72 *The expression "too late" is a leitmotif*: Coulter, p. 182.
72 *It was a huge blunder*: Ratner, p. 108.
73 *reliable estimates put it at between $1 billion and $1.5 billion*: Schwab, pp. 301ff.
73 *cruel capitalism practiced by the North*: Ratner, p. 107.
74 *The south's distinctive feelings of pessimism*: See Woodward, *The Burden of Southern History*.

Chapter 4: "There Is No Tax More Equal"

The descriptions of New York's prosperity at the height of the Civil War are drawn heavily from *Gotham*, by Edwin Burrows and Mike Wallace, a magisterial history of New York City. I have also indulged myself perhaps in quoting at length from Samuel Chase's memoirs, among the most interesting documents from the Civil War era. Like many in the circle around Lincoln, Chase did not think highly of the President and assumed that he could do a better job than Lincoln at saving the Union. In the end, however, his insights tend to elevate Lincoln in the reader's eyes, perhaps because we can see a man struggling toward a successful and tragic conclusion, whereas those around him saw a mere politician overwhelmed by the tide of events.

75 *"we shall find Negroes among us"*: Burrows and Wallace, *Gotham*, p. 865.
76 *"Oh, indeed, is that so?"*: Ibid., p. 867.
77 *"Our streets are crowded"*: Ibid., p. 877.
79 *"the rich went on a shopping spree"*: A wonderful description by Burrows and Wallace, ibid., p. 878.
80 *the $3,000 paid by Treasury Secretary Chase:* Ibid., p. 888.
81 *"Gold, gold, gold, gold"*: Richardson, *The Greatest Nation*, p. 95.
81 *Lincoln was said to have banged his fist:* Boritt, Lincoln and the Economics, p. 207.
81 *"It should never be so"*: Ibid., p. 219.
81 *"I have always felt for them"*: Ibid., p. 221.
81 *"You understand these things"*: Donald, *Lincoln*, p. 449.
82 *"the darkest period in the financial history"*: Ratner, *American Taxation*, p. 80.
83 *"Whence the money to carry on?"*: Ibid., p. 81.
83 *"Oh! For energy & economy"*: These quotations are from Chase's correspondence. Niven, ed., *The Salmon P. Chase Papers: Correspondence*, vol. 4, pp. 154–55.
84 *tolerated corruption and fraud:* Niven, *Salmon Chase*, p. 347.
84 *"like the bluebottle fly, lay his eggs"*: Donald, *Lincoln*, p. 480.
84 *the new Internal Revenue Commissioner, Joseph J. Lewis:* In Boutwell's reminiscences, he asserts that his successor was given his job in part because of his laudatory biography of Lincoln. After resigning in 1863, Boutwell was elected to the House from Massachusetts. There he helped handle the impeachment case against President Andrew Johnson in 1867. He served as Treasury Secretary under President Ulysses S. Grant and then as a U. S. senator from 1873 to 1877.
84 *"The larger tax we pay at this time"*: Ratner, p. 83.
85 *"vicious" and "unjust" theory:* Ibid.
85 *"no less than a confiscation of property"*: Ibid.
85 *"Go to the Astors and Stewarts"*: Stanley, *Dimensions of the Law* p. 33.
85 *"I can speak fairly on this subject"*: Ratner, pp. 83–84.
86 *"fighting to protect the millionaires"*: Ibid., p. 85.
87 *"Can we keep Grant & Sherman"*: Niven, ed., *The Salmon P. Chase Papers: Journals*, vol. 1, p. 461.
87 *"What can be done to arrest the decline"*: Ibid., p. 467.
87 *"As a whole, and taking it alone"*: Ratner, p. 90.
88 *"I thought I could not stand it any longer"*: Niven, *Salmon Chase*, p. 366.
88 *"Have you resigned?"*: Recounted in Niven, ed., *Chase Journals*, vol. 1, p. 470. Also in Jellison, *Fessenden of Maine*, p. 180.
88 *embarked on a "timid & almost proslavery course"*: Niven, ed., *Chase Journals*, vol. 1, p. 477.
89 *"He cannot sympathize with my desires"*: Ibid., p. 473.
89 *"no more of finances than a post"*: Donald, *Lincoln*, p. 508.
89 *After a meeting at the White House to discuss the job:* the story of how Lincoln delivered the news to Tod is recounted in a fascinating portion of John Sherman's reminiscences (p. 338). Tod informed Sherman later that he

had been invited to dine with the President and arrived to see him with a group of politicians. Soon everyone joined in telling humorous stories, laughing, trading anecdotes and enjoying each other's company. At the end of a session that Tod thought would include the President offering him the Treasury Secretary's job, Lincoln turned to Tod and said, "Well, governor, we have not had a chance to talk about the war, but we have had a good time anyway; come and see me again." Afterward, Sherman writes, it "dawned on the governor" that the entire evening had been a ploy to avoid offering him the job. Whether Lincoln was being shrewdly diplomatic or incapable of delivering bad news is not clear, but the message was sent and Tod withdrew from consideration for the job.

89 *"exceedingly probable" that he could be defeated:* Donald, *Lincoln,* p. 529.

90 *"the blessings of good government":* Ratner, p. 96.

90 *"the same uneasy struggle between capital and labor":* Ibid., p. 98.

91 *enough resources to "maintain the contest indefinitely":* McPherson, *Battle Cry of Freedom,* p. 816.

91 *These were the final weeks of the war:* According to Donald (*Lincoln,* pp. 560–61), Davis sent emissaries to negotiate, and by some accounts Lincoln was willing to make a deal in which southerners would be compensated for their slaves if they surrendered, costing the Union as much as $400 million. That would have been a considerable sum for the Union treasury. Donald says the proposal reflected Lincoln's "generosity of spirit," as well as his "desperate sense of urgency" to finish the war. The cabinet protested the proposal. Lincoln shelved it, telling them: "You are all against me."

91 *"digging gold to pay the National debt":* Ibid., p. 576.

92 *Only the prospect of peace dominated his thinking:* Ibid., p. 583.

94 *The subsequent scandals of the post bellum period:* Ratner, p. 113.

94 *"the accumulated wealth of the country":* Ibid.

95 *"until and including the year 1870 and no longer":* Ibid., p. 114.

97 *the progress made under President Johnson:* Ibid., p. 123.

98 *"the men of gigantic capital":* Ibid., pp. 122–25.

98 *"the most just and equitable tax":* Ibid., p. 127.

100 *"to require property to contribute":* Ibid., p. 134.

101 *"one of the most powerful instruments in America":* Ibid., p. 141.

101 *accounted for about a fifth of federal revenues:* Ibid., 139–41. Also Brownlee, *Federal Taxation in America,* pp. 27ff.

102 *it made him feel "important":* Acosta, *IRS Service,* p. 37.

103 *"We tax the tea, the coffee, the sugar":* Quoted by Stanley, p. 19.

104 *"You will hear clamor":* Ibid., p. 22.

Chapter 5: "The Communism of Combined Wealth"

The indispensable biography of Grover Cleveland is *Grover Cleveland: A Study in Courage,* by Allan Nevins. As the title implies, this book, along with a separate study by Rexford G. Tugwell, sees its subject as a principled, honorable President engulfed by economic and political turmoil. Matthew Josephson's *The Politicos* offers a lively, more skeptical view of Cleveland and the men of wealth he chose around him. The authoritative biography of William Jennings Bryan remains that by Paolo E. Coletta. I also found Louis Koenig's "political biography" extremely useful. I am indebted to Shearman & Sterling, the law firm, and especially to Edward J. Burke and Joseph Markulin, for providing me with its history and for tracking down materials on the life and writings of the law firm's founder, Thomas Shearman.

105 *A freak late-winter storm:* This description and that following was drawn from the *New York Times* coverage of the inauguration, March 5, 1893.

109 *Descended from a long line of Puritan ministers:* Cleveland's life in these pages is drawn from Nevins's biography, *Grover Cleveland.*

112 *"Communism is a hateful thing":* Ibid., p. 444.

112 *Returning to private life, Cleveland moved:* Ibid., pp. 443–59.

112 *"the only Democrat who could be elected":* Josephson, *The Politicos,* p. 490.

113 *"Corruption dominates the ballot-box":* Donnelly, quoted in Blum et al., *The National Experience,* p. 506.

114 *"In the south the impression of you":* Josephson, *The Politicos,* p. 508.

114 *"The wants of our people arising from the deficiency":* Ibid., p. 512.

114 *"I have not been consulted at all":* Ibid., p. 515.

116 *"I am very sorry for President Harrison":* Ibid., p. 517.

116 *"I only wish":* Ibid., p. 518

117 *"ruin and disaster run riot over the land":* Stanley, *Dimensions of Law,* p. 111.

117 *"I cannot get the men I want":* Nevins, *Grover Cleveland,* p. 511.

119 *"One morning in May 1893":* Cleveland's extraordinary operation described in ibid., pp. 529–33.

120 *the law raised the effective tariff rates from 44 to:* Ratner, *American Taxation,* p. 159.

120 *"Cleveland's troubles":* Nevins, *Grover Cleveland,* p. 611.

120 *One "battalion" departed from Massillon:* There are several good books about Coxey's army. The one I used is by Carlos Schwantes.

122 *One of the most respected surveys:* Shearman's fascinating biography was provided by, among others, a privately produced history of the law firm of Shearman & Sterling.

123 *it listed the wealthiest people in America:* See Shearman, "The Owners of the United States."

124 *Shearman was among those summoned:* Shearman & Sterling found the testimony for me.

124 *"The most effective weapon against":* The letter from Charles Jones is typed out and found in the Bryan papers of the Library of Congress.

125 *Yet in this great expanse of land:* The Federal Writers Project description of Nebraska is informative and stirring.

126 *From his earliest days in prep school:* The pages at the end of this chapter are drawn from Coletta, *William Jennings Bryan,* and Louis Koenig, *Bryan.*

Chapter 6: "Fraught with Danger . . . to Each and Every Citizen"

In this chapter, I again relied on Coletta and Koenig for Bryan, Nevins for Cleveland and Josephson for the political clash between them and their forces. The centerpiece, however, is the legal battle over the Pollock decision rejecting the income tax as unconstitutional. Owen Fiss's study of the Fuller court, *Troubled Beginnings of the Modern State*, was indispensable. The portraits of Fuller and other lawyers and justices were drawn from the equally indispensable *Dictionary of American Biography* and various studies of the Supreme Court, including Bernard Schwartz's *A History of the Supreme Court*. The Pollock decisions are available on Lexis. Alan Westin's essay "The Supreme Court, the Populist Movement and the Campaign of 1896" tells the gripping story of how the Pollock decision played a perhaps underappreciated role in the election that year.

132 *"a small tax upon incomes":* Ratner, *American Taxation*, p. 174.

133 *The proposal by Bryan and McMillin:* Studenski and Kroos, *Financial History of the United States*, p. 222; see also Ratner, p. 189.

133 *"Vote for free sugar":* Blakey and Blakey, *The Federal Income Tax*, p. 15; see also Josephson, *The Politicos*, pp. 543ff.

134 *"Richard Croker never said anything to me":* Connable and Silberfarb, *Tigers of Tammany*, p. 197. This book provides a very useful description of the inner workings of the Democratic organization in New York at the end of the nineteenth century.

135 *In a debate held by the Democratic caucus:* The description of the debate at the caucus and the ensuing section quoting from various participants was drawn from microfilm of the *New York Times* of January and February 1894. See also Ratner, pp. 172–90.

136 *The* New York World: Cited by Stanley, *Dimensions of Law*, p. 114.

136 *McMillin opened the debate:* Recounted in ibid., p. 116.

137 *In the debate over the tax:* New York Times, January 24, 1894, and following.

138 *"a measure to kill anarchy":* Stanley, p. 117.

139 *The long and dramatic debate:* New York Times, January 31, 1894, and following.

142 *women had to be carried away:* Stanley, p. 100.

142 *"The Democratic hen":* Blakey and Blakey, p. 15.

143 *"But I cannot afford to oppose and be beaten":* Ratner, citing Carnegie autobiography, p. 182.

143 *"go ahead and do the best they could":* Josephson, *The Politicos*, p. 550.

144 *undermine business confidence:* Stanley, p. 131.

144 *"little squads of anarchists":* Ibid., p. 119.

145 *"party perfidy and party dishonor":* Josephson, *The Politicos*, p. 552.

145 *his most important legislative accomplishment:* Koenig, *Bryan*, p. 133.

145 *all "gains, profits and income derived":* Studenski and Kroos, p. 223.

145 *Also exempt were states:* Ratner, p. 191.

146 *"I won't appoint a man to be Chief Justice":* Nevins, *Grover Cleveland*, p. 446.

147 *"Fuller came to a court that wondered":* Quoted in Schwartz, *A History of the Supreme Court*, p. 175.

147 *"I suspect that it would be easier to get a man"*: Quoted in Fiss, *Troubled Beginnings of the Modern State*, p. 27.

149 *No sooner had the income tax passed:* See ibid., pp. 75–106; see also Paul, *Taxation in the United States.*

152 *"a doctrine worthy of a Jacobin Club"*: Paul, p. 55.

152 *"the only path of safety"*: Fiss, p. 83.

156 *"what was intended as a tax on capital"*: Ibid., p. 91.

159 *"Felix Frankfurther once said"*: Quoted in Schwartz, p. 179.

159 *"Each Court viewed itself as the guardian"*: Fiss, p. 10. I found his analysis of the thinking of the Fuller court to be most persuasive.

160 *"an institution devoted to liberty"*: Ibid., p. 12.

160 *Whatever the logic of the justices:* Discussed by Ratner, p. 212–14.

160 *"Thanks to the court, our government is not to be dragged"*: Quoted by Westin, "The Supreme Court, the Populist Movement and the Campaign of 1896," p. 23. Westin's essay on the populist outcry over the Supreme Court was most striking. Most historical accounts of the 1896 campaign highlight the free silver issue, not the Pollock decision and the Supreme Court.

161 *"On a wintry morning in early February"*: Josephson, *The Politicos*, p. 596. Nevins, *Grover Cleveland*, p. 660; see also Strouse, *Morgan*, pp. 573–96.

164 *"He is an old bag of beef"*: Williams et al., *A History of the United States (Since 1865)*, p. 202.

165 *"You have asked me the impossible"*: Koenig, p. 155.

166 *"You are young yet"*: Ibid., p. 170.

167 *"due proportion of the expense of the government"*: Westin, p. 31.

167 *"So that you both may sleep well"*: Koenig, p. 192.

170 *"Hebrew race" could sympathize:* Ibid., p. 246. There is a long debate over whether Bryan's comments, including his "Cross of Gold" speech, were anti-Semitic. They perhaps were not directly meant that way, but many historians have regarded their implications as unmistakable.

171 *a kind of October surprise:* The strange turnaround in the economy recounted by Josephson, *The Politicus*, p. 701.

171 *"one man, but such a man!"*: Koenig, p. 254.

Chapter 7: "A Peculiar Obligation to the State"

The turbulent life of Theodore Roosevelt has been thoroughly examined by generations of biographers and historians. Yet the more one reads and thinks about him, the more of a puzzle he remains. One of the things that make Roosevelt so compelling, from the perspective of this book, is that his passionate denunciations of the excesses of capitalism and of wealth itself seem rooted in his life's experiences. Yet the actual sources of his antipathy toward "great wealth" are not obvious. I have tried in this chapter to trace what might have been some of the origins of his attitudes toward wealth itself in an already well-scrutinized life. The two volumes on Roosevelt by Edmund Morris dramatically recount his life's story, but I found Henry Pringle's somewhat more skeptical biography, from an earlier generation, of greater use. H. W. Brands's *T.R.: The Last Romantic* also contains useful information about Roosevelt's personal finances. There is a tendency to see T.R. as a children's storybook hero. John Morton Blum's *The Republican Roosevelt*, sees him as a professional Republican politician whose grandiose pronouncements have to be measured against the compromises and tactical maneuverings of a pragmatic President. The reader will also note that this author has placed considerable confidence in Richard Hofstadter's thesis that the Progressive Era resulted—partly, of course—from the middle and upper classes' feeling that their status was threatened by the sudden emergence of a powerful and hugely wealthy business elite. The life of Theodore Roosevelt in the middle ranges of New York's gentry seems to support that explanation.

174 *Although American businessmen feared:* See Ratner, *American Taxation*, p. 226.

174 *The cause of the explosion remains a mystery:* The preponderance of belief after many decades of study is that the blast was caused not by a mine, as charged and generally believed at the time, but by an accidental explosion inside the *Maine*'s hull. This was the conclusion, for example, of an engineering study conducted by Admiral Hyman Rickover, published in 1976. A group of experts assembled by the National Geographic Society in 1998 leaned the same way.

175 *"the advance agent of prosperity":* Williams et al., *A History of the United States*, p. 221. See also Ratner, pp. 217ff. on McKinley's significance.

176 *the traditional method of raising revenue, tariffs:* Ratner, p. 222.

177 *Faced with no possibility of an income tax:* Ibid., pp. 234–37.

179 *By 1890, it was $65 billion:* Ratner, p. 219.

180 *but workers and farmers felt overmatched:* Paul, *Taxation in the United States*, pp. 66ff.

180 *"full of hates and ebullient, evanescent enthusiasms":* Quoted in Hofstadter, *The Age of Reform*, p. 132.

181 *"upheaval of status":* Ibid., pp 131–46.

182 *"solid, respectable and a little complacent":* Pringle, *Theodore Roosevelt*, p. 7.

183 *a man of cultivation and achievement:* Ibid., pp. 18ff.

184 *"Free Trade, Free Press and Free Beer":* Ibid., p. 22.

184 *"He never had any idea":* Ibid., p. 39.

184 *"I have been spending money":* Brands, *T.R: The Last Romantic*, p. 109.

185 *"Mr. Speak-ah":* Pringle, *Theodore Roosevelt*, p. 47.

185 *When a woman fell to the pavement:* Ibid., p. 52.

186 *"Black care rarely sits":* Ibid., p. 65.

186 *his few years in the West were a disaster:* Brands, pp. 208–10.

187 *"You are not the timber":* Pringle, *Theodore Roosevelt*, p. 81.

188 *"How many of them do you think you can pay?":* Brands, p. 250.

188 *"The trouble is that my career":* Ibid., p. 256.

188 *"a very hotbed of knavery, debauchery and bestiality":* Pringle, *Theodore Roosevelt*, p. 93.

188 *"I'll beat myself. See?":* Ibid., p. 108.

189 *"The truth is, Will":* Ibid., p. 115.

190 *"the right of a man to run his own business":* Ibid., p. 146.

190 *"that's an Acceptance Hat"*: Ibid., p. 154.
191 *"it represents an effort on my part"*: Ibid., p. 159.
192 *J. P. Morgan cursed, staggered to his desk:* Ibid., p. 167.
192 *"entered the presidency with any deliberately planned"*: Williams et al., p. 284.
194 *"a remarkable exercise in dialectical ingenuity"*: Ratner, p. 245.
195 *"the plain people," "the common man"*: Hofstadter, *Age of Reform*, p. 173.
196 *"There is nothing more intrinsically"*: Williams et al., p. 295.
197 *"a wicked falsehood"*: Pringle, *Theodore Roosevelt*, p. 250.
197 *"can only be secured through the continuance in power"*: Brands, p. 510.
198 *The revelations persuaded Roosevelt:* See Robert E. Mutch's *Campaigns, Congress, and Courts.*
199 *"an increase in the supervision"*: Pringle, *Theodore Roosevelt*, p. 360, 1931 edition.
199 *Roosevelt told his friend Nicholas Murray Butler:* Blum, *The Republican Roosevelt*, pp. 76–78.
199 *"less an objective than a device"*: Ibid., p. 77.
200 *"Somehow or other"*: Pringle, *Theodore Roosevelt*, p. 259.
200 *"great increase in the socialistic propaganda"*: Ibid., p. 290.
201 *The tax had also been adopted:* Keller, *Regulating a New Economy*, p. 212.
202 *"The President seemed to be delighted"*: Blakey and Blakey, *The Federal Income Tax*, p. 21.
202 *"more encouragement to state socialism"*: Ratner, p. 260.
203 *"Roosevelt did little to deprive the privileged"*: Paul, p. 90.
204 *To stave off the panic:* See Strouse, *Morgan.*
206 *"I am simply unable to understand"*: Roosevelt, *The Autobiography of Theodore Roosevelt*, p. 243.
206 *"a professional Republican politician"*: Blum, *Republican Roosevelt*, p. 7.
206 *"grief and sorrow"*: Pringle, *Theodore Roosevelt*, p. 337.

Chapter 8: "The Congress Shall Have Power . . ."

The life of President Taft is amply documented in Henry Pringle's 1939 biography, *The Life and Times of William Howard Taft*. It is a study both sympathetic and unsparing of Taft's many shortcomings, though it sees the President as somewhat more in control of his dealings with Congress than was the impression of other observers. This chapter relies heavily on Pringle's book and on the essay by Paolo Coletta on the 1908 presidential election in *History of American Presidential Elections*, edited by Arthur M. Schlesinger et al. Also useful was the work of George Mowry in two books, *Theodore Roosevelt and the Progressive Movement* and *The Era of Theodore Roosevelt.*

207 *"I am not a politician and I dislike politics"*: Coletta, "Election of 1908," p. 2062.
208 *"A national campaign for the Presidency to me"*: Ibid.
209 *"I haven't a word to say"*: Ibid., p. 2074.
210 *"a kindly, well-meaning, emotional man"*: Ibid., p. 2053.
211 *"reasonable profit" to American industries:* Ratner, *American Taxation*, p. 268.

211 *He had earlier been on record:* Stanley, *Dimensions of Law,* p. 187.
211 *"I believe that an income tax":* Paul, *Taxation in the United States,* p. 91.
212 *"the most conservative countries in the old world":* Stanley, p. 186.
212 *"well and good, but that is uncertain":* Blakey and Blakey, *The Federal Income Tax,* p. 23.
212 *"the unconditional surrender of the capitalist class":* Coletta, "Election of 1908," p. 2069.
213 *"Hit them hard, old man!":* Pringle, *The Life and Times of William Howard Taft,* p. 359.
214 *Among the presumed insults:* Ibid., p. 391.
214 *"the lawlessness and abuses of power":* Ratner, p. 269.
214 *"correct in principle and as certain and easy of collection":* Seligman, *The Income Tax,* pp. 591–92.
214 *"I turn to see whether you are not":* Pringle, *Taft,* pp. 399–400.
215 *The new President had no love for Cannon:* Ibid., 402–11.
215 *he had the disconcerting habit:* Ibid., p. 402.
216 *"unless they are coming in to do the square thing":* Ibid., p. 405.
216 *He had brazenly used his position:* Ibid., pp. 412–14.
216 *"a man with whom I don't always agree":* Ibid.
217 *"He acts with promptness and vigor . . .":* Butt quoted by Blum et al., *The National Experience,* p. 565.
217 *"I fear that a large part of the public":* Williams et al., *History of the United States,* pp. 306–7.
218 *"Where did we ever make the statement":* Pringle, *Taft,* p. 429.
219 *"with their aggregated billions of hoarded wealth":* Ratner, p. 272.
219 *"every attempt to impose upon them their proper share":* Stanley, p. 188.
219 *"spirit of reform now sweeping the country":* Stanley quoting Kinsman, 189.
220 *"I ask, who are the consumers?":* Williams et al., p. 308.
221 *The noisiest and most emotional of the progressives:* See Nancy Unger, *Fighting Bob La Follette.*
222 *With the help of Democrats:* Williams et al., p. 307.
222 *"We are but servants":* Unger, p. 188.
222 *"Saw Taft—he is with us":* George E. Mowry, *Theodore Roosevelt and the Progressive Movement,* p. 56.
222 *other rabble-rousers in the progressive movement:* Williams et al., p. 309.
223 *"If I were counsel for the rich":* Stanley, p. 193.
223 *In a memorandum to the economic historians:* Blakey and Blakey, pp. 30–35.
224 *Newly elected but nationally famous:* See J. Anthony Lukas, *Big Trouble,* for Borah's role in prosecuting the Steunenberg murder.
224 *"a little revenue for the Government":* Stanley, p. 193.
224 *"It was never so intended":* Blakey and Blakey, p. 38.
226 *"But, really, Senator Aldrich is steering her":* Ibid., pp. 31–32.
226 *Taft went "deathly pale":* Quoted in Pringle, *Taft,* pp. 442–43.
226 *The balance of power in the Senate:* Ibid., pp. 434ff.
227 *"Nothing has ever injured the prestige":* Blakey and Blakey, p. 45.
227 *"the independence, the dignity, the respect, the sacredness":* Paul, p. 95.
228 *"of being in the saddle":* Pringle, *Taft,* p. 435.

228 *"The situation is not one of my yielding":* Ibid.
228 *"supervisory control" through the tax system:* Blakey and Blakey, p. 43.
228 *"madder than hornets":* Quoted in ibid., p. 51.
229 *"It will tax tens of thousands of stockholders":* Quoted in ibid., p. 45.
229 *only twelve states to block ratification:* Ratner, p. 289.
230 *"I shall vote for a corporation tax":* Ibid., p. 288.
230 *"I care not":* Ibid., p. 290.
231 *"Well, good friends, this makes me happy":* Pringle, *Taft,* p. 441.
231 *"leave us in a mess":* Ibid., p. 437.
231 *"to rob and plunder industrious consumers":* Ratner, p. 279.
231 *"a sincere effort on the part of the Republican party.":* Williams et al., p. 309.
232 *a bitter pill for Taft:* Ratner, p. 279.
233 *"I would not mind in the least":* Blakey and Blakey, p. 57.
234 *the Finance Committee simplified the language:* Stanley, p. 198.
234 *"The success of any given amendment is very improbable":* Blakey and Blakey, p. 60.
235 *The letter K became an evil symbol:* Pringle, *Taft,* p. 447.
235 *Traveling the country to try to sell his policies:* Ibid., pp. 451–68. The lengthy, irresistible account of this trip in Pringle's book offers a wonderful glimpse into politics of the era.
236 *"On the whole, however":* Ibid., pp. 453–54. Taft's comment on the tariff is widely described as one of the great gaffes of the era, offering a good illustration of the emotion surrounding the subject.
236 *"I cannot be mistaken in finding":* Ibid., p. 468.

Chapter 9: "It Will Lighten the Burdens of the Poor"

The conflict between Taft and Roosevelt, one of the richest chapters in American political history, reflects a strange mixture of personality and issues. Sorting them out is not easy from the distance of a century. The biographies of Roosevelt and Taft by Henry Pringle were very helpful, as was George Mowry's essay on the 1912 election. The definitive biography of Woodrow Wilson remains that of Arthur Link. But I found the little volume by Louis Auchincloss a useful summary of his life. I relied heavily on these sources. For the discussion of the ratification of the Sixteenth Amendment, the best work is John Buenker's *The Income Tax and the Progressive Era,* especially the section on New York, printed also in the *New-York Historical Society Quarterly* of April 1968. My thanks also to Kay Shatraw of the *New York Times* Albany Bureau for locating biographical material from the 1911–12 legislative handbook on Governor John Dix.

240 *"little short of a revolutionist":* Williams et al., *History of the United States,* p. 313.
240 *not "big enough":* Mowry, "Election of 1912," p. 2141.
241 *Roosevelt's strategy:* Ibid.
242 *"We stand at Armageddon":* Ibid., p. 2153.
245 *without ever setting foot in the Capitol:* P. Johnson, *A History of the American People,* p. 633.

247 *"stagger like France through fields of blood"*: Auchincloss, *Woodrow Wilson*.
248 *no candidate had a majority*: Mowry, "Election of 1912," pp. 2147ff.
248 *"we are chosen to show the way"*: Auchincloss, p. 44.
248 *"God ordained that I should be the next"*: Ibid., p. 45.
249 *"I've been growing more radical"*: Mowry, "Election of 1912," p. 2159.
251 *A good example of the regional dynamics*: See Buenker, "Progressivism in Practice," *New-York Historical Society Quarterly*, April 1968.
252 *"Every time wealth invades"*: Stanley, *Dimensions in Law*, p. 203.
252 *"When a man has accumulated a sum"*: Ratner, *American Taxation*, p. 304.
252 *"If once you give the power to the nation"*: Ibid., p. 303.
253 *What saved the amendment*: See the analysis of Buenker, "Progressivism."
253 *Wisconsin adopted the first permanent income tax*: See John O. Stark, "The Establishment of Wisconsin's Income Tax," *Wisconsin Magazine of History*, Autumn 1987.
254 *As the Wisconsin Supreme Court declared*: Stanley, p. 208.
255 *The Empire State*: This section is drawn from Buenker, "Progressivism."
257 *He also declared that the amendment should have*: See also Ratner, p. 304. In opposing ratification, the governor showed the conservative states' rights ideology he would follow in the 1930s when, as Chief Justice, he guided the Supreme Court to strike down much of Franklin Roosevelt's New Deal legislation. But while serving as an associate justice in 1916, Hughes would uphold the constitutionality of the income tax.
259 *"divide the population into two classes"*: Stanley, p. 226.
259 *Henry Stimson, a New York City corporate lawyer*: Stimson was later Secretary of War for Taft, Secretary of State for Herbert Hoover, and Secretary of War during World War II under Franklin Roosevelt.
260 *Dix preceded his run with a listening tour*: Murlin, *The New York Red Book*, pp. 25–28.
260 *a freak snowstorm*: *New York Times*, November 9, 1910.
261 *forty of the nation's forty-six legislatures were to meet*: Buenker, *The Income Tax*, pp. 138–381.
262 *"to invade its territory"*: Blakey and Blakey, *The Federal Income Tax*, p. 70.
262 *"When they are in a position to repay me"*: Buenker, *The Income Tax and the Progressive Era*, p. 325.

Chapter 10: "Here at Last Was Fruition . . ."

Woodrow Wilson's presidency marked the most dramatic transformation in American politics and government since the Civil War. I have relied on Arthur Link's incomparable biography and again on Louis Auchincloss for particular insights. In trying to tell the story of some of these years through Wilson's Treasury Secretary, I have relied on *Crowded Years: The Reminiscences of William G. McAdoo* and on John Broesamle's excellent biography, *William Gibbs McAdoo; A Passion for Change, 1863–1917*. The selections of Wilson's speeches are drawn from his papers, edited by Link. Of particular interest in understanding this period are the memoirs of Cordell Hull, a two-volume work that extends through his long service as Franklin Roosevelt's Secretary of State.

269 *"my second personality"*: Auchincloss, *Woodrow Wilson*, p. 35.

269 *"I wish it clearly understood"*: Link, *Wilson*, vol. 2, *New Freedom*, p. 5.

270 *"I don't want a banker or financier"*: McAdoo, *Crowded Years*, p. 178.

270 *"cuts us off from our proper part"*: Acosta el al., *IRS Service*, p. 86.

270 *"My head is with the progressives"*: Williams et al., *History of the United States*, p. 329.

270 *The President's firmest advocate*: McAdoo, pp. 193ff.

271 *"a brick couldn't be thrown"*: Ratner, *American Taxation*, p. 322. See also Auchincloss, p. 53.

272 *By September, the Senate passed*: Ratner, pp. 322–23.

272 *Born in a log cabin*: Hull, The *Memoirs of Cordell Hull*, vol. 1, pp. 3–75. The Hull material here is drawn from these interesting memoirs.

273 *"the great middle class"*: Ibid., p. 45.

274 *"Prepare for the funeral"*: Ibid, p. 48.

274 *he had studied the history*: Ibid.

274 *"It was inconceivable to me"*: Ibid, p. 49.

274 *"by those least able to bear them"*: Ibid, p. 58.

275 *"for me the opening of a new era"*: Ibid, p. 69.

275 *"Here at last was fruition"*: Ibid, p. 70.

276 *"individual judgments will naturally differ"*: Brownlee, *Federal Taxation in America*, p. 44.

276 *Hull delivered a sweeping address*: Ratner, p. 326.

277 *it would reduce taxpayers' annoyance*: Blakey and Blakey, *The Federal Income Tax*, p. 80.

277 *"taxation of the few for the benefit"*: Paul, *Taxation in the United States*, p. 102.

278 *On May 8, 1913, the House approved*: Ratner, p. 329.

278 *limited the dependents' exemptions*: Witte, *The Politics and Development of the Federal Income Tax*, p. 77, see also Ratner, p. 330.

279 *"confiscation of property under the guise of taxation"*: Witte, p. 77.

279 *"The Democratic Party never has done it"*: Paul, p. 103.

280 *"I guess you will have to go to jail"*: Ibid., p. 102.

280 *"utterly impossible to write provisions in general law"*: Buenker, *The Income Tax and the Progressive Era*, p. 367.

280 *signed the final tax and tariff bill*: Ratner, p. 333.

281 *In terms of rates, the tax*: Ratner's analysis, pp. 333ff.

283 *But the court was unmoved*: See Ibid., p. 337.

284 *"disturbing incidents and events"*: Blakey and Blakey, p. 72.

285 *"absolute divorce of the Treasury from Wall Street"*: Broesamle, *William Gibbs McAdoo*, p. 145.

285 *But these steps only accelerated complaints*: Wiebe, *Businessmen and Reform*, pp. 143–44.

287 *"Don't shoot. He's doing his damndest"*: Auchincloss, p. 55.

287 *"He was the best judge of measures"*: Williams et al., p. 328.

287 *"just a line to congratulate you"*: Hull, vol. 1, p. 74.

288 *"And then in June"*: Ibid.

Chapter 11: "What Did We Do? What Did We Do?"

This chapter again draws heavily from the Wilson biography by Link and from Auchincloss. The general studies of preparedness and America's entry into World War I by David Kennedy (*Over Here: The First World War and American Society*) and Meirion and Susie Harries (*The Last Days of Innocence: America at War: 1917–1918*) were also very helpful. The essay by Arthur Link and William J. Leary, Jr., on the 1916 election in the *History of American Presidential Elections* (edited by Schlesinger et al.) was also very helpful. Page Smith's lively volume 7 in his people's history series, *America Enters the World: A People's History of the Progressive Era and World War I*, is also well told. Phyllis Lee Levin's *Edith and Woodrow: The Wilson White House* offers an extraordinary glimpse into the life and work of a solitary president.

290 *A study published in 1915:* Ratner, *American Taxation*, pp. 307–9.
291 *A study of the nation's total wealth:* Harries and Harries, *The Last Days of Innocence*, p. 8.
292 *"Conditions have arisen which no man":* Link, *Wilson*, vol. 3: *The Struggle for Neutrality 1914–1915*, p. 102.
292 *"more sleepless nights":* Ibid, p. 98.
292 *"It is not a question of sympathy":* Ibid., p. 95.
293 *"within the limitations of economic law and safe finance":* Ibid., p. 96.
293 *"the thing that is giving us the greatest concern":* Ibid, p. 98.
293 *"in three generations":* Ibid, p. 102.
294 *The final tax bill produced:* Ratner, p. 342.
294 *Wilson rushed back from the golf course:* Link, *Struggle*, p. 104.
295 *"There is such a thing":* Auchincloss, *Woodrow Wilson*, p. 72.
296 *"Pacifist that I am":* Ratner, p. 344.
296 *"I was like a sea captain":* McAdoo, *Crowded Years*, p. 187.
297 *"Isn't it wonderful?":* Broesamle, *William Gibbs McAdoo*, p. 139.
297 *"Oh, my God, what am I to do?":* Auchincloss, p. 60.
297 *"my perfect playmate":* Ibid., p. 62.
298 *McAdoo is said to have devised:* Levin, *Edith and Woodrow*, pp. 109–10.
298 *"I knew his mental habits":* McAdoo, p. 512.
299 *DO AND DARE:* Broesamle, p. 14.
300 *McAdoo's good fortune turned up:* The story of McAdoo's involvement in the Hudson River tunnels is well told in ibid., pp. 17–24.
301 *"hen cars":* Ibid., p. 27.
301 *"the hero of life in New York":* Ibid., p. 31.
301 *"the most ambitions, aggressive, and domineering":* Link, *Woodrow Wilson and the Progressive Era*, pp. 27–28.
302 *"Borrowing money is short-sighted finance":* Ratner, p. 344.
302 *"the character of ward politics . . .":* Blakey and Blakey, *The Federal Income Tax*, p. 107.
303 *"the single most important financial decision . . .":* Brownlee, *Federal Taxation in America*, p. 49.
303 *"My conscience and judgment":* Johnson and Malone, eds, *The Dictionary of American Biography*, vol. 10, p. 439.

303 *"I never knew a man"*: Ibid., p. 440.

304 *"Preparedness is demanded by wealth . . ."*: Link, *Wilson and Progressive Era*, p. 94.

304 *"If the forces of big business are to plunge"*: Link, *Wilson*, vol. 4, *Confusion and Crises 1915–1916*, p. 61.

305 *"The Supreme Court's decision has unfettered"*: Hull, *The Memoirs of Cordell Hull*, p. 76.

305 *"the best labor and best thought . . ."*: Blakey and Blakey, p. 114.

305 *"The bill had four parts"*: Ratner, p. 352.

306 *As for the inheritance tax*: Ibid., p. 354.

306 *"something must be done to discourage . . ."*: Blakey and Blakey, p. 113.

306 *"An irrepressible conflict has been raging . . ."*: Ratner, p. 348.

307 *the new Senator from Alabama, Oscar W. Underwood*: Blakey and Blakey, p. 118.

307 *The Senate passed the bill*: Ratner, pp. 349–52; also Blakey and Blakey, p. 120.

308 *"The principle of the income tax was now permanently established . . ."*: Hull, p. 81.

308 *Wilson was so preoccupied with the war . . ."*: Link, *Confusions and Crises*, p. 65.

309 *One study, by an independent group*: Ratner, p. 355.

310 *"What did we do? What did we do?"*: Link and Leary, "Election of 1916," p. 2253. Some versions have it that the speaker shouted, "What did we do?" and the audience replied, "We didn't go to war."

311 *got a curt acceptance*: Ibid., p. 2252.

311 *Hughes laid out his case*: Ibid., p. 2255.

312 *Wilson went to bed*: Ibid, p. 2269.

Chapter 12: "The Dawn of a Day of Righteousness"

The story of America's entry into the war, Wilson's leadership, the transformation of American society and the battle over the League of Nations draws on the same materials as the previous chapters. David M. Kennedy's *Over Here* is especially authoritative on the American economic and military mobilization.

316 *"bring home to the minds of a great number"*: cited by Ratner, *American Taxation*, p. 365.

316 *"You can tell your people"*: Blakey and Blakey, *The Federal Income Tax*, p. 123.

317 *"a mysterious, a rather Olympian personage"*: Auchincloss, *Woodrow Wilson*, p. 75.

317 *"War means autocracy"*: Ratner, p. 369.

318 *As the President spoke*: Unger, *Fighting Bob La Follette*, p. 348–50.

318 *"I thought he was too refined"*: Cited by Auchincloss, p. 84.

318 *On the mobilization side*: Kennedy, *Over Here*, pp. 93–143.

320 *"a little shiver of premonitory dread"*: T. S. Adams, in *The New Republic*, April 7, 1917, pp. 292–94.

320 *"a pretty clear idea of what not to do"*: McAdoo, *Crowded Years*, p. 374.

321 *"If you take the whole of a man's surplus"*: Ibid., p. 384.

321 *"nothing short of the economic crime"*: Unger, p. 252.

322 *"the wealthier classes"*: Seligman, in Ratner, p. 382.

322 *Another powerful argument*: O. M. W. Sprague in *The New Republic*, February 24, 1917, and July 14, 1917.

323 *"war weary, jangled, nervous"*: Harries and Harries, *The Last Days of Innocence*, p. 152.

324 *"We went direct to the people"*: McAdoo, p. 378.

325 *"Not one man"*: Ratner, p. 373. See also Blakey and Blakey, p. 169.

325 *"I quarreled and fought"*: Blakey and Blakey, p. 358.

326 *"war profits" or "excess profits"*: Ratner, p. 372.

327 *in a compromise, House and Senate tax-writers*: Ibid., p. 375.

327 *The War Revenue Act signed by Wilson*: Ibid.

328 *"This is the high water mark thus far reached"*: Ibid., p. 376.

330 *"characteristic of the want of foresight"*: Blakey and Blakey, p. 158.

333 *The same situation . . . applied to Eastman Kodak*: Ibid., pp. 65–66.

333 *"a function of taxation to bring all profits down"*: Ibid., p. 165.

333 *"the rich and well-to-do classes"*: Ratner, p. 390.

333 *"It is a poor man's war"*: Ibid.

337 *During the interregnum*: Blakey and Blakey, pp. 179ff.

338 *"no intellectual integrity"*: Auchincloss, p. 105.

339 *"Never! Never!"*: Williams et al., *History of the United States*, p. 406.

340 *"I am not interested in the President"*: Ibid.

340 *After some weeks, Wilson reappeared*: The best and most dramatic description of the power that Edith Wilson wielded in this period is in Levin's *Edith and Woodrow*, pp. 350–98.

341 *"a tragic mystery, a mystery that now"*: Auchincloss, p. 125.

343 *"an army of pompous phrases moving across"*: Williams et al., p. 422.

Epilogue

350 *"destructive of business activity"*: John F. Witte, *The Politics and Development of the Federal Income Tax*, p. 88.

351 *"a means of confiscating wealth"*: Blum et al., *The National Experience*, p. 624.

351 *"The fairness of taxing more lightly incomes"*: Witte, p. 90.

352 *In the mid-1930s, Roosevelt shifted gears*: Brownlee, *Federal Taxation in America*, p. 74.

353 *Yet Roosevelt became a Keynesian*: Brownlee, p. 88.

356 *"an across the board, top to bottom cut"*: Witte, p. 158.

356 *"could almost have been written by Andrew Mellon"*: Witte, p. 159.

357 *"By re-creating the incentive to work, save invest"*: Cited by Witte, p. 217.

359 *"reduced the role of the income tax"*: Brownlee, p. 117.

BIBLIOGRAPHY

I. General

Acosta, Ernest, chief of editorial board. *IRS Service* (in-house magazine). Inaugural edition celebrating 125 years of service to America. Washington, D.C.: Internal Revenue Service, reprint of Summer 1987 issue.

Adams, Charles. *Those Dirty Rotten Taxes: The Tax Revolts That Built America.* New York: The Free Press, 1998.

Beard, Charles A., and Mary R. Beard. *The Rise of American Civilization.* 1933. Reprint, New York: Macmillan Co., 1956.

Blakey, Roy G., and Gladys C. Blakey. *The Federal Income Tax.* New York: Longmans, Green and Co., 1940.

Blum, John M., Bruce Catton, Edmund S. Morgan, Arthur M. Schlesinger, Jr., Kenneth M. Stampp and C. Vann Woodward. *The National Experience: A History of the United States.* New York: Harcourt, Brace and World, 1968.

Brinkley, Alan. *Liberalism and Its Discontents.* Cambridge, Mass.: Harvard University Press, 1998.

Brownlee, W. Elliot. *Federal Taxation in America: A Short History.* Cambridge and Washington, D.C.: Woodrow Wilson Center Press and Cambridge University Press, 1996.

Burrows, Edwin G., and Mike Wallace. *Gotham: A History of New York City to 1898.* New York and Oxford: Oxford University Press, 1999.

Carson, Gerald. *The Golden Egg: The Personal Income Tax: Where It Came from, How It Grew.* Boston: Houghton Mifflin Co., 1977.

Collins, Gail. *Scorpion Tongues: Gossip, Celebrity and American Politics.* New York: William Morrow and Co., 1998.

Davis, Shelley L. *IRS Historical Fact Book: A Chronology, 1646–1992.* Washington, D.C.: Internal Revenue Service, Department of Treasury, 1992.

Fogel, Robert W., and Stanley L. Engerman, eds. *The Reinterpretation of American Economic History.* New York: Harper and Row, 1971.

Friedman, Milton. *Money Mischief: Episodes in Monetary History.* San Diego: Harcourt, Brace and Co., 1994.

————, and Anna Jacobson Schwartz. *A Monetary History of the United States, 1867–1960*. Princeton, N.J.: Princeton University Press, 1963.

Garraty, John A., and Mark C. Carnes, eds. *The Dictionary of American Biography.* Supplement 8. New York: Charles Scribner's Sons and Collier Macmillan, under the auspices of the American Council of Learned Societies, 1988.

Garraty, John A., and Edward T. James, eds. *The Dictionary of American Biography.* Supplements 4, 5, 6 and 7. New York: Charles Scribner's Sons, under the auspices of the American Council of Learned Societies, 1974–1981.

Gordon, John Steele. *Hamilton's Blessing: The Extraordinary Life and Times of Our National Debt.* New York: Penguin Books, 1997.

Graetz, Michael J. *The Decline (And Fall?) of the Income Tax.* New York: W.W. Norton and Co., 1997.

James, Edward T., ed. *The Dictionary of American Biography.* Supplement 3. New York: Charles Scribner's Sons, under the auspices of the American Council of Learned Societies, 1973.

Johnson, Allen, and Dumas Malone, eds. *The Dictionary of American Biography.* 20 vols. New York: Charles Scribner's Sons, under the auspices of the American Council of Learned Societies, 1930–1936.

Johnson, Paul. *A History of the American People.* New York: HarperCollins Publishers, 1997.

Lee, Susan Previant, and Peter Passell. *A New Economic View of American History.* New York: W.W. Norton and Co., 1979.

Lindsey, Lawrence. *The Growth Experiment: How the New Tax Policy Is Transforming the U.S. Economy.* New York: Basic Books, 1990.

McIntyre, Robert S., and Dean C. Tipps. *Inequity and Decline: How the Reagan Tax Policies Are Affecting the American Taxpayer and the Economy.* Washington, D.C.: Center on Budget and Policy Priorities, 1983.

Myers, Margaret G. *A Financial History of the United States.* New York: Columbia University Press, 1970.

Paul, Randolph E. *Taxation in the United States.* Boston: Little, Brown and Co., 1954.

Porter, Glenn, ed. *Encyclopedia of American Economic History: Studies of the Principal Movements and Ideas.* 3 vols. New York: Charles Scribner's Sons, 1980.

Ratner, Sidney. *American Taxation: Its History as a Social Force in Democracy.* New York: W.W. Norton and Co., 1942.

Schlesinger, Arthur M. Jr., Fred L. Israel and William P. Hansen, eds. *History of American Presidential Elections, 1789–1968.* Vol. 3, *1900–1936.* New York: Chelsea House Publishers, 1971.

Schuyler, Robert Livingston. *The Dictionary of American Biography.* Vol. 22 (Supplement 2). New York: Charles Scribner's Sons, under the auspices of the American Council of Learned Societies, 1958.

Sease, Douglas R., and Tom Herman. *The Flat-Tax Primer: A Nonpartisan Guide to What It Means for the Economy, the Government—and You.* New York: Viking, 1996.

Seligman, Edwin Robert Anderson. *The Income Tax: A Study of the History, Theory, and Practice of Income Taxation at Home and Abroad.* New York: Macmillan Co., 1914.

Stanley, Robert. *Dimensions of Law in the Service of Order: Origins of the Federal Income Tax, 1861–1913.* New York and Oxford: Oxford University Press, 1993.

Starr, Harris E., ed. *The Dictionary of American Biography.* Vol. 21 (Supplement 1). New York: Charles Scribner's Sons, under the auspices of the American Council of Learned Societies, 1944.

Strouse, Jean. *Morgan: American Financier.* New York: Random House, 1999.

Studenski, Paul, and Herman E. Kroos. *Financial History of the United States.* New York: McGraw-Hill Book Co., 1963.

Taussig, Frank. *The Tariff in United States History.* New York: Augustus M. Kelley, 1967.

Thayer, George. *Who Shakes the Money Tree? American Campaign Financing Practices from 1789 to the Present.* New York: Simon and Schuster, 1974.

Weatherford, Jack. *The History of Money: From Sandstone to Cyberspace.* New York: Three Rivers Press, 1997.

Webber, Carolyn, and Aaron Wildavsky. *A History of Taxation and Expenditure in the Western World.* New York: Simon and Schuster, 1986.

Williams, T. Harry, Richard N. Current and Frank Freidel. *A History of the United States (Since 1865).* New York: Alfred A. Knopf, 1959.

Witte, John F. *The Politics and Development of the Federal Income Tax.* Madison: University of Wisconsin Press, 1985.

II. Civil War

Boritt, Gabor S. *Lincoln and the Economics of the American Dream.* Urbana: University of Illinois Press, 1994.

Boutwell, George S. *Reminiscences of Sixty Years in Public Affairs.* 2 vols. New York: McClure, Phillips and Co., 1902.

Brodie, Fawn M. *Thaddeus Stevens, Scourge of the South.* New York: W.W. Norton and Co., 1959.

Capers, Henry D. *The Life and Times of C. G. Memminger.* Richmond, Va.: Everett Waddey Co., 1893.

Catton, Bruce. *The Centennial History of the Civil War.* 3 vols. Garden City, N.Y.: Doubleday, 1961–1965.

Coulter, E. Merton. *The Confederate States of America, 1861–1865.* Vol. 7 of *A History of the South.* Edited by Wendell Holmes Stephenson and E. Merton Coulter. Baton Rouge: Louisiana State University Press and The Littlefield Fund for Southern History of the University of Texas, 1950.

Donald, David Herbert. *Lincoln.* New York: Touchstone Books, 1996.

———, ed. *Why the North Won the Civil War.* New York: Touchstone Books, 1996.

Dunbar, C. F. "The Direct Tax in 1861." *Quarterly Journal of Economics* 3 (October 1, 1886): 444–51.

Ellis, Elmer. "Public Opinion and the Income Tax, 1860–1900." *Mississippi Valley Historical Review* Vol. 27 (September 1940): 225–42.

Ferleger, Herbert Ronald. *David A. Wells and the American Revenue System 1865–1870.* Ann Arbor, Mich.: Edwards Bros., 1942.

Fessenden, Francis. *Life and Public Services of William Pitt Fessenden.* 2 vols. Boston: Houghton Mifflin Co., 1907.

Foner, Eric. *Free Soil, Free Labor, Free Men: The Ideology of the Republican Party Before the Civil War.* New York and Oxford: Oxford University Press, 1995.

———. *Reconstruction: America's Unfinished Revolution 1863–1877.* New York: Harper and Row Perennial Library, 1989.

Foote, Shelby. *The Civil War: A Narrative.* 3 vols. New York: Random House, 1958–1974.

Hammond, Bray. *Banks and Politics in America: From the Revolution to the Civil War.* Princeton, N.J.: Princeton University Press, 1991.

Hyman, Harold. "Election of 1864." In *History of American Presidential Elections 1789–1968.* Vol. 2. Edited by Arthur M. Schlesinger, Jr. New York: Chelsea House Publishers, 1971.

Jellison, Charles A. *Fessenden of Maine, Civil War Senator.* Syracuse, N.Y.: Syracuse University Press, 1962.

Korngold, Ralph. *Thaddeus Stevens: A Being Darkly Wise and Rudely Great.* Westport, Conn.: Greenwood Press, 1955.

Larson, Henrietta M. *Jay Cooke: Private Banker.* 1936. Reprint, New York: Greenwood Press, 1968.

McPherson, James M. *Battle Cry of Freedom: The Civil War Era.* New York: Ballantine Books, 1989.

———, ed. *For Cause and Comrades: Why Men Fought in the Civil War.* New York and Oxford: Oxford University Press, 1997.

Martin, Edgar Winfield. *The Standard of Living in 1860: American Consumption on the Eve of the Civil War.* Chicago: University of Chicago Press, 1942.

Mayr, Otto, and Robert C. Post, eds. *Yankee Enterprise: The Rise of the American System of Manufactures.* A symposium sponsored by the United States Chamber of Commerce. Washington, D.C.: Smithsonian Institution Press, 1981.

Morison, Elting. "Election of 1860." In *History of American Presidential Elections 1789–1968.* Vol. 2. Edited by Arthur M. Schlesinger, Jr. New York: Chelsea House Publishers, 1971.

Nevins, Allan. *The Ordeal of the Union.* 4 vols. New York: Charles Scribner's Sons, 1959–1971.

Niven, John. *Salmon Chase: A Biography.* New York and Oxford: Oxford University Press, 1995.

———, ed. *The Salmon P. Chase Papers: Correspondence.* Vol. 3, *1858–March 1863;* vol. 4, *April 1863–1864.* Ashland, Ohio: Kent State University Press, 1996–1997.

———, ed. *The Salmon P. Chase Papers: Journals.* Vol. 1, *1829–1872.* Ashland, Ohio: Kent State University Press, 1993.

North, Douglas C. *The Economic Growth of the United States 1790–1860.* Englewood Cliffs, N.J.: Prentice-Hall, 1961.

Oberholtzer, Ellis P. *Jay Cooke: Financier of the Civil War.* 2 vols. Philadelphia: G.W. Jacobs and Co., 1907.

Pessen, Edward. *Riches, Class and Power: America Before the Civil War.* New Brunswick, N.J.: Transaction Publishers, 1990.

Potter, David M. *The Impending Crisis 1848–1861*. Edited and completed by Don E. Fehrenbacher. New York: Harper and Row, 1976.

Richardson, Heather Cox. *The Greatest Nation of the Earth*. Cambridge, Mass.: Harvard University Press, 1997.

Safire, William. *Freedom A Novel of Abraham Lincoln and the Civil War*. Garden City, N.Y.: Doubleday and Co., 1987.

Schwab, John Christopher. *The Confederate States of America, 1861–1865: A Financial and Industrial History of the South During the Civil War*. New York: Charles Scribner's Sons, 1901.

Sharkey, Robert P. *Money, Class, and Party: An Economic Study of Civil War and Reconstruction*. Baltimore: The Johns Hopkins Press, 1959.

Sherman, John. *John Sherman's Recollections of Forty Years in the House, Senate, and Cabinet*. Chicago: The Werner Company, 1895.

Soltow, Lee. *Men and Wealth in the United States 1850–1870*. New Haven, Conn.: Yale University Press, 1975.

Stampp, Kenneth M., ed. *The Causes of the Civil War*. New York: Touchstone Books, 1991.

Todd, Richard C. *Confederate Finance*. Athens: University of Georgia Press, 1954.

Ward, Adolphus William, G. W. Prothero and Stanley Mordaunt Leathes. "The South During the War (1861–1865)." In *The Cambridge Modern History*. Vol. 7, *The United States*. New York: Macmillan Co., 1934.

Woodburn, James Albert. *The Life of Thaddeus Stevens*. Indianapolis: Bobbs-Merrill Co., 1913.

Woodward, C. Vann. *The Burden of Southern History*, New York: New American Library, 1968.

III. The 1890s

Alexander, DeAlva Stanwood. *Four Famous New Yorkers: The Political Careers of Cleveland, Platt, Hill and Roosevelt*. New York: Henry Holt and Co., 1923.

Anderson, William. *Laura Ingalls Wilder: A Biography*. New York: HarperCollins Publishers/Harper Trophy, 1995.

Beer, Thomas. *The Mauve Decade: American Life at the End of the Nineteenth Century*. Garden City, N.Y.: Garden City Publishing Co., 1926.

The Biographical Dictionary and Portrait Gallery of Representative Men of Chicago, St. Louis and the World's Columbian Exposition. Chicago: American Biographical Publishing Co., 1893.

Bryan, William Jennings. Papers, 1877–1940. Archival Manuscript Material (Collection). Washington, D.C.: Library of Congress.

Cashman, Sean Dennis. *America in the Gilded Age: From the Death of Lincoln to the Rise of Theodore Roosevelt*. New York: New York University Press, 1993.

Chernow, Ron. *The House of Morgan: An American Banking Dynasty and the Rise of Modern Finance*. New York: Atlantic Monthly Press, 1990.

Coletta, Paolo E. *William Jennings Bryan*. Vol. 1, *Political Evangelist 1860–1908*. Lincoln: University of Nebraska Press, 1964.

Connable, Alfred, and Edward Silberfarb. *Tigers of Tammany: Nine Men Who Ran New York*. New York: Holt, Rinehart and Winston, 1967.

Federal Writers' Project of the Works Progress Administration for the State of Nebraska. *Nebraska: A Guide to the Cornhusker State*. American Guide Series. Sponsored by the Nebraska State Historical Society. New York: Viking Press, 1939.

Fiss, Owen M. *Troubled Beginnings of the Modern State, 1888–1910*. Vol. 8, *The Oliver Wendell Holmes Devise, History of the Supreme Court of the United States*. New York: Macmillan Publishing Co., 1993.

Fite, Gilbert C. "Election of 1896." In *History of American Presidential Elections 1789–1968*. Vol. 2. Edited by Arthur M. Schlesinger, Jr. New York: Chelsea House Publishers, 1971.

Glad, Paul W. *The Trumpet Soundeth: William Jennings Bryan and His Democracy, 1896–1912*. Lincoln: University of Nebraska Press, 1960.

Goldin, Claudia, and Hugh Rockoff, eds. *Strategic Factors in Nineteenth Century American Economic History*. Chicago: University of Chicago Press, 1992.

Goldman, Eric F. *Rendezvous with Destiny: A History of Modern American Reform*. Rev. ed., abridged by author. New York: Vintage Books, 1956.

Green, Constance McLaughlin. *Washington, Capital City 1879–1950*. Princeton, N.J.: Princeton University Press, 1963.

Hofstadter, Richard. *The Age of Reform: From Bryan to F.D.R.* New York: Vintage Books, 1955.

———, and Beatrice K. Hofstadter, eds. *Great Issues in American History*. New York: Vintage Books, 1982.

Holmes, George K. "The Concentration of Wealth." *Political Science Quarterly* 8, no. 4 (December 1893): 589–600.

Hurd, Charles. *Washington Cavalcade*. New York: E.P. Dutton and Co., 1948.

Jensen, Erik M. "The Apportionment of 'Direct Taxes': Are Consumption Taxes Constitutional?" *Columbia Law Review* 97 (December 1997): 301–86.

Josephson, Matthew. *The Politicos: 1865–1896*. New York: Harcourt, Brace and World, 1938.

———. *The Robber Barons*. New York: Harcourt, Brace and Co., 1962.

Kazin, Michael. *The Populist Persuasion: An American History*. New York: Basic Books, 1995.

Keller, Morton. *Affairs of State: Public Life in Late Nineteenth Century America*. Cambridge, Mass.: The Belknap Press of Harvard University Press, 1977.

Kirkland, Edward C. *Industry Comes of Age: Business, Labor, and Public Policy 1860–1897*, Vol. 6 of *The Economic History of the United States*. New York: Holt, Rinehart and Winston, 1961.

Koenig, Louis W. *Bryan: A Political Biography of William Jennings Bryan*. New York: G.P. Putnam's Sons, 1971

McLaughlin, Andrew C. *A Constitutional History of the United States*. New York: D. Appleton-Century Co., 1936.

McMath, Robert C. Jr. *American Populism: A Social History 1877–1898*. New York: Hill and Wang, 1993.

Merwin, C. L. Jr. "American Studies of the Distribution of Wealth and Income by Size," *Studies of Income and Wealth*. The Conference on Research in National Income and Wealth. New York, 1939.

Morgan, H. Wayne. "Election of 1892." In *History of American Presidential Elections 1789–1968*. Vol. 2. Edited by Arthur M. Schlesinger, Jr. New York: Chelsea House Publishers, 1971.

Nevins, Allan. *Grover Cleveland: A Study in Courage*. New York: Dodd, Mead and Company, 1966.

Parlin, Charles. *Shearman and Sterling 1873–1973*. Published by Charles P. Young for the Shearman & Sterling law firm. New York, 1973.

Schwantes, Carlos A. *Coxey's Army: An American Odyssey*. Lincoln: University of Nebraska Press, 1985.

Schwartz, Bernard. *A History of the Supreme Court*. New York and Oxford: Oxford University Press, 1993.

Shannon, Fred A. *The Farmer's Last Frontier, Agriculture, 1860–1897*. Vol. 5 of *The Economic History of the United States*. Armonk, N.Y.: M.E. Sharpe, 1945.

Shearman, Thomas G. "A Just and Practicable Income Tax." Testimony before Committee on Ways and Means, October 16, 1893. Washington, D.C.: Archives of Shearman & Sterling law firm.

———. "The Owners of the United States." *The Forum*, November 1889, 262–73.

Skocpol, Theda. *Protecting Soldiers and Mothers: The Political Origins of Social Policy in the United States*. Cambridge, Mass.: The Belknap Press of Harvard University Press, 1992.

Spahr, Charles B. *An Essay on the Present Distribution of Wealth in the United States*. 1896. Reprint, New York: Johnson Reprint Corp., 1970.

Steffens, Lincoln. *The Autobiography of Lincoln Steffens*. Vol. 1. New York: Harcourt, Brace and World, 1931, 1958.

Supreme Court of the United States. *Pollock v. Farmers' Loan and Trust Company*. No. 893; 157 U.S. 429; 15 S. Ct. 673; 1895 U.S. Lexis 2215; 39 L. Ed. 759; 3 A.F.T.R. (P.H) 2557; Argued March 7, 8, 11, 12, 13, 1895; April 8, 1895, Decided.

———. *Pollock v. Farmers' Loan and Trust Company* (Rehearing). *Hyde v. Continental Trust Company* (Rehearing). Nos. 893, 894.; 158 U.S. 601; 15 S. Ct. 912; 1895 U.S. Lexis 2280; 39 L. Ed. 1108; 3 A.F.T.R. (P-H) 2602; Argued May 6, 7, 8, 1895; May 20, 1895, Decided.

Tugwell, Rexford Guy. *Grover Cleveland*. New York: Macmillan Company, 1968.

Watkins, G. P. "The Growth of Large Fortunes." *Publications of the American Economic Association*. 3d series. Vol. 8, no. 4 (1907): 735–904.

Werner, M. R. *Tammany Hall*. Garden City, N.Y.: Doubleday, Doran and Co., 1931.

Westin, Alan Furman. "The Supreme Court, the Populist Movement and the Campaign of 1896." *The Journal of Politics*. The journal of the Southern Political Science Association. Vol. 15 (1953): 3–41.

Williams, Wayne C. *William Jennings Bryan*. New York: G.P. Putnam's Sons, 1936.

IV. The Progressive Era

Acheson, Sam Hanna. *Joe Bailey, The Last Democrat.* New York: Macmillan Company, 1932.

Auchincloss, Louis. *Woodrow Wilson.* New York: Lipper/Viking Books, 2000.

Blum, John Morton. *The Progressive Presidents: Roosevelt, Wilson, Roosevelt, Johnson.* New York: W.W. Norton and Co., 1980.

———. *The Republican Roosevelt.* Cambridge, Mass.: Harvard University Press, 1954.

———. *Woodrow Wilson and the Politics of Morality.* Boston: Little, Brown and Co., 1956.

Bolles, Blair. *Tyrant from Illinois: Uncle Joe Cannon's Experiment with Personal Power.* New York: W.W. Norton & Co., 1951.

Brands, H. W. *T.R.: The Last Romantic.* New York: Basic Books, 1997.

Broesamle, John J. *William Gibbs McAdoo: A Passion for Change, 1863–1917.* Port Washington, N.Y.: National University Publications/Kennikat Press, 1973.

Brownlee, W. Elliot. *Progressivism and Economic Growth: The Wisconsin Income Tax, 1911–1929.* Port Washington, N.Y.: Kennikat Press, 1974.

Buenker, John D. *The Income Tax and the Progressive Era.* New York: Garland Publishers, 1985.

———. "Progressivism in Practice." *The New-York Historical Society Quarterly.* 52, no. 2 (April 1968): 139–69.

Bullock, C. J. "Conscription of Wealth." *North American Review* 205 (June 1917): 859–904.

Carnegie, Andrew. *The Gospel of Wealth and Other Timely Essays.* Edited by Edward C. Kirkland. Cambridge, Mass.: The Belknap Press of Harvard University Press, 1962.

Clark, Champ. *My Quarter Century of American Politics.* New York: Harper and Brothers, 1920.

Coletta, Paolo E. "Election of 1908." In *History of American Presidential Elections 1789–1968.* Vol. 3 *1900–1936.* Edited by Arthur M. Schlesinger, Jr., Fred L. Israel and William P. Hansen. New York: Chelsea House Publishers, 1971.

Croly, Herbert. *The Promise of American Life.* New York: Capricorn Books, 1964.

Dawley, Alan. *Struggles for Justice: Social Responsibility and the Liberal State.* Cambridge, Mass.: The Belknap Press of Harvard University Press, 1991.

Duffy, Herbert S. *William Howard Taft.* New York: Minton, Balch and Co., 1930.

Faulkner, Harold U. *The Decline of Laissez Faire 1897–1917.* Vol. 7 of *The Economic History of the United States.* Armonk, N.Y.: M.E. Sharpe, 1951.

George, Henry. *Progress and Poverty.* New York: Robert Schalkenbach Foundation, 1956.

Harbaugh, William H. "Election of 1904." In *History of American Presidential Elections 1789–1968.* Vol. 3, *1900–1936.* Edited by Arthur M. Schlesinger, Jr., Fred L. Israel and William P. Hansen. New York: Chelsea House Publishers, 1971.

———. *Power and Responsibility: The Life and Times of Theodore Roosevelt.* New York: Farrar, Straus and Cudahy, 1961.

Harries, Meirion and Susie. *The Last Days of Innocence, America at War, 1917–1918.* New York: Random House, 1997.

Hull, Cordell. *The Memoirs of Cordell Hull.* 2 vols. New York: Macmillan Co., 1948.

Keller, Morton. *Regulating a New Economy: Public Policy and Economic Change in America, 1900–1933.* Cambridge, Mass.: Harvard University Press, 1990.

———. *Regulating a New Society: Public Policy and Social Change in America, 1900–1933.* Cambridge, Mass.: Harvard University Press, 1994.

Kennedy, David M. *Over Here: The First World War and American Society.* New York: Oxford University Press, 1980.

Kinsman, Delos O. "Genesis of Wisconsin's Income Tax Law." *The Wisconsin Magazine of History.* 21, no. 1 (September 1937): 3–15.

———. "The Present Period of Income Tax Activity in the American States." *Quarterly Journal of Economics*, no. 23 (1909): 296ff.

LaFeber, Walter. "Election of 1900." In *History of American Presidential Elections 1789–1968.* Vol. 3, *1900–1936.* Edited by Arthur M. Schlesinger, Jr., Fred L. Israel and William P. Hansen. New York: Chelsea House Publishers, 1971.

Levin, Phyllis Lee. *Edith and Woodrow: The Wilson White House.* New York: Scribner, 2001.

Link, Arthur S. *Wilson.* Vol. 1, *The Road to the White House.* Princeton N.J.: Princeton University Press, 1947.

———. *Wilson.* Vol. 2, *The New Freedom.* Princeton, N.J.: Princeton University Press, 1956.

———. *Wilson.* Vol. 3, *The Struggle for Neutrality 1914–1915.* Princeton, N.J.: Princeton University Press, 1960.

———. *Wilson.* Vol. 4, *Confusions and Crises 1915–1916.* Princeton, N.J.: Princeton University Press, 1964.

———. *Wilson.* Vol. 5, *Campaigns for Progressivism and Peace 1916–1917.* Princeton, N.J.: Princeton University Press, 1965.

———. *Woodrow Wilson and the Progressive Era 1910–1917.* New York: Harper and Brothers, 1954.

———, and William M. Leary, Jr. "Election of 1916." In *History of American Presidential Elections 1789–1968.* Vol. 3, *1900–1936.* Edited by Arthur M. Schlesinger, Jr., Fred L. Israel and William P. Hansen. New York: Chelsea House Publishers, 1971.

Lukas, J. Anthony. *Big Trouble.* New York: Simon & Schuster, 1997.

McAdoo, William G. *Crowded Years: The Reminiscences of William G. McAdoo.* Cambridge, Boston and New York: Houghton Mifflin Co./The Riverside Press, 1931.

McCoy, Donald R. "Election of 1920." In *History of American Presidential Elections 1789–1968.* Vol. 3, *1900–1936.* Edited by Arthur M. Schlesinger, Jr., Frank L. Israel and William P. Hansen. New York: Chelsea House Publishers, 1971.

Miller, Nathan. *Theodore Roosevelt: A Life.* New York: Quill/William Morrow, 1992.

Morris, Edmund. *The Rise of Theodore Roosevelt.* New York: Ballantine Books, 1979.

———. *Theodore Rex.* New York: Random House, 2001.

Mowry, George E. "Election of 1912." In *History of American Presidential Elections 1789–1968.* Vol. 3, *1900–1936.* Edited by Arthur M. Schlesinger, Jr., Frank L. Israel and William P. Hansen. New York: Chelsea House Publishers, 1971.

———. *The Era of Theodore Roosevelt, 1900–1912.* New York: Harper and Brothers, 1958.

———. *Theodore Roosevelt and the Progressive Movement.* New York: Hill and Wang, 1946.

Murlin, Edgar L. *The New York Red Book: Portraits and Biographies of the U.S. Senators, Governor, States Officers and Members of the Legislature, Etc.* Albany, N.Y.: J.B. Lyon Company, 1911.

Mutch, Robert E. *Campaigns, Congress, and Courts: The Making of Federal Campaign Finance Law.* New York: Praeger, 1988.

Pringle, Henry. *The Life and Times of William Howard Taft.* 2 vols. New York: Farrar and Rinehart, 1939.

———. *Theodore Roosevelt: A Biography.* 1931. Reprint, New York: Konecky and Konecky, 1955.

Roosevelt, Theodore. *The Autobiography of Theodore Roosevelt.* Edited by Wayne Andrews. New York: Charles Scribner's Sons, 1958.

Seligman, E.R.A. "Taxes vs. Bonds." *New York Times,* April 15, 1917.

Smith, Page. *America Enters the World.* Vol. 7, *A People's History of the Progressive Era and World War I.* New York: McGraw-Hill Book Co., 1985.

Sprague, Oliver M. W. "The Conscription of Income." *New Republic,* February 24, 1917, pp. 92–97.

———. "Conscription of Wealth Once More" *New Republic,* July 14, 1917, pp. 300–301.

Stark, John O. "The Establishment of Wisconsin's Income Tax." *Wisconsin Magazine of History* 71, no. 1 (autumn 1987): 27–45.

Stephenson, Nathaniel Wright. *Nelson W. Aldrich: A Leader in American Politics.* New York: Charles Scribner's Sons, 1930.

Unger, Nancy C. *Fighting Bob La Follette: The Righteous Reformer.* Chapel Hill: University of North Carolina Press, 2000.

Wiebe, Robert H. *Businessmen and Reform: A Study of the Progressive Movement.* Chicago: Quadrangle Books, 1962.

———. *The Search for Order, 1877–1920.* New York: Hill and Wang, 1967.

ACKNOWLEDGMENTS

—⁓—

This book is a product of four years of research and writing, and more than thirty years of work and education at the *New York Times* while covering politics, government, economics and international affairs. I am enormously indebted to many colleagues who have helped and taught me in both endeavors, and I am extremely grateful for their assistance and support.

Alice Mayhew, editorial director of Simon & Schuster, had long encouraged me to write a book, finally suggesting that I look for themes of interest not in the contemporary arena but in the politics of the Progressive Era. It had never occurred to me to write about history. But with Alice as an incomparable editor, teacher and collaborator, I have found it tremendously rewarding to try. Roger Labrie of Simon & Schuster has been a perceptive and patient editor of my words and ideas. I could not have pulled this book together without him.

I am indebted to my niece, Lisa Cope, who as an assistant editor at Simon & Schuster and a researcher at ABC News helped tremendously and cheerfully in tracking down books and doing research. Her work and support helped get this book off the ground. I also thank David Rosenthal, publisher at Simon & Schuster and my old comrade in arms covering City Hall in the 1970s; Jonathan Jao; Toni Rachiele and Martha Schwartz, copyediting supervisors, and Virginia Croft, my copyeditor; Victoria Meyer and Aileen Boyle, who have worked on publicity; and Michael Accordino, who oversaw the design of the dust jacket.

My agent and friend, Amanda Urban, has been waiting for this book for a long time. Without her encouragement, enthusiasm and sense of humor my energies would have flagged. Daniel Yergin has been my closest intellectual partner and guide in this enterprise and many others. His editing suggestions breathed life into many of its pages.

It was humbling to attempt to write history, and I am grateful to several historians who encouraged me. John Morton Blum, Sterling professor of history emeritus at Yale, under whom I studied as an undergraduate, spent many hours reading this book and helping me avoid a multitude of errors and thickets. Harold Holzer and Gabor S. Boritt carefully read the Civil War chapters and discerned many mistakes and cases of clumsy thinking. They are not responsible, of course, for any errors that remain. Alan Brinkley and David Rothman at Columbia University encouraged me to think that I could bring something original to the job. Ellen Chesler has long studied the Progressive Era and helped me understand it. David Greenberg also offered encouragement and advice. My friend Richard Reeves taught me how to write about politics at the beginning of my career and, more recently, how to move from journalism to history. Walter Isaacson has been a guide on the same journey.

I have been lucky to work at the *Times* under a succession of brilliant and supportive editors. Most of all I thank Howell Raines, who for more than twenty years has been my colleague, friend, editor and teacher. Gail Collins, fellow traveler in history, has given me the gift of her humor, curiosity and enthusiasm. I thank Arthur O. Sulzberger, Jr., for his friendship and encouragement at the *Times*. I am grateful to many editors and colleagues who have granted me opportunities over the years, especially A. M. Rosenthal, Arthur Gelb, Max Frankel, Joseph Lelyveld, Bill Kovach, John Finney, David Jones, Warren Hoge and Bernard Gwertzman. Among the many past and present colleagues at the *Times* from whom I have learned the craft are Frank Clines, John Darnton, E. J. Dionne, Linda Greenhouse, Charles Kaiser, David Sanger, James

Sterngold, Terence Smith, Richard Bernstein, Barbara Crossette, Paul Goldberger, Maureen Dowd, Eden Lipson, Sheldon Binn, Bill Borders, John Lee, Clyde Haberman, Jim Greenfield, Katy Roberts, and Michael Oreskes. My colleagues on the editorial board at the *Times* have been constant sources of encouragement on this book, especially Philip Taubman, Philip Boffey, Eleanor Randolph, Brent Staples, Terry Tang, Verlyn Klinkenborg, Robert Semple, Tina Rosenberg, Andres Martinez, David Unger, Dorothy Samuels, Michael Weinstein and Floyd Norris. Brian Zittel, Maureen Muenster, Peter Catapano, Rosemary Shields and Marion Greene have helped in countless ways. Kay Shatraw in the Albany Bureau helped track down some important materials for me. Among those on the library and research staff at the *Times*, I thank Linda Amster, John Motyka, Monica Borkowski, Barclay Walsh, Marjorie Goldsborough, Lora Korbut, Marilyn Annan, Judy Greenfeld, Linda Lake and Michael Porter.

Starting in the 1970s, I have been fortunate to learn about the interrelationship between politics and finance from many people. I am grateful especially to two brilliant teachers, Felix Rohatyn and Peter Goldmark. Many other friends and colleagues have helped me understand the world and culture of politics, or of books, especially Hendrik Hertzberg, David Freeman, Judy Gingold, Ken Auletta, Steven Rattner, Maureen White, Meryl Gordon, Walter Shapiro, Stephen Kessler, Matthew Mallow, Fred Wertheimer, Judy Miller, Peter and Susan Osnos and Victor and Betsy Gotbaum. A special group of friends who have watched me struggle every weekend and offered encouragement deserve special thanks. They include Cathy Isaacson, Amy and Chick Entelis, Andrew and Betsy Lack, David and Sherrie Westin, Caroline and Haywood Miller, Jack and Candy Weiss, Priscilla Painton and Tim Smith, Nancy Gibbs and Waits May and Marc and Susan Epstein.

I also thank the friends and colleagues who have offered encouragement and conversation about the subjects in this book over many years. They include Angela Stent, Michele Slung, Ron

Rosenbaum, Strobe Talbott, Brooke Shearer, Steven Isenberg, Michael Mandelbaum, Eugene Keilin, Sidney Blumenthal, Geraldine Baum, Robert Greenstein, Robert McIntyre, Ellen Nissenbaum, Alex Garvin, Ray Horton, Rahm Emanuel, Jeffrey Garten, M. J. Akbar, Carter Wiseman, Reed Hundt, Henry Scott Stokes, James Kugel, Richard Leone, Leo Braudy, Richard Brodhead, Robert Deans, Rone Tempest, Fred Hiatt, Margaret Shapiro, Amitav Ghosh, Patsy Glazer, Richard Mittenthal, Derek Shearer, Ruth Goldway, Elaine Kagan, Jonathan Lear, Chris and Kathy Matthews, Ben Bradlee and Sally Quinn, Daniel Patrick Moynihan, Elizabeth Moynihan, Maura Moynihan, Bim Bissell, Robert Reischauer, Edward Rollins, Karen Sulzberger, Eric Lax, Leon Wieseltier, Marc Roth, Shashi Tharoor and Jean Vallely. Among the friends and mentors who I wish could have seen this book are A. Bartlett Giamatti, John Scanlon, John Bissell and John Rosemond. I thank Senator Charles Schumer for his friendship and I thank Brad Tusk, Elizabeth Alexander, and Rick Castellano in his office for helping me thread the mysteries of the Library of Congress; Marvin Kranz, the American history specialist at the Library of Congress; and innumerable and unfailingly helpful staff members at the New York Public Library and the New-York Historical Society. I also thank, for their help, Edward J. Burke and Joseph Markulin at the law firm of Shearman & Sterling; Noel C. Holobeck of the St. Louis Area Studies Center of the St. Louis Public Library; David Lowery of the University of North Carolina Political Science Department; Mike Keane of the Wisconsin Legislative Reference Bureau; Karen Van Rossem; Charlie Murphy of Scenic Hudson, Inc.; and Steven Pyrek of the Internal Revenue Service. I also am indebted to Ron Skarzenski and Jim Mulcahy for rescuing me from many computer meltdowns.

I am grateful for the encouragement of my family. I dedicate this book to my mother and my late father, who have taught me strength, tolerance and understanding all my life. My brother Michael and sister Lynn have always given me their love and support. My niece Annie Weisman is my co-conspirator in writing. I am grateful for the encouragement given me by Betsy Weisman, Greg Weisman, Gunhild and Jack Rose, and Ted and Ruth Ann Bumiller.

My children Madeleine and Teddy have been more generous, loving and understanding than they can know, even when they wondered who would read a book on taxes. Finally, of course, I thank my wife, Elisabeth Bumiller. Without her love, partnership, strength, patience (and impatience), incomparable understanding of words, and humor, I could never have struggled through this project. She is the vital center of my existence and she has made my life whole and this book possible.

INDEX

African Americans, 80, 92, 96, 97, 299, 334

Aldrich, Nelson: and banks, 284; and corporate tax, 221, 227–29; and income tax debate, 225–28, 225–28, 229–30, 251, 254, 262; and inheritance tax, 221; personal and professional background of, 216; and railroads, 200; Taft's relations with, 215, 216, 217–18, 220–21, 228, 231, 236, 238; and tariffs, 143, 196, 216, 217–18, 220–21, 225, 226, 230, 231, 238

Altgeld, John, 121–22, 161, 165, 166, 169

American Revolution, 102–3

"American System," 16–17, 21

Astor, William B., 34, 100, 103, 123

Bailey, Joseph W., 177, 223–25, 226, 229–30, 231, 234, 251, 261–62

banks/bankers: in Civil War Era, 9, 10–11, 25, 26, 35, 37, 38, 40, 48, 49, 52, 53, 55, 56, 63, 72, 77, 82; and Cleveland, 161–64, 170; and cotton trade, 292, 293; in early 1890s, 127, 128; and elections, 114, 241; and legacy of Civil War, 93; and Panic of 1893, 108, 117, 118, 119–20; and Panic of 1907, 203–5; and Sixteenth Amendment, 251; in South, 52, 53, 55, 56, 63, 72; and Wilson, 268, 270, 284–85, 286; and World War I, 292, 293, 295. *See also specific person*

Baruch, Bernard, 319, 329, 341

Belmont, August, Jr., 80, 114, 162, 163

Bethlehem Steel Corporation, 304, 334–35

"Black Friday" (September 24, 1869), 83–84, 100

Bland-Allison Act (1878), 118

Blum, John Morton, 199, 206, 267

Borah, William E., 222, 224, 226–27, 229, 240, 252, 278–79

Boutwell, George S., 43–44, 45, 46, 99

"bracket creep," 358, 363

Britain: and Civil War, 37, 50, 56–57, 73, 76, 78, 79, 90; class issues in, 57, 90, 322–23; imports from, 25; and Panic of 1893, 117; taxes in, 32, 141, 178, 201, 219, 276, 277, 281, 309, 316, 322, 328; and *Trent* affair, 37; U.S. relations with, 312; U.S. surpasses industrial might of, 13; wealth in, 123; and World War I, 289, 290, 291, 294, 295, 330, 331, 335–36

Brownlee, W. Elliot, 102, 302–3, 329, 354, 359

Brushaber v. Union Pacific Railroad Co. (1916), 283–84

Bryan, William Jennings: Allen selected for senate over, 144; and corporate tax, 228; enemies of, 165; and Federal Reserve Board, 284; Hull's admiration for, 273, 274; and income tax debate, 5, 129, 133, 135, 137–38, 139, 140–42, 145, 165, 169, 170, 211–12, 261, 274, 279; Jones' letter to, 124–25, 131; personal and professional background of, 125–27; popular votes for, 250,

ABOUT THE AUTHOR

STEVEN R. WEISMAN has covered politics, economics, and international affairs for *The New York Times* for more than thirty years. Previously a deputy foreign editor at the *Times*, he now writes editorials for the paper about government, politics, and international subjects, including the battles over taxes in the last two presidential elections. He lives with his wife, Elisabeth Bumiller, and family in the Washington, D.C., area.